HUMAN RIGHTS AND
AMERICAN FOREIGN POLICY

Human Rights and American Foreign Policy

EDITED BY

Donald P. Kommers
and
Gilburt D. Loescher

UNIVERSITY OF NOTRE DAME PRESS
NOTRE DAME   LONDON

Copyright © 1979 by
University of Notre Dame Press
Notre Dame, Indiana 46556

Library of Congress Cataloging in Publication Data
Main entry under title:

Human rights and American foreign policy.

  Bibliography: p.
  Includes index.
  1. Civil rights—Addresses, essays, lectures.
2. United States—Foreign relations—1974-
—Addresses, essays, lectures. I. Kommers,
Donald P. II. Loescher, Gil.
JC571.H768.7   323.4   78-62966
ISBN 0-268-01071-4

Manufactured in the United States of America

Contents

Preface   ix

PART ONE
Human Rights Around the World

Introduction   2

1. Human Rights: A Global Assessment
   A. H. Robertson   5

   Bibliography   29

PART TWO
Individual and Group Rights

Introduction   32

2. The Individual, The State, and Ethnic Communities in Political Theory
   Vernon Van Dyke   36

3. Minority Rights and Self-Determination
   Ben Whitaker   63

   Bibliography   77

PART THREE
Human Rights: Conflicting Ideologies

Introduction   80

4. A First World View
   Rita E. Hauser   85

5. A Third World View
   Eddison J. M. Zvobgo   90

   Bibliography   107

   PART FOUR

   Human Rights: The Soviet Union and Helsinki

   Introduction   110

6. Theory and Practice of Human Rights in the Soviet Union
   Peter B. Reddaway   115

7. The Helsinki Agreement and Human Rights
   A. H. Robertson   130

   Bibliography   149

   PART FIVE

   International Monitoring Agencies

   Introduction   152

8. Monitoring Human Rights by the U.N. System and Nongovernmental Organizations
   Nigel S. Rodley   157

9. Monitoring Human Rights Violations: The Role of Nongovernmental Organizations
   Laurie S. Wiseberg and *Harry M. Scoble*   179

   Bibliography   209

   PART SIX

   American Foreign Policy and Human Rights

   Introduction   212

10. Human Rights Decision-Making in the Executive Branch: Some Proposals for a Coordinated Strategy
    Roberta Cohen   216

11. Congress's Role in the Making of International
    Human Rights Policy
    Donald M. Fraser   247

    Bibliography   255

PART SEVEN

Human Rights and Priorities in American Foreign Policy

Introduction   258

12. On a Collision Course: The American Campaign
    for Human Rights and the Antiradical Bias in the
    Third World
    Tom J. Farer   263

13. A United States Policy of Humanitarian
    Intervention and Intercession
    Richard B. Lillich   278

    Bibliography   299

APPENDICES

Commencement Address at the University of
Notre Dame
President Jimmy Carter   302

Law Day Address on Human Rights Policy
Cyrus R. Vance   309

Universal Declaration of Human Rights
U.N. General Assembly   316

Biographical Sketches   321

Index   325

Preface

THIS BOOK CONSTITUTES A STUDY OF HUMAN RIGHTS AS A SIGNIFIcant component of American foreign policy. A product of the international symposium "American Foreign Policy and Human Rights" held by the Law School Center for Civil Rights at the University of Notre Dame, it is a unique scholarly collaboration and a contribution to the significant emerging literature on U.S. human rights policy. The authors of the chapters represent national and international nongovernmental human rights organizations, the Department of State, and the scholarly community. This collaboration of academicians, governmental officials, and representatives of nongovernmental organizations has resulted in a judicious blending of theoretical knowledge and practical experience. Indeed, the book represents a diversity of views on the question of what should be the specific content of a U.S. human rights policy and how that policy might be implemented. It is directed not only to the academic and policy making communities but also to the general but sophisticated observer of American foreign policy and international affairs.

The book includes chapters dealing with ideas, institutions and processes most relevant to the formulation of American human rights policy. In Part One, A. H. Robertson (formerly director of Human Rights of the Council of Europe and currently professor of law at the University of Paris) presents a general picture of the condition and protection of human rights in the world today.

Part Two is an attack on the Western liberal tradition for its exclusive concern for individuals and for its neglect of groups. It argues that groups have not only legal but also moral rights that theorists, foreign policy-makers, and international diplomats ought to take into account. The arguments on behalf of group rights are advanced by Vernon Van Dyke (professor of political science, University of Iowa), a leading American human rights scholar, and Ben

Whitaker (director, Minority Rights Group), a long time defender of group rights before various international human rights agencies.

In Part Three, Rita E. Hauser (U.S. Representative to the United Nations Commission on Human Rights from 1969 to 1972 and a member of Department of the State's Advisory Panel on International Law) and Eddison Zvobgo (Deputy Secretary-General of the Zimbabwe African National Union and a board member of Amnesty International [USA]) advance sharply conflicting views about the significance of politico-civil and socio-economic rights in the First and Third worlds.

Part Four is a discussion of human rights in the Second World, which we broadly identify with the Soviet Union and other nations with advanced communist political systems. Peter Reddaway (professor of government, University of London), a well-known authority on the Soviet Union, discusses the condition of human rights within the USSR, while in a second paper A. H. Robertson draws upon his considerable skills as an international lawyer and human rights scholar in the discussion of the Helsinki Agreement.

Part Five reflects the practical wisdom of a British lawyer professionally involved in human rights litigation and the scholarly research of two leading U.S. authorities on nongovernmental human rights organizations. Nigel Rodley (legal advisor, Amnesty International) presents a paper on the work of official international human rights agencies, while Laurie Wiseberg and Harry Scoble (professors of political science, University of Illinois at Chicago Circle) give us their critical analysis of the role of nongovernmental human rights organizations in the making of American foreign policy.

Part Six includes papers by two long-time and widely respected authorities on human rights violations around the world. Both are Americans vitally concerned with the United States human rights policy-making process. Roberta Cohen (executive director, International League for Human Rights), who is involved in the direction of this country's most influential nongovernmental human rights organization, discusses and proposes improvements in the human rights policy-making role of the Executive Branch. Donald Fraser (U.S. Representative from Minnesota), recognized as the House's most influential Congressman in the field of human rights, considers the role of Congress in the formulation of a U.S. human rights policy.

Part Seven concludes with papers on human rights and priorities in American foreign policy by two distinguished law professors widely known for their scholarly writing and public activity in the international human rights field. Tom J. Farer (professor of law, Rutgers

University, and American representative on the Inter-American Commission on Human Rights) is concerned with the human rights implications of what he perceives as the American tendency to oppose radical regimes around the world. Richard B. Lillich (professor of law, University of Virginia) offers specific suggestions for a U.S. policy of humanitarian intercession and intervention.

For the convenience of the reader the editors have written rather substantial introductions to all of the aforementioned parts of the book. We have also supplied a short bibliography at the end of each part. Finally, we have included in the appendices to this volume President Carter's commencement address at the University of Notre Dame and Secretary of State Cyrus Vance's Law Day speech on human rights at the University of Georgia.

The editors would like to acknowledge and thank the following persons for their substantial contributions to the international symposium out of which this book evolved: Allard Lowenstein (U.S. Representative to the United Nations Commission on Human Rights), Ernst Benda (President, West German Federal Constitutional Court), John Brademas (Majority Whip, U.S. House of Representatives), William Butler (President, American Association for International Commission of Jurists), Charles Runyon III (assistant legal advisor for human rights, U.S. Department of State), Julian Friedmann (professor of political science, Syracuse University), Frederick J. Crosson (professor of philosophy, University of Notre Dame), Reverend Joseph Gremillion (former director of the Pontifical Commission on Justice and Peace and coordinator of the Interreligious Peace Colloquium), and Stephen D. Kertesz (professor emeritus of government and international studies, University of Notre Dame).

We also want to thank the following persons from the University of Notre Dame for their generous help and advice: George A. Brinkley (director, Institute for International Studies), James R. Langford (director, University of Notre Dame Press), James H. Powell (assistant director, Center for Continuing Education), Charles K. Wilber (chairman, Department of Economics), Frederick Crosson, Joseph Gremillion, and Stephen Kertesz.

We are also indebted to Reverend Theodore M. Hesburgh, C.S.C. (president), Reverend James T. Burtchaell, C.S.C. (provost), and David T. Link (dean of the Law School). Last, but certainly not least, the editors are grateful to Barry O'Connor, Catherine Flanagan, Norma Silvers, Dean F. Richardson, Eugenia Schwartz, Mary Walsh, and other members of the staff of the Center for Civil Rights for their valuable assistance and cooperation in the preparation of this manuscript. We also want to acknowledge the generous support of The Ford Foundation, whose assistance made the symposium and book possible. Lastly, we are grateful to the *Notre Dame Lawyer* for its permission to publish the two articles by A. H. Robertson.

Donald P. Kommers
Gilburt D. Loescher

HUMAN RIGHTS AND
AMERICAN FOREIGN POLICY

PART ONE
Human Rights Around the World

Introduction

ON DECEMBER 10, 1948, THE GENERAL ASSEMBLY OF THE UNITED Nations adopted the Universal Declaration of Human Rights and proclaimed it "a common standard of achievement for all peoples and all nations." The declaration begins with the proclamation that "all human beings are born free and equal in dignity and rights" (Article 1) and that every person is entitled to all of its rights and freedoms without regard to "race, color, sex, language, religion, political or other opinion, national or social origin, property, birth, or other status" (Article 2). Articles 3 to 21 speak of personal, civil, and political rights. These include (1) rights to life, liberty, property, personal security and honor, and equal protection under law, (2) freedom of conscience and religion, speech, assembly, association, and movement, (3) rights to personal privacy including the right to marry and found a family, (4) guarantees of a fair trial in criminal proceedings, and (5) the right to vote for political leaders in free and periodic elections.

In addition to these classical liberties rooted in the political tradition of the West, Articles 22 to 27 provide for certain economic and social rights. These include the rights to employment and choice of work, safe and healthy working conditions, rest and leisure, medical care, security in old age, and education, together with the right of parents to choose the kind of education that shall be given to their children and participation in the cultural life of the community.

Finally, Articles 28 to 30 assert that the aforementioned rights, freedoms, and guarantees can be protected only within an international order based on peace, justice, and the rule of law.

But 30 years after the adoption of the Universal Declaration this international order of peace, justice, and the rule of law is still a dream. Torture, terrorism, violence, political repression, and hunger continue to stalk the earth. In the late 1970's all of the rights mentioned in the declaration—civil and political no less than social and economic—are under assault somewhere in the world. Indeed, as A. H. Robertson notes in the chapter to follow, the available figures on rights violations "paint a somber picture of the condition of human rights."

Robertson's "global assessment" does not dwell at length on human rights violations around the world. The short summary at the beginning of his paper is intended merely to call attention to the scale and variety of abuses currently inflicted upon human beings. No useful purpose would be served in stringing out the parade of horrors that could be mounted with the known facts about these abuses in the world today. More important for his purposes is what governments are doing, singly and multilaterally, to reduce and ultimately to eliminate at least the more flagrant human rights violations. The author's main concern is to trace the main developments in the international protection of human rights during the last 30 years.

These developments include the adoption and entry into force of several international human rights charters and conventions, the creation of corresponding international and regional agencies charged with the implementation of guaranteed rights, and the successful operation within individual states of the institution of the ombudsman. While these international charters and conventions have been inadequately implemented, the author finds in the 30-year record as a whole a source of cautious optimism.

In Robertson's view, the most effective system for the international protection of human rights is located in Europe. Under the European Convention for the Protection of Human Rights and Fundamental Freedoms governments have the right to file complaints with the European Commission on Human Rights and ultimately, should its good offices fail to conciliate the problem, to have their cases heard by the European Court of Human Rights, whose decisions are binding on all signatory states. In the Americas, on the other hand, where authoritarian governments predominate, little progress has been made in protecting the rights of persons against torture, summary executions, and long detention without trial. The same could be said of Africa, which has yet to develop instruments to deal with such invasions of human freedom and dignity.

The record of U.N. agencies, such as the Committee on Human Rights and the Committee on the Elimination of Racial Discrimination, has fallen far short of original expectations. Robertson finds their procedures cumbersome, their deliberations marred by ideological cleavage and interbloc rivalry, and their decisions judicially unenforceable. Yet he attaches important symbolic value to the ratification by 40 states of the U.N. International Covenants on Civil and Political

Rights and Social, Economic, and Cultural Rights as well as the ratification by 92 states of the U.N. International Convention on the Elimination of All Forms of Racial Discrimination. These ratifications suggest a wide consensus among countries on all continents about the basic principles that should influence the treatment of persons by government. As he states, "Virtually everyone today is in favor of human rights" just as "no government or political leader today dares to admit publicly to being an opponent of civil liberties."

In the end, the author feels that the moral force of world public opinion growing increasingly sensitive to human rights violations "is the key to the human rights balance sheet" of the future. But whether "world public opinion" can be mobilized effectively against offending governments is a question that yields no immediate answer. Nevertheless, it is possible to argue that the climate of public opinion is today more congenial than ever to the development of better machinery and procedures for the protection of human rights, both within and among nations. But we are left with the realization, as Robertson seems to suggest in his concluding remarks, that progress in the international legal protection of human rights is to be measured in decades, not years or months. The Universal Declaration of Human Rights would not have commanded the assent of humankind a century or even a half century ago. It does today, and that in the perspective of history (and of diplomats) is progress.

Where does the United States fit into this picture? Many take the view that as one of the two most powerful nations in the world, the United States is in a position to exert constructive and forceful leadership in furthering the international protection of human rights. Some suggest that the United States could play a leading role in strengthening U.N. machinery for protecting human rights. Others note that the United States needs to win credibility within the United Nations and throughout the world by proceeding to ratify, without delay, the International Covenants on Human Rights, the Genocide Convention, and the Convention on the Elimination of All Forms of Racial Discrimination. Still others insist that in addition to these symbolic acts of ratification the United States, prior to assuming any meaningful leadership role in the human rights field, would have to put its own house in order and see to it that the commands and ideals of the U.S. Constitution are fully realized.

1: Human Rights: A Global Assessment

A. H. ROBERTSON

I. Introduction

Any attempt to undertake a "global assessment" of the situation of human rights in the world is fraught with difficulty and danger. The difficulty is immense because the situation varies so much from country to country and continent to continent. No one person, even in an age of computers, can possess all of the information necessary to form a balanced—let alone comprehensive—view of a situation of such complexity. The danger also is great because any account which is incomplete is likely to be criticized by some as both partial in its selection of material and as tendentious as well. Nevertheless, the task is not without attraction because so many of us who usually are forced by circumstances to concentrate our attention and our work on some particular facet or aspect of a global problem rarely have the time or the opportunity to try to formulate a comprehensive view. We rarely see the wood for the trees.

The following essay might be thought of as a "State of the Union" message on the situation of human rights in the world today. But since this must be one brief article rather than a documented report of several hundred pages, the essay will have the character of a summary rather than of a Presidential communication. Moreover, because it is bound to be subjective, it cannot do more than recount the impressions of one interested observer. What follows, then, is a summary of the impressions gleaned from many sources and assembled by one individual.

II. The Negative Aspects

Never before have newspapers carried so much information about human rights—articles both about violations and about interventions designed to protect such rights.[1] Indeed, as one looks around the world today as it is portrayed in the press or in reports of both official and nongovernmental international organizations, one cannot help being depressed by the mass of information about flagrant violations of human rights that is being published constantly.

It is neither the purpose nor function of this essay to prepare an indictment against any particular country. But it would be unrealistic and irresponsible to ignore the evidence. Without passing judgment on any particular situation, one is still obliged to draw attention to substantial evidence of what is called in the United Nations "a consistent pattern of gross violations" of human rights in many quarters. For example, anyone who has attended sessions of the Commission on Human Rights in recent years cannot help but be aware of the constant emphasis placed on the problem of racial discrimination in southern Africa. By definition, the policy of apartheid involves racial discrimination and therefore violation of human rights. The reports issued by the ad hoc group of experts to investigate apartheid appointed by the Commission in 1967[2] leave little doubt on this score.

Because of the particular situation in Namibia, the International Institute of Human Rights, which was founded by M. René Cassin, organized a special conference at Dakar in January 1976 under the auspices of the U.N. High Commissioner for Namibia. This conference led to similar conclusions which have been brought to the attention of the Security Council.[3] In many other countries in Africa there is a sad record of detention without trial and of executions for political opinion. The most glaring recent cases have been in Uganda, where Amnesty International has reported more than 50,000 summary executions. The Ugandan situation led to an unsuccessful British proposal to the Commission on Human Rights in 1977 that it investigate the situation: This proposal was made nearly three years after the massive expulsion from Uganda of thousands of persons of Asian origin in a striking example of "racial discrimination in reverse."

Studies of South America also have provided extensive evidence of systematic human rights violations in Chile collected by the Commission on Human Rights of the Organization of American States and by the U.N. Commission. In compliance with a resolution of the General Assembly adopted in 1974, the U.N. Commission established an ad hoc working group of five members to inquire into the present situation of human rights in Chile.[4] In spite of an initial promise to cooperate, the Chilean government refused the group admittance to the country at the last moment. The group subsequently collected such information as it could from many sources, including Chilean exiles and witnesses who were sent to meetings in Geneva by the

Chilean government. The group has since reported to the General Assembly[5] and to the Commission on Human Rights[6] on the extensive violations of human rights thus established. At its session in 1977, the Commission considered an additional report[7] and, in accordance with a proposal made by Cuba and the United States, sent a telegram to the Chilean government calling on it to restore respect for human rights, to stop the practice of torture, and to release political prisoners. The attempts of the Human Rights Commission of the Organization of American States have been equally frustrating, so much so that in 1976 the Commission's Executive Secretary submitted his resignation.

Much evidence has been collected by nongovernmental organizations, particularly Amnesty International, about the regular use of torture in various Latin American countries, particularly Brazil. The Brazilian bishops and the Vatican have protested against this situation. The human rights records of Argentina and Uruguay are so deplorable that President Jimmy Carter has reduced American aid. Finally, in Cuba there are reported to be between 4,000 and 5,000 political prisoners, while in Guatemala, about 15,000 persons are believed to have been killed by political terror squads during the last six years.[8]

Other continents cannot be omitted from this gloomy catalog. In a number of Asian countries abundant evidence exists of prolonged detention without trial, of inhuman prison conditions, and of executions. Indonesia, Iran, and Iraq are those countries most frequently accused of such violations. Wholesale massacres in Cambodia have been reported.

The revelations of Solzhenitsyn concerning conditions in detention camps in the Soviet Union are well known as are the charges of other Russian dissidents, both inside and outside the USSR, who have appealed to the Western democracies for help.[9] It is widely believed that there are 10,000 political prisoners in the Soviet Union, yet the recent U.S. proposal that the U.N. Commission on Human Rights request information about the situation in the USSR had to be abandoned for lack of support.

All these indications paint a somber picture of the condition of human rights. A global assessment of human rights in the world today demands an account of the negative aspect and a recognition that violations are widespread and flagrant. There are probably more countries where fundamental rights and civil liberties are systematically violated than there are countries where they are effectively protected. Amnesty International estimates that there are 60 countries which employ systematic use of torture and that the number of political prisoners worldwide approaches half a million.[10] Therefore, the general picture is in many respects both discouraging and alarming. It is believed that the principles of liberal democracy, with its respect for fundamental rights, are observed in fewer than 30 countries today.

III. Some Positive Aspects

The human rights picture is not entirely bleak, however. A number of positive features will give comfort to those who are concerned about the state of human rights in the world.

A. *The United Nations*

The most important recent development on the international scene is, of course, the entry into force of the two United Nations covenants: the International Covenant on Economic, Social, and Cultural Rights and the International Covenant on Civil and Political Rights.[11] These covenants were approved by the General Assembly on December 16, 1966, but required ratification by 35 states before entering into force. As a result, it was nearly ten years before the Covenant on Economic, Social and Cultural Rights entered into force on January 3, 1976, and the Covenant on Civil and Political Rights entered into force on March 23, 1976. The first Covenant protects ten economic, social, and cultural rights, while the second protects 23 civil and political rights; the rights of all peoples to self-determination and to the free disposition of their natural wealth and resources are common to both.

These treaties, however, are not merely reaffirmations of rights already proclaimed in earlier texts. Each covenant contains its own system of so-called "measures of implementation," the object of which is to ensure that the obligations assumed by states are effectively carried out. The point of departure for this system of international supervision is the agreement of each state to submit reports to the United Nations on the manner in which they have discharged their obligations as outlined in the covenants.

In the Covenant on Economic, Social, and Cultural Rights the obligation is stated as an undertaking "to take steps . . . with a view to achieving progressively the full realization of the rights recognized in the present Covenant"; the national reports will relate to "the measures which they [the individual states] have adopted and the progress made in achieving the observance of the rights recognized herein."

Copies or extracts from these reports will be sent to the pertinent Specialized Agencies and also may be sent to the Commission on Human Rights. The comments of these bodies and of the states parties will be considered by the Economic and Social Council, which will receive the national reports and may submit its own reports "with recommendations of a general nature" to the General Assembly.

The obligations resulting from the Covenant on Civil and Political Rights are somewhat more stringent. First, the undertaking "to respect and ensure . . . the rights recognized in the present Covenant" is of more immediate application than the corresponding provision in the first Covenant. Second, there is a similar undertaking to "submit reports on the measures which [the states parties] have adopted which give effect to the rights recognized herein and on the progress made in the enjoyment of those rights." Third, provision is made for a new Human Rights Committee of 18 members, serving in a personal capacity, which will study the reports submitted by the states parties. The committee is empowered to send its own reports and "such general comments as it considers appropriate" to the states parties and to the Economic and Social Council. In addition, the Human Rights Committee will submit an annual report on its activities through the Council to the General Assembly.[12]

There is also an optional procedure for handling interstate complaints or "communications" concerning human rights. This procedure applies only to states that have expressly accepted it and goes into effect only when ten states have done so. The procedure includes bilateral negotiations between the states concerned; the use of the good offices of the Human Rights Committee, which will examine the communications and written or oral submissions of the states concerned in closed meetings; and the possibility of recourse to an ad hoc Conciliation Commission if both parties agree. An optional protocol to the second Covenant (which also requires ten ratifications to enter into force) establishes a procedure whereby the Human Rights Committee can consider communications from individuals who claim to have been victims of a violation of any of the rights set forth in the covenant.[13]

By the end of 1977, 46 states had ratified the covenants and accepted their obligations: nine "Western" states,[14] ten states of the Soviet bloc,[15] ten African countries,[16] six Asian countries,[17] six Latin American countries and five Caribbean countries.[18] Only three countries had accepted the optional procedure for interstate communications;[19] this procedure, therefore, is not yet in force. Seventeen states had ratified the optional protocol authorizing the Human Rights

Committee to consider communications from individuals,[20] with the result that the protocol entered into force at the same time as the Covenant on Civil and Political Rights.

The new Human Rights Committee was elected by the states parties to the second Covenant on September 29, 1976, and held its first meeting in March 1977. The committee includes six members from the "Western" states,[21] four from Eastern Europe,[22] three from African countries,[23] two from Asian countries,[24] and three from Latin American countries.[25]

The birth of this new system for the international protection of human rights represents the results of labors extending over a period of 30 years, beginning with the drafting of the Universal Declaration in 1946. Of course, it is too early to say how effective the new covenant will be, though it is evident that they will be less effective than the system instituted by the European Convention. They do not approach a system of judicial control. The essence of the procedure lies in the submission and examination of reports, the formulation by the Human Rights Committee or by the Economic and Social Council of such recommendations "of a general nature" as they consider appropriate and, in the case of states which have accepted one or both of the optional procedures, the proposal of good offices and attempts at conciliation in response to specific allegations of violation.

It would be a mistake to expect more stringent obligations in the heterogeneous community of the United Nations. Nonetheless, some critics, when considering the human rights record of some of the states which have ratified the covenants, will conclude that the procedures are likely to remain ineffective and that, even after ratification, a state may continue to violate human rights with impunity. But such criticism is unduly pessimistic and should not deter us from trying to make the system work as its authors intended or from urging governments which have not yet ratified or adhered to the covenants to do so without further delay. It is encouraging that President Carter, in his statement to the United Nations in New York in 1977, expressed the intention of signing and of asking Congress to ratify the two covenants, and they were in fact signed by the United States in October of that year. If they are ratified, this will strengthen the moral force of the initiatives taken by the U.S. government in favor of the protection of human rights throughout the world.

Another more limited, but nevertheless useful, development in the United Nations is the work of the Committee on the Elimination of Racial Discrimination. This committee was established under the provisions of the International Convention on the Elimination of All

Forms of Racial Discrimination, which was approved by the General Assembly on December 21, 1965, and entered into force on January 4, 1969. By December 31, 1977, nearly 100 states had ratified or acceded to this convention. The committee consists of 18 experts who serve in a personal capacity and have the task of reviewing the application of the convention on the basis of reports submitted by the contracting states. The committee reports annually to the General Assembly and may make its own suggestions and general recommendations.

Although the results of the work of this committee have not been spectacular, they are interesting in several respects. The subject matter—the prevention of racial discrimination—is one which, quite rightly, commands ready support in all organs of the United Nations. About two-thirds of the total membership of the United Nations have ratified this convention, substantially more than the number who have ratified the Human Rights covenants. Perhaps the most positive achievement of the committee so far has been to secure the acceptance by the contracting states not only of the practice of transmitting written reports but also of sending representatives to discuss the content of these reports with the committee. The dialogue that results is in itself a favorable development because it relates to matters which some states previously would have considered as falling essentially within their domestic jurisdiction; and therefore outside the competence of the United Nations under Article 2(7) of the Charter.

Some of the problems discussed but not yet solved by the committee include the question of whether the principle of nondiscrimination permits differentiation between citizens and foreigners in any given country. While the committee does not question the right of a state to reserve certain rights such as voting to its own citizens, the problem arises in regard to such matters as employment and wages. The question has arisen as to whether "positive discrimination" in favor of minority groups is permissible or whether the aim of those working against racial discrimination should be the integration of the minority into the majority.

A less happy development in the United Nations involves the procedure for dealing with individual communications relating to violations of human rights. The Secretary General receives many thousands of such communications each year. For many years the Commission on Human Rights insisted that it had "no power to take any action in regard to any complaints concerning human rights." This attitude was approved by the Economic and Social Council in 1947[26] and reaffirmed in 1959.[27] Various attempts to reverse this negative approach followed in subsequent years but were regularly countered by the argument, advanced by the Soviet Union in particular, that the consideration of individual complaints by the Commission would constitute "intervention in matters which are essentially within the domestic jurisdiction of states" in violation of Article 2(7) of the Charter.

Nevertheless, the Commission on Human Rights, at its twenty-sixth session in 1970, worked out a procedure whereby it would be authorized to examine "communications, together with replies of governments, if any, which appear to reveal a consistent pattern of gross violations of human rights." It is significant that this proposal was approved by a vote of 14 in favor, 7 opposed, and 5 abstentions. Later in the same year the Economic and Social Council in turn approved the proposal and authorized the Commission on Human Rights to act accordingly.[28]

It seemed at first that this decision represented an important breakthrough that would change an attitude which had been described by the Secretary General in 1949 as one which "is bound to lower the prestige and authority not only of the Commission on Human Rights but of the United Nations in the opinion of the general public."[29] These hopes, however, were short-lived, because a triple-screening process was to be involved in the operation of the procedure: these screenings were to be accomplished, first, in a working group of the Sub-Commission on Prevention of Discrimination and Protection of Minorities; second, in the subcommission itself; and, finally, by the Commission on Human Rights, which still would not be obliged to consider the complaints filtered to it but could decide whether the complaints required a thorough study and whether they should be the object of an investigation by an ad hoc committee "to be appointed by the Commission after obtaining the consent of the state concerned."

In fact, the Commission on Human Rights later inserted a fourth stage in the procedure when it appointed a five-member group of its own members to examine in detail all matters submitted to it by the subcommission. The results of this cumbersome system have been largely negative and have consisted for the most part of references from one group to another for further study.[30] Moreover, under the terms of the decision of the Economic and Social Council in 1970, the whole procedure is to be reviewed after the entry into force of the Covenant on Civil and Political Rights and the establishment of the new Human Rights Committee. Thus it is difficult to be optimistic about the future effectiveness of this procedure as a means of examining individual complaints about violations of human rights.

B. In Europe

The most effective system yet developed for the international protection of human rights is that established by the European Convention for the Protection of Human Rights and Fundamental Freedoms and which was concluded by the member states of the Council of Europe and signed in Rome on November 4, 1950. It is perhaps particularly significant that its origins were intimately linked with the movement for European Unity after the end of World War II.

It was in 1942 that Winston Churchill first proposed the creation, after the end of hostilities, of a Council of Europe as a remedy for Europe's incessant strife and as a means of restoring its former greatness. At Zurich in 1946 he elaborated this "sovereign remedy." At the Congress of Europe at The Hague in 1948 nearly 700 Europeans from 16 countries called for the creation of a United Europe "throughout whose area the free movement of persons, ideas, and goods is restored" and of a "Charter of Human Rights guaranteeing liberty of thought, assembly, and expression as well as the right to form a political opposition."

The Council of Europe was founded a year later, on May 5, 1949, at St. James's Palace in London as an association of democratic states seeking greater unity between its members and devoted to the maintenance of the rule of law and the protection of fundamental freedoms. Indeed, Article 3 of the statute stipulates that respect for these principles is to be a condition for membership.[31] The Charter of Human Rights followed in 1950 and contained a guarantee of 12 of the rights and freedoms fundamental to a democratic society. The contracting states undertook to ensure these rights to everyone within their jurisdiction. A Commission and a Court of Human Rights were established to provide a remedy for anyone who believed his or her rights and freedoms, as defined in the convention, had been violated.

All of these arrangements were made in conscious reaction to the bitter experiences of the previous decade. Never had human rights been violated so deliberately and systematically as had been done by the Nazi and Fascist regimes. In an attempt to prevent the gradual resurgence of dictatorships, the Western powers believed it was necessary to institute a system of international control "which will sound the alarm to the minds of a nation menaced by this progressive corruption."

The rights and freedoms guaranteed in the European Convention are taken from the Universal Declaration of Human Rights of 1948 and include such basic civil liberties as freedom of speech, assembly, association, conscience, and religion; freedom from torture, compulsory labor, and inhuman treatment; the right to liberty, habeas corpus, and a fair trial; and the right of privacy. Later protocols have added the right of property, the right to education, the holding of free elections, and the right to freedom of movement. (Economic and social rights are protected by the European Social Charter of 1961, described below.)

Any state party to the convention—and all members of the Council of Europe are parties except Portugal and Spain, who have signed but not yet ratified—can refer an alleged violation of the convention to the Commission of Human Rights. This procedure allowed the three Scandinavian governments, along with the Netherlands, to bring a case against the Greek military government in 1967. On the basis of the Commission's report, the Committee of Foreign Ministers determined that the Greek government had violated ten articles of the convention. Had the Greeks not resigned from the Council of Europe and denounced the convention in December 1969, they would have been expelled as a result of their disregard for human rights. Happily, a democratic Greece reratified the Convention on Human Rights in 1974 and was readmitted to the Council of Europe.

This same interstate procedure was employed by the Republic of Ireland against the United Kingdom in a case that began in 1971. The case concerns the problem of internment without trial and methods of interrogation in Northern Ireland. The proceedings have been protracted; many witnesses have been examined in Strasbourg and at an airfield near Stavanger in Norway. In January 1976 the Commission of Human Rights submitted its report, in which it expressed the opinion that, in certain respects, violations had occurred. Early in 1978 the Court decided that the British security forces in Northern Ireland had been guilty, in a limited number of cases, of inhuman treatment, but not of torture.

But these are examples of rare instances when one government will bring a case against another. Such cases are not only rare, they are also undesirable except in highly unusual circumstances. The great majority of suspected violations concern miscarriages of justice due to gaps in the law, archaic procedures, administrative delays, overcomplicated administration, or other similar unintentional causes. It would be absurd to turn these individual problems into disputes between states. But it is necessary for the aggrieved individual to have a remedy and to be able, as a private citizen, to bring his or her case before the European Commission. The great merit of the European Convention is that—for almost the first time in history—it grants the individual access to an international organ which can investigate the complaint, provided that the state concerned has accepted the "right of individual petition." It is to their credit that thirteen countries—Austria, Germany, Belgium, the Netherlands, Luxemburg, Norway, Sweden, Denmark, Iceland, Ireland, Italy, Switzerland, and the United Kingdom—have accepted this right. This remedy is thus available to 200 million people within the jurisdiction of these 13 states.

However, before an individual can exercise the "right of individual petition," one must "exhaust his local remedies." Thus, before one can appeal to an international body, one must first seek a remedy before a national court. It would be unfair to engage the international responsibility of the state if a national remedy is available but has not been used. Other rules exist to determine what cases are "admissible"; for example, they must not be anonymous, abusive, or manifestly ill-founded. These rules are applied strictly and, consequently, the great majority of complaints received in Strasbourg are ruled inadmissible at this preliminary stage. By December 1977, of the more than 8,000 individual applications that had been filed with the commission, only 174 had been declared admissible.

Once a case has been admitted, the Commission of Human Rights has three distinct functions: to establish the facts, to try to reach a friendly settlement, and—if this effort fails—to draw up a report setting out its opinion on the question of violation. The Commission has no power to take a decision.

A decision is taken subsequently either by the European Court of Human Rights—if the state concerned is one of the 14 which have accepted its jurisdiction—or by the Committee of Foreign Ministers. For example, the Court of Human Rights has held that a two- or three-year period of detention before trial constituted a violation of the convention; it was the Committee of Foreign Ministers which took the decision in the Greek case mentioned above. Whichever body takes the decision, the governments have agreed to accept it as binding.[32] By the end of 1977, the court had given judgment on 18 cases while the Committee of Ministers had made decisions on 24 cases. On a number of occasions several applications involving the same issue were joined together in one case.

Problems that have been raised before the Strasbourg organs include detention without trial in times of emergency (in the Republic of Ireland and in Northern Ireland), methods of interrogation of prisoners (in Northern Ireland), permissible limitations on freedom of expression (in Belgium, the Netherlands, and the United Kingdom), the right to a fair trial (in several countries), the right to a fair trial in criminal appeals (in Austria), laws on the use of languages in education (in Belgium), the right to trial within a reasonable time (in

Austria and the Federal Republic of Germany), the use as evidence of a clandestinely made tape recording (in Austria), trade union rights (in Belgium and Sweden), sex education in schools (in Denmark), the right of a detained person to consult a lawyer in order to institute a civil action (in the United Kingdom), and the question of military discipline (in the Netherlands). The Greek case revealed violations of ten different rights, including the use of torture and the suppression of democratic institutions. As a result of cases brought before the Strasbourg bodies, changes in the law and administrative practices have been effected in a number of countries. Norway has even changed its constitution in order to respect the right of freedom of religion. Switzerland also has altered its constitution to grant women the right to vote in federal elections.

In this way standards are being established in Europe to protect citizens' rights that are increasingly threatened by the growing power of the modern state. Though it is sometimes troublesome for a particular country to be subjected to a system of international supervision, this is the price which must be paid in order to secure the respect for fundamental freedoms throughout the democratic countries of Europe. As the Commission said on one occasion, the purpose of the states that concluded the convention "was not to concede to each other reciprocal rights and obligations in pursuance of their individual national interests, but to establish a common public order of the free democracies of Europe with the object of safeguarding their common heritage of political traditions, ideals, freedom and the rule of law."[33]

Thus, in formulating a global assessment of the present state of human rights protection in the world, we can record a considerable measure of positive achievement in the framework of the Council of Europe. In November 1975 a colloquy was held in Rome to celebrate the twenty-fifth anniversary of the signature of the European Convention. When their work was finished, the participants were received in the Vatican by Pope Paul VI, who referred to the European system as "an important step towards greater justice, not only because it enables injustices to be rectified, but also because it encourages a search for justice." The Pope asked, "Should not Europe set an example of a truly human civilization which is not merely concerned with economic and technological development, but also make it a point of honor to defend the rights of human beings?"[34] This question might be asked today not only of Europe but of the whole world.

Three other developments in Europe must be mentioned briefly. The first is the European Social Charter. While the Convention on

Human Rights protects civil and political rights, the Social Charter, concluded in 1961, protects economic and social rights in the member states. This charter specifically protects 19 separate rights.[35] It provides an arrangement for progressive implementation, establishes a system of international supervision which is largely inspired by the practice of the International Labor Organization (ILO), and is based on the submission of reports by governments and the examination of these reports and the comments of employers and trade unions by a committee of independent experts. Finally, it provides for subsequent discussion of the issues raised by the competent organs of the Council of Europe; such discussion may result in necessary recommendations being made to governments by the Committee of Ministers.[36]

By the end of 1977, eleven states had ratified the Social Charter.[37] It has been in force for over ten years and has led to a number of changes, which have constituted improvements in social policy and administration, in the states which are parties to the charter. As examples one might mention improvement of systems of social security, increased maternity benefits, new regulations for the protection of young workers, arrangements for the admission of the families of migrant workers into specific countries, and the introduction of equal pay for men and women.[38]

The second development concerns the law of the European Communities created by the Paris treaty of 1951 and the two treaties of Rome of 1957. Each of the nine states which comprise the communities are also members of the Council of Europe and are parties to the European Convention on Human Rights. In addition, eight of these states have constitutional guarantees of human rights in their national constitutions. It is therefore to be expected that the institutions of the European Communities should respect basic human rights and fundamental freedoms. Yet a number of questions arise: How is this to be achieved? What is the relationship between the Human Rights Convention of 1950 and the European Economic Community (EEC) treaty of 1957? Since the European Communities have established their own legal order which is interpreted by their own Court of Justice in Luxemburg, what is the relationship between EEC law and European human rights law?

The Luxemburg Court has tackled these questions in an interesting way in recent years. In the Internationale Handels-gesellschaft Case in 1970 the court ruled that "respect for basic rights forms an integral part of the general principles of law whose observation is ensured by the Court of Justice" and continued: "the protection of these rights, consonant with the constitutional traditions common to member states, must be assured within the context and aims of the Community."

In the Nold Case in 1974 the court reaffirmed this principle and elaborated it by stating that the court must be guided by the constitutional traditions of member states as well as by international treaties on human rights of which the member states are signatories—an obvious reference to the European Convention.

In the Ruttili Case in 1975 the Luxemburg Court went further and specifically cited several articles of the European Convention and of its Fourth Protocol as a basis for its reasoning. It is evident therefore that the human rights standards of the European Convention are gradually finding their way into community law; a measure of interpenetration of the two systems may be expected in the future.[39]

The interest of the communities in ensuring the effective protection of human rights is further illustrated by an important report prepared by the Commission at the request of the European Parliament in 1976,[40] by references to the question by the Commission and the Court of Justice in their reports on European union during the previous year,[41] and by the importance attached to "a citizen's Europe" and "the protection of rights" by Leo Tindemans, the Belgian prime minister, in his "Report on European Union" prepared for the European Council at the request of the "Summit Meeting" of Heads of Government in Paris in December 1974.[42]

The third major development in Europe in recent years is, of course, the signature of the Final Act of the Helsinki Conference on August 1, 1975, and the subsequent reactions to it in Eastern Europe, in the West, and in the United States. This is discussed in a later chapter.

C. In the Americas

In the western hemisphere there is considerable cause for concern at the slow progress made toward bringing into force the American Convention on Human Rights concluded in San José de Costa Rica on November 22, 1969, resulting from a decision taken in 1959.

Even earlier, in 1948—seven months before the General Assembly of the United Nations approved the text of the Universal Declaration—the Organization of American States had adopted in Bogotá the American Declaration on the Rights and Duties of Man. At a consultation meeting of the Ministers for Foreign Affairs at Santiago in 1959 the participants decided to establish an Inter-American Commission on Human Rights and to charge the Inter-

American Council of Jurists to prepare a draft convention. The draft thus prepared, as well as two other drafts submitted by Chile and Uruguay, was discussed at the Organization of American States (OAS) Conference in Rio de Janeiro in 1965. Then, after further discussions and a revision of the draft convention effected by the Inter-American Commission, a Specialized Conference on Human Rights was held in San José, November 7 to 22, 1969, at the conclusion of which the convention was signed by the representatives of 12 states.[43]

The American Convention[44] is in many respects similar to the European Convention, although it includes additional rights and some of the definitions it employs are more liberal than those in its European counterpart. It includes a system of international control which will function through the existing Inter-American Commission and a new Inter-American Court of Human Rights. The most important difference, however, is that acceptance of the competence of the Commission to consider individual petitions is not an optional provision (as in the European Convention and in the U.N. optional protocol) but is a binding obligation that follows automatically from ratification. On the other hand, the procedure of interstate complaints is optional and only applies to those states which have expressly indicated their agreement to this procedure.

The American Convention on Human Rights requires 11 ratifications to enter into force. This number was obtained on 18 July 1978, with the ratifications of Colombia, Costa Rica, Dominican Republic, Ecuador, Guatemala, Haiti, Honduras, El Salvador, Granada, Panama, and Venezuela. And is it too much to hope that favorable action might be taken on President Carter's request to the Congress to ratify the American Convention? Such action would constitute a significant step toward the more effective protection of human rights in the western hemisphere.

D. The Institution of the Ombudsman

The institution of the ombudsman, although not consciously conceived as a mechanism for the protection of human rights as such, is a valuable means of protecting the citizen against maladministration on the part of public authorities.

The institution of the ombudsman originated in Sweden as early as 1809. Thus, since the Swedish ombudsman is the prototype, it is appropriate to define the ombudsman by describing his functions. The ombudsman is an independent, high-level official, appointed by and responsible to the parliament, who supervises the observance of the law by all executive officials and the judiciary. The Constitution of 1809 prescribed that the Riksdag (parliament) should appoint a *justitieombudsman* of known legal ability and outstanding integrity to serve as representative of the Riksdag. The first ombudsman was appointed in the following year.

In order to fulfill his obligations the ombudsman may receive complaints from citizens who feel that they have been unfairly treated by government departments. The ombudsman then investigates the charges and tries to arrange a satisfactory solution, usually by making an appropriate recommendation. It is important to note that the ombudsman does not have power to give instructions to executive agencies, although he does have great power of persuasion backed up by the right to report his findings to parliament if he is dissatisfied with the action taken on his recommendation.

The ombudsman system has evolved over the years. In 1915 the Riksdag appointed a separate *militieombudsman* (military commissioner) to supervise the action of the military authorities. However, since the end of World War II the work of the *militieombudsman* has diminished, while that of the *justitieombudsman* has increased. Consequently, in 1967 the Riksdag undertook a radical reform of the system. The two existing offices were merged into one post, but three persons, each with the title of *justitieombudsman* and with a common staff of assistants, were appointed by the Riksdag for terms of four years each. Today the ombudsmen have a staff of 50, about half of whom are lawyers. The ombudsmen constitute a triumvirate with equal powers and divide the work among themselves according to its substance. One ombudsman supervises the courts of justice, the public prosecutors, the police, and the armed forces; the second supervises the field of social welfare, insurance, and education; the third handles cases relating to taxation, execution of judgments, and other matters of civil administration.

Today the supervisory competence of the ombudsman extends, with few exceptions, to the acts of all national and municipal officials, but not to those of members of the government. The purpose of this supervision is to ensure that laws and statutes are observed and that officials perform their duties properly. In particular, the ombudsmen are required to ensure that no unlawful constraints are imposed on personal liberty. If in the course of their work they observe defects or omissions in the law, they are required to draw attention to these problems and to make suitable recommendations.

In order to discharge his functions, the ombudsman has access to all official files and documents. No document may be kept from the ombudsman on grounds of secrecy. All officials are obliged by law to surrender any information or other assistance required.

In serious cases of breach of duty or improper administration, the ombudsman may institute a prosecution; but this action occurs rarely—only about six times a year. In less serious cases the ombudsman issues an admonition; this is a more effective sanction than one might suppose, for such decisions are reported in the press and recorded in the published annual report to the parliament. If the ombudsman considers an act of a public official inadequate or unwise even if it is not illegal, he can issue a recommendation to solve the problem and to improve the procedures of the department involved in the future. The ombudsman also may support a claim for compensation if the victim has suffered injury or a request for retrial if the ombudsman thinks that the accused has been wrongly convicted.

Anyone may complain to the ombudsman without restriction regarding nationality or residence, direct interest in the matter, or exhaustion of other remedies.

When adopting the ombudsman law of 1967 the Riksdag emphasized the importance of the ombudsman's undertaking investigations on his own initiative. Such investigations constitute an important part of the work; they may relate to matters revealed incidentally during the examination of a complaint, to matters discovered during an inspection, or to allegations originally made in the newspapers or other sources.

Another function of the ombudsman is the inspection of courts, prisons, administrative boards, and agencies, including those of the central government departments in Stockholm. Each of the three ombudsmen spends about 30 days a year on such inspections, which usually take several days. The inspections extend to courts, prosecutors, police authorities, prisons, mental homes, and military establishments as well as executive agencies. The inspection usually begins with the people in charge and includes interviews with members of the staff and—in the case of prisons and mental homes—with the inmates. At the end of the inspection the ombudsman makes any recommendations deemed appropriate.

This activity undoubtedly has a preventive value in that it helps to prevent situations from arising which, if unchecked, might give rise to violations of citizens' rights and the filing of complaints. Since so much of human rights law is concerned with protection of the rights of individuals against improper interference by public authorities and with guarantees that officials ensure and respect the rights of citizens, it is evident that there is much common ground in the two systems, even though ombudsmen (as well as persons exercising similar functions but with different titles) also are called upon to deal with problems outside the scope of human rights law.

From this summary account of the institution of the ombudsman in Sweden, several conclusions can be drawn:
1. The system has amply justified itself over a period of more than 150 years.
2. The system affords a simple and inexpensive remedy to any individual who believes his or her rights have been violated by the public authorities.
3. The system of investigation and inspection on the ombudsman's own initiative means that there is a permanent watchdog over the acts of the administration in the interests of the individual.
4. The institution of the ombudsman affords an additional and important guarantee of the rights and liberties of the citizen.

The institution of the ombudsman has spread rapidly around the world in recent years.[45] The system has been adopted with local variations in Finland, Denmark, Norway, the Federal Republic of Germany (for the armed forces), the United Kingdom (in the form of the "Parliamentary Commissioner for Administration," with separate "local commissioners" for local government), in Northern Ireland, in France (in the person of the *médiateur*), and in Switzerland (for the city of Zurich).

These developments have not been limited to Europe. In a 1962 act of Parliament, New Zealand became the first *common law* country to introduce the institution.[46] Israel introduced a variation in 1971 whereby the state comptroller was given jurisdiction, as public complaints commissioner, over complaints against acts of the administration. In Canada the function of ombudsman has been introduced in most of the provinces. At the federal level a "commissioner of official languages" already exists, while proposals for an ombudsman with general competence have been introduced in Parliament. In the United States there is no ombudsman in the classic sense at the federal level, although a number of government departments and commissions have appointed "executive ombudsmen" with the specific task of handling complaints against the administration in which they serve. There are, however, persons discharging the functions of ombudsmen in a number of the states (notably Hawaii, Nebraska, Iowa, Alaska, and Michigan), while many big cities have appointed a senior official in the mayor's or city manager's office either to deal directly with citizens' complaints or to afford citizens redress. Similar examples exist in other parts of the world.[47]

The institution of the ombudsman and its introduction, with local variations, in so many countries in recent years affords one more proof of the widespread awareness of the necessity to protect the citizen against the ever-present danger of misuse of power, or even simple mistakes, on the part of public authorities and is a recognition that the measures taken for this purpose constitute additional safeguards for human rights and fundamental freedoms.

IV. Balance Sheet

How can we strike a balance between the negative factors and the positive aspects of the condition of human rights in the world today? For that matter, is it possible to strike such a balance? It certainly is not possible to do so with any degree of precision or certainty. It does seem desirable, however, to formulate certain indications that may help the reader to come to his or her own conclusions.

The first point is perhaps more of a psychological than of a concrete nature: it is the recognition that nowadays virtually everyone is in favor of human rights. Although deeds do not always correspond to professions of faith, few governments or political leaders today dare to admit publicly to being opponents of civil liberties. Attempts may be made to justify or excuse violations; arguments may be used to explain—perhaps tendentiously or even hypocritically—that certain categories of rights are more important than others. But world public opinion is such that no one dares deny the basic article of faith that (in the words of the Universal Declaration) "every individual and every organ of society ... shall strive ... to promote respect for these rights and freedoms and ... to secure their universal and effective recognition and observance."

Many factors have contributed to this situation. One might mention the Charter of the United Nations itself, the Universal Declaration of 1948, the U.N. covenants of 1966, various resolutions of the General Assembly,[48] the papal encyclical *Pacem in Terris*, the work of the Vatican Commission on Justice and Peace, declarations of other churches, the statutes of regional organizations, and the provisions of many national constitutions.[49] It may be objected that this lip service to human rights is valueless when practical realities do not correspond to public declarations. But this would be a mistake, because the constant reaffirmation of the obligation to respect human rights is something new in the second half of the twentieth century and constitutes an important element in the formation of public opinion throughout the world.

This reference to public opinion is the key to the human rights balance sheet. Gloomy as the human rights picture is in many parts of the world, anyone who has studied history will know that it has been worse at most periods in the past. It is sufficient to recall the institution of slavery which existed for many centuries in most parts of the world, the fact that torture was the standard accompaniment of interrogation in the middle ages, the atrocities inflicted on civilian populations during the religious wars of the sixteenth and seventeenth centuries, the burning at the stake of religious dissidents during the counter-reformation, and the absence of rules of humanitarian law until Henry Dunant founded the Red Cross just over a century ago. These forms of cruelty and inhumanity were not generally regarded as exceptional or even as reprehensible by many people. They were usual practice; burnings and hangings were a public show—often the occasion for a public holiday. Even in our own time, who can forget the death camps and the gas chambers of World War II?

It would be facile and overoptimistic to assert that these conditions have changed completely. But something has changed: World public opinion has changed. In most countries national opinion has changed; and for many millions of people throughout the world, individual opinion has changed. Here the mass media have played a cardinal role. In my view they are playing it well. When new evidence of massive violations of human rights is uncovered, this is reported throughout the world, at least where there is freedom of expression. When President Carter receives a Soviet dissident or makes proposals to the United Nations to strengthen its human rights machinery, the fact is known from Alaska to Australia within a matter of hours.

The concern of the average citizen is the best hope for the future. In this context, I must mention the work and influence of the numerous nongovernmental organizations which are tireless in their work for human rights. Three in particular—Amnesty International, which is concerned with prisoners of conscience and the abolition of torture; the International Commission of Jurists, which is devoted to the observance of the rule of law and the right to a fair trial; and the International Institute of Human Rights, which by its publications and annual teaching sessions is spreading the gospel in many countries—deserve special mention. Many other organizations do similar yeoman work. It is undeniable that there is a public conscience which is slowly but surely making itself felt.

Governments and intergovernmental organizations, of course, must play the principal role and, in the third part of this essay, I have tried to indicate some of the ways in which they are doing so. Other important developments are the Final Act of the Helsinki Conference, the reactions to the Helsinki Agreement both in the

East and the West, and President Carter's proposals to the United Nations on March 17, 1977. One can reach a provisional conclusion regarding a global assessment of human rights. Though there are many somber aspects of the human rights situation in the world, never in recorded history have so many individuals, organizations, and governments labored so constantly to secure the universal and effective recognition and observance of human rights throughout the world as at the present time. That is the basis of hope for the future.

NOTES

1. I have derived much information during recent months from the columns of *The Times* (London), the *International Herald-Tribune* (Paris), *Le Monde*, and *Le Figaro*. Particular mention should be made of B. Gwertzman, "Human Rights: As Others See Them," *Herald-Tribune*, March 9, 1977, and of Raymond Aron, "Diplomatie americaine et droits de l'homme," *Le Figaro*, March 14, 1977.
2. Resolution 2 (XXIII), March 6, 1967 and Resolution 5 (XXIII), March 16, 1967 (U.N. Commission on Human Rights).
3. Dakar International Conference on Namibia and Human Rights (International Institute of Human Rights, 1977); see also *A Trust Betrayed: Namibia* (U.N. Office of Public Information, 1974).
4. Resolution 8 (XXXXI), 1974 (U.N. Commission on Human Rights). There is also a special committee to examine Israeli practices affecting the human rights of the population of the territories occupied by Israel in 1967 created by the General Assembly on December 19, 1968. See M. Schreiber, "La Pratique recente des Nations Unies dans le domaine de la protection des droits de l'homme," *Recueil des cours de l'academie de droit international*, 1975, vol. 2: 368–371.
5. U.N. Doc. A/10285 (1975) and A/31253 (1976).
6. U.N. Doc. E/CN.4/1188 (1976).
7. U.N. Doc. E/CN.4/1221 (1977).
8. See B. Gwertzman, *supra* note 1.
9. One recalls particularly the television interview of Andrei Sakharov broadcast in the United States in February 1977; President Carter's letter to Sakharov of February 5, 1977; Vladimir Bukovsky's reception in Washington later that month; the attempt of Andrei Amalrik to see President Giscard d'Estaing in Paris on February 14, 1977; and the meeting in Prague at the beginning of March between Max van der Stoel, the Dutch Foreign Minister, and the late Professor Jan Patocka, leader of the "Charter 77 Campaign."
10. See *Report on Torture* (Amnesty International, December 1973) on the occasion of their Paris conference.
11. The history and contents of the two covenants are summarized in A. H. Robertson, *Human Rights in the World* (Manchester; England: Manchester University Press, 1972), pp. 22–48.

12. These procedures are described in greater detail in M. Schreiber, *supra* note 4, pp. 338–342 and 362–365.
13. See A. H. Robertson, *supra* note 11 and M. Schreiber, *supra* note 4.
14. Canada, Cyprus, Denmark, Finland, the Federal Republic of Germany, Norway, Spain, Sweden, and the United Kingdom. In addition, Australia and the Philippines are parties to the first but not to the second covenant.
15. Bulgaria, Byelorussia, Czechoslovakia, the German Democratic Republic, Hungary, Poland, Romania, the Ukraine, the USSR, and Yugoslavia.
16. Guinea, Kenya, Libya, Madagascar, Mali, Mauritius, Rwanda, Tanzania, Tunisia, and Zaire. Senegal ratified on February 13, 1978.
17. Iran, Iraq, Jordan, Lebanon, Syria, and Mongolia.
18. Barbados, Chile, Colombia, Costa Rica, Dominican Republic, Ecuador, Guyana, Jamaica, Panama, Surinam, and Uruguay.
19. Denmark, Norway, and Sweden.
20. Barbados, Canada, Colombia, Costa Rica, Denmark, Dominican Republic, Ecuador, Finland, Jamaica, Madagascar, Mauritius, Norway, Panama, Surinam, Sweden, Uruguay, and Zaire. Senegal also ratified the protocol on February 13, 1978.
21. Canada, Cyprus, Denmark, the Federal Republic of Germany, Norway, and the United Kingdom.
22. Bulgaria, the German Democratic Republic, Romania, and the USSR.
23. Mauritius, Rwanda, and Tunisia.
24. Iran and Syria.
25. From Colombia, Costa Rica, and Ecuador.
26. Resolution 75 (V), August 5, 1947 (U.N. Economic and Social Council).
27. Resolution 728 F (XXVII), July 30, 1959 (U.N. Economic and Social Council).
28. Resolution 1503 (XLVIII), May 27, 1970 (U.N. Economic and Social Council). These developments are described in detail in L. Sohn and T. Buergenthal (eds.), *International Protection of Human Rights* (Indianapolis: Bobbs-Merrill Co., 1973), pp. 739–855.
29. Report by the Secretary General on the present situation with regard to communications concerning human rights, *U.N. Doc.* E/CN.40165 (1949).
30. M. Schreiber, *supra* note 4, pp. 354–359.
31. The origins, functions, and achievements of the Council of Europe are described in A. H. Robertson, *The Council of Europe,* 2d ed. (London: Stevens, 1961) and *Manual of the Council of Europe* (1970). The original member states were Belgium, Denmark, France, Ireland, Italy, Luxemburg, the Netherlands, Norway, Sweden, and the United Kingdom. The following subsequently acceded: Greece, Turkey, Iceland, the Federal Republic of Germany, Austria, Switzerland, Cyprus, Malta, Portugal and Spain.
32. The operation of the European Convention is described in detail in J. E. S. Fawcett, *The Application of the European Convention on Human Rights* (Oxford: Clarendon Press, 1969); F. Jacobs, *The European Convention on Human Rights* (Oxford: Clarendon Press, 1975); and A. H. Robertson, *Human Rights in Europe,* 2d ed. (Manchester, England: Manchester University Press; New York: Oceana, 1977). The more important decisions of the Commission, the Court, and the Committee of Ministers are published in the *Yearbook of the*

European Convention on Human Rights (The Hague: Martinus Nijhoff, annually).

33. "Decision of the Commission as to the Admissibility of Application No. 788/60 lodged by the Government of the Federal Republic of Austria against the Government of the Republic of Italy," *Yearbook of the European Convention on Human Rights* (1961), pp. 116-182.

34. *Proceedings,* Fourth International Colloquy about the European Convention on Human Rights (Council of Europe, 1976), pp. 289-291.

35. Seven rights are considered of particular importance: the right to work, the right to organize, the right to collective bargaining, the right to social security, the right to social and medical assistance, the right of the family to special measures of protection, and the rights of migrant workers.

36. The history and content of the Social Charter are described in chapter eight of A. H. Robertson, *Human Rights in Europe,* 1st ed. (Manchester, England: Manchester University Press; New York: Oceana, 1963).

37. Austria, Cyprus, Denmark, France, the Federal Republic of Germany, Iceland, Ireland, Italy, Norway, Sweden, and the United Kingdom.

38. H. Wiebringhaus, "La Convention européenne des droits de l'homme et la charte sociale européenne," 8 *Human Rights Journal* (1975): 527-544. F. Sur, "La Charte sociale européene—dix anées d'application," 22 *European Yearbook* (1974): 88-136 (summary in English).

39. These developments are summarized more fully in A. H. Robertson, *supra* note 32, pp. 286-291, and analyzed in depth in H. G. Petersmann, "The Protection of Fundamental Rights in the European Communities," 23 *European Yearbook* (1975): 179-206.

40. "Protection of Fundamental Rights in the European Communities," *Bulletin of the European Communities Supplements,* no. 5 (1976).

41. *Bulletin of the European Communities Supplements,* nos. 5 and 9 (1975).

42. *Bulletin of the European Communities Supplements,* no. 1 (1976); 23 *European Yearbook* (1975): 3.

43. Chile, Colombia, Costa Rica, Ecuador, El Salvador, Guatemala, Honduras, Nicaragua, Panama, Paraguay, Uruguay, and Venezuela. The history of the convention and its contents are summarized in A. H. Robertson, *supra* note 11, pp. 111-139.

44. *Ibid.,* pp. 249-273.

45. On the ombudsman in general, see D. Rowat, *The Ombudsman—Citizen's Defender,* 2d ed. (London: Allen and Unwin, 1968); W. Gellhorn, *Ombudsmen and Others* (Cambridge: Harvard University Press, 1966); A. Legrand, *Ombudsman scandinave: Études comparées sur le controle de l'administration* (Paris: Librairie générale de droit et de jurisprudence, 1970); B. Frank, "The Ombudsman Revisited," *International Bar Journal* no. 48 (1975).

Much detailed information on the ombudsmen and parliamentary commissioners in European countries may be found in *Council of Europe Parliamentary Assembly: Meeting of the Legal Affairs Committee with the Ombudsmen and Parliamentary Commissioners in Member States* (Strasbourg's Council of Europe, 1974). Information on ombudsmen throughout the world is published in *Reports and Newsletter of the Ombudsman Committee* of the International Bar Association (Allentown, Pa.); hereinafter cited as *Ombudsman Committee.* See also A. H. Robertson, *The Ombudsman in Comparative Law* (Strasbourg: International Faculty for the Teaching of Comparative Law, summer 1975 no. 1213).

46. D. E. Paterson, "The New Zealand Ombudsman as a Protector of Citizen's Rights," 2 *Human Rights Journal* (1969): 395.

47. In Tanzania, Guyana, Mauritius, and Zambia see *Ombudsman Committee, supra* note 45; A. H. Robertson, *supra* note 45.

48. For example, the Declaration on Colonialism of 1960 (reaffirmed in 1962 by 101 votes in favor, with one against and four abstentions) stated that "all states shall observe faithfully and strictly the provisions of the Universal Declaration of Human Rights."

49. At the International Conference on Human Rights at Teheran in 1968, the Secretary General of the United Nations, U Thant, stated that there were 43 constitutions adopted in recent years which were clearly inspired by the Universal Declaration (*U.N. Doc.* A/Conf. 32/41).

Bibliography

BROWNLIE, I. (ed.), *Basic Documents on Human Rights* (Oxford, 1971).
CAREY, J., *International Protection of Human Rights* (New York, 1968).
CLAUDE, R. P. (ed.), *Comparative Human Rights* (Baltimore, 1976).
DOMINQUEZ, J., et al., *Enhancing Global Human Rights* (New York, 1979).
ERVING, W. C., and Veenhoven, W. A. (eds.), *Case Studies on Human Rights and Fundamental Freedoms: A World Survey*, 5 vols (The Hague, 1976).
HESBURGH, T. M., *The Humane Imperative* (New Haven, 1974).
International Human Rights: A Bibliography 1965-1969 (Notre Dame, Ind., 1976).
International Human Rights: A Bibliography 1970-1976 (Notre Dame, Ind., 1976).
International Protection of Human Rights, hearings before the Subcommittee on International Organizations and Movements of the Committee on Foreign Affairs, U.S. House of Representatives, 93rd Congress (Washington, D.C., 1974).
LILLICH, R. B., and Newman, F. (eds.), *International Human Rights: Problems of Law and Policy* (New York, 1977).
MOSKOWITZ, M., *International Concern with Human Rights* (New York, 1975).
ROBERTSON, A. H., *Human Rights in the World* (Manchester, 1972).

PART TWO
Individual and Group Rights

Introduction

WHAT ACTUALLY IS A HUMAN RIGHT? WHAT IS THE BASIS OF A CLAIM to a human right? Do human rights exist outside the structure of positive law or in the absence of their juridical enforcement? How do human rights differ from other kinds of rights, such as *civil* rights? Can a human *need* properly be treated as a human *right*? When does a human need translate into a right that is the object of a just claim? Modern rights theorists have only begun to struggle with these questions and to restore some conceptual order to a very muddled philosophical landscape. In spite of their importance these questions are treated only tangentially in Part Two, where the focus, as in the remainder of this volume, is on certain practical problems or difficulties arising out of prevailing human rights theory.

The editors take it for granted that the rights enumerated in existing human rights charters and covenants are human rights deserving universal respect and implementation. Indeed, if the Universal Declaration does in fact reflect a common understanding of humankind regarding those rights which are necessary for living a truly *human* life, then there would seem to be broad agreement in the world on the kinds of rights that are in need of protection. These rights form three groups: fundamental intellectual, spiritual, and political freedoms; procedural guarantees that respect the bodily integrity and personal dignity of prisoners; and basic socio-economic needs. While governments differ in their interpretations of these rights and in the extent to which they can be realized in given social contexts—a matter taken up in Part Three—all governments seem to agree that they are intrinsic to the *individual* because of his or her personal dignity and being as a human person. The emphasis upon individual rights is, of course, strongest in the Western liberal-constitutionalist tradition. The inadequacies of this tradition as the basis for a theory or a policy of rights is explored in the chapters by Vernon Van Dyke and Ben Whitaker.

Van Dyke contends that liberalism, which focuses exclusively on the relationship between the individual and society, has failed to provide an adequate theory of the state. Contractarian, utilitarian, and natural right theories of government are all individualist prescriptions that are unable theoretically to cope with the serious and very real problems arising out of discrimination against ethnic, racial, religious, and linguistic communities in many parts of the world. And so he introduces the notion of "group rights" and argues, persuasively, that "ethnic communities and other groups, in addition to individuals, [be] acknowledged as right-and-duty-bearing units." That groups do have rights, suggests Van Dyke, is also a legitimate inference from the explicit recognition in the U.N. Charter and the two international covenants on human rights of the right of "all peoples" to self-determination.

After an attempt to define the communities that might be justified in staking out a moral and legal claim to group rights, the author proceeds to cite historical precedents and modern practices to support his thesis. Several of his illustrations are drawn from heterogeneous societies in which cultural minorities are corporately recognized in systems of political representation, in the distribution of social benefits, or in the assignment of territory within which the group or community enjoys complete or partial autonomy. Discussed, too, are those situations where the principle of free government might require the informed consent of whole groups, such as American Indians or other ethnic and cultural minorities. He also sets forth the argument that black Americans, because they have suffered repression and discrimination as a group, might well establish a moral claim to a group right that would conceivably involve the adoption of racial quotas and other compensatory programs for improving the group's position in society.

Finally, Van Dyke suggests that the concept of groups as "right-and-duty-bearing units" would furnish political theorists and statesmen alike with an "intellectually defensible doctrine ... which would respond to practical problems." It could contribute to the well-being and psychological health of insular minorities, safeguard the independence and integrity of minority cultures, facilitate the adoption of affirmative action policies in the United States, provide a coherent rationale for exempting certain communities (such as the American Amish) from the application of general law, and fashion a tool for dealing with many problems of justice and peace in the world.

Ben Whitaker, who shifts our attention to specific problems of justice and peace, tells of the efforts of the United Nations and individual countries to grant self-determination to suppressed peoples and minorities with serious grievances against the dominant majority within nations. For the most part, these efforts seem to have floundered on the inability of U.N. delegates to agree on a definition of a minority group or on what rights minorities should have apart from those they may actually claim. Such agreement is surely necessary before minority rights could be enforced by any international agency.

"Subordinate peoples" are to be found in many countries today, as Whitaker notes. But he omits several minorities with severe grievances against the dominant majority, such as blacks in the United States and foreign workers long resident in West Germany. Presumably, the author does not wish to describe all minorities as "subordinate peoples." But the wide variety and different historical experiences of all these groups compound the difficulty inherent in attempting to define rights universally applicable to minorities. Yet many minorities and some governments are searching for ways to accommodate the legitimate demands of these groups. Strategies of accommodation range from plans for withdrawal of minorities into autonomous enclaves of separate development, including secession from existing nation-states, to full political integration into the national community subject only to the condition that the minority be allowed to preserve and foster its cultural, religious, linguistic, or ethnic identity.

Of course there are difficult problems, acknowledged by both Van Dyke and Whitaker, in working out a standard to govern the treatment of minorities by dominant majorities. That no universal standard is available for application is surely a possible reply to the problem, and difficulties in this area may have to be resolved on a case-by-case basis. For one thing, there are situations where individual rights might well conflict with group rights. Which should prevail? For another, minority rights have been perceived in some situations as conflicting with the principle of self-determination of peoples, leading to the breakup of the nation-state and the consequent curtailing of the socio-economic development that may be necessary to fulfill basic human needs. Yet the search for community in the modern world is an intense one and is symptomatic of the identity crisis through which many minorities are passing.

There is considerable disagreement over which groups should be entitled to claim rights and which groups' rights should be entitled to recognition. Should group rights be accorded to insular minorities in the United States? Van Dyke, notwithstanding his references to recent U.S. Supreme Court decisions granting recognition to the rights of cognizable groups, wonders whether it is justifiable to emphasize the notion of group rights within the United States. It is difficult to formulate a satisfactory theory of group rights in societies where minority groups not only accept the individualistic ethic of the dominant society but also prefer full assimilation into that society. But in other regions of the world, where minorities are against assimilation and suffer persecution because of their desire for autonomy, the principle of self-determination of peoples is sharply in conflict with the notion of group rights. This is particularly true of Africa, where developing countries and new nations strongly resist tendencies toward internal disunity and territorial fragmentation.

Should the rights of oppressed minorities around the world be acknowledged by U.S. foreign policy-makers? Nearly everyone agrees that racial majorities suppressed by minority governments should be regarded as oppressed minorities and that the United States should by word and deed support the claims of these minorities. But what of other insular groupings and subordinate peoples? Here there is no consensus on the feasibility of an American policy. Even in meritorious cases, where minorities are the victims of injustice, an American silence, owing to geopolitical and ideological realities, may be preferable to any kind of action. The ethnic separatism occurring in Ethiopia is a current example of where an official silence may be the best policy. Support by the United States of secessionist Eritreans or of Somali rebels in Ogaden could, given the pattern of alliances in this region of the world, affect chances for peace in the Middle East, jeopardize American-Soviet cooperation on arms reduction, or intensify Ethiopia's armed conflict with Somalia. Problems such as these, it seems, can be resolved only through international standards governing the treatment and disposition of minorities living within national boundaries.

2: The Individual, The State, and Ethnic Communities in Political Theory

VERNON VAN DYKE

SINCE THE TIME OF HOBBES AND LOCKE, LIBERAL POLITICAL theorists have made it their primary purpose to explore relationships between the individual and the state.[1] Problems in these relationships pervade the writing of academic theorists, and pronouncements about them are central features of historic documents. The truths that Thomas Jefferson held to be self-evident are truths concerning the individual and the state: All men have inalienable rights, and governments derive their just powers from the consent of the governed. Similarly, the French revolutionaries, though also concerned with the nation, proclaimed the rights of man and of the citizen. The tradition is carried on in contemporary international declarations and covenants on human rights, because—with certain exceptions—the rights enumerated are those of individuals in relation to the state.

The argument here will be that the liberal conception—an individualist one—is unduly limited. It is not enough to think in terms of two-level relationships, with the individual at one level and the state at another; nor is it enough if the nation is added. Considering the heterogeneity of humankind and of the population of virtually every existing state, it is also necessary to think of ethnic communities and certain other kinds of groups and to include them among the kinds of right-and-duty-bearing units whose interrelationships are to be explored. The question is whether ethnic communities that meet certain criteria should be considered units (corporate bodies) with moral rights and whether legal status and rights should be accorded to them.

The first step in the argument, after the definition of crucial

This chapter first appeared in 29 *World Politics*, no. 3 (April, 1977). Copyright © 1977 by Princeton University Press.

terms, is to show that the liberal emphasis on the individual even precludes a proper theory of the state, which suggests in principle that liberalism cannot be trusted to deal adequately with the question of status and rights for ethnic communities, most of which are minorities within the state.

The second step is to cite practices relating to ethnic communities and other groups—practices that at the very least raise questions about the adequacy of the liberal individualistic prescription. They suggest that liberalism needs supplementing.

The third step elaborates on the second, citing the right of nations or peoples to self-determination as the right of groups rather than of individuals, and therefore as a right for which liberalism does not offer a clear basis. In some cases the rights that groups exercise are perhaps reducible to individual rights and can thus be brought within the framework of liberal theory, but in other cases the rights belong to groups as corporate units.

The fourth step is to note an implication of the third: The usual assumption that the consent of the governed is the consent of individuals is open to question, and the consent that counts may come from groups.

The final step is to ask what difference it makes if ethnic communities and other groups, in addition to individuals, are acknowledged as right-and-duty-bearing units.

The Meaning of Crucial Terms

By ethnic community I mean a group of persons, predominantly of common descent, who think of themselves as collectively possessing a separate identity based on race or on shared cultural characteristics, usually language or religion. They may or may not think of themselves as a nation, a concept with stronger implications for political autonomy or independence.

In asking whether ethnic communities should be considered to have rights, I am asking about moral rights—that is, about morally justified claims.[2] Whether a claim is morally justified is, I assume, a question for individual judgment, though of course many persons need to concur in the judgment before meaningful social recognition of the claim is likely to occur. In fact, one of the common issues in politics is whether a justified moral claim (a moral right) exists that ought to be reinforced by law—that is, by being made a legal right as well.

The above implies that rights may be moral or legal or both. To classify them in additional ways is to raise questions, some of which will be argued below. Rights may belong either to individuals or to groups as units. I do not have an exhaustive list of the kinds of groups that ought to be considered in this connection. I would surely include the following as potential or actual right-and-duty-bearing units: ethnic communities, nations, and the populations of political dependencies and sovereign states. I would also include trade unions, though they do not figure in my present argument. I would exclude chance aggregations and even social and economic classes, considered as such; they may have group interests, but not group rights. What to say about other sorts of groups is a question I leave unexplored.

Rights that belong to individuals may go to them either as human beings or as members of a group. The Universal Declaration of Human Rights enumerates rights of the first sort; they go to "everyone ... without distinction of any kind, such as race, color, sex, language, religion, political or other opinion, national or social origin, property, birth or other status." No comparable enumeration exists of rights of the second sort, going to individuals as members of a group; they are illustrated by the right to vote, which as a rule goes only to citizens.

Rights that belong to a group may be either derivative or intrinsic. A group right is derivative if it is delegated by one or more of the original holders of the right—for example, the members of the group or perhaps the state; it is intrinsic if it is aboriginal to the group. To hold that a group right is derivative, and most particularly to hold that it is derived from individuals, is compatible with liberal individualistic theory because the group right is then reducible to an individual right. To hold that a group right is intrinsic, however, requires a modification of individualism in some degree.

The statement that groups have moral and legal rights (are right-and-duty-bearing units) inevitably threatens to revive the old question of whether there is such a thing as a real "group-person" with human qualities such as a mind or a spirit.[3] I reject the thought but will not argue the question in this brief statement of crucial definitions. What I have in mind is suggested by the idea of a corporation, which has rights and liabilities distinct from those of the persons composing it. It is suggested, for that matter, by the state itself, because *it* is a kind of corporation. At the same time, ethnic communities are unlike corporations in that they are not the creatures of law or the state. They come into existence—as nations sometimes do—independently of the state, raising the question of whether they may have moral rights and a capacity to advance moral claims regardless of their legal status.

Liberal Theory on the Individual and the State

Among liberal political theorists the focus on the individual and the state is so prominent and obvious that it seems almost superfluous to cite supporting evidence. But the focus is important, and so is the related fact that the emphasis on individualism leaves liberals without a proper theory of the state.

Both the focus and the related fact are apparent in works stressing the idea of the social contract. Hobbes and Locke, for example, make it clear that individuals (men, in fact) are parties to the contract—men who act for themselves and presumably for associated women and children. They do not act as representatives of ethnic or other groups. According to Hobbes, "A commonwealth is said to be instituted when a multitude of men do agree."[4] Hobbes provided no place for associations or groups at the intermediate level between the individual and the commonwealth.

As Sabine puts it, "There is [for Hobbes] no middle ground between humanity as a sand-heap of separate organisms and the state as an outside power."[5] Similarly, Locke spoke of an "original compact [through which] any number of men ... make one community or government wherein the majority have a right to act and conclude the rest."[6] Later Rousseau, too, spoke of a number of men establishing the state through a social compact. He was explicit about eliminating associations intermediate between the individual and the state, holding that "if ... the general will is to be truly expressed, it is essential that there be no subsidiary groups within the State." Each citizen was to "voice his own opinion and nothing but his own opinion."[7]

The most recent major exponent of a contractarian point of view, John Rawls, likewise assumes that the parties in the original position, who work out the principles of justice, are individuals who speak for themselves. Moreover, the justice that they seek is only for individuals. Rawls shows concern for social classes (that is, for "the least advantaged"), but he does not raise the question of whether ethnic communities should be considered as entities with claims to justice.[8]

Emphasis on the individual is not confined to those who assume a social contract. In speaking of the greatest good of the greatest number, utilitarians obviously have individuals in mind. Those who focus on the common good or on the nature of political obligation are thinking of individuals. Those who speak of the consent of the governed usually take it as an obvious assumption that the consent is to come from individuals. Those who deal with the concepts of one man-one vote, one vote-one value, and of majority rule clearly have individuals in mind. And references to equality can be assumed to be references to the equality of individuals unless it is specified otherwise, as in references to the sovereign equality of states.

Stressing individualism, liberals have no proper theory of the state. As indicated above, Hobbes spoke of a "multitude of men" and Locke of "any number of men" making a covenant. Neither attempted to characterize the men—not saying, for example, whether the men shared a common language or religion. They evidently thought of the question of how some men acquired a moral right to make a covenant that would bind dissenters, because they both specified that the covenant was to have unanimous consent—not asking how probable it was that unanimous consent could be obtained. They did not bother, however, to say how women and children came to be bound. Rousseau's solution to the problem was in a way more forthright. He stated that those who did not consent became foreigners and could leave; if they remained, consent was implied.[9] At the same time Rousseau's solution assumes that those making the contract somehow had a right to impose change on others.

More recent liberal authors handle the problem in different ways. Ernest Barker, considering Locke's position, says that two steps are necessary to a social contract: Preceding the contract that establishes a government is an earlier contract that establishes a society. "There must already be something in the nature of an organized community" before there can be a contract.[10] This is an ingenious, if not a disingenuous, solution to the problem; it suggests infinite regress. Rawls's solution to the problem is simpler: He just takes the state for granted, as a kind of happening, and goes on from there.

Some associate the state with the nation. That is the case with John Stuart Mill and with Ernest Barker (when speaking for himself and not commenting on Locke). Both are concerned, as Barker puts it, with the maximum development of the capacities of the greatest number of individuals, and both therefore favor a democratic state. Thus they are concerned about the conditions prerequisite to democracy, and this leads them to insist that the boundaries of the nation determine the boundaries of the state. Mill's statement, descriptive in form but prescriptive in intent, is as follows:

> Free institutions are next to impossible in a country made up of different nationalities. Among a people without fellow-feeling, especially if they read and speak different languages, the united public opinion, necessary to the working of representative government, cannot exist.... [I]t is in general a necessary condition of free institutions that the boundaries of governments should coincide in the main with those of nationalities.[11]

Barker also is both descriptive and prescriptive. "[M]ost States," he says, "are what we call 'national States.'" The assertion was highly questionable when he made it (his book was published in 1951) and surely is untrue today. Speaking of the United Kingdom, he equated it with England. He spoke of the "general structure of English life" and said that "we start from the primary fact of the existence of national society."[12]

> The reason why the nation is generally the basis of a State is simple. There must be a general social cohesion which serves as it were, as a matrix, before the seal of legal association can be effectively imposed on a population. If the seal of the State is stamped on a population which is not held together in the matrix of a common tradition and sentiment, there is likely to be a cracking and splitting, as there was in Austria-Hungary.[13]

Barker acknowledges that "the modern State is not always a unitary national society. It may contain national minorities."[14] But rather than adjusting his theory to this fact, he treats it as an "addition," tacked on and left as an anomaly.

Though Barker thinks that the state should be based on a national society, he does not grant the nation a moral right to statehood any more than he accepted Locke's apparent assumption that "any number of men" in a state of nature had a moral right to make a contract of government without having made a prior contract of society. In fact, Barker refuses to attribute moral rights (or what he calls "quasi-rights")[15] to groups of any sort. Aggregations of individuals may form groups, such as trade unions, and carry on activities; and the aggregations may be regarded as bodies or "wholes." But they are not to be regarded as persons and not to be accepted as possessing moral claims or "quasi-rights." Moral rights belong only to individuals.

If the state were regarded as a moral person, *étatisme* would be fostered and might issue in "a philosophy of the total and engulfing State whose will is the peace—and the tomb of its members."[16] If groups other than the state were regarded as moral persons, the authority of the state would be threatened. According to Barker, the state and nonstate groups are to be legal persons only. How "any number of men" or a nation acquires a moral right to establish a state is a question left without a satisfactory answer. And the point has an implication: Those who do not see a moral basis for the establishment of the state are not likely to see a moral basis for the claims of ethnic communities.

One wonders what Barker's answer would have been had he

thought of the question of whether, in international politics, one state might in principle have a moral claim against another or whether the people of a colony might collectively have a moral claim against their imperial overlord. For that matter, one wonders what his answer would have been if he had thought of the question whether the citizens of a state, who in his eyes constitute a corporate unit with collective legal rights and responsibilities while it exists, also constitute a corporate unit with a collective moral right to reestablish the state if it were somehow dissolved. To be consistent he would have had to say no to all these questions—unless in the third case he chose to suggest a prior contract of society. He concedes moral rights to individuals but offers no basis for saying that some individuals have a moral right to impose change on others or to restrict their liberty.

Historic Precedents and Contemporary Practices

Historic precedents exist and contemporary practices are followed that go against the liberal individualistic position. They reflect the granting of both legal and moral rights to groups. In some cases it seems clear that the group rights are not reducible to individual rights. In other cases the question can be answered, in a Kuhnian sense, in terms of the paradigm one adopts. Those who insist on an individualistic paradigm can find a basis for arguing that what is ostensibly a group right is reducible; and those who reject an individualistic paradigm as inadequate can contend (as I do) that it is preferable to adopt a more complex paradigm permitting individual and group rights, both legal and moral, to exist side by side.

The great historic precedent, of course, is the establishment of the state itself. As suggested above, the notion that all individuals somehow consent to the jurisdiction of the state is an obvious fiction. A more tenable position (though none is entirely satisfactory) is that human needs exist at various levels (for example, at the level of the individual and at the level of the community) and that the existence of needs implies a right to meet them. Essentially the same principle can be expressed in terms of the good: The good can be sought for units at various levels, and there is a right to promote the good.[17] This principle justifies individual rights, and it also justifies the rights of communities, including the communities (or the communities of communities) that constitute states. At no level are the rights absolute. At each level and between levels rights and their exercise are limited by other rights. Within limits reached after considering the relevant rights, the meeting of the needs of the community—or the promotion of the good of the community—justifies restrictions on the behavior of individuals, whether they consent or not.

Precedents in specific circumstances were set in connection with the American and the French revolutions. In the same declaration in which Jefferson and his associates proclaimed the inalienable rights of all men, they also proclaimed the right of "one People to dissolve the Political Bands which have connected them with another, and to assume . . . the separate and equal Station to which the Laws of Nature and of Nature's God entitle them." The wording permits a choice between paradigms. Jefferson spoke of "one People" and of "them." Those impressed by the term "them" can say that the laws of nature and nature's God conferred the right on individuals severally, who then acted through representatives in exercising it. Those impressed by the term "one People" can say that the right was conferred aboriginally on the community as a kind of corporate unit and that the right of individuals was simply to participate in the decision of the corporation.

The French revolutionaries were clearer. They proclaimed the rights of man, but they also proclaimed that "all sovereignty resides essentially in the nation." The statement presumably means that the nation has a collective right to act as a unit, and the word "essentially" suggests that the right is intrinsic, not delegated by individuals and not reducible.

Elsewhere I have described contemporary practices with regard to the legal rights of groups.[18] Ethnic communities are sometimes treated as political units within countries, both through territorial delimitations and through the use of separate electoral rolls. Thus communities as units are accorded representation in the various branches of government. Different communities sometimes live under different sets of laws—for instance, in the field of family law. It is not at all uncommon for ethnic communities to operate their own school systems, with tax support. Ethnic communities in many countries are differentially treated with respect to rights of property and residence; it is not only a question of territorial reservations for the indigenous but also a question of special measures designed to make it possible for the communities to preserve their distinctive identity. And in the case of less advanced groups, or of groups that have suffered discrimination, it is now not uncommon to give them a right to expect special measures (affirmative action) designed to promote their equality, for example, in the economic and educational realms.

Of the various questions that attend these practices, two will be considered here. The first concerns reducibility: whether the communities have the rights as units, and whether the rights of the communities are reducible to the rights of individuals as members. The second is whether the legal rights should be thought of as reflecting moral claims. I will argue that the communities have the rights as units, that in some cases the rights are irreducible, and that in principle they may well reflect moral claims.

With respect to the first question, some of the clearest illustrations come from British colonial practices. In setting up legislative councils in colonies, the British regularly faced the problem of disparate ethnic communities—a relatively small but economically and politically powerful European (mainly British) community, one or more "native" communities, and perhaps a non-European immigrant community (for instance, in East Africa, an Asian community). Cultural differences were often acute. In such circumstances, the British thought explicitly in terms of communities, and perhaps in terms of "interests." In Tanganyika, for example, they thought in terms of three communities: European, Asian, and African—in 1948 numbering 11,000, 57,000, and 7 million, respectively.

A British commission charged with recommending a system of representation at the end of World War II apparently did not even think of assuming that what should be represented were individual inhabitants. Instead, it thought in terms of the "claims of the communities" and the relative importance of those claims. Further, professing an inability to assess their relative importance, it saw "no logical alternative to equal representation."[19] There would be what other British spokesmen have called "parity," that is, each community would count as one. There would be a "partnership" of communities in a "multiracial" society.[20] The words implied that the communities would retain their separate identities, being treated as distinct units. Individuals would have the right to help elect the representatives of the community to which they belonged. The British did this kind of thing not only in Tanganyika, but in other dependencies as well.[21]

That the British conferred legal rights on the communities as units is plain. And it is difficult to see how the community rights can be reduced to individual rights. The best reductionist argument would presumably be that each voter, or each adult inhabitant, was given a right to expect that his or her racial group would be represented as indicated. Individualists would be uncomfortable in making the argument, however, if their individualism included even an elementary variety of egalitarianism, because the arrangement made each European equivalent to about 5 Asians or 636 Africans. It is more comfortable and sensible to hold that the British looked at the problem of representation much as they and others look at it in international politics. Between states, regardless of their size, the problem of representation is solved by the parity rule: one state–one vote. The British simply treated the communities of Tanganyika like states.

Practices analogous to those followed in British colonies are followed today in a number of countries. Fiji provides an example—not surprisingly, perhaps, because it was a British dependency not long ago. Its population is racially divided. Approximately 50 percent are Indian; 42 percent, Fijian; and 8 percent, European and other. Voters register on racial electoral rolls, and each racial group has a quota of seats in the two houses of the central legislature. The House of Representatives consists of 52 members, with Indians, Fijis, and Europeans and others entitled to 22, 22, and 8 seats, respectively. No provision exists for changing the quotas as the distribution of the population changes.

Again, a reductionist could argue that the arrangement gives each voter or adult a right to expect that his or her group will be represented as indicated, and the departure from the requirements of egalitarianism is not so egregious as in Tanganyika. Moreover, the third racial roll (European and other) is not strictly a community roll, though the British are the dominant element. At the same time, a modification of the international analogy applies in a credible way: The Fijian constitution (conferred by Britain) assumes the existence of three communities and assures them representation as such. The right of the individual is to participate in selecting those who represent not individuals, but the community.

In Fiji five-sixths of the land is owned by over 6,600 Fijian landowning units and is administered by a Native Land Trust Board. The constitution includes special protection for this arrangement, providing that any bill affecting it must be approved by at least six of the eight senators appointed in accordance with the advice of the Great (Fijian) Council of Chiefs.[22] The arrangement is obviously communal, giving land rights to the community as such on a collective, corporate basis. To seek to reduce these communal rights to individual rights is to strain to preserve a paradigm that does not fit.

In Belgium the linguistic communities have rights. The constitution itself says that "Belgium comprises three cultural communities.... Each community enjoys the powers invested in it by the Constitution or by such legislation as shall be enacted by virtue thereof." Clearly each community is here treated as a unit—potentially as a right-and-duty-bearing unit. The cultural communities are identified by language. Each has its own region, and a fourth region (Brussels-Capital) is bilingual. Within each region language regulations prevail. The language of instruction in the schools, for example, must be the language of the region if tax support is to be forthcoming and if diplomas granted are to be recognized. The Belgians speak specifically, in official publications, of assuring "the territorial integrity of the cultural communities."[23] According to the constitution,

> The boundaries of the four regions may only be altered or amended by an act of Parliament passed on a majority vote in each linguistic group of each of the Houses, on condition that the majority of the members of each group are present and that the total votes in favour within the two linguistic groups attain two-thirds of the votes cast.

French and Dutch Cultural Councils are established, made up respectively of the French- and Dutch-speaking members of parliament, and limited legislative powers are devolved upon them. The constitution specifies that "with the possible exception of the Prime Minister, the Cabinet comprises an equal number of French-speaking and Dutch-speaking Ministers." Clearly these provisions confer rights on the communities as units. Determined individualists can of course argue that the community rights are reducible to individual rights and that the moral claim is that of individuals rather than of the group. The argument would be that individuals have a right to expect that the territorial integrity of their linguistic community will be maintained, that within their region their language will be used, and that members of their linguistic community will share in governmental offices. In contrast, those who accept a paradigm including group rights can say that when the Belgians themselves officially speak of the rights of communities, it is gratuitous to allege that this cannot be what they mean and that the rights really go to individuals. Moreover, the requirements that the language of the community be used and that the linguistic communities be represented in the cabinet are not suggestive of individualism.

Community rights are recognized even in the United States. Individualism is dominant, of course, but there are exceptions to it and inconsistencies in it, and references to groups and their rights are increasing. The clearest case is that of the Indian tribes—"subordinate and dependent nations," enjoying those powers of sovereignty that Congress has not taken away.[24] Legislation concerning the Indians reflects different and contradictory principles, but some of it assumes that the tribes are like sovereign states in being irreducible right-and-duty-bearing units.

In the United States courts refer increasingly to groups. In 1938 the Supreme Court spoke of the possibility that "prejudice against discrete and insular minorities" might call for especially searching judicial inquiry.[25] Subsequently, the Court noted that "the economic rights of an individual may depend for the effectiveness of their enforcement on rights in the group, even though not formally corporate, to which he belongs."[26] In one of the landmark cases on school integration, a federal district court quoted a statement asserting that "[S]egregation is a group phenomenon. Although the effects of discrimination are felt by each member of the group, any discriminatory practice is directed against the group as a unit and against individuals only as their connection with the group involves the antigroup sanction."[27] In the 1960's the terms "identifiable minority" and "cognizable group" began appearing in cases involving desegregation,[28] housing legislation,[29] jury selection,[30] and racial gerrymandering. With respect to the latter, one court pointed out that "the gerrymander... does not directly or necessarily affect the individual right to vote. It is aimed at groups of citizens and is intended to diminish the likelihood that their candidate will be elected."

"There is no principle," the court held, "which requires a minority racial or ethnic group to have any particular voting strength reflected in the council [of the City of Chicago]. The principle is that such strength must not be purposefully minimized on account of their race or ethnic origin."[31] Earlier the Supreme Court had declared that "the Equal Protection Clause of the Fourteenth Amendment... protects voting rights and political groups... as well as economic units, *racial communities,* and *other entities.*"[32] In the numerous ratio-hiring cases, the regular practice is to require that minority groups (perhaps including women) be represented in specified kinds of municipal or state employment in rough proportion to their numbers.[33]

These various judicial references to group rights of course are inconclusive. A Procrustean insistence that the evidence fits liberal individualist theory is possible. But the incongruities of that theory with respect to the equal protection of the law are receiving increased attention. Thus Owen M. Fiss urges that, with respect to the interpretation of the equal protection clause, the "antidiscrimination principle" (which focuses on the individual) ought to be abandoned and that in its place a "group-disadvantaging principle" ought to be adopted. "The concern," he says, "should be with those laws or practices that particularly hurt a disadvantaged group."[34] An individualist interpretation of equal protection provides a questionable basis for affirmative action—for example, when benefits go to persons who have not suffered discrimination themselves.

Rights for groups or communities are recognized not only at the domestic, but also at the international level. International action relating to Cyprus provides the clearest illustration of the assertion of irreducible community rights. The 1960 constitution of Cyprus, reflecting agreement among Britain, Greece, and Turkey, starts right out defining "the Greek community" and "the Turkish community"; numerous provisions treat these communities as corporate entities. Moreover, a resolution of the Consultative Assembly of the Council of Europe relating to Cyprus calls explicitly for the protection of two kinds of rights on the island: "The human rights of all inhabitants," and "other rights belonging to the communities."[35]

Other actions at the international level, though clearly providing for group rights, are not so clear on the question of reducibility. A resolution of the U.N. Sub-Commission on Prevention of Discrimination and Protection of Minorities, for example, speaks of minorities that "wish for a measure of differential treatment in order to preserve basic characteristics which they possess and which distinguish them from the majority of the population." It says that "differential treatment of such groups or of individuals belonging to such groups is justified."[36] And the U.N. Convention on the Elimination of All Forms of Racial Discrimination stipulates that parties "shall, when the circumstances so warrant, take ... special ... measures to ensure the adequate development and protection of certain racial groups or individuals belonging to them for the purpose of guaranteeing them the full and equal enjoyment of human rights."

The second question is whether the legal rights that are accorded should be thought of as reflecting moral claims. Barker's negative answer, noted above, is surely inconclusive. His assumption that the authority of the state should be safeguarded against the claims of nonstate groups is an assumption that those concerned with minorities may or may not share. And even he did not allege that *étatisme* necessarily follows an acceptance of the state as a moral person. Evils may flow, of course, from almost any kind of political arrangement, including the recognition of group rights. The parity arrangement in Tanganyika, for example, is not suggestive of moral sensitivity. But no reason is evident for rejecting out of hand the view that groups, considered as units, may have moral rights. On the contrary, the granting of legal status and rights to groups—as in Belgium, Cyprus, Fijii, and the United States—may well be in response to a moral claim. Why should the possibility be ruled out that the authority of the state should be limited not only by the moral rights of individuals ("inalienable" or human rights), but also by the moral rights of groups?

Self-Determination as the Moral Right
of Dependent Peoples

As noted above, Mill and Barker speak of the desirability of making the state coextensive with the nation. The view is relevant to the idea of self-determination, which has been advanced since the time of the French Revolution, though more in the political than in the intellectual realm; and self-determination has often been described as a *right*. "Every people," Woodrow Wilson said, "has a right to choose the sovereignty under which they shall live."[37] The Charter of the United Nations speaks of the *principle* of self-determination, and the two human rights covenants speak of the *right*. Speaking of it as a right, Wilson sometimes attributed it to *peoples* and sometimes to *nations*. The common reference in the interwar years was to *national* self-determination, but the U.N. Charter and the two human rights covenants revert to the term *people*. "All peoples," the covenants say, "have the right of self-determination." Who constitutes a *people* is left vague.

Like the legal rights of communities, the right of nations or peoples to self-determination raises a question about the adequacy of the liberal focus on the individual and the state. Of course it might be argued that the right of a nation or people is reducible to an individual right—that what is really recognized is the right of individuals to choose the sovereignty under which they will live or the right to be governed (if they choose) along with others of their own kind. Such arguments, however, are not persuasive. Wilson's statement was not that every *person* but that every *people* has a right to choose the sovereignty under which to live. At most, the individual has a right to participate in the decision—and to leave the group if he does not like the outcome. Approximately the same rejoinder applies to the thought that individuals have a right to be governed together with their own kind. In contrast, a strong argument can be advanced that self-determination is the right of a group, of a corporate unit. The argument rests on words chosen when the right is asserted, on logic, and on an examination of practice.

The words chosen are sometimes ambiguous, as when Jefferson spoke of the right of "one People"—especially since the pronoun that he associated with "one People" was "them." At other times the words chosen leave no doubt. Thus in 1975 the General Assembly adopted a resolution calling for measures "to enable the Palestinian people to exercise *its* inalienable national rights."[38] A just collective claim is here assumed.

Logic supports the point more strongly. Where an individual right is at stake, such as the right of free speech, violation is a possibility, and preventive or protective measures can be taken; and if a violation occurs, redress can be sought. If self-determination were an individual right, comparable statements could be made. But, in fact, comparable statements cannot be made. There is never a thought that, when a people exercises its right of self-determination, the outcome might violate an individual right. No violation occurs even in the case of those who oppose the outcome. They retain the right to leave the group, but they have no right of protection against the group's decision and no right of redress. The only individual right that might be violated is the right to participate in the decision. The foregoing suggests that it is the corporate unit that enjoys the right; the most that an individual can claim is a right to participate in the corporate choice.

That self-determination is the right of a corporate unit is also suggested by the way in which the right has been implemented. After World War I it was simply assumed that certain components of the Russian and Austro-Hungarian empires were nations entitled to independent statehood. Individual voters in Finland, Poland, Czechoslovakia, and so forth were not asked to choose. The victorious powers simply dealt with leaders of these entities whom they recognized and arranged for independence. Even if there had been plebiscites giving individuals an opportunity to participate in the decision, they would have been within national units, and a majority vote would presumably have determined the fate of the entire unit, regardless of the wishes of the minority. In the few border areas where plebiscites in fact occurred, individuals voted not so much in their own right as to help in the settlement of conflicting claims between the adjacent nation-states. After World War II the implementation of the right of self-determination continued to be on a group basis. The dominant view in the United Nations is that a "people" is to be defined as the population of a political dependency as a whole. In most cases the imperial power endorsing self-determination and granting independence has dealt with whatever central authority it recognized in the dependency, though in some cases special votes or referenda have been held. Whatever the procedure, the "self" that is "determined" is always a group as a unit.

When we speak of a group's right of self-determination, what kind of a right is at issue? The question is important, especially in the light of Barker's view that moral rights should not be attributed to groups. It is, perhaps, not surprising that Barker did not analyze the notion of a right of self-determination. Although self-determination might be a legal right (it is nominally a constitutional right in the USSR), assertions of the right rarely give it this quality. When Jefferson asserted the right of "one People" he described it as a right "to which the Laws of Nature and of Nature's God entitle them." The right that he had in mind should thus be classified as natural or divine or moral. Similarly, when the General Assembly adopts a resolution speaking of "the Palestinian people" and "*its* inalienable national rights," it is not speaking of legal rights; rather, it is asserting that "the Palestinian people" have a moral claim. Even when a state ratifies one of the covenants, saying that "all peoples have the right of self-determination," it is not conferring a legal right on them. Rather, it is committing itself to the position that peoples have the moral right in question.

Assuming that self-determination is essentially the moral right of a group—of a collective entity, a unit, a corporate body—what is its basis? Several answers are possible. Those who believe that the individual's rights are natural or God-given can extend that belief to the rights of groups; they can say that the right comes into existence along with the group itself. Those who believe that the moral claims of individuals rest simply on a critical judgment about what ought to be can well say the same of the rights of groups. Both these answers are compatible with a third possible answer, given earlier: The existence of needs implies a right to act (within limits) to meet them, or a conception of the good has a corresponding implication.

The Consent of the Governed: Can It Come from Groups?

The view that government derives its just power from the consent of the governed is noted above, along with the related tacit assumption that "the governed" are individuals. The question now is whether that tacit assumption is justifiable.

The assumption is understandable if the population of the state is homogeneous, sharing a common culture. But if the population is divided into different communities, each cherishing and wanting to preserve its distinctive identity, why should it be assumed that the consent that counts comes from individuals? Can entire communities not give or withhold consent as collective units?

The question calls for additional comment on the right of nations or peoples to self-determination. Although the usual outcome of an exercise of the right is independence (sovereign statehood), that is not the only possibility. Puerto Rico has chosen commonwealth status, giving it a considerable measure of autonomy while remaining under the flag of the United States. The same kind of status is contemplated for the people of the Northern Marianas Islands. The people of the Cook Islands have obtained a similar status in relation to New Zealand; and the people of the island of Mayotte have voted to remain a part of France rather than join the other Comoros Islands in an independent state. Every minority that has any kind of special status might in principle have obtained it through an exercise of self-determination.

Moreover, nothing prevents an exercise of self-determination from leading to a decision to drop all claim to distinctive status and to accept assimilation into, or fusion with, another society. Whatever the outcome, as already indicated, the decision is that of a collectivity. Even if the entity exercising self-determination is somehow split, with different parts choosing different futures for themselves, the decision is collective; it is the consent of the respective parts that is obtained. And if the group or part of it chooses to remain within an existing state, why should it not be said that the consent of the governed is the consent of a collectivity? Individuals may consent, too, if only by submitting, but this does not deny the separate consent of the group. And if, in connection with self-determination, the consent of the group as a unit can be obtained by deliberate design, why can the consent of other groups not be given in less formal ways? Individuals may, of course, protest the consent that the group gives and may leave the group, but the group's decision stands.

The Question of Exceptions

In the light of the statement made at the outset—that modern liberal political theorists focus on relations between the individual and the state as if no groups count that are intermediate—let it be acknowledged that social classes and interest groups are commonly recognized. That fact, however, is beside the point, because the consideration given to social classes and interest groups has little to do with the consideration that ought to be given to ethnic communities. To be sure, social classes in Europe (as "estates") were once differentially treated for political purposes, and in some countries a social class is at the same time an ethnic community. Moreover, an ethnic community may be an interest group. But liberal political theorists, apparently regarding selected aspects of the North Atlantic world as typical of the whole world, tend to ignore the possibilities suggested by these facts.

Assuming that social and political arrangements within the state are arrangements for individuals, they treat social classes and interest groups as aggregations of individuals struggling with other such aggregations. They take it for granted that the various aggregations are integral parts of the society and polity, destined to remain so. They do not seem to think of the exceptional cases of aggregations that are culture groups with a corporate claim to differential political status and rights. Thus the consideration that they give to social classes and interest groups is not on a continuum with the consideration they give to states as corporate units, or to nations or "peoples." If one starts with the fact that states exist as corporate units and goes on to a consideration of the claims of nations or "peoples," logical continuity is broken if the next step is to social classes and interest groups as they are usually considered. Logical continuity requires that the next step be a consideration of ethnic communities.

Are the theorists known as "pluralists" exceptions to the generalization that an unjustifiable leap occurs from a consideration of the state, nation, or "people" to a consideration of the individual?

In terms of the English pluralists (for example, Figgis, Laski, Cole, and Maitland) and of the German pluralist Gierke, who influenced them, the answer might go either way. Of course, all of them intimate a framework, however vaguely, into which special status and rights for ethnic communities could perhaps be fitted. This is particularly true of Figgis, who concerned himself especially with the church and who spoke of the state as a *communitas communitatum*. Laski, too, made comments of an incidental sort suggesting some degree of autonomy for the countries which comprise the United Kingdom and for the Flemish and Walloons in Belgium. But it is abundantly clear that Laski and the other English pluralists, except Figgis, were thinking primarily if not exclusively of classes and interest groups that pursue individualistic values. They were not thinking of ethnic groups or culture groups that seek some kind of collective autonomy within a larger society or that seek to participate in the larger society as entities with status and rights. Their pluralism was the pluralism of economic associations and interests.

The principal steps beyond a recognition of the state and nation toward the recognition of status and rights for other comparable groups have been taken by scholars outside the mainstream of political theory—scholars whose orientations are predominantly empirical. Furnivall is credited with coining the term "plural society," and others influenced by him (notably M. G. Smith, Leo Kuper, and Leo A. Depres) are obviously concerned about the status and role (if not the status and rights) of ethnic groups. In the field of comparative politics, Arend Lijphart ("consociational democracy"), Val R. Lorwin ("segmented pluralism"), Hans Daalder, and others have similar concerns. Kenneth D. McRae, whose background is in political theory, belongs on the same list. A literature is growing that does not proceed on the assumption that once the state and nation have been recognized, the remaining questions concern relationships between the individual and the state.

What Difference Does It Make?

What difference does it make? Why is it important that, alongside the principle that individuals are right-and-duty-bearing units, a comparable principle should be accepted for the benefit of ethnic communities? The answer has a number of parts.

1. Whether communities as well as individuals are considered as potential right-and-duty-bearing units should make a difference in intellectual inquiry. The traditional and present stress on the individual leads to a failure even to think about groups in some contexts where the omission is obviously deplorable, or to a gross neglect of groups. According to prevailing norms it is all right to think of differential treatment for the population of states and for nations but not for other communities or groups with a distinctive identity. Put somewhat differently, a stress on the individual and on the principle of equal treatment tends to promote the view that it is improper even to think about differences of race, sex, language, and religion unless it be to combat discrimination based on these characteristics. It tends to promote blindness to group differences and a kind of unspoken assumption either that societies are homogeneous or that right-thinking persons will treat them as if they were.

Illustrations of these tendencies are not hard to find. They are present, for example, in John Rawls's *A Theory of Justice*. As noted earlier, Rawls is wholly preoccupied with the question of justice for individuals. He does not deal with the problem of ethnic communities. He takes no note at all of differences of language. He mentions race only to rule it out as a basis for discrimination, and he mentions religion out of concern for the individual believer rather than for religious communities. He mentions self-determination not as the right of a group to choose whether or not to be a sovereign state, but as the right of a state to be free of external intervention. The society to which his theory of justice applies is a society of individuals; he assumes that all societies are alike in that they consist of individuals and not of groups.

Similar statements apply to Hanna Pitkin's *The Concept of Repre-*

sentation. Pitkin seems to take into account only British and American experience—and only those aspects of that experience that other political philosophers and theorists have noted. The representation of which she speaks is of individuals, of constituencies, of interests, and of the "nation" as a whole. Of course, the "persons" of whom she speaks might be artificial or corporate, but she does not seem to think of this possibility. She does not acknowledge that representation might go to racial communities (as it does in Fiji and New Zealand) or to religious communities (as it has in Lebanon) or to linguistic communities (as it does in the Belgian Cabinet) or to ethnic communities of any sort.

Carole Pateman's *Participation in Democratic Theory* also illustrates the point. Pateman assumes that the only participants are individuals. One can read her book without finding any reason why seats in the House of Commons are allocated on a quota basis to the English, the Scots, the Welsh, and the Irish, respectively, or even an acknowledgment that this happens.

J. P. Plamenatz's *Consent, Freedom, and Political Obligation* reinforces the point. Plamenatz does not even mention the possibility that consent might come from a group as a collective unit, that freedom (i.e., "national liberation") might be desired by a group or that political obligation might rest on a group.

In each of these cases, individualistic assumptions, combined with the dichotomy between the state and the individual, lead to inattention to practices that go counter to those assumptions. It is not that the practices are rejected; they simply are not considered. Vision is narrowed, and those studying the subjects treated are not reminded of and instructed on possibilities that they ought to take into account.

2. If, in principle, communities as well as individuals were accepted as right-and-duty-bearing units, the chance would be increased that a coherent and intellectually defensible doctrine or set of doctrines could be developed which would respond to practical problems. Individuals want freedom and equality, to be sure, but there is also a "quest for community."[39] To focus only on the rights of individuals is to focus only on forces making for atomization and estrangement and to ignore primordial collective sentiment and group loyalties. Because of the failure to consider the appropriate role of communalism in the scheme of things, theory and doctrine go along one line and practice often goes along another; and individualism is assumed while anomie is bewailed. The thinking that occurs is compartmentalized—or cynical or naive.

3. If ethnic communities as well as individuals were explicitly accepted as right-and-duty-bearing units, it would probably make a

difference in their representation in various activities. To be sure, individualism and even the principle of treatment according to merit are often modified in practice in favor of group claims, as in affirmative action programs. Nevertheless, individualism gives an advantage to members of the dominant group. Their cultural characteristics permit them to establish rapport most easily with those who already have influence and power. They command the dominant language. These qualities are likely to make them seem most suitable for appointive and elective offices and for leadership positions in all walks of life. Thus they tend to obtain disproportionate representation in the various elites. Persons from the minorities who become members of an elite may or may not be representative of their own culture group; they are likely to be co-opted, perhaps because they have more or less abandoned the culture from which they sprang.

4. If ethnic communities as well as individuals were accepted as right-and-duty-bearing units, it should make a difference to the fate of communities that are nondominant and to the psychological health of their members. Individualism, combined with the usual stress on personal merit, is destructive of cultures other than the majority or dominant culture. The schools—at every level—are likely to promote the dominant culture and to undermine all others. The standards and the procedures for recruiting elites are likely, as indicated above, to favor persons who belong to the dominant culture or are willing to assimilate into it. The minority person who adheres to a minority culture is likely to be looked upon as second class and second rate, his or her culture disparaged as unworthy. The whole attitude is an attack on the existence of the group and the self-respect of its members. It means oppression and perhaps exploitation as well.

5. It would facilitate affirmative action if ethnic communities were accepted as right-and-duty-bearing units. After all, the discrimination for which affirmative action is compensatory was directed against individuals because of their membership in certain communities, and through them against the community as such. The discrimination was in a sense impersonal. It was not that a given person was to be denied certain opportunities and thus be excluded or kept down but rather that the whole community was to be kept in its place. The reciprocal of this is to take compensatory action for the whole community and to let individual members benefit even if they have not personally suffered discrimination.

Such action is hard to justify, however, if the focus is simply on the individual and the state. It is hard to justify especially if affirmative action includes the preferential treatment of some, and therefore the prejudicial treatment of others. The point is brought out in the

DeFunis case—where a white claimed that he was denied equal protection when the Law School of the University of Washington denied him admission while granting admission to apparently less qualified blacks. The case went into the courts, but the issue was never resolved because it had become moot by the time the Supreme Court was ready to act. The issue would be much easier to handle—in fact, it would probably not arise—if it were accepted that communities as well as individuals are entitled to certain kinds of status and rights.

6. As already indicated, to accept communities as right-and-duty-bearing units would provide a more satisfactory doctrinal basis for some actual practices; it would also open up the question of engaging in comparable additional practices. For example, as noted above, American courts are treating certain groups as "cognizable." In the name of the principle that the state shall not discriminate against individuals, the courts are ordering measures benefiting members of such groups, whether or not they have suffered discrimination. Moreover, corrective equity for a cognizable group may impair the interests, if not the rights, of a group that is noncognizable. For instance, a community of Hasidic Jews in the Williamsburg district of New York could be divided against its will between two electoral districts so as to undo the effects of discrimination against blacks.[40] An exclusive emphasis on individualism thus leads to paradoxes that need to be resolved.

Soul City offers another paradox. It is being developed in North Carolina under black leadership, the idea being that it is to be mainly for blacks. But undiscriminating individualism makes it impossible to state this explicitly or officially. The merits of the project can scarcely even be debated in terms of the principle relevant to it—that communities as such (in this case the black community) deserve consideration and may have rights.

Still another paradox appears in the case of the Old Order Amish in Wisconsin.[41] The issue was whether the religious community had a right of survival that modified the right of the child to an education. The Amish were willing to send their children to public schools through the eighth grade but feared that their community might be destroyed if the law requiring attendance to the sixteenth year were enforced against them. In this case, interestingly enough, the Supreme Court gave precedence to the right of the religious community. But the Court acted on the basis of the First Amendment guarantee of freedom of religion, leaving the presumption untouched that nonreligious ethnic communities do not have a comparable right.

7. A doctrine accepting both individuals and communities as

right-and-duty-bearing units is susceptible to universal application, whereas a doctrine focusing on individuals is not. Even if the melting pot could produce homogeneity in the United States, it could not possibly do so in most countries of the world. Actually, it is out of the question in the United States, too. All countries of the world are to some degree heterogeneous. The tendency to think of states as if they were nation-states is highly misleading, because scarcely a state qualifies for the label.[42] Virtually all states are polyglot in the sense that they are multilingual, multiracial, multireligious, or multinational. If every culture group in the world were assumed to be a "nation" entitled to be a state, it would mean the division of virtually every existing state and the creation of ministates numbering in the thousands.

To have a doctrine that responds to the heterogeneity of the world it is necessary to provide a place for (that is, to permit the grant of status and rights to) groups that are intermediate between the individual and the state. Choices can then be deliberately made concerning the relative emphasis on the two principles. Sometimes the emphasis will properly be on individual rights and therefore on equal treatment regardless of ethnic differences. Sometimes the emphasis will properly be on the rights of ethnic communities and therefore on the differential treatment of members and nonmembers. The implication is that the state should not be conceived as a monolithic unity but as an agency for recognizing groups, determining what legal status and rights they shall have, supervising and coordinating their interrelationships, and itself conducting certain kinds of functions in which all have a common interest.

8. If communities as well as individuals were accepted as right-and-duty-bearing units, there would be consequences for both justice and peace.

In principle, the granting of status and rights to ethnic communities on an intermediate basis should extend justice by giving minorities their due and reducing the discrimination and oppression to which they are commonly subjected. At the same time, this consequence cannot simply be assumed. After all, the concept of status and rights for communities does not mean simply status and rights for *minority* communities. Dominant or majority communities would necessarily also have status and rights and would have an opportunity to influence the decisions that are made. It is too much to expect that, as a rule, they would be magnanimous and benign. The problem would be to induce them to be fair.

In a sense, dominant communities now commonly arrogate special privilege to themselves under the cover of individualism and the principle of treatment according to merit, and the temptation to do this might or might not be reduced if community rights as such were explicitly considered. The record of the whites of South Africa, who endorse the idea of rights for different ethnic communities, is appalling. It is at least arguable that even if justice calls for community rights in principle, it would be better strategy in practice for minority communities to forgo their claims and to concentrate instead on the principle of nondiscrimination. But this would have to be a short-run strategy, for certain countries only; as already indicated, it would not provide a suitable universal basis for organizing humankind.

In principle, too, the grant of status and rights to communities on an intermediate basis should make for peace—on the assumption that justice is one of the conditions of peace. But it is unrealistic to expect the prompt achievement of justice even if just rules are accepted. Struggle is likely to be necessary. Hope for justice might actually increase violence, as surer and more rapid change is demanded by some and resisted by others. In the long run, however, it seems probable that the interests of peace as well as the interest of justice would be served.

Two Caveats

Two caveats are in order. First, no criticism is intended of the idea of individual human rights. They are precious. And defense of them might need to be even more vigilant where groups enjoy status and rights, because groups as well as the state might violate them. The point here is not that the problem of equal treatment for individuals should be ignored, but that the rule of equal treatment must be interpreted in the light of a counterpart: that ethnic communities—as well as states, nations, and "peoples"—may also have just claims. Reasonable classification is accepted as compatible with equal treatment, and for certain purposes it should be regarded as reasonable to classify people into groups by language, race, or religion. In appropriate circumstances the relevant claims should be interpreted and applied in the light of each other. Thus, as in the Old Order Amish case, the right of a child to an education and the right of the state to require school attendance until the sixteenth year would be considered in terms of the right of a community to preserve itself. And the right of an individual to freedom of expression might be interpreted in terms of the right of a linguistic community to preserve its language.

The second caveat is that the case made here is general in its terms and leaves many questions unresolved. The criteria for deciding whether a community should be recognized and what status and rights it should have are left virtually unexplored. It is obviously not the argument that just any combination of persons is entitled to call itself a group and to have whatever status and rights it wants. Present practices over the world are suggestive of what might be desirable, but much examining and appraising need to occur before generally applicable standards of judgment can be worked out.

Conclusion

The requirements of logic and the long-term requirements of universal justice commend the idea of accepting communities as right-and-duty-bearing units. It is quite logical to take the view that only states, nations, and "peoples" are entitled to be treated as entities and that lesser groups are not. It is illogical to jump from the state, nation, or "people" on the one side to the individual on the other and to say that the ethnic communities that exist in between do not deserve consideration. Not only is it illogical, it is also unjust. It is unjust to accept or assume status and rights for states, nations, and "peoples," but to reject them for ethnic communities that are also historically constituted. And it is even unjust to individuals to say that those who belong to dominant groups can enjoy the attendant advantages and satisfactions, whereas those who belong to nondominant and minority groups must either abandon their culture or accept second-class status. It is not enough for political theorists to contemplate simply the individual and society or relationships between persons and the state. It is time for them to contemplate humankind in its great variety.

NOTES

1. Though not presuming to classify Dante Germino ideologically, I might cite his statement that "the primary purpose of a political philosopher is to explore the individual's relationship to society." See his contribution, "The Contemporary Relevance of the Classics of Political Philosophy," in F. I. Greenstein and N. W. Polsby (eds.), *Political Science: Scope and Theory*, Vol. 1, *Handbook of Political Science* (Reading, Mass.: Addison-Wesley, 1975), p. 259.

2. *Cf.* M. Ginsburg, *On Justice in Society* (Ithaca: Cornell University Press, 1965), pp. 74–75; S. I. Benn and R. S. Peters, *The Principles of Political Thought* (New York: Free Press, 1965), pp. 107–116.

3. *Cf.* O. Gierke, *Natural Law and the Theory of Society 1500 to 1800*, trans.

with an introduction by E. Barker (Cambridge: Cambridge University Press, 1934), Vol. I: lxiv, lxxxvii, 174, 175; F. W. Maitland, *Collected Papers* (Cambridge: Cambridge University Press, 1911), Vol. III: 304-320; M. R. Cohen, *Reason and Nature: An Essay on the Meaning of Scientific Method*, 2d ed. (Glencoe, Ill.: Free Press, 1953), pp. 388-397; H. J. Laski, "Morris Cohen's Approach to Legal Philosophy," 15 *University of Chicago Law Review* (Spring 1948): 577-582; L. C. Webb, "Corporate Personality and Political Pluralism," in Webb (ed.), *Legal Personality and Political Pluralism* (Melbourne: Melbourne University Press, 1958), pp. 45-65; D. Jellema, "Abraham Kuyper's Attack on Liberalism," 19 *Review of Politics* (October 1957): 482-485; B. Zylstra, *From Pluralism to Collectivism: The Development of Harold Laski's Political Thought* (Assen, The Netherlands: Van Gorcum, 1968), pp. 25, 38-39, 50-53.

4. *Hobbes' Leviathan* (Oxford: Clarendon Press, 1909), chap. xviii, p. 133.

5. G. H. Sabine, *A History of Political Theory* (New York: Holt, 1950), p. 475.

6. E. Barker (ed.), *Social Contract: Essays by Locke, Hume, and Rousseau* (New York: Oxford University Press, 1962), pp. 56-57.

7. *Ibid.*, p. 194.

8. V. Van Dyke, "Justice as Fairness: For Groups?" 69 *American Political Science Review* (June 1975): 607-614.

9. E. Barker, *supra* note 6, pp. 272-273.

10. *Ibid.*, p. xii.

11. J. S. Mill, *Considerations on Representative Government* (Indianapolis: Bobbs-Merrill, 1958), pp. 230-233.

12. E. Barker, *Principles of Social and Political Theory* (Oxford: Clarendon Press, 1951), pp. 3, 42.

13. *Ibid.*, p. 55.

14. *Ibid.*, p. 56.

15. *Ibid.*, p. 139.

16. *Ibid.*, p. 71.

17. *Cf.* the definition of a *right* offered by Plamenatz: "A right is a power which a creature ought to possess, either because its exercise by him is itself good or else because it is a means to what is good, and in the exercise of which all rational beings ought to protect him." J. P. Plamenatz, *Consent, Freedom, and Political Obligation* (London: Oxford University Press, 1938), p. 82.

18. V. Van Dyke, "Human Rights and the Rights of Groups," 18 *American Journal of Political Science* (November 1974): 725-741.

19. Great Britain, Parliamentary Papers, "Inter-territorial Organization in East Africa," *Colonial No. 191* (December 1945), p. 8.

20. *Cf.* Tanganyika, *Report of the Committee on Constitutional Development 1951* (Dar es Salaam: Government Printer, 1951), pp. 2, 18-19; C. Pratt, "Multi-Racialism and Local Government in Tanganyika," 2 *Race* (November 1960): 35-36; Y. Tandon, "A Political Survey," in D. P. Ghai (ed.), *Portrait of a Minority: Asians in East Africa* (Nairobi: Oxford University Press, 1965), p. 79.

21. *Cf.* V. Van Dyke, "One Man One Vote and Majority Rule as Human Rights," 6 *Revue des droits de l'homme*, nos. 3 and 4 (1973): 456-458.

22. Great Britain, *Fiji Independence Order 1970*, "The Constitution of Fiji," Articles 45 and 68.

23. R. Senelle, "The Revision of the Constitution, 1967-1971," *Memo From Belgium*, nos. 144-145-146, January-February-March 1972 (Ministry of Foreign Affairs, External Trade and Cooperation in Development), p. 130.

24. *Native American Church* v. *Navajo Tribal Council*, 272 F.2d 131 (10th

Cir. 1959). U.S. Department of the Interior, Office of the Solicitor, F. S. Cohen, *Handbook of Federal Indian Law* (Washington, D.C., 1942), pp. 122–123, 278.

25. *United States* v. *Carolene Products Co.*, 304 U.S. 144 (1938), at 153, fn. 4.

26. *Beauharnais* v. *Illinois*, 343 U.S. 250 (1951), at 262.

27. *United States* v. *Jefferson County Board of Education*, 372 F.2d 836 (1966), at 866, quoting note, 20 *University of Chicago Law Review* (1953): 577.

28. *Cisneros* v. *Corpus Christi Independent School Dist.*, 324 F.Supp. 599 (1970), at 606, 627; *United States* v. *State of Texas*, 342 F.Supp. 24 (1971), at 24.

29. *Hunter* v. *Erickson*, 393 U.S. 385 (1969), at 393.

30. *Hernandez* v. *Texas*, 347 U.S. 475 (1954) at 478; *United States* v. *Hunt*, 265 F.Supp. 178 (1967), at 188.

31. *Cousins* v. *City Council of City of Chicago*, 466 F.2d 830 (1972), at 843, 851. *Cf. Sims* v. *Baggett*, 247 F.Supp. 103 (1965); *Howard* v. *Adams County Board of Supervisors*, 453 F.2d 455 (1972), at 457; *Graves* v. *Barnes*, 343 F.Supp. 704 (1972), at 728, 730; *Klahr* v. *Williams*, 339 F.Supp. 922 (1972); *White* v. *Regester*, 412 U.S. 755 (1972), at 765; *Beer* v. *United States*, 374 F.Supp. 363 (1974), at 393.

32. *Williams* v. *Rhodes*, 393 U.S. 23 (1968), at 39; emphasis added.

33. See, for example, *Officers for Justice* v. *Civil Service Commission, C. & C. San Francisco*, 371 F.Supp. 1328 (1973), at 1332.

34. O. W. Fiss, "Groups and the Equal Protection Clause," 5 *Philosophy and Public Affairs* (Winter 1976): 157.

35. Council of Europe, Consultative Assembly, Sixteenth Ordinary Session, *Resolution 290* (1965).

36. U.N. Doc. E/CN.4/Sub.2/40/Rev.I (June 1949), 2. *Cf.* U.N. Doc. E/CN.4/641 (October 25, 1951).

37. M. Pomerance, "The United States and Self-Determination: Perspectives on the Wilsonian Conception," 70 *American Journal of International Law* (January 1976): 2.

38. U.N. Doc. A/Res/3375, XXX (November 13, 1975); emphasis added.

39. R. A. Nisbet, *The Quest for Community* (New York: Oxford University Press, 1953).

40. *United Jewish Organization of Williamsburgh, Inc.* v. *Wilson*, 377 F.Supp. 1164 (1974); 500 F.2d 434 (1974).

41. *Wisconsin* v. *Yoder*, 406 U.S. 205 (1972).

42. W. Connor, "Ethnic Nationalism as a Political Force," 133 *World Affairs* (September 1970): 91–98; W. Connor, "Nation-Building or Nation-Destroying?" 24 *World Politics* (April 1972): 320; W. Connor, "The Politics of Ethnonationalism," 27 *Journal of International Affairs* (1973): 1–2.

3: Minority Rights and Self-Determination

BEN WHITAKER

It was Gandhi who said that civilization should be judged by its treatment of minorities. Since almost all politics are concerned with some form of majorities and minorities, reconciling their conflicting interests is an endemic as well as an inescapable problem in society. In this chapter the focus of concern is on the concept of minority in its qualitative rather than quantitative sense. Hence, the definition also embraces those numerical majorities which today are oppressed in various areas of the world (such as Namibia or Burundi) by minorities. Many of the problems of minorities are residual legacies of colonialism, with its arbitrary establishment of boundaries, motivation of economic exploitation, importation of labor, and employment of the historic technique of keeping power by playing off one race or tribe against another. Nonetheless, antisemitism, apartheid, and the "double minority" of Northern Ireland remind us that wholesale violations of human rights can always occur in allegedly developed countries as well.

I. Defining Minorities

The problems of minorities begin with the difficulty of defining them. Although the United Nations has been confronted with this problem since 1947, until now it has been unable to agree upon any definition of a minority, let alone upon the principles that should govern minority rights. One basic division of opinion arises over the question of whether the definition should be objective or subjective. Should the definition be agreed upon by consensus or be perceived solely by a group's members? A delegate at the 1974 U.N. seminar at Ohrid, Yugoslavia, suggested that the definition should be "a group of citizens, sufficient in number to pursue the aims of the group, but numerically smaller than the rest of the people linked together by historical, ethnic, cultural, religious or linguistic bonds and wishing to preserve such bonds, which are different from those of the rest of the people."[1]

As the United Kingdom's delegate to the U.N. Human Rights Sub-Commission in 1975, I suggested the following definition: "A minority group is any group who, because of their physical or cultural characteristics, are singled out from others in the society in which they live for differential and unequal treatment."[2] Another member of the commission noted that "The common denominator of all minorities, however, was the desire to preserve the characteristics of the group."[3] In 1951, at its fourth session, the subcommission suggested that "the term minority included only those non-dominant groups in a population which possess and wish to preserve stable ethnic, religious or linguistic traditions or characteristics markedly different from those of the rest of the population."[4]

Francesco Capotorti, the special *rapporteur* of the subcommission's study of Article 27 of the U.N.'s International Covenant on Civil and Political Rights—which deals with ethnic, linguistic, and religious minorities—adopted as his working definition "a group numerically smaller than the rest of the population of the State to which it belongs and possessing cultural, physical or historical characteristics, a religion or a language different from those of the rest of the population."[5] And, in a paper soon to be published by the Minority Rights Group, Claire Palley stresses the factor of the imbalance of power: "A minority is any relatively permanent racial, tribal, linguistic, religious, caste, nationality or regional group dominated by, or perceiving itself as dominated by or as having its aims frustrated by, other groups or by those in control of the state."

Article 27 of the International Covenant on Civil and Political Rights contains the only reference to minority rights as such in the main international human rights instruments of the United Nations. It gingerly describes the rights of minorities in these minimal and defensive terms:

> In those States in which ethnic, religious or linguistic minorities exist, persons belonging to such minorities shall not be denied the rights, in community with the other members of their group, to enjoy their own culture, to profess and practice their own religion, or to use their own language.

In addition, the covenant guarantees those rights—such as freedom of opinion, of expression, of thought and religion, from arbitrary interference in family life, and of association—which are important to the preservation of minority culture.

II. Strategies of Self-Preservation

Minority groups today are beginning to assert themselves as never before and vigorously to defend their rights, including the right to group autonomy. Because of the rise of pluralist tensions in the world a growing number of such groups are unwilling to continue playing the role of victim, whether by being oppressed or by being patronized. Economic recession in many developed countries has severely exposed the vulnerability of weak and visible minorities, some of which are fighting back. In Europe, for example, there is a new interest among Scots, Bretons, and Basques in regional devolution while other groups are experimenting with various forms of neighborhood or community organizations.

The awakening of many minority groups seems coincident with the erosion of the belief in the necessity for the garrison state, particularly in the face of 30 years of peace on the continent of Europe. Jean-Paul Sartre reminds us that all big nations contain internal colonies with frontiers they themselves have drawn, although the U.N.'s decolonization lobby is reluctant to recognize this. Nonetheless, a group of various West European separatist political parties (campaigning on a platform of the right of all people to self-government and protection of their identity in the realm of language and culture and the right of all people to set up social, economic, and commercial structures to resist abuse of power by supranational corporations) ultimately seeks to replace the existing nine-member states of the European Community with between 15 and 20 "national communities."[6]

The plight of minority groups is most often traceable to the attitude of the dominant majority. The presence of minority cultures is challenging and disturbing to the majority, both socially and psychologically, but generally they are a positive value to the larger society. For one thing, they serve to remind us that each human being in some respect belongs to a minority. There is, of course, no rule of human nature that equates minorities with virtue. The culture of any group, small or large, may include one or more systematic violations of basic human rights; some small religious cults, for example, have practices which seem discriminatory and even oppressive to nonmembers. It is difficult to argue that anyone should acquire a special right or privilege any more than any inherent disadvantage simply through membership in a minority group. Toleration must be mutual and must be based on responsibilities as well as on rights.

But, obviously, most small groups do remain physically vulnerable. After all, governments exist to protect minorities, because majorities, such as the loved and the rich, need no protection. The condition of minority groups raises the controversial question of the ethics and desirability of positive or reverse discrimination, or affirmative action. It is easier for a social reformer to find justifiable special treatment or beneficial discrimination to rectify the past's injustices than for a lawyer to do so, but both social reformers and lawyers must remember that many racial groups and castes have a long historical backlog of unfairness to make up.

Conor Cruise O'Brien argues that it is a mistake to speak either of minority or majority rights. "Rights," he suggested in the 1972 Minority Rights Group Annual Lecture, "are best thought of as inherent in each human being, irrespective of what kind of cultural grouping he or she may belong to."[7] The notion of minority rights may indeed be used as a convenient tool for denying general rights to people as a whole and as individuals, thus resulting in the continual stigmatization of the minority group. It is probably for this reason that the Universal Declaration of Human Rights addresses itself to the rights of individual human beings instead of group rights.

This is also the approach that has been favored at the United Nations, and there is much difference of opinion between the various blocs and between developed and underdeveloped countries about this matter. On the whole, "developed" nations are more sympathetic to group rights than are "underdeveloped." This fact may seem surprising for more than one reason. The language of the Universal Declaration, which people of so many cultures appear to find acceptable, is clearly the product of one special culture, namely, that of Western Europe and the Europeans of North America. In fact, it has been argued powerfully by some people from the Third World that this generalized and abstract concern with human rights as defined by Europeans has become an instrument, consciously or unconsciously applied, for the disruption of other people's cultures.

For practical reasons rights are often inevitably determined for and by groups: The machinery of courts can scarcely cope with a plethora of individual cases. I believe that to view all minority rights simply in terms of individual rights is too legalistic. It is a view which would be perfectly tenable were one beginning human society *ab initio*, without the political reality that some groups inescapably have inherited disadvantages. Nevertheless, the individual must equally be allowed the right to secede by voting with his or her feet.

The Roots of Prejudice and Discrimination

Of course, majorities have their rights as well as their responsibilities. One of the most practical measures that would benefit minorities is effective research into the whole phenomenon of group stigmatization and the reasons why some minority groups are seen as threats or scapegoats while others are tolerated by the majority. We recognize that historical myths, often based on doubtful evidence, continually impinge on contemporary intergroup relations. Ethnocentrically biased books and newspapers lend not only authority but also permanence to prejudice and discrimination. Not infrequently, such prejudices are then used as pretexts for denigrating political, social, or economic opponents and are seized upon by demagogues as excuses for exploiting classes, races, or women.

Long before Hitler, unscrupulous political manipulators were using minorities in bids for popular support by channeling public emotion against vulnerable scapegoats. Such dehumanization is a particular danger in times of inflation and other apparently insoluble economic problems. Because of their own need for security, easily led members of majorities are tempted to seek shelter behind blinkers and can be diverted or at least distracted from focusing upon the real reasons for their troubles. Hence, to the general public, minorities often reveal social problems and become identified with the causes of those problems. Much interethnic conflict in fact is due to society's imbalances of power rather than to pluralism as such.

Assimilation or Integration

In the face of such disparate pressures, it is not surprising that the response of minorities themselves has been far from unified. Their individual members are divided in their personal reactions and also in the reactive policies they advocate. Many, but not all, minority group members prefer mutual tolerance to assimilation in a society: They seek not assimilation but integration in the sense of equal opportunity accompanied by cultural diversity in an atmosphere of tolerance. (It is interesting that in the United Kingdom some of the people who complain most loudly about the failure of immigrants to become gray British stereotypes are themselves Britons who would never have dreamed of adopting the local majority's customs, clothing, food, or even language when they were inhabiting former British colonies abroad.) In some American schools ethnicity syllabi have been adopted which attempt to educate children from diverse backgrounds to accept and respect their own rights and at the same time to learn that the differences of others imply no inferiority. Such action is in striking contrast to previous efforts to pressure minority members to shed their roots and to be fused into an all-American identity—one which in reality was a scarcely concealed euphemism for white Anglo-Saxon Protestant values.

At any one time different members of the same minority group may be pursuing diametrically conflicting goals in relation to assimilation. Some may be aspiring to social integration into a wider society as relief from prejudice and a means to upward social mobility. Others, such as many Chinese-Americans and Pakistanis of Britain, may prefer to seek economic and functional integration—including equality of access to training and promotion—but stop short of fuller social assimilation. Some minority members have used economic advance in the host society as a tactical stepping stone in order to seek additional political rights. Still other individuals may from the outset advocate the antithesis of integration: separate development with or without ultimate secession. I myself believe that the decision whether to integrate or assimilate must be one for the individual, but the availability of real options must be a prerequisite for any such choice.

The Problem of Secession

It is the option of secession that makes minority rights such a sensitive subject. Here lies the real reason for reluctant discussion in international forums such as the United Nations. Many international jurists believe that while minorities should be allowed to seek varying degrees of internal autonomy, they should not have the right to challenge a nation's territorial boundaries, except in the face of the most gross and persistent oppression. Such a challenge should be the ultimate resort in defense of rights. This view was expounded most eloquently by the founders of the United States and subsequently by Americans at the time of the Civil War. O'Brien, with first-hand knowledge of the problems of Ireland and elsewhere, remarked in his Minority Rights Group lecture, "Secession is a very unpopular idea... since it threatens the life of a state and threatens public order. Yet hardly anyone I think would claim that there is no such thing as a right to secede in any circumstances at all."[8] But the right of secession has been applied in varying ways. After commenting on the American and Latin American experiences during the eighteenth and nineteenth centuries, he spoke of the distinction affirming "that it was all right to secede from the things called empires but all wrong to secede from the things called republics."[9] He also noted that after World War I, Woodrow Wilson's principle of the self-determination of nations was used to break up the defeated empires by building "the new states as far as possible around historical, cultural and linguistic groupings," whereas after World War II, "the arbitrary assumption was made . . . that the various colonial administrative territories, all of short duration and some of vast extent, now constituted nations and were exercising self-determination."[10] Then too there are the more recent examples of Bangladesh and Biafra, where secession was legitimate in the first case but not in the latter. O'Brien's assessment of the meaning of all this deserves extended quotation:

> It is hard to see, if we are putting the question on a moral plane (as I suppose we must if what we are attempting to discuss is rights), why self-determination should be right in the one case and necessarily wrong in the other. I believe that secession is an evil, or rather the recognition of an evil, a breakdown in human relations. I also believe that no minority is likely to have recourse to it, with all its dangers, unless the pressures on it are felt to be intolerable and unless also other conditions apply in terms of numbers, terrain, diplomatic conjuncture and other apparently propitious factors. It would be uselessly pedantic, I believe, to draw up rules for when secession is right. It is enough to say that no minority is likely to attempt anything like this unless it or a substantial section of it has been driven desperate by events.[11]

In considering secession in terms of human rights, there is also the practical problem of where if ever to stop subdividing. The so-called "double minority" problem of Northern Ireland illustrates that it is rare indeed for a partitioned or secessionist state not to contain within its new boundaries minorities who may still be disaffected in varying degrees.[12] It is always difficult to lock human beings into membership in any one group. It is true that the governments of large federal units may indeed exercise greater tolerance than smaller local governments. For example, for many years blacks had more allies in Washington, D.C., than in the Alabama or Mississippi state governments, and it was London rather than Belfast which put through measures aimed at removal of the disadvantages of Catholics in Northern Ireland.

Other Demands of Beleaguered Minorities

The world's minority groups include more than 600 million persons. But the ethnic picture in some countries is very complex. For instance, in Kenya the Luo is only the most obvious example of the many tribes that may feel oppressed by Kikuyu preeminence. Another example is the Philippines, which includes not only the Southern Muslims or Moros, who have made outstanding claims upon the government, but also a large number of lesser-known, potentially separatist groups.[13] But any list of dependent peoples would also include those minorities which occupy more than one country. This of course presents another special problem. The international conventions and covenants of human rights rarely take any notice of men and women living outside a nation: The people of nations that have been dispossessed or overrun fall within such conventions, but people who refuse to align with any nation do not.

Each minority situation is a unique amalgam of its own distinct historical, economic, psychological, social, and political factors, so generalized remedies are rarely helpful in solving minority problems. A report by the U.N. Secretary General lists the following as the most frequent demands of minorities seeking to preserve their way of life:

> The "positive services" and "special rights" which such minorities feel they must have if their equality within the State is to be real, vary greatly, but usually include one or more of the following:
> a. Provision of adequate primary and secondary education for the minority in its own language and its cultural traditions;
> b. Provision for maintenance of the culture of the minority through the establishment and operation of schools, libraries, museums, media of information, and other cultural and educational institutions;
> c. Provision of adequate facilities to the minority for the use of its language, either orally or in writing, in the legislature, before the courts, and in administration, and the granting of the right to use that language in private enterprise;
> d. Provision for respect of the family law and personal status of the minority and their religious practices and interests;
> e. Provision of a certain degree of autonomy.[14]

Each of these demands is a source of tension and controversy between minority groups and the prevailing culture in which they find themselves.

The International Commission of Jurists, at its meeting on the protection of minorities in Vienna in April 1977, concluded that the chief factors uniting a minority are language, culture, and religion. "Where a minority has a different language from the majority," it was said at the meeting, "it tends to be at once the strongest bond uniting the minority and the source of the greatest problems for the government of the state and for the relationship between the minority and the majority. On this point it was further stated:

> The right to use of their own language in primary education has long been claimed by minority groups to ensure the preservation

of their culture and avoid the handicap for their children of having to be taught in the majority tongue. But governments face many problems complicating the achievement of minority desires. National unity and national communication [are] of fundamental importance to national integration and development. This problem can sometimes be overcome, where resources both material and human are adequate, by bilingualism or even multilingualism. But some states contain fifty or more mutually unintelligible languages, creating an impossible burden upon the state in financing and coordinating a system to teach these myriad languages. Recognition of language to be used in official matters has political as well as practical aspects.[15]

But minority cultures are not always linked to a minority language. And even where there is a common language, remarked a participant in the ICJ meeting:

> ... a minority will sometimes have its own historical and cultural traditions, with its own songs, music, dances, and other art forms; different social habits; different values; and perhaps a different religion, all of which tend to produce a sense of separate identity and loyalty from that of the nation as a whole. It is now generally recognized in principle, though often not given effect in practice, that the preservation of minority cultures is of paramount importance to the happiness and well being of the individuals who belong to the minorities and contributes to the enrichment of the life of the nation as a whole.[16]

Article 18 of the U.N. Universal Declaration of Human Rights proclaims: "Everyone has the right to freedom of thought, conscience and religion; this right includes freedom to change religion or belief, and freedom, either alone or in community with others and in public or private, to manifest his religion or belief in teaching, practice, worship and observance." Article 18 of the International Covenant on Civil and Political Rights carries this statement further with a provision against coercion impairing freedom to choose one's religion or to manifest one's religion or belief and a guarantee of respect for the freedom of parents to ensure the religious and moral education of their children in conformity with their convictions.

Practical Application

It is perhaps salutary to step down from the rarified language of international idealism to consider a few of the practical problems arising in this area. Two recent individual cases, one in the United

States and the other in Britain, illustrate the complexities that can arise in practice. The first case involved members of the so-called Unification Church led by Reverend Sun Myung Moon. In March 1977 a San Francisco judge ordered five members of Moon's flock— three women and two men between the ages of 21 and 26—to be handed over to their parents for 30 days of "deprogramming." It was reported that witnesses for the parents, many of them former followers of Moon who had turned against his church, said that new members of the church were coerced by poor diets and lack of sleep. A spokesman for the church countered that the five young people were genuine converts and that it was the deprogrammers who were the brainwashers. In his ruling Judge Vavuris said, "[This is a case] about the very essence of life here, mother, father, and children. There's nothing closer in our civilization [than the family]." The judge continued: "So the law looks at that binding thing between a parent and a child. It is never ending. No matter how old we are, it's there."[17]

The five all opposed their parents' move and played music or read poetry in court as a way of proving that their powers of creativity had not been impaired by church membership. After the hearing, one of the five, 23-year-old John Hovard, said, "This is very scary. This is like the mental institutions where they put dissidents in Russia." The legal battle about this very fundamental issue of human rights continued, fought on the parents' side by an organization called the Freedom of Thought Foundation of Tucson, Arizona, while groups like the American Civil Liberties Union filed briefs, *amicus curiae,* on behalf of the children. Judge Vavuris's decision was reversed by the California State Court of Appeals on April 11, 1977.[18]

In the second case, and during the same month, the English Court of Appeal dismissed the claim of a London Muslim schoolteacher that the school authority's refusal to allow him time off from his duties for 45 minutes every Friday to pray in a nearby mosque amounted to religious discrimination. Lord Alfred Thompson Denning, giving the majority view of the judges, said, "It would do the Muslim community no good or any other minority no good, if they were to be given preferential treatment over the great majority of the people. If in the name of religious freedom they were given special privileges or advantages it would provoke discontent, and even resentment among those with whom they worked. And so the cause of racial integration would suffer."[19]

But where, it might be asked, does preferential treatment begin? In Britain many factories do allow persons to take time off during the working day for religious reasons. In exchange, these persons (e.g., Muslims and Jews) are required to make up that lost time by working later or through lunch hours. But that is not possible in a profession such as teaching, where working hours are determined by the attendance of other people. In this situation there may be no easy solution and no possible way clearly to distinguish between legitimate toleration of alien customs and unfair preferential treatment of minority groups. The *London Times* remarked, "It is essential for the sake of racial peace and harmony that those groups and individuals wanting concessions should not pitch their demands too high, and that those in a position to grant them should be seen to be sympathetic and flexible, but careful of the consequences of seeming to give too much away."

In a dissenting opinion Lord Justice Leslie George Scarman said that a narrow construction of the United Kingdom's Education Act would mean that a Muslim who took his religious duties seriously could never accept employment as a full-time teacher but would have to be content with the lesser emoluments of part-time service. "In modern British society—with its elaborate statutory protection of the individual from discrimination arising from race, color, religion, or sex—and against the background of the European Convention, I find this unacceptable, inconsistent with the policy of modern statute law, and almost certainly a breach of our international obligations."[20] The judge considered that under the act a teacher was not to receive a smaller salary simply because he or she attended religious worship during school hours. Lord Justice Scarman said the choice forced upon the Muslim teacher by the Inner London Education Authority was tantamount to dismissal from full-time employment. It was unfair, and the teacher was entitled to reinstatement or compensation.

How are these conflicting viewpoints to be resolved? So far no adequate answer has been forthcoming.

III. Conclusion

The "right of self-determination of peoples" is proclaimed in both of the International Covenants on Human Rights, but the meaning and scope of this right has not yet been authoritatively defined. At the United Nations, self-determination has usually been invoked exclusively in relation to the granting of independence to colonial and other dependent or occupied territories. So long as the delegates at the United Nations and other international bodies continue to represent national governments that have a natural antipathy to secession, this fact is inevitable—at least until the United Nations succeeds in reforming itself so as to give practical expression to the concept of the initial words of its charter: "We the peoples of the world." Over time, the word "peoples" has been subtly changed into "We the governments...." Meanwhile, it is interesting to note that Article 26 of the Declaration on the Rights of Peoples formulated at Algiers suggested that a right to independence under the principle of self-determination should be revived in any case where the democratic rights of a minority people have been so consistently denied and repressed by the state as to make it intolerable for the people to continue to remain under the domination of the majority.

Since recognition of any such right is generally likely to take second place to the overriding priority of the state's cohesion for reasons of development and internal security, it is necessary to consider what safeguards, both at a national and at an international level, can be given without secession to minorities. In the future the successful reconciliation of civil and political with economic and social human rights is the most important task facing society.

At the national level some disadvantaged minorities may require special constitutional safeguards in addition to the bedrock protection of all individuals' fundamental human rights. Intangible prejudice and discrimination can be the hardest of all to rectify, and we should not forget that minorities can suffer from continual discrimination in a democracy just as much as in a dictatorship. International protection depends, in the short term, upon making the U.N. Human Rights Commission at least minimally effective; in the medium term, upon the development of the committee charted with overseeing the new covenants; and in the long term, upon the establishment of an effective U.N. high commissioner for human rights who could act as a world ombudsman both for groups and individuals.

For such progress to occur a major change of political will is required. In the present absence of any effective international machinery, a particular responsibility falls upon nongovernmental organizations and the voices of an informed press and public opinion. I would like to suggest the value in setting up an unofficial international "shadow" model of the human rights machinery that would be needed in the United Nations, a human rights tribunal and/or commissioner for human rights who could hold public hearings, conducted judicially with cross-examination of witnesses. Such a model could serve three purposes: it could act as a working experimental model to refine techniques, it could prompt the reform of the official machinery, and it could use the sanction of publicity against violators.

In his initial address to the United Nations in 1977 President Carter remarked: "All the signatories of the U.N. Charter have pledged themselves to observe and respect basic human rights. Thus, no member of the U.N. can claim that mistreatment of its citizens is solely its own business. Equally, no member can avoid its responsibilities to review and speak when torture or unwarranted deprivation of freedom occurs."[21] President Carter's courageous words give a welcome lead to the long—and long overdue—process of changing national politicians' attitudes toward human rights and have already lent heart to some timid governments even though others still need pressure from public opinion. But the reported protests of some U.S. companies (such as DuPont, the Chicago Bridge and Iron Company, and Control Data Corporation) that President Carter's stance on human rights is likely to endanger their commercial prospects overseas show the pitfalls of unilateral action by any one nation, especially when that nation's commercial competitors have no such principled policy. Hence, there is urgent necessity for progress toward internationalizing action on human rights, so that sanctions against flagrant transgression can be applied more effectively against the recalcitrant and with fewer unfair penalties to those countries which practice what they preach.

NOTES

1. *U.N. Doc.* E/CN.4/Sub.2/SR 695, at 36 (1975).
2. *U.N. Doc.* E/CN.4/Sub.2/SR 720, at 57 (1975).
3. *U.N. Doc.* E/CN.4/Sub.2/SR 721, at 64 (1975).
4. *U.N. Doc.* E/CN.4/Sub.2/149, at 26 (1952).
5. *U.N. Doc.* CN.4/Sub.2/L 595, at 128 (1974).
6. The parties referred to here are the Scots, Bretons, and Basques.
7. G. Ashworth, *World Minorities* (London: Quartermaine House, 1977), p. xvii.
8. *Ibid.*, p. xiii.
9. *Ibid.*, p. xiv.
10. *Ibid.*
11. *Ibid.*, pp. xiv–xv.
12. See H. Jackson, *The Two Irelands: The Problem of the Double Minority—A Dual Study of Inter-Group Relations,* Revised Report No. 2, May 1972 (London: Minority Rights Group).
13. For a discussion of Kenyan and Philippine minorities see, respectively, *The Asian Minorities of East and Central Africa,* Report No. 4, April 1971 (London: Minority Rights Group) and *The Chinese in Indonesia, the Philippines, and Malaysia,* Report No. 10, June 1972 (London: Minority Rights Group).
14. "Definition and Classification of Minorities," 14 *U.N. Public Sales No. 50,* 3, at 37.
15. Committee No. Three on Minority Rights, *Working Paper* (Geneva: International Commission of Jurists, 1977).

16. *Ibid.*
17. See *Jacqueline Katz et al* v. *The Superior Court of the City and County of San Francisco,* 73 Cal. App. 3rd 963 (1977), at 964, note 3.
18. *Ibid.,* p. 964.
19. *Ahmed* v. *Inner London Education Authority,* 1976 I.C.R. 461, E.A.T.
20. *Ibid.*
21. Address by President Carter before the United Nations, March 17, 1977.

Bibliography

ARENS, R., *Genocide in Paraguay* (Philadelphia, 1977).

ASHWORTH, G., and O'Brien, C. C. (eds.), *World Minorities* (London, 1977).

FLATHMAN, R., *The Practice of Rights* (Cambridge, 1976).

GOTLIEB, A. (ed.), *Human Rights, Federalism, and Minorities* (Toronto, 1970).

HAKSAR, U., *Minority Protection and International Bill of Human Rights* (Bombay, 1974).

HOROWITZ, I. L., *Genocide: State Power and Mass Murder* (New York, 1976).

HOWARD, J. R. (ed.), *Awakening Minorities: American Indians, Mexican Americans, Puerto Ricans* (Chicago, 1970).

KING, R. R., *Minorities under Communism: Nationalities as a Source of Tension among Balkan Communist States* (Cambridge, 1973).

KUNSTADTER, P. (ed.), *Southeast Asian Tribes, Minorities and Nations*, 2 vols. (Princeton, 1968).

MILLER, D., *Social Justice* (Oxford, 1976).

SUNDBERG-WEITMAN, B., *Discrimination on the Grounds of Nationality* (Amsterdam, 1976).

VAN DYKE, V., "Self-determination and Minority Rights," 13 *International Studies Quarterly* (June 1969): 223-253.

―――, "Human Rights and the Rights of Groups," 18 *American Journal of Political Science* (November 1974): 725.

―――, "Human Rights Without Distinction as to Language," 20 *International Studies Quarterly* (March 1976): 3-38.

PART THREE
Human Rights: Conflicting Ideologies

Introduction

MOST DISCUSSIONS ABOUT HUMAN RIGHTS BEGIN AND END IN A quandary over a definition of the term. As A. H. Robertson noted in his chapter in Part One, observance of human rights poses problems everywhere, and no country, be it highly industrialized or economically underdeveloped, possesses a faultless record in this regard. The different interpretations of human rights that separate the First and the Third worlds is now one of the key issues of international politics.

The espousal of human rights by First World nations, especially by the United States, has tended to reflect a peculiarly Western concern with limiting the power of government over the rights of the governed. The West traces its concern for human rights to the Magna Carta (1216), the English Petition of Right (1628), the English Bill of Rights (1689), the French Declaration of the Rights of Man (1791), and the American Bill of Rights (1791). This tradition of political freedom in Western Europe and North America rests on a series of procedural safeguards of due process of law. Westerners in general, and Americans in particular, have long been vitally concerned with how individual citizens can be protected by law from the encroachment of governmental tyranny. For example, to protect the civil and political rights enshrined in their Bill of Rights, Americans have shaped a tradition of an independent judiciary; the right to legal counsel; the right to a fair, speedy, and public trial by an impartial jury of one's peers; the right of protection against arbitrary arrest and imprisonment; and the prohibition against cruel and unusual punishment. Other Western nations also have made significant advances in guaranteeing freedom of religion, speech, press, assembly, and political participation, about which the American Bill of Rights was created.

Rita Hauser not only argues that political and civil rights have a primacy in the political system and thinking of the West, but also states emphatically that these rights should exist in non-Western nations as well. The fundamental irreducible political rights to which Hauser refers are freedom from arbitrary imprisonment, freedom of life and liberty, and freedom—at least to some degree—of thought and expression. Although it is clear that not all people agree on the range and importance of human rights, people do care about having fulfilled those basic rights relating to integrity of the person and the value of life.

In this chapter Eddison Zvobgo points up the different perspective from which Africans (and other non-Western peoples) view humankind. Obviously, the values of one culture cannot be applied to another automatically, and every country has evolved in a different way in response to different conditions. Nevertheless, Third World nations share a number of common characteristics in their view of human rights. As Zvobgo illustrates, concern for the human condition in Asia, Africa, and Latin America predated the colonial period, but regard for political and civil rights in the classical sense often originated in many less-developed countries during the Western imperialist era. Many Third World leaders and intellectuals first became acquainted with classical human rights either in the metropolitan capitals of the colonial empire or in local schools and universities that were permeated by European political thought and ideals. When Third World countries sought independence from their Western masters, these same leaders and intellectuals called on the Europeans to apply their liberal principles in the colonial context.

Most Third World leaders argue that economic and social rights are necessary companions to classical civil and political rights. In a similar manner, the human rights covenants put into final form by the United Nations in 1966 stressed the importance of the interrelationship between civil and political rights and economic, social, and cultural rights. Though all of these human rights are regarded as important, in the minds of the Third World leaders, economic, social, and cultural rights are by far the more important. Such rights are exemplified by the right to work, the right to social security, and the right to education. Therefore, the principles of self-determination and racial equality as well as insistence upon the economic foundations of human rights are the essential elements to Third World thinking on human rights.

Even while recognizing the interdependence of all human rights, many poor societies remain under great pressure from internal and external problems that seem more pressing than ensuring human rights. In many developing countries, economic resources are few, and the majority of people, who live on the margin of subsistence, are often oppressed by privileged groups and unjust structures. In addition, many of these countries face the implacable enemies of poverty, illiteracy, and disease. Some Third World leaders maintain that under such circumstances, basic economic and social needs (e.g., welfare, nutrition, and income distribution) must be met before people can enjoy political freedoms and self-government. Some argue further that in regions of the world where standards of living are so low that most people regard human rights as a virtually meaningless concept, economic development is the only priority. In such cases, formal human rights in practice can be temporarily curtailed.

For example, Zvobgo argues that both the recent history and present state of African economic systems behoove African states to order their agendas in such a way as to give primary attention to economic development. Some African states, such as Tanzania, place a higher value on human needs than on political liberties as we in the West know them. In many African cultures, group identity and loyalty are emphasized more than the role of the individual. Thus, for example, Tanzania is characterized not only by single-party political dominance and a controlled press, but also by generally humane treatment of its people and a national commitment to the alleviation of the poverty of its citizens. Tanzania is driving itself toward self-sufficiency, sustained growth, and the placing of its people in a position where they can be in control of their own resources.

Thus Western concern over the violation of civil liberties in developing countries is viewed with great skepticism by most of the Third World. Many countries resent the practices of the Western powers in their colonies in the past and particularly the degradation and exploitation which they once suffered at the hands of Western rulers. The Third World views as hypocritical the concern for the rule of law in their countries that the West has evidenced since independence. This concern seems particularly hypocritical in light of the racism, forced labor, and expropriation in which the West engaged before independence. There also exists the feeling that First World societies will resort to the use of emergency powers and the curtailment of civil liberties during periods such as war, which they deem critical, even while they fail to accept famine and underdevelopment as being crises of equal rank. Finally, the Third World realizes that Western governments tend to become sensitive to human rights violations only when a client regime threatens to break away from a strategic alliance or to block access to foreign investment.

At the international level, Third World states insist that worldwide redistribution of economic, social, and political resources is very much a part of human rights. A recent vehicle for expressing the poor countries' aspirations for justice and equality is the Declaration on the Establishment of a New International Economic Order (NIEO). This declaration is viewed by the Third World as an important complement to the Universal Declaration of Human Rights. The NIEO declaration balances the primarily political liberties of the Universal Declaration with extensive affirmations of economic rights. It also places human rights in a global context of justice. Because international inequities and structural impediments have called into question the ability of many less-developed countries to survive, leaders of Third World nations often use U.N. forums to expound their demands for a greater share of the world's wealth, greater access to technology and markets, debt moratorium and cancellation, and international aid given both on a multilateral basis and on a large scale. The less-developed countries argue that the integrity of humanity can be achieved only by working to ensure that the attainment of political freedom is always coupled with that of economic justice. At the international level, then, the Third World uses human rights to measure the level of injustice and as norms for the redress of their grievances.

The emphasis placed on political liberties by the United States and the industrial world is viewed by many poor countries as an effort to sidetrack attention from Third World demands for a new international economic order based on global redistribution of the world's resources, which are now held largely by the northern democracies. They insist that the American emphasis on procedure and political form is not sensitive enough to broader mass-based freedoms and rights (i.e., freedom from premature death, freedom from hunger, and freedom from inadequate clothing and shelter). Many of the most humane leaders of the Third World cannot understand why the concern for political rights appears to be greater in the West than the concern about poverty and the needs of the poor.

It is in the context of North-South relations that the human rights policy of the United States faces its most critical test of relevance. How much the United States can and should respond to Third World demands for a new international economic order is a matter not easily settled. However, Washington should consider seriously the fact that human rights also encompass human needs and that while encouragement of formal rights and the emphasis on procedure are important, they are inadequate without working for the substantive freedoms that have the most relevance and meaning for Third World peoples. Without establishing the notion of minimum substantive rights (food, shelter, and employment) for all people, attaining the procedural rights (freedom of speech, press, religion, and thought) that Westerners cherish will remain an irrelevant and unattainable goal for a majority of the world.

If America is to have any credibility in promoting and protecting civil liberties throughout the world, it must demonstrate its interest in supporting the economic development that reaches the poorest elements of the population in the less developed countries. In the absence of tangible evidence of American support for the economic and social dimension of human rights, such as significant increases in U.S. aid to basic human needs, American concern for civil and political rights is not likely to strike others either as morally compelling or as relevant to the needs of the majority of the human race. (These issues will be discussed in greater detail in Parts Six and Seven.)

Industrialization in the large Western countries was carried out at a time when a great degree of inequality was taken for granted. It may be that civil and political rights are bound to be abused until a certain level of development is reached, at which point classical rights come to have some meaning for the mass of the population. Like other states, the developing countries suffer the incompatibilities that exist between the principles espoused by their statesmen in international bodies and the backward socio-economic structure of the states concerned. Over the long term, in order to set standards, national progress on the human rights front must be brought into better relation with international efforts. In human rights matters, standards have tended to move too far ahead of the political and social facts of many societies.

4: A First World View

RITA E. HAUSER

The fundamental emphasis of human rights in the First World is on liberty of the person: the right to physical security and protection of basic intellectual beliefs. To assure such liberty, those possessing the power of the state (regardless of how the term has been defined over the course of history) must necessarily be restricted in the application of that power by rules inhibiting arbitrary and uncontrolled behavior. Certain actions of the state, under this scheme of things, are absolutely forbidden; others are severely constrained; and yet others may be exercised only in the face of a perceived danger to the state or the collective citizenry. In other words, restricted or limited government is the hallmark of the First World, although clearly the line defining the limitations has altered over the centuries and under divergent political philosophies.

Both the Old and New Testaments, the underpinning of Western law, are grounded on the concepts of human freedom: That which is nonvolitional in nature is immoral and may be negated. Indeed, the Bible is replete with tales of freedom-fighters, to use a modern term, all of whom rose up against the imposition of arbitrary rule and human degradation. A concomitant to freedom is justice: That which endures must be right in the eyes of God and in accordance with His law.

These concepts of freedom, justice, and morality impregnate the history of the Western World throughout its diverse stages. In modern times the Magna Carta and, later, the French Revolution with its enunciation of the rights of man denominate continued efforts to restrict the power of the monarch and assure basic human liberty. The American Declaration of Independence is the apogee of this development, and still remains the best articulation of the idea that man is born free, imbued with human dignity and freedom, destined to pursue his life in accordance with the laws of God and nature.

From these overriding precepts, the history of the Western World is a long story of the development of practical procedures to ensure limitations on the state's powers and the institutions necessary to ensure the sanctity of the procedures. Due process of law becomes the centerpiece of this development; the compelling view is that the state is subject to the rule of law and may not act other than in accordance with the law. An independent and respected judiciary, free of state control, assures the process of law.

This brief sketch helps to place the emphasis that First World nations place on certain fundamental human rights, enunciated in the Universal Declaration of Human Rights as the most basic and on which, in the Western view, all other rights are premised. These rights include

—Right to life, liberty, and security of the person.
—Freedom from subjection to torture or to cruel, inhuman, or degrading treatment or punishment.
—Freedom from arbitrary arrest, detention, or exile.
—Right to freedom of thought, conscience, and religion.
—Right to freedom of opinion and expression.

It is only when these rights are secured (discussed below) that one may begin to address other needs that are essentially economic and social in nature. Indeed, despite the fact that these needs are enumerated as rights in the Universal Declaration of Human Rights, there are many Western jurists who would still dispute their juridical nature. Surely, until the adoption of the Universal Declaration, the quest for economic security, a decent education, protections in case of sickness and in old age, and other similar assurances for the well-being of the person were considered in the First World as elements of social bargaining between those who did not possess such protections as against those who could afford to provide them. Trade unionism began as a collective effort to force the employer, until very recently almost always a private rather than a public entity, to grant some of these protections, especially those related to employment. Fair wages and decent working conditions, including rest periods and paid holidays, were the object of early collective bargaining efforts. Only after a long and arduous battle in almost all Western states did the basic ability to group and bargain collectively through trade unions come to be recognized as a legal right protected by special legislation.

From that, once the trade union movement became an established fact, it was an easy leap in the West to demands that only the state could provide: insurance against disability, unemployment, sickness, provisions for retirement, and other benefits. In some, but not all Western states, a system of national health was provided, soon expanded to include maternity benefits, which inured to all citizens of the state regardless of need or ability to pay. All Western states provide universal free education up to a point; some provide free or low-cost housing to those in need. Some more "advanced" or socialist states in the First World assure employment through various devices for the majority of its nationals or sufficient state payments in case of unemployment to ease or eliminate the burden of job loss.

Whether or not they are recognized as legal rights, such protections and benefits provided by the state are characteristic of much of the First World. The United States probably affords the smallest range of state benefits, still behaving as if it were a laissez-faire economy in contrast to overtly socialist states such as England, France, or Sweden, but even guarantees of minimum social benefits are extensive in America. On the whole, it is fair to say that since the end of World War II, the First World nations have all moved toward some form of welfare state in which the economic and social rights of the Universal Declaration are provided in one manner or another. The degree and extent of these benefits are the subject of political dispute within the various Western states, but few would argue today that the state should have a minimal role or no role in providing these benefits to all residents of the nation.

The basic political and civil rights listed above nevertheless remain the centerpiece of attention in any review of human rights in the Western World. Failure to assure such rights for the broadest number of people is taken to be a sign of ill health in the polity, and nonobservance of them on a sustained basis by any Western nation would place it well outside the accepted spectrum. Greece under the military junta, Spain and Portugal under their respective past dictators, even France under an authoritarian de Gaulle, were viewed as deviants from the normative. It is not an acceptable affirmative defense in such instances to plead that economic or social conditions of the citizenry have advanced under such rule. That argument is not acceptable to the majority of First World persons because political and civil freedoms cannot be compromised.

Freedom of conscience, free speech and press, protection against arbitrary police action, and a guarantee of free elections are viewed as fundamental to the very existence of the state. Without such freedoms, the state is acting without the consent of the governed, and all its actions, no matter how beneficial they may be in certain realms, are illegitimate and need not be obeyed. Indeed, the right to overturn the government of such a state can then be properly asserted. The fundamental political rights must be assured in the First World if the state is to enjoy the support of its citizens and the legitimacy that derives from such support.

The most difficult problem in the First World lies in the fact that not all citizens may enjoy the basic protections and rights afforded by law to the same degree. This is particularly true as to racial, religious, or ethnic minorities within the state who, by virtue of state-encouraged or state-tolerated discrimination, are deprived of the full exercise of their rights. Thus the right to vote in free elections was respected in the United States, with various qualifications, from the origin of the nation, but not all citizens were able to exercise suffrage equally. Only in recent years has the state adopted legislation to assure this basic political right to all, with power of enforcement against those who seek to deny the right to members of minority groups.

In many western European countries basic political rights have been denied in some instances to aliens residing in the nation, particularly migrant laborers brought from poorer countries who constitute a pool of "different" people in terms of race, religion, language, or ethnicity. International treaties and, to some extent, local legislation have sought to overcome this situation with varying degrees of success. Unless the state takes affirmative action in these instances, the natural propensity to discriminate, seen in all countries, would prevail. Thus political freedom for all requires the intervention of the state, seen here as a positive force although it may necessitate the coercion of those who prefer to segregate others, across the broad range of activities. A delicate balance is required between the intervention of the state for positive purposes and the assurance to every citizen that his or her liberty will not be diminished to an unacceptable degree. The latter balance, of course, is defined by the pull and tug of politics and social discourse, and it is clear that prevailing standards of right and wrong on these issues can shift rather quickly, as was true, for example, in the United States in the 1955-1965 period.

Thoughtful people in the First World nations worry today about the concentration of power in the state due to welfarism, defense, and security needs and the growth everywhere toward strong executive leadership. The minimal state has passed into history. Whatever the degree of effective power exercised by the state, citizens of the First World would not tolerate systematic torture, physical abuse, arbitrary imprisonment, crooked trials, or other direct attacks against the integrity of the person. Covert abuse, usually condoned in the name of national security, is tolerated in most but not all countries; thus electronic spying, telephone tapping, and other indirect devices that infringe on personal liberty are accepted practices in many Western nations although the law permits them only under very restricted and controlled circumstances. How deeply people care about these abuses determines their course, as the current furor in America over the excesses of the CIA and the FBI has shown. The level of tolerance is always extended in times of armed conflict or great internal disarray.

For the First World, the content of human rights will always be defined by political and civic rights. Economic and social rights are viewed as derivative; they are important but do not rise to the level of significance of those rights on which the very legitimacy of the state is premised. Political freedoms, the protection of the person, and the enjoyment of liberty—these are the fundamental rights well protected in most of the First World nations. These nations are called democracies, and the failure in any of them to assure such rights on a broad scale results in the loss of that appellation.

A developed nation in the economic and social sense which practices authoritarianism is a suspect member of the First World, its credentials lacking. The history of the Western World compels this conclusion. Whether other nations with different histories and institutions can be persuaded to follow this path is the central drama of our times. Some countries, such as the People's Republic of China, have made great economic and social gains in the absence of liberty; indeed, coercion of the citizenry was the core ingredient for these developments although the country in many respects is still very backward. Most countries where deprivation of liberty is practiced have witnessed few economic and social gains. Freedom, it would seem, is conducive to human development, and it is in this respect that the First World nations have excelled.

5: A Third World View

EDDISON JONAS MUDADIRWA ZVOBGO

I.

While many Third World rulers and academics are aware of the worldwide crusade for the observance and promotion of human rights, few have joined this crusade to the extent that many of their colleagues in the western and northern hemispheres have done. This fact, however, should not imply a lesser concern or interest on the part of the Third World in this important area of human values. Rather it may, as I propose to argue, be indicative, *first*, of the fact that priorities as set forth on the First World's agendas are often different from those of the Third World's and, *second*, of the fact that the socio-cultural heritages significantly separate peoples in this as in other areas of human activity.

The belief that human beings have or are entitled to certain rights is neither new nor controversial. It is universal. Practically all peoples, races, and religions have conceded this through the centuries. What is controversial, though not new, is the origin and nature of those rights. Anglo-Saxons, for example, never tire—nor should they—of pointing to the Magna Carta of 1215 as the abiding evidence of their commitment to human rights. They point out, rightly in my opinion, that while the growth of royal absolutism of the fifteenth, sixteenth, and early seventeenth centuries constituted a serious assault upon the faith in human rights in England as well as in much of the rest of Europe, the effort merely managed to stifle but not extinguish the spirit of Runnymede.

As evidence, they point to the epic revolts against absolutism in England and Europe during the seventeenth, eighteenth, and nineteenth centuries which resulted in the vesting of sovereignty in the people. These victories, some would argue, were made possible only by the fact that the humanist/naturalist movement had roots that could be traced to the Magna Carta and had been sustained and nourished by an "egalitarian" Judeo-Christian environment. Although the extent to which Christianity served as a catalyst is not clear—particularly in light of its monarchical structure and arbitrary procedures—it can hardly be denied that the Christian religion contributed significantly to the naturalist argument.

The triumph of the humanist/naturalist argument in Europe remained largely inchoate as turmoil and revolutions continued and as the sovereign peoples groped for permanent structures that internalized the newly won values. It is to the credit of the American founders that they managed in the eighteenth century, by sheer force of will and intellect, to design, institutionalize, and internalize in a new environment those ideas which had been distilled by the humanist/naturalist protagonists in Europe. Hence, the U.S. Constitution and Bill of Rights constitute a new and important beacon on Western mankind's road to self-realization and self-fulfillment.

This march was blurred by World War I in this century. But this vision appears to have been regained, as evidenced by President Woodrow Wilson's Fourteen Points. However, the League of Nations proved to be an inadequate tool for ensuring that peace without which respect for human rights is but a dream. But the fact of the League of Nations was further evidence that the quest was alive.

It was not until history's worst catastrophe—World War II—that the First World finally was able to press forward more vigorously to assure the continuing observance of human rights everywhere through the establishment of the United Nations. But there was never any doubt that the "human rights" that the United States, France, Britain, and their allies sought to universalize were those which were consistent with their own values and traditions. The *travaux preparetoires* of the U.N. Charter leaves no doubt that the United States was *primus inter pares* at San Francisco. President Franklin Roosevelt's "Four Freedoms," as elucidated by Secretary of State Stettinius in plenary sessions, were clearly the source of those charter provisions which refer to human rights. Coming from the Third World, one may be forgiven for asserting that if President Wilson had sought to make the world safe for democracy after World War I, President Roosevelt sought to make it more Western, if not specifically American,[1] after World War II.

Once concern for human rights had become entrenched in the U.N. Charter—the first universal, multilateral treaty to embody that concern—only enforcement provisions remained to be written. The question of what actually were the human rights referred to in the charter was a pressing one after 1945. The supplementary questions of who was to be bound by the human rights provisions of the charter and how were the provisions to be enforced were equally pressing.

Both were answered by the General Assembly's "Universal Declaration of Human Rights" of December 10, 1948. All the "human rights" envisaged under the charter were spelled out therein, and the declaration was proclaimed as

> ... the human standard of achievement for all nations to the end that every individual and every organ of society keeping this Declaration constantly in mind shall strive, by teaching and education, to promote all these rights and freedoms and by progressive measures, national and international, to secure their universal and effective recognition and observance, both among the people of Member States themselves and among the peoples of territories in their jurisdictions.

Whether the declaration is binding law under U.N. jurisprudence is an interesting issue but not one which is relevant here. Suffice to say that not one member or nonmember of the United Nations has ever asserted that it violates human rights because it is not bound by the declaration which is merely a resolution of the General Assembly. Rather, the practice of the state is to deny guilt of any alleged violation.

The U.N. Charter's provisions on human rights and the declaration have enjoyed enormous prestige worldwide and have been the inspiration behind the numerous conventions and draft conventions in this area.[2]

II.

Among most of the nations of the Third World, the people have always been the primary cultural reality. In African culture, the following sayings (expressed variously according to language and community experiences) are instructive of this view:

"*The king is people.*" This statement means that if one is king and wishes to reign for a long time, he should treat people humanely and kindly.

"*A prince in his own home is a subject out of it.*" This statement means that one should not swagger, be overbearing, or be arbitrary with other people, even if one is the prince, because others are also princes in their own right, depending on their circumstances.

"*We will touch each other's buttocks when crossing the river.*" This means one should never forget that people need each other in adversity; therefore, one should treat everyone with dignity and respect today.

"*Power migrates; many people take turns at it.*" This means that one may be the ruler today, but tomorrow it may be someone else's turn. Consequently, one should treat people kindly and with humanity.

These and similar adages go back to the recall of oral tradition. Although expressed differently, such notions are not alien to Asian peoples. Respect for senior citizens by the young and for the young by seniors; respect for rulers by subjects and for subjects by rulers; preoccupation with maintaining a good name, generosity, and reputation; and commitment to family, relatives, clan, community, and country—all these values are enmeshed in the cultures of Third World peoples. The peoples' devotion to "human rights" is self-evident even though the Third World may not be able to point to a Magna Carta, a Bill of Rights, "Fourteen Points," or "Four Freedoms" as enshrining them.

This is not to say that Third World peoples have never known brutal and cruel rulers. In Africa we have had our Tshakas, as Europe has had its Napoleons; we have had our Amins, as Europe has had its Hitlers and Mussolinis. The same is true of Asian peoples. But these rulers and the periods of their regimes have been interludes in an otherwise impressive history of devotion to human value.

There is, however, one fundamental difference between Third World peoples and those of the northern hemisphere including Anglo-Saxons. Most African and Asian peoples, because of culture, history, and peculiar socio-economic factors sharpened by their new sense of nationalism in the postcolonial era, have experienced very little, if any, movement from what Sir Henry Maine called *status* toward *contract*. Except for the small crowds of ruling elites who have been exposed to Western values, the bulk of Africans and Asians remain culture-bound. To most of them, the concept of the human being as an autonomous, separate, and self-determining actor is as nonexistent as it is absurd. Such a person,—separate and alone, pursuing a self-determined path to happiness and self-fulfillment—would be curious to them.

"Rights" from a Third World view do not exist as an integral part of human nature. They arise from a person's destiny of living in a relationship with family, friends, ethno-linguistic groups, and nation. They are incidental, unavoidable, and necessary, but not an attribute of being human. No rights can be exercised apart from one's relationship with another. In isolation an African has, because of his or her humanity, the potential of enjoying rights. However, the occasion and the opportunity for such enjoyment does not arise until contact and intercourse with others has been made. This is not the Lockean "man" and, in this view, lies the essence of the difference between the Third World and the First World.

It is important for us to note in this regard that the Western dual theories of rights—freedom *from* and freedom *of* or *to*—which are central to the U.S. Constitution, the Bill of Rights, the Universal Declaration of Human Rights, and the European Convention of Human Rights, postulate the Lockean "man." By contrast, an African and Asian can only be said to have a "right-with" as a precedent without which other "right-actualizations," such as *to, from,* or *of,* are impossible.

III. The U.N. Charter (Human Rights Provisions), the Declaration of Human Rights, and the Third World

It is important to bear in mind that there were only 50 charter members of the United Nations. Of these nations only two, Ethiopia and Liberia, represented the whole of black Africa. Apart from China, only India "represented" Asia. The Western allied powers were the dominant group. When one recalls that the Latin-American republics always echoed the U.S. position during the Cold War, the so-called First World enjoyed a comfortable majority in the world body.

The situation has changed a great deal in the wake of the decolonization of Africa and Asia and the emergence of Arab republics in the Middle East. Black Africa is now represented by 37 independent states. Fourteen Arab republics have come into being in the Middle East, while twelve new sovereign states have come into existence in Asia, excluding Australia and New Zealand but including Indonesia and Papua New Guinea. Consequently, the total membership of the United Nations has risen from 50 in 1945–1946 to 138 in 1977.

The important questions which are rarely raised and never pressed seriously are these: Granted that the U.N. Charter is a multilateral treaty binding on every new member who chooses to subscribe to the treaty and is admitted to membership, what is the U.N.'s binding moral authority over the two-thirds of the present membership that did not exist at the time the United Nations was organized solely because their territories and peoples were under the colonial bondage of the principal charter members? Can it be argued seriously that Malawi or Botswana or Burundi could, upon admission, have expressed reservations to the charter, assuming there were articles in it to which they objected? Is the U.N. Charter not in truth a treaty or contract of the adhesion which a new member must accept or reject as it stands? These and similar questions have not been asked largely because membership, for a small Third World state, has come to be viewed as the act of recognition of its own sovereignty. For such states the advantages outweigh any disadvantages.

I am convinced that were the Universal Declaration of Human Rights to be debated again in the General Assembly, the final draft would be significantly different from that which was adopted in 1948.[3] Article 1, for example, which imposes the Western "Rousseau-Lockean" view on all states and peoples, could be omitted since the observance of human rights is not dependent upon its acceptance. Thus those states and peoples who subscribe to the "social origin" of rights theory would not need to abandon their position in order to comply fully with the spirit of the declaration. Articles 2-16, 19, and 23-26 are neutral on their face. In any event, since much of their substance has been enshrined in the *International Covenant on Civil and Political Rights,* they would raise no difficulties.

The real problems would be in Article 17, which seeks to impose free enterprise and capitalism on the rest of the world; in Article 18, the spirit of which—if not the letter—would outlaw "one-party" states and domestic legislation requiring permits for political rallies and demonstrations against the government; and in Article 21, which seeks to universalize Western-style elections. It is debatable whether the rights protected in these articles are in fact natural rights which flow naturally from the assumption of Article 1.

No Afro-Asian leader has publicly challenged the U.N. Charter or the Universal Declaration of Rights in regard to their source or their articulation of the nature of human rights. There are four reasons for this inaction: First, such a statement could easily be misunderstood by the electorate and the world-at-large as a signal of an intention to violate human rights generally. Second, African states have found these and similar instruments useful in their campaign against colonialism, apartheid, and imperialism. Third, the majority of Afro-Asian rulers are in fact Western-educated and/or trained elites; the majority are neocolonial agents or puppets of one or the other Euro-American powers. They believe it pays to see humankind and the world as those powers do. Finally, and more generously, it may be that no one sees any value to be gained in fighting over the philosophical questions of "origin" or rights and "the proper scope" of those rights so long as the objective is one that is in the interests of humanity.

Most Afro-Asian Republics, liberated from British, French, or Belgian colonialism, not only have publicly embraced the Universal

Declaration of Human Rights as it stands, but also have enshrined it in part or in whole in their constitutions.[4] The Charter of the Organization for African Unity has made the recognition of human rights a major objective.[5] At the United Nations, Afro-Asian states have played an impressive activist role because of their numbers in pushing through the General Assembly several resolutions that promote human rights. Invariably, their spokespersons at the United Nations have cited the fact that the U.N. Charter mentions human rights seven times; they repeatedly have pointed to the declaration in terms which suggest that their states regard it as binding over both member and nonmember nations.[6]

On the whole, however, Third World states have tended to limit their activism to the promotion of decolonization (in Zimbabwe, Namibia and, until 1974, Portuguese Angola, Mozambique, and Guinea-Bissau) and condemnation of Apartheid. The African position has invoked sharp criticism from scholars and writers who feel that Africa's record on human rights at the United Nations demonstrates an unacceptable double standard[7] or that it amounts to unpardonable selectivity.[8] These criticisms may stem from a failure to appreciate the essential differences between the denial of human rights in black Africa and the denial of human rights in white-ruled Africa (Rhodesia and South Africa).[9] This distinction is treated below.

IV. Human Rights and the Third World Environment

The African view of the value and sanctity of people and of human rights has been suggested in the preceding sections. It has been argued that, generally, the African view approximates the representative Third World vision. In this segment I propose to argue that because of the recent history of the Third World and because of the enormous problems which confront each Third World state in the postcolonial era, certain human rights as declared by the U.N. declaration are in very grave danger.

Most Third World nations are small in territory and in population. Until two decades ago, most were colonies of the Euro-American powers—a few for as long as 600 years and many for at least a century. The colonial powers have uniformly, with differences mainly of style and nuance, pursued and practiced harsh, repressive, oppressive, and suppressive policies over the native inhabitants. All of the colonial powers practiced policies of large-scale exploitation in the areas of labor and natural resources. Racism was the bedrock of colonial policy. Only meager efforts were made to develop economic infrastructures in the colonies, and human resources were wasted without much regard to the future needs of the postcolonial era.

When the moment of decolonization finally came, several colonial powers ruined the little capital structures that did exist out of pique. However, all the colonial powers made sure that they "bequeathed" to their erstwhile colonies replicas of their own constitutional structures, even though they bore little, if any, resemblance to traditional institutions. For example, "opposition parties" on the Westminister model were encouraged—at least in British Africa and Asia. Legislatures—replete with speakers, sergeants-at-arms, and clerks—were installed. Some were even complete with British wigs and gowns! The new institutions were not only alien, but were in fact obscene in an African or Asian environment.

The new leaders found a plethora of urgent problems staring them in the face. Illiteracy, disease, inadequate housing, malnutrition, poor communications, ailing agricultural systems, European-style educational systems which were totally irrelevant to their needs, lack of educated or trained personnel, and monetary reserves and currencies tied to the apron strings of the former colonizer were all problems to be faced. The list is endless. These and other realities of independence required the new states to arrange priorities in a manner that sometimes was not based on a rational cost-benefit analysis.

One African president put it this way to the author: "No one but us understands the motives upon which we act. Imperialists talk about human rights, drinking tea or sipping champagne. They can afford to—after all, they have it made. If we had had slaves for 200 years to build our roads, build our homesteads, sow our fields; if we had had multinationals for 300 years looting wealth from other people's lands; if we had literate, healthy, well-fed citizens—if we had a diversified economy and people had jobs—we too could talk human rights from our air conditioned offices and homes. But we can't do it; we have nothing."

A junior minister present joined in: "You know, professor, we wish imperialists could understand that the sick and hungry have no use for freedom of movement or of speech. Maybe of worship! Hunger dulls hearing and stills the tongue. Poverty and lack of roads, trains, or buses negate freedom of movement. You know, freedom to own property alone is demanded by less than 1 percent here—those who had collaborated with imperialists in robbing the poor masses. The poor are grateful and glad to share.[11]

Above all, a new African state faces ethno-linguistic problems in the political arena. Political competition among ethno-linguistic groups as well as among the small coteries of ruling elites—especially in multiparty environments—has been endemic in Africa. Between 1958 and 1970 there were 36 "communal instabilities" of various kinds in Burundi, Cameroun, Chad, Congo (now Zaire), the People's Republic of the Congo, Dahomey, Ethiopia, the Ivory Coast, Kenya, Malawi, Mali, Mauritania, Niger, Nigeria, Rwanda, Senegal, Sierra-Leone, Somalia, Sudan, Togo, Uganda, and Zambia. Some instabilities involved tribal conflict; others, church-state struggles, struggles between trade unions and state, struggles between parties and, finally, struggles between the executive and the military. In addition, between 1958 and 1970 there were 40 successful *coups d'etat*, 17 attempted ones, and 5 assassinations of heads of government.[10]

This is not the place for an inquiry into the causes of such instability. However, a few reasons may be suggested: the loss of political influence by elites and opposition groups barred from political activity, the decline in status and influence felt by middle-class groups as that of the working class and party member groups increased, the progressive taxation of the wealthy and regressive taxation of the poor, and corrupt, ostentatious living by the bourgeois leadership.

In the face of such conditions the reality which suddenly dawns on the president-monarch of an African state is that the government's hold on power is tenuous. There usually are not enough police and armed forces to insure peace, law, and order. The courts left behind by the colonizers, which are presided over by British, French, or Belgian trained lawyers, insist upon intricate Anglo-American or French or Belgian rules of procedure regarding admissibility and "sufficiency" of evidence which in turn assures disposition of cases at a snail's pace. In the end the president-monarch resorts to "preempting trouble" on the theory that "prevention is better than cure." At this point human rights come into jeopardy.

These conditions have resulted in the creation of powerful presidents both in Africa and in Asia. Although the president is a creature of an alien constitution, "the legitimacy crisis" has compelled every chief executive to draw heavily upon three sources of support: tradition, the political party, and the army.

First, the president-monarch invariably benefits from what Ali Mazrui has termed the deeply rooted "elder tradition." As elder the president is the resurrected traditional ruler; he is the paramount chief, king, or emperor. The fact that Khama, Jonathan/Moshoeshoe, and Sobhuza/Dhlamini are actual traditional rulers is not without significance. As elder the president is not *primus inter pares;* he is *primus.* He may be perceived as Osagyego (Nkrumah), Old Man/Big Man/ Teacher (Kaunda or Touré), Mzee (Kenyatta), Mwalimu (Nyerere), Ngwazi/Mukango/Tambala or merely Kamuzu (Banda), or the most authentic Sese-Soko (Mobutu). The African masses generate power, and, by tradition, they know their duties vis-à-vis the ruler. As the Ngwazi, Dr. Kamuzu Banda always reminds his subjects in his radio broadcasts, those duties comprise an inseparable trilogy: "loyalty, obedience, and dedication." These three qualities African president-monarchs get in abundance whether or not they deserve them.

Second, provided there is no military rule, the president-monarch normally presides over the vanguard movement responsible for liberating the country (KANU/Kenyatta, TANU/Nyerere, UNIP/Kaunda, Mbokodvo/Sobhuza, DPG/Touré, FRELIMO/Machel, Democratic Party/Mobutu, etc.). As president and/or secretary-general of the only lawful party in the country, the president-monarch has a monopoly of power and of access to the masses through the party. Invariably the party is elevated to a position of primacy over the government. At this point the civil servants become party functionaries. Kaunda took the matter a stage further: In order to mobilize party power, only he and the secretary-general/prime minister are both members of the party's Central Committee and of government. Since the party directs the government, his ministers, because they are not party officers, are reduced to the level of boot-lickers.

Where there have been successful *coups d'etat* (Burundi, Zaire, Congo/Brazzaville, Dahomey, Chad, Ethiopia, Ghana, Lesotho, Mali, Niger, Nigeria, Sierra-Leone, Somalia, Sudan, Swaziland, Togo, Uganda, and Upper Volta) the president-monarch also has monopolized dominance over the bureaucracy—a significant source of power. The legislature, where this organ of state exists, has been reduced (except in Tanzania, Botswana, and Kenya) to a mere rubber-stamp role.

Third, and finally, in the fashion of American and French presidential models, the African president-monarch is both head of state and head of government. For example, in the former British colonies the constitutions make it a crime to insult or to ascribe improper motives to the actions of the president; such a statute borrows both from English and African customary law. As head of state, the president is the statesman who receives and accredits diplomats and is commander-in-chief of the armed forces. He assents to bills, issues proclamations or decrees, and alone has the monopoly of declaring states of emergency without having to demonstrate "clear and present danger" to the state. In this type of environment the potential for abuse of power is self-evident.

V. Third World "Domestic Human Rights" Practice: The Nyerere Declaration Tested

On the occasion of Tanganyika's admission to the United Nations on December 14, 1961, Prime Minister Julius Nyerere, now president of Tanzania, told the General Assembly of the United Nations:

> Nonetheless the underlying theme of the Universal Declaration, that of human brotherhood, regardless of race, color, or creed, is the basic principle which we ourselves in Tanganyika and, we believe that other people in Africa and other parts of the world, have been struggling to implement.... We are conscious that the implementation of the spirit underlying lofty ideas is not always achieved without some difficulty.... But any apparent deviation from the articles of the declaration will be an honest attempt on our part to balance conflicting interests while preserving the major principle itself.

There is no doubt that in enunciating the doctrine of "apparent deviation" in an attempt to "balance conflicting interests" President Nyerere had in mind the problems and pressures set out in Section IV above. The real question is, looking at Africa and Asia from the vantage point of the 1970's, can we say that such violations of human rights as have occurred have amounted to no more than "apparent deviations" from the declaration while "preserving the major principle itself?" In addition, can we say with Nyerere that such "deviations" as have occurred have been inspired solely by "an honest attempt... to balance conflicting interests"?

The first question, I submit, may be answered with a qualified "yes" for the Third World as a whole, but with an unequivocal "no" in respect to three or four African cases. The second question can be answered by either a "yes," a "no," or both.

First, let us turn to Africa's worst cases:
1. Rwanda's massacre of Tutsi people (1964).[11]
2. Burundi's massacre of the Hutu (1972–1973).[12]
3. Uganda's explusion of Asians (1971), and General Amin's campaign of brutality and terror.[13]
4. Ghana's explusion of West African aliens.[14]
5. Zambia's conflict with the Lumpa Church of Alice Lenschina.[15]

6. Ethiopia's summary killing without trial of all suspected enemies of the military regime.[16]
7. The Ian Smith (Rhodesia) and John Vorster (South Africa) regimes, and their campaigns of murder and terror.[17]

These cases are well known and do not need restatement. The only case on the list which may not have been a direct breach of the Declaration of Human Rights is Ghana's expulsion of West African aliens; this instance is distinguishable on the facts from Uganda's manner of, if not the fact of, expelling Asians.

Rarely has human-made tragedy—save in war—approached the cases of Rwanda, Burundi, and Uganda. In the first two the immediate cause was competition for political control on the basis of the ethno-linguistic factor. In Amin's case the frequent reports of horrors do not seem to suggest any distinct rational purpose, although it is possible that Amin himself perceives personal danger in every human face that does not belong to one of his immediate allies. These three cases can rightly be said to be noncharacteristic of the Third World.

The usual forms of deprivation of rights are (1) arresting real, suspected, or potential political opponents and putting them on trial on fabricated evidence, (2) arresting and charging someone with a crime without obtaining a normal warrant, on the orders of the president or one of his principal ministers (usually the minister of justice or home affairs), and (3) committing a person to "detention" without trial at the pleasure of the regime. Such "detainees" often are committed to specially prepared detention camps or are confined to regular prisons. They usually are treated as unconvicted prisoners. A fourth form of human rights deprivation involves arrests on police initiative and confinement to police lockup stations.

Unusual methods of human rights violations involve arrests but also include beatings, isolation, and torture. Such procedures may be added where the prisoners are regarded as important. Banishment, or so-called restriction to some forest area, has been used in Kenya, Zambia, Rhodesia, and South Africa.

Between black Africa and white-ruled Africa there is a "duration" difference in the periods to which opponents tend to be rusticated. In Rhodesia and South Africa, political prisoners may "disappear" forever without leaving any trace. Those opponents who do not "disappear" are detained "for good." In both countries some detainees are in the fifteenth, sixteenth, and seventeenth years of detention without trial. John Vorster Square (Johannesburg), Cornmara (Rhodesia), Khami Prison (Rhodesia), and Salisbury Maximum Security Prison are in fact graveyards. Many detainees die there because the tenure of their detention is without end.

By contrast, denials of human rights in black Africa tend to occur in spurts of limited duration. A few examples can underscore the difference:

1. In the Cameroun, Amnesty International estimated that there were close to 5,000 detainees, mostly from the Bassa and Bamileke communities, at Poli and Mantoum in 1973. As the Union des Populations (UPC) continued its guerrilla struggle against the regime, more detention centers were opened at Tcollire, Lomie, and Yoko. The regime did put many opponents, including the UPC leader Ernest Quandie, on trial. Torture was alleged and probably was practiced. Since 1973, however, several hundred people have been released.
2. In Ghana, although Nkrumah detained his opponents, he killed no one and, except for Dr. Dankwa, who died in prison, all such prisoners were eventually released. Following Acheampong's coup, in January 1972, Amnesty International's headquarters received reports of the torture of prisoners. But in June 1973 an amnesty was proclaimed which resulted in the release of most of the detainees. Since then, a number of persons have been arrested, tried, and sentenced by military courts for political offenses. The military government subsequently has reduced many of these sentences.
3. In the Ivory Coast, Amnesty International was aware of 300 persons under detention in 1973. In December 1973 an amnesty was proclaimed that resulted in the release of 100 political prisoners.
4. In Kenya the former president is credited for releasing Oginga Odinga and other KPU leaders, such as Ochola Ogaye Mak'-Anyengo. The total number of detainees in Kenya is probably less than ten.
5. Presidents' birthdays are frequently used as occasions for releasing detainees in black Africa. Following the arrest and detention of hundreds of Jehovah's Witnesses, lawyers, and former civil servants in Malawi in 1972, 1973, and 1977, President Banda chose May 14, his birthday, and July 10, the tenth anniversary of Malawi's independence, to release political prisoners.
6. Amnesties also have been proclaimed in Senegal, Swaziland (for the release of Dr. Zwane), Tanzania, and Zambia (for the release of Alice Lenschina, Nalumino Mundia, Simon Kapwepwe, and others).

This evidence permits me to assert that African president-monarchs do not appear to have as high a tolerance for the nasty business of detention without trial as do the South African and

Rhodesian regimes. African president-monarchs are conscious both of the injustice of unlawful detention and of the fact that their people identify the weapon with colonialist tactics.

The Procedure-Remedy Difference

It generally is conceded that human rights tend to be better protected in those countries where, by law, procedural rules are deemed important and where, by law, persons deprived of their rights are entitled to judicial recourse. Procedural rules are meaningless without judicial recourse. No matter how scrupulously rules are observed, they provide no protection unless a citizen can approach the courts for remedy when his or her rights are violated. By the same token, however, it is meaningless for a state to proclaim that every person shall have recourse to the courts unless the procedures for doing so exist and can be readily utilized.

In South Africa and Rhodesia the regimes have made a fetish of procedural rules. Every detainee is "served" with an order signed personally by the Minister of Justice. The order lists the statutory provision under which the minister is acting and intimates in broad generalities the "reason" for the minister's action. However, the specifics of the charges are seldom revealed to the detainee "because of their confidential character." In the case of Rhodesia the detainee is informed in writing that he or she may appeal to the minister stating the reasons for the appeal within seven days following the serving of the order. But this right of appeal is a farce. Not being privy to the information available to the minister, the applicant is unable to answer whatever allegations are being made.

In Rhodesia there is also a "detainee's tribunal" chaired by a judge of the High Court which is convened annually to hear "appeals" from detainees. This procedure is a travesty of justice. I appeared before such a tribunal in 1969. The secret police submitted to the tribunal a thick file containing more than 100 allegations against me, yet all that was required of me was to answer "yes" or "no" to each charge. The police did not produce their informers, and there was no one to cross-examine.

Both in South Africa and in Rhodesia indemnity acts have been passed that make it impossible for anyone to sue any police officer, prison official, or government official for irregular or unlawful acts against a detainee. This fact negates any value that may have been derived from the regime's fetish for procedural propriety.

African practice has varied considerably. Zambia, for example, permits detainees to institute actions in the courts of law to seek an answer to torture or other brutalities inflicted upon them (Simon Kapwepwe was awarded a considerable sum of money for assaults upon his person while in detention). In Malawi, Kenya, and Tanzania it appears that it is possible to sue the government, although it is difficult to hazard the outcome. African governments often can be faulted for failing to adhere to their own procedures and laws. But by and large their established procedures and legal framework permit judicial recourse.

The Infrastructure Difference

It takes a fairly high degree of organizational, technological, and educational development to implement and sustain a program of terror, torture, and degradation on a massive scale. Such a program also calls for a significant outlay of financial resources. Most African states, with the possible exception of Nigeria, do not have either the monetary or the human resources to pursue a permanent policy of terror. In most African states such abuse of prisoners as exists is quite unprogramed and lacking in central direction. Amin's Department of Research has made terror its speciality, but even in Uganda the indications are that repression is haphazard and unsystematic.

By contrast, in Rhodesia and South Africa there exist highly centralized regimes with sophisticated infrastructural supports. Here the application of terror and torture is scientific. In 1965, at Alexander Mashawira's inquest, a Salisbury magistrate confessed that the method of torture used in the prison cells was so sophisticated that it reminded him of Nazi Germany. Mashawira had been beaten all over with an instrument, but that instrument left no external marks, even though it caused 64 hemorrhaging lacerations inside the body. The use of dark cells, fridge rooms, electric shock gadgets, and nine-hour nude sessions in sieve floor wet rooms are as yet unknown in black Africa. These forms of torture call for a certain perverse sense of brutality that only a people with its back to the wall can be capable of. Amin is said to have ordered the execution of many people—some by having their heads pounded into pulp and others by having pieces of their anatomy cut and cooked. If this is so, it would single out Amin even more from his African peers. Amin and his practices represent a mutation, an aberration, *not* a norm.

NOTES

1. See Preamble, and Articles 1, 13, 55, and 56 of the U.N. Charter.
2. For example, a UNESCO sponsored Convention Relating to the Status of Refugees (1951); ILO sponsored Human Remuneration Convention (1951); Convention on the Political Rights of Women (1952); Convention on the Status of Stateless Persons (1954); Supplementary Convention on the Abolition of Slavery, the Slave Trade, and Institutions and Practices Similar to Slavery (1956); Convention on the Nationality of Married Women (1956); Convention on the Abolition of Forced Labor (1957); ILO Discrimination (Employment) Convention; Convention Against Discrimination in Education (1960); Convention on the Reduction of Statelessness (1961); Convention on Consent to Marriage, Minimum Age of Marriage, and Registration of Marriage (1962); Employment Policy Convention (1964); International Convention on the Elimination of all Forms of Racial Discrimination (1965); and Genocide Convention (1948).
3. See a restatement of most of the provisions in *The International Covenant on Civil and Political Rights* opened for signature on December 16, 1966 (adopted with the approval of Third World states).
4. E. Schwelb, "The United Nations and Human Rights," 2 *Howard Law Journal* (Spring 1965): 355-372; and D. F. Keys, *Human Rights: Present and Future* (New York: The International League for the Rights of Man, 1968).
5. Boutros-Ghali, "The Addis Ababa Charter," no. 546 *International Conciliation* (January 1964).
6. See, generally, D. Kay, "The Politics of Decolonization: The New Nations and the United Nations Political Process," 21 *International Organization* (1967): 786-811.
7. See, for example, L. S. Wiseberg, "Human Rights in Africa: Toward the Definition of the Problem of a Double Standard," 6 *Issue* (Winter, 1976): 3-10.
8. See, for example, W. Weinstein, "Africa's Approach to Human Rights at the United Nations," 6 *Issue* (Winter 1976): 16-17.
9. See E. J. M. Zvobgo, "The Abuse of Executive Prerogative: A Purposive Difference between Detention in Black Africa and Detention in White Racist Africa," 6 *Issue* (Winter 1976): 38-43.

For whatever it is worth, the author's data also shows that by 1970 no successful coup had been carried out in Niger, Liberia, the Ivory Coast, the Republic of Guinea, Tanzania, Malawi, Rwanda, Kenya, Zambia, Mauritania, Gambia, Botswana, and the Camerouns—all states where there was either one party (*de facto* or *de jure*) or where the opposition parties were so weak they were soon eclipsed. By contrast, successful coups occurred in every African state where there was a strong opposition party (or parties).

10. D. G. Morrison *et al.*, *Black Africa: A Comparative Handbook* (New York: Free Press, 1972).
11. J. Vanderunden, *La Republique rwandaise* (Paris: Berger-Levrault, 1970); and, specifically, see A. Segal, "Massacre in Rwanda," 240 *Fabian Research Series* (April 1974).
12. M. A. Weinstein, "Ethnicity and Conflict Regulation: The 1972 Burundi Revolt," 9 *Afrika Spectrum* (1974); and M. A. Weinstein *et al.*, *Selective Genocide in Burundi* (London: Minority Rights Group, 1974).

13. M. Posner, *Violations of Human Rights and the Rule of Law in Uganda* (Geneva: International Commission of Jurists, 1974).
14. M. Peil, "The Expulsion of West African Aliens," 9 *Journal of Modern African Studies* (August 1971).
15. E. J. M. Zvobgo, "Zambia: Problems of Survival," unpublished paper.
16. *Amnesty International Report 1977*, pp. 69–72.
17. E. J. M. Zvobgo, "The Abuse of Executive Prerogative," *supra* note 9.

Bibliography

BERLIN, I., *Four Essays on Liberty* (London, 1969).

BYSTRICKY, R., "Universality of Human Rights in a World of Conflicting Ideologies," *International Protection of Human Rights* no. 83.

CLAUDE, R. P., "The Classical Model of Human Rights Development," in Claude, R. (ed.), *Comparative Human Rights* (Baltimore and London, 1976), pp. 6-50.

CRANSTON, M. W., *What Are Human Rights?* (London, 1973).

EIDE, A., "Universality of Human Rights and the Widening Agreement on Their Contents," *International Protection of Human Rights* no. 269.

EMERSON, R., "The Fate of Human Rights in the Third World," 27 *World Politics* (January 1975): 201-226.

HAUSER, R. E., "Forward: Universal Declaration of Human Rights," 11 *Columbia Journal of Transnational Law* (1972): 1-13.

———, "U.N. and Human Rights: A Long and Winding Road," 8 *Vista* (September-October 1972): 81.

HENDERSON, C., "Underdevelopment and Political Rights: A Revisionist Challenge," 12 *Government and Opposition* (Summer 1977): 276-292.

MOWER, A. GLENN., "Human Rights in Black Africa: A Double Standard?" 9 *Human Rights Journal* (January-March 1976): 33-70.

RAPHAEL, D. D. (ed.), *Political Theory and the Rights of Man* (Bloomington, 1967).

UNESCO, *Human Rights: Comments and Interpretations* (Westport, Conn., 1973).

WISEBERG, L., and Weinstein, W. (eds.), "Human Rights in Africa," 6 *Issue* (Winter 1976).

PART FOUR
Human Rights: The Soviet Union and Helsinki

Introduction

HUMAN RIGHTS ARE AS IMPORTANT AN ISSUE IN EAST-WEST RELAtions as they are in North-South relations. The Soviet constitution guarantees freedom of speech, freedom of the press, freedom of assembly—including the right to hold mass meetings—and freedom of street demonstrations. Soviet law also recognizes both the freedom to worship and the freedom to disseminate antireligious propaganda. In practice and in law, however, civil freedoms are curbed by the state in the Soviet Union mostly in the name of the defense of socialism. Because of these theoretical guarantees the civil rights movement in the USSR centers on enforcement of those rights listed in Soviet law and publicizes and documents actions that appear to be in violation of these laws.

In his chapter Peter Reddaway illustrates the acknowledgment by Soviet spokespersons of their government's restrictive attitude toward civil rights. These people contend that freedom of expression should be restricted in order to prevent its abuse to the detriment of Soviet society and state. Moreover, Moscow argues that the exercise of free expression should be permitted only when it is of positive value to the public interest as defined in official party policy. Thus the Communist Party of the Soviet Union cannot bring itself to tolerate the expression of dissent beyond certain restricted limits.

Since the communist system rests on the assumption that the party represents the interests of all the people and is the ultimate repository of all authority and wisdom, dissent from the party's positions must be wrong and conflicts of interests must be allowed to appear only in limited spheres. Therefore, in spite of constitutional guarantees, there is no right of dissent in the Soviet Union. Individual rights thus have had little place in the traditionally authoritarian Soviet political system, and Soviet leaders have acted as if they regarded the survival of the state as being in danger as a result of the actions of a small minority of intellectuals and aspiring emigrants.

Moreover, since Soviet law is the servant of the party and an expression of the political authority, it can be used against anyone who questions this authority. Soviet criminal law specifies penalties for exceeding the approved limits of freedom of expression. The two provisions most commonly used against dissidents are Articles 70 and 190-191 of the criminal code. Article 70 prohibits "anti-Soviet agitation and propaganda" and provides for up to seven years' imprisonment and five years' exile for violations. Article 190-191 prohibits the circulation, either by mouth or in writing, of fabrications which consciously defame the Soviet system. Article 190-191 provides for up to three years' imprisonment for violations. In addition to these legal safeguards for the state, the USSR also has a series of graded sanctions that can be brought to bear against dissenters, because in an authoritarian system, the individual is dependent on the state for employment, housing, the education of children, permission to reside in a certain place, and passport and travel documents.

Although the USSR is a signatory to the U.N. Charter, has ratified the two U.N. covenants on economic, social, and cultural rights, and most recently has signed the Helsinki declaration, Moscow also has insisted on the primacy of social and economic rights over political and civil rights. Moscow thus emphasizes what it considers to be advances in genuine human rights in its own country while ignoring areas that other nations might consider important. For example, the Soviet constitution lays particular emphasis on the guaranteed right to work, to education, to leisure, and to social security. Soviet spokespersons argue with the Western concepts of dignity and liberty are "bourgeois" in character and devoid of meaning without the prior recognition and fulfillment of the essential human rights of food, shelter, and education. In the area of social and economic rights, Moscow feels that it has succeeded in fulfilling many human rights more than the political democracies of the West have. Soviet spokespersons argue that people are not dying of drug addiction or suffering from hunger, inadequate medical care, or unemployment in their country.

Just as the Soviet communists view the meaning and functions of domestic law differently from the West, much the same holds true of the Soviet attitude toward international agreements and obligations. The Final Act of the Conference on Security and Cooperation in Europe (CSCE), signed in Helsinki on August 1, 1975, is a case in point. Although, as A. H. Robertson states, the Helsinki Agreement is not a treaty with binding obligations in international law, it is a firm declaration of intentions which each participating state can expect all parties to honor. Human rights were a central issue at the 1975 CSCE talks. While the Helsinki Agreement was concerned principally with subjects such as strategic arms limitations and the status of national borders in Europe, humanitarian provisions of the third basket of the agreement included measures to increase freedom of movement, dissemination of information in all of Europe, and cultural exchange and cooperation. The overriding interest of the USSR at Helsinki was the fixing of the postwar European borders, an act which, in Soviet eyes, would secure Western acceptance of the status quo in Europe and thereby eliminate the major cause of East-West tension. Basket Three was the price the Soviet Union paid for Western recognition of Soviet dominance in Eastern Europe.

Although Western governments traditionally have asserted that access to information, the freedom to travel, and the right to emigrate are fundamental and universal human rights, before the CSCE Conference in Helsinki these rights had not been viewed as appropriate issues for international negotiations by either East or West. The traditional view was that these issues were domestic affairs that had no impact on international relations, and thus any formal diplomatic discussion of human rights beyond a general declaration of support for them would constitute external intervention in another state's internal affairs. However, by making human rights a formal component of the CSCE, the precedent was set for including human rights as a subject for international negotiations. The result was to legitimize human rights as a subject on the East-West agenda and to establish standards of behavior to which the West could hold the Soviet Union and East European governments accountable.

The Helsinki declaration has had serious repercussions both in the Soviet Union and in Eastern Europe. Robertson has noted that the wide publicity given to the Helsinki declaration in the Communist states has prompted many citizens in these countries to demand that the rights their governments have guaranteed them on paper be implemented in practice. Domestic critics have organized themselves into monitoring groups and charged their governments with specific human rights violations. These groups have found external support for their struggle from the Euro-communists. The communist parties of France, Spain, and Italy have become increasingly independent and critical of the suppression of dissent and of the restrictive measures prevalent in Eastern Europe and the USSR. The dissidents also have found support for their cause in the West and have come to expect the Western nations to hold the socialist bloc accountable for the practical application of the commitment it adopted in Helsinki.

Soviet and East European implementation of the CSCE final act has been minimal, especially in the area of human rights. The Russians claim that by streamling visa regulations for journalists, by relaxing travel restrictions, and by simplifying emigration procedures, they have observed their Helsinki obligations. In fact, Moscow complains that the Western nations place more barriers on free travel than the Soviet Union does. However, progress on human rights has indeed fallen far short of the standards envisaged in the agreement. During the first months of the Carter Administration, Soviet repression of dissidents was the worst it had been in many years. Soviet dissidents were persecuted for invoking and monitoring the Helsinki Agreement, and the Carter Administration was highly critical of the arrest of dissidents, deteriorating working conditions for Western journalists in the East, tightening of visa requirements for businesspeople, and a slowdown of commercial and economic information from Moscow. East European governments, mindful of past events in Budapest and Prague and already concerned about the considerable pressures of nationalist feelings and economic discontent, moved quickly to quell any rebelliousness.

The reaction of the Soviet Union and some Eastern European countries to Western charges and criticism of violation of human rights has been to defend themselves by claiming that the interest expressed by the West in their domestic affairs runs counter to one of the central provisions in the Helsinki declaration. Moscow also has charged the West with failing to meet all the requirements of the agreement and has compiled vast dossiers of real and imagined U.S. and Western violations. In the Soviet mind, deficiencies in Western societies, such as poverty and unemployment and the British policy in Northern Ireland and the treatment of political dissidents and minorities in the United States, are violations of the Helsinki declaration.

United States policy toward the socialist bloc undoubtedly will continue to emphasize the desire for greater observance of human rights in communist countries. As Robertson points out, it is entirely legitimate for the United States to comment publicly on human rights violations in other countries. On certain matters the Soviet bloc has accepted obligations in international law by signing the U.N. Charter and U.N. agreements and has given firm expression of intentions by agreeing to the Helsinki declaration. Hence these matters cease to be questions solely within their domestic jurisdiction. Thus the question is not whether it is desirable for the United States to comment on human rights problems in communist countries, but rather how and when to do so.

It is encumbent on the United States as a great power to calculate the potential consequences of its actions both for the continued maintenance of the central balance of power and for the peoples of the USSR and Eastern Europe. The crux of the U.S. human rights policy vis-à-vis the USSR and Eastern Europe hinges on the key question of how to ensure necessary leverage to translate exhortations into practical results without jeopardizing the strategic arms talks. If the Jackson-Vanik and Stevenson amendments are precedents, the strict linkage of commercial or strategic issues with progress on human rights observance is likely to be counterproductive and may, in fact, hinder America's arms control objectives. The United States must manage its human rights policy in a balanced context in which the essence of détente, the possibility of progress toward arms control, and the prospect of commercial relations will be preserved. Another important consideration for U.S. policy-makers is the potential effect of human rights diplomacy on political developments in Eastern Europe. The communist governments of Eastern Europe fear external human rights pressures that could lead to domestic strife and Soviet military intervention. Hence any American support for dissidents in a region of the world where our ability to help people is limited must take into account the danger of external intervention by Moscow in the defense of socialism.

Human rights is an issue that is likely to remain prominent in East-West relations. If nothing else, the 1975 Helsinki declaration has made human rights a matter of legitimate international concern and responsibility. This is substantial progress over past diplomatic practice.

6: Theory and Practice of Human Rights in the Soviet Union

PETER B. REDDAWAY

Introduction

If one can be expert about only one of the Marxist-Leninist states, then the Soviet Union is perhaps the most suitable choice. It is by far the oldest such state so, not surprisingly, the influence of its political, constitutional, and legal arrangements on those of almost all the other Marxist-Leninist regimes has been great. Nearest to the Soviet model probably are Bulgaria, Czechoslovakia, Hungary, East Germany, Romania, and Poland; then would come Yugoslavia, Albania, China, North Korea, Vietnam, and Cuba; finally, there are the new Marxist-Leninist states such as Cambodia, Laos, Mozambique, and Angola, where it is still too early to predict to what extent they will adopt Soviet-type patterns.

There is a further advantage in focusing on the human rights situation in the USSR: It is the only one of all the Marxist-Leninist states that contains a wide variety of groups which openly criticize official theory and practice in different areas of human rights. Thus a voluminous uncensored literature exists alongside the official materials, and by reading both one can study many situations in detail.

Russian Traditions and Culture

For the first three centuries of its existence as a state, Kievan Russia was in many ways part of Europe. Then, however, the Mongol invasions of the thirteenth century subjugated it and cut it off from Europe. Russia was not to experience the Renaissance; rather, while Western European culture was reborn, Russia stagnated. Only around 1700 did Peter the Great set about the task of rejoining Russia to Europe and—by making up the enormous social, cultural, and economic lag—"catching Europe up."

However, the desire and impetus for this enterprise was not organic in the Russian nation. Russian commerce was weak, education was primitive, culture was not much beyond the folk level, and communications—in a vast land—were rudimentary. Moreover, the Orthodox Church concentrated mostly on the Liturgy and had little concern for social matters or "the Protestant ethic." So Peter took a path followed since by many underdeveloped countries: He built up the state and the armed forces in order to harness *them* to his purposes. In turn, the bloated state bureaucracy had to harness—and usually coerce—the backward population to achieve progress. For the next two centuries the modernization of Russia was conducted not by merchants, industrialists, big landowners, and rich patrons of education and the arts, but primarily by the state. Most of the nonserf population became part of the state bureaucracy.

It is not hard to see the implications of all this for human rights. Individualism, weak to begin with and little nourished by commercialism or a legal tradition of respect for private property, faced the steadily increasing power of the state and its police—a power which rulers justified by reference to Russia's continuing vulnerability to foreign invaders.

Only in the second half of the nineteenth century did the tsarist autocracy begin to realize that its ambition to "catch up" with Western Europe—an ambition reinvigorated by the desire to compete with other empires in imperial self-aggrandizement—positively necessitated economic modernization and that such modernization in turn required a measure of liberalization in culture, law, and politics. As the emerging intelligentsia—many of whom were concerned with the individual, conscience, and human rights—had been demanding all these measures for some time, it is not surprising that deep social transformations began to take place, often at a rapid pace, during the last 60 years of tsarist rule. Although considerable economic control remained in the hands of the government, the relation between the individual and the state shifted markedly in favor of the former.

Soviet Theory Affecting Human Rights— The Historical Background

In 1917 two revolutions took place in Russia. The first saw the autocracy crumble; the second resulted in power being seized by a far-left group whose ideological roots were in that part of Russian intellectual culture which was *not* concerned with the rights of individuals. The Bolsheviks were Marxists, but they also were Jacobins.

Although Lenin publicly rejected this link to the radicals of the French Revolution, he implicitly acknowledged it on many occasions when he declared that the Bolshevik revolution would soon perish and be overthrown unless it was quickly supported by socialist revolutions in the advanced countries of Western Europe. He firmly believed that it was here that revolutions were due, not in backward peasant Russia where the Bolsheviks' only justification for having taken power was the appearance of a unique chance to "break the capitalist chain at its weakest link" and then to "hang on" grimly until the imminent Western revolutions could take place and shore up the Bolsheviks.

In these circumstances the Bolsheviks proclaimed "the dictatorship of the proletariat" in orthodox Marxist fashion in order to disarm the exploiting classes and destroy the old order, but, in a much less orthodox move, they declined to share power with other proletarian parties in exercising the dictatorship. They justified this action ideologically by stating that their party represented "the vanguard of the proletariat" and that, therefore, only they could understand correctly the laws of social and historical development and rule in accordance with those laws.

Thus legal theory was from the start rendered wholly subordinate to Bolshevik ideological doctrines, and these in turn were influenced by the exigencies of the need to remain firmly in power. Stalin, for example, changed a central ideological principle in 1924 when he departed from Leninist orthodoxy about the dependence of the Bolshevik revolution on Western revolution to develop the new doctrine of the possibility—indeed necessity—of building socialism in the USSR, even though such development would mean that revolution elsewhere would have to be delayed and the "capitalist encirclement" would continue for the indefinite future. This change, though it smacked of unorthodoxy, made it easier for him to justify a strong "dictatorship of the proletariat."

The notion of dictatorship had, we should note, ruled out from the start any possibility of applying any liberal principle like the separation of powers. Such a principle could easily have weakened the unity of the dictatorship's authority. In any case, the Bolsheviks maintained, the rights of working people by definition could not be violated by a people's government.

It was not difficult for the Bolsheviks to argue this case, because their ideology divided people into classes, not individuals. Moreover, it held that the socio-economic "infrastructure" of society determined the political and legal "superstructure." Thus, if the working people possessed the socio-economic rights that the Bolsheviks were steadily giving them, their political and legal rights would automatically be safeguarded, too.

In the constitutional field, then, there was to be no separation of powers. More fundamentally, though, the state itself and law with it were destined to "wither away," according to Marxian prescription, as socialism and then communism were built. During the dictatorship of the proletariat, law would still be needed, but the most important point about its application would be that judges, in interpreting its deliberately vague formulations, should apply their "revolutionary consciousness." In other words, they were to disregard formal legal requirements and the interests of the defendant if the interests of the revolutionary state could thereby be advanced.[1]

The Soviet state had, in its rulers' eyes, much greater responsibilities than had the imperial Russian state. The main task was no longer to catch up with the Western world in order to take part in the imperial race; now the task was to act as the bulwark for an ideology destined by history both to triumph throughout the world and to transform human nature. As socialism and communism were built the "new socialist man" would develop. In the words of the Communist Party *Programme*, the new man would "harmoniously combine spiritual wealth, moral purity and a perfect physique."[2]

The argument so far helps to explain how the Bolsheviks justified their overwhelming reconcentration of political, legal, economic, and social power in the hands of the state and how the previous trend of an increase in rights for the individual was sharply reversed. It also helps to explain how Stalin's regime could carry out the forcible collectivization of agriculture and the "Great Terror" of the 1930's and the postwar years. In this period, 6 to 7 million people died in the artificial famine of 1932–1933, more than 1 million were shot, and more than 10 million died in concentration camps. Most of these people had been falsely accused of counterrevolutionary crimes. Human rights in the Soviet Union had almost ceased to exist. From 1934 on people could be—and in large numbers were—peremptorily tried by three-man tribunals and executed without right of appeal; many others were legally sent to concentration camps for being relatives of "enemies of the people." From 1938 on torture by state officials was legalized.[3]

Although the successful completion of the construction of socialism had been proclaimed in 1934 and enshrined in the 1936 constitution which appeared to guarantee many human rights, Stalin justified the continued terror by a new doctrine that held that the class struggle suddenly grows more intense in the period just prior to its disappearance. On this basis the dictatorship of the proletariat remained in force until, in 1961, Nikita Khrushchev announced that it had come to an end, that there were no exploiting elements left in society, and that the workers, the peasants, and the intelligentsia were at last friendly to each other. Consequently, there was no need for any more dictation by the proletariat. Instead, the Soviet Union had become "a state of the whole people."

The party *Programme* of 1961 did, however, include one qualification with reference to both the USSR and the people's democracies:

> Changes in the domestic or external situation may cause the class struggle to intensify in specific periods. This calls for constant vigilance in order to frustrate in good time the designs of hostile forces within and without, who persist in their attempts to undermine people's power and sow strife in the fraternal community of socialist countries.[4]

Nonetheless, the legal and political reforms of the Khrushchev period were of great importance. The powers of the security police were reduced, torture was outlawed, and the Criminal Code and the Code of Criminal Procedure were completely revised to provide more specific definitions of crimes and less fragile procedural safeguards.[5] The principle of "guilt by analogy"—that is, the notion that one could be guilty of a crime even if that crime was not specified in the Criminal Code, provided that the crime was analogous to a specified offense—was abolished. Also abolished was the law permitting the imprisonment of innocent relatives of "enemies of the people."

Despite these comprehensive revisions, the Soviets did, and still do, hold that law will eventually wither away along with the state. When this happens the party will supervise the "communist self-government of the people"; law will be superceded as, in the party *Programme*'s words, "universally recognized rules of the communist way of life will be established whose observance will become an organic need and habit with everyone."[6] Although crimes may still be committed, criminals, as Khrushchev stated, will be "people of abnormal mind."[7]

These developments are, however, a matter for the indefinite future. Khrushchev's few tentative innovations in this direction, such as the comrades' courts and the people's volunteer police, have not been extended by his successors. Nor have Soviet leaders since Khrushchev made much reference to Khrushchev's cautious formula concerning the withering of the state or the process which governs the general pace of change toward "communist self-government": "To ensure that the state withers away completely, it is necessary to provide both internal conditions—the building of a developed communist society—and external conditions—the victory and consolidation of socialism in the world arena."[8]

All this, then, provides the ideological framework in which Soviet law operates and indicates the intended direction of change. However, the present reality is governed by the legal codes revised at the end of the 1950s, and, as law in the Soviet Union has no real autonomy from politics, by the party's current policies.

In the field of human rights this reality was conveyed with some accuracy in a speech in 1975 by Andropov, head of the security police (KGB) and member of the party's Politbureau:

> Any citizen of the Soviet Union whose interests coincide with the interests of society enjoys the whole range of our democratic freedoms. It is another matter if these interests in certain instances do not coincide. Here we say straight out: priority must be given to the interests of society as a whole, of all working people, and we consider this principle fully just.... Soviet authority has not only formally proclaimed the democratic rights of the citizens of our country, but has also guaranteed their observance in practice. In addition to political rights, guaranteed also are socio-economic rights—the rights to work, to leisure and education, to welfare in old age. Without these rights all declarations about political freedoms and civil rights turn into hot air.[9]

One of Khrushchev's lieutenants, Leonid Ilichev, made the same point more bluntly and succinctly when he stated: "We have complete freedom to struggle for communism. We do not have, and cannot have, freedom to struggle against communism."[10]

The Emergence of Unofficial Rights Movements

The discussion of human rights in the Soviet Union to date should help to explain the emergence of unofficial rights movements in the Soviet Union in the 1960s. The last decades of tsarism had seen the development of numerous and varied movements of dissent and opposition in Russia, many of which the new Soviet regime held up as worthy of admiration as forerunners or comrades in the anti-tsarist struggle. This regime proved, however, to be even more tyrannical than that of the tsars. When Stalin's terror ended with his death in 1953 and nearly 10 million prisoners were released from concentration camps, there was strong pressure brought to bear on Khrushchev to liberalize the system and to make amends to Stalin's victims. Khrushchev raised many hopes by taking certain actions in this direction. He denounced Stalin for his "crimes" and set in motion the huge (and still uncompleted) task of legally rehabilitating millions of innocent victims (in many cases posthumously) and financially compensating those who had survived.[11]

But Khrushchev's measures were merely half measures; he and his colleagues soon came to feel that anything more thoroughgoing would in the long run threaten their power. In several fields he even put his liberalization into reverse. Between 1958 and 1964 he conducted a new campaign of harassment and persecution against Christianity and other religions. It was this action which provoked the emergence of the first religious dissent movement—among Soviet Baptists.[12] In 1960 and 1961 he launched a thinly disguised long-term policy of assimilating all national minorities into the Russian nation. This action provoked the first nationalist dissent movement based in one of the 15 union-republics—the Ukraine.[13]

Specific nationalist movements had in fact first appeared several years earlier. In 1955 and 1956 the government had legally rehabilitated most of the minority peoples deported by Stalin during World War II and allowed the majority to return to their homes. However, among those not allowed to return were the Crimean Tatars, the Soviet Germans, and Meskhetians. These peoples launched organized movements of protest; as a result, the Germans achieved rehabilitation in 1964 and the Crimean Tatars in 1967. But none of these groups has yet obtained its principal goal of returning home from exile.[14]

Khrushchev was cautious about excessively alienating the independent-minded section of the intelligentsia; therefore, he avoided arresting individuals with a prominent public reputation. It was this new degree of personal security which his successors began to undermine in 1965 when they arrested intellectuals in Moscow and the Ukraine.[15] This action provoked the emergence of the human rights movement which came to maturity in 1968. Given additional courage by the fact that 1968 had been proclaimed International Human Rights Year by the United Nations, the new movement's members began to issue the *Chronicle of Current Events,* an unofficial typescript or *samizdat* journal which has published more than 40 issues to date,[16] as a forum for their views.

This journal contains a factual presentation of all newsworthy material on Soviet human rights cases and issues that is available to the editors. This material as a rule has not already appeared in the official censored press. Second, the journal includes summaries of statements, articles, and books on a wide range of subjects which cannot be published because of censorship and which have begun to circulate "*in samizdat.*"[17] When read along with related documents,[18] the *Chronicle* makes it possible to gain a clear, if complex, picture of the various groups and movements of dissent that have come into existence in the last decade. Most of these are understandably much more informal and loosely structured than their equivalents would be in liberal democracies—so that it is more difficult for the security police to charge participants with "anti-Soviet activity." The movements are usually held together by shared values, shared persecution, and personal ties.

Among the religious groups or movements are those of the Russian Orthodox, the Georgian Orthodox, the Ukrainian Uniate Catholics, the Lithuanian Catholics, the Pentecostals, and the Adventists. The latter two groups, along with the Baptists, are concerned exclusively with obtaining greater religious freedom. The other denominations are all closely intertwined with the corresponding nationalist movement and, therefore, demand in addition to religious liberty more freedom to express national identity in the spheres of culture, language, and even politics and economics.[19]

Among the other nationalist movements are those of the Armenians, the Estonians, and the Latvians; all of these are presently weak. In addition, there are those special groups which have had the principal goal of emigration: the Jews[20] and, since the early 1970's, the Germans.

There also are groups and individuals who are concerned with censorship and cultural freedom; these groups include artists, writers, film-makers, and historians.[21] Other groups are concerned with political dissent or opposition,[22] with worker's rights,[23] with legal rights and law reform,[24] with the abuse of psychiatry,[25] and with humanitarian aid to prisoners of conscience and their relatives.[26]

The Soviet human rights movement is a loose "umbrella" whose main, broad purpose is to aid in whatever ways possible all individuals and groups who are being persecuted for their beliefs. Movement activists intercede with the authorities, for example, or organize material aid or legal advice. But the most important single method used is to gain publicity for these people through the *Chronicle* and through written appeals to foreign organizations and eminent individuals. This material is sent out of the USSR and given to foreign journalists. Once abroad, it is broadcast back to the Soviet Union where, despite official jamming of radio lines, it is widely heard.[27] The human rights movement is, in fact, a type of informal civil liberties group, aiding and lobbying for the persecuted and serving as a sounding board to amplify their grievances.

The Soviet Attitude to International Agreements Concerning Human Rights

Considering developments such as those discussed above and the history of human rights in Russia and the USSR, it is hardly surprising that the Soviet government is wary of the philosophical and political liberalism that underlies most international agreements concerning human rights. Its general pattern has been to try to appear liberal by signing such agreements—including the U.N.'s International Covenant on Civil and Political Rights (though not the Optional Protocol)—but then maneuvering vigorously to ensure that there is never any accountability under any of them. The Soviet government also strives to prevent the United Nations from acting vigorously on human rights in any country because it fears that precedents might be set which might one day facilitate effective action against its own abuses. When attempts are made to take steps which the USSR disapproves of, its leaders assert a doctrine of virtually total sovereignty of individual states.[28] For example, notwithstanding the Soviet signature on various relevant agreements, the Soviet ambassador could write in a 1973 letter to the U.N. Secretary General: "As regards the departure abroad of citizens of this or that state and their return to their own country, these matters relate wholly and completely to the internal competence of the state in question."[29]

In recent years the Soviet government has found itself under particular pressure in the International Labor Organization, in the U.N. Human Rights Commission's Sub-Commission on Prevention of Discrimination and Protection of Minorities, and within the context of the Helsinki Conference on Security and Cooperation in Europe.

Areas of Particular Regime-Dissenter Conflict over Human Rights

To bring the human rights situation in the USSR into sharper focus, we will now look in more detail at a few particularly prominent issues. Most basic of all for the rights groups are the closely interrelated freedoms of press, speech, and association. The Soviet constitution stipulates that these freedoms are guaranteed to citizens by law "in accordance with the interests of the working people and for the purpose of strengthening the socialist order."[30] Most of the dissenters argue that they exercise the freedoms in this spirit and that it is the security police who, by arresting them for doing so, are breaking the law, discrediting socialism, and weakening the socialist order. They also refer to documents such as the Universal Declaration of Human Rights, in which Article 19 concerns freedom of opinion and the free flow of information and has served as the epigraph on each issue of the *Chronicle*. However, when human rights activists are charged with a crime, party-approved judges refuse to accept these arguments and invariably see in the evidence what is only rarely there. For example, judges may accuse activists of "knowingly false fabrications which defame the Soviet political and social system" (Article 190–1 of the RSFSR Criminal Code) or of deliberate intent to undermine the regime through "anti-Soviet agitation and propaganda" (Article 70).[31]

Freedom of movement, especially for the purpose of traveling abroad or emigrating, is another issue of intense concern especially, but not exclusively, to the militant and partially successful Jewish and German emigration movements. Here the Soviet authorities are especially sensitive, because foreign governments become directly involved and are therefore less inhibited in applying diplomatic and other pressures. Correspondingly, Soviet laws and the constitution are restrictive; emigration, for example, normally is permitted only to reunite a separated family. In contrast, though, would-be emigrants refer in self-justification to more liberal documents ratified by the Soviet government, such as the International Covenant on Civil and Political Rights (Article 12) or the Helsinki CSCE "Final Act."

The freedom sought by dissenting religious groups is of many kinds. They ask to be allowed to print their own Bibles, prayer books, and other literature; to import literature from abroad; to communicate freely with co-religionists abroad; to be free of pervasive discrimination in education and jobs; to appoint their own clergy and hierarchy without state vetoes; to train adequate numbers of their own independent new clergy in seminaries; and to bring up their children in their own faiths. They point out that the state restrictions applied in many of these fields stem from legislation that directly violates the constitutional principles of freedom of conscience and separation of church and state and that the constitution is, in theory, of higher status than the law. They also point to various international documents, such as the UNESCO Convention and Recommendation Against Discrimination in Education, which categorically forbid the signatories, including the USSR, to discriminate against people on grounds of religion or to prevent them from educating their children as they wish.[32]

However, Soviet courts frequently convict believers of anti-Soviet activities, using in particular two vaguely formulated articles of the Criminal Code, Numbers 142 and 227.[33]

Areas of Lesser Conflict

There are, of course, some areas of human rights where Soviet citizens are content, or at least passive. The rights to employment and social security, for example, and to equal rights for women are, broadly speaking, implemented. Although the right to strike does not, conspicuously, exist, strikes are rather rare at present. So is underground trade union activity by workers who regard the official unions with scepticism.

Demands for full political freedoms such as the right to form political parties and groups are also unusual. One of the reasons for this is that the authorities tolerate no open activity at all in these areas, so demands of this sort tend to seem unrealistic and premature.

Sanctions Against Dissenters

Sanctions against dissenters are finely graded. They are almost always organized, if not directly applied, by the KGB. First come warnings; then perhaps demotion at work; then, if applicable, expulsion from the Party, the Young Communist League, or a professional union; then a house search, which usually involves the confiscation of compromising materials; and then unpleasant KGB interrogations. Sometimes, and increasingly often in the last few years, an act of physical intimidation or assault may take place at this stage. Finally, if the dissenter refuses to be intimidated into silence or emigration and has no influential foreign or domestic "protectors," he or she is arrested. But the KGB evidently has orders to avoid arrests whenever possible; and although it is impossible to estimate reliably the total number of prisoners of conscience, it appears to be only in the rough order of 10,000.

Following arrest, the dissenter is subjected to more intensive pressures to persuade him to "recant" and repent for what he has done. In this case, providing that he adheres to his line in court, he may receive a light sentence of one or two years or possibly only exile. Otherwise, he probably will receive three years under Article 190-1 or about four to seven years (plus two to three of exile) under Article 70. For the most serious offences—such as forming an anti-Soviet group, treason, or fleeing abroad—ten to fifteen years is the norm, with very occasional use of the death penalty. A variant to all these penalties is internment in a prison mental hospital, with the risk of forcible drug treatment and with an indefinite "sentence" to be served amid violent psychotics.[34]

The forced labor camps where most prisoners of conscience serve their sentences are the scene of a continued struggle for human rights. This is the struggle against inhumane treatment, malnutrition, and compulsory labor and for the formal status of political prisoner. These concerns are strongly supported by the human rights movement as a whole, which has built up a persuasive case, with numerous references to both Soviet law and international conventions.[35]

Conclusion

By putting forward persuasive moral and legal cases based on Soviet and international law for their claims, the Soviet rights groups appear to have chosen a reliable method. By also appealing for support to communists and noncommunists in the West and to international organizations, they have refined a second method, which has become more effective as the West has increased its concern for human rights (spurred most recently by President Carter), and thereby unwittingly assisted the development of the important—to Soviet dissenters—phenomenon of "Euro-communism." Especially significant here have been Andrei Sakharov's arguments about the interdependence of a stable peace and a wider respect for human rights which contributed to his being awarded the Nobel Peace Prize in 1975.[36]

One of the major problems for the dissenting groups is the inertia and passivity of the general Soviet public, whose legal culture is virtually nonexistent and who have retained no viable independent values from the past.[37] And while the number of groups has, through force of example, steadily increased, they constitute that minority in the population which *has* retained such values, and their numbers may be fast running out. The other main problem is the conservative, often reactionary, opposition to change of most of the Soviet leadership and bureaucracy. These circles appear to believe the unlikely proposition that the introduction of mild liberalization could lead to a situation like that in Czechoslovakia in 1968.

However, it is possible that Soviet officials may soon begin to feel pressures analogous to those experienced by Alexander II in the 1860s, pressures which may become irresistible. In order, in fact, to catch up with the West in living standards—something Khrushchev often promised to achieve without delay—and in order to compete effectively with the United States for a dominant influence in world affairs, modernization of the economy and of society as a whole would become essential. This, again, is what Sakharov, Roy Medvedev,[38] and others have argued. Finally, the development of human rights movements in Eastern Europe could add still more pressure.

If all this were to happen, then the stoic persistence of most of the rights groups might gradually gain some reward, because Soviet society would at last loosen up. Reward also could come if, even without liberalization from above, the working class were to start to follow the dissenters' example and to form independent trade unions. For the moment, however, the remorseless, grinding struggle continues between the groups and a regime deeply hostile to the classical human rights of the "First World," with neither side giving the impression that it sees any resolution in sight.

NOTES

1. See the chapter "Lenin, Law and Legality" by I. Lapenna, in L. Schapiro and P. Reddaway (eds.), *Lenin: The Man, the Theorist, the Leader* (London: Pall Mall, 1967).
2. *Programme of the Communist Party of the Soviet Union* (Moscow: Foreign Languages Publishing House, 1961), p. 109.
3. See R. Conquest, *The Great Terror* (London: Macmillan, 1968), and A. Solzhenitzyn, *The Gulag Archipelago*, Vols. 1–3 (London: Collins/Harvill, 1974/1978).
4. *Programme, supra* note 2, p. 24.
5. See H. Berman and J. Spindler, *Soviet Criminal Law and Procedure* (Cambridge: Harvard University Press, 1966), for the texts of the new codes and a commentary on them.
6. *Programme, supra* note 2, pp. 96–97, 99.
7. Speech reported verbatim in *Pravda*, May 24, 1959. For commentary on this statement see S. Bloch and P. Reddaway, *Psychiatric Terror: How Soviet Psychiatry Is Used to Suppress Dissent* (New York: Basic Books, 1977), chap. 3.
8. *Programme, supra* note 2, p. 99.
9. *Izvestiya*, June 10, 1975.
10. Speech reported in *Pravda*, December 22, 1962.
11. See, for example, the experience as a rehabilitation official of Nikolai Danilov in P. Reddaway, *Uncensored Russia: The Human Rights Movement in the Soviet Union* (London: Cape, 1972), pp. 382–383.
12. See M. Bourdeaux, *Religious Ferment in Russia: Protestant Opposition to Soviet Religious Policy* (London: Macmillan, 1968).
13. See M. Browne, *Ferment in the Ukraine* (London: Macmillan, 1971) and V. Chornovil, *The Chornovil Papers* (Toronto: McGraw-Hill, 1968).
14. See numerous issues of the *Chronicle of Current Events* (note 16 below) and A. Sheehy, *The Crimean Tatars, Volga Germans and Meskhetians: Soviet Treatment of Some National Minorities* (London: Minority Rights Group, 1973).

15. See V. Chornovil, *supra* note 13, and L. Labedz and M. Hayward, *On Trial: The Case of Sinyavsky (Tertz) and Daniel (Arzhak)* (London: Collins/Harvill, 1967).

16. Issue nos. 1 to 11 of the *Chronicle of Current Events* have been published in English in Reddaway, *supra* note 11, and nos. 16 to 47 (with more to come) as booklets by Amnesty International Publications, London. Nos. 28 to 47 have been published in the original Russian by Khronika Press, 505 Eighth Avenue, New York, N.Y. 10018.

17. *In samizdat* means in any do-it-yourself form, most often in typescript but sometimes in photographic reproduction or as printed by a homemade duplicator or printing press (ownership of either machine is illegal for unauthorized individuals).

18. The largest repository of these, containing some 3,000 items varying from brief statements to long books, is the Samizdat Archive of Radio Liberty in Munich. Most of the archive's materials are available in selected libraries, including the Library of Congress and the British Museum.

19. See the quarterly journal *Religion in Communist Lands,* published by Keston College, Kent, U.K.; and also M. Bourdeaux, H. Hebly, and E. Voss (eds.), *Religious Liberty in the Soviet Union: WCC and USSR: A Post-Nairobi Documentation* (Kent, U.K.: Keston College, 1976).

20. See L. Schroeter, *The Last Exodus* (New York: Universe Books, 1974).

21. See, for example, the report on a campaign by artists to exhibit their work without censorship in the *Chronicle of Current Events* no. 34.

22. See, for example, P. Reddaway, *supra* note 11, chaps. 4, 5, 8, and 19.

23. *Ibid.,* pp. 290–291.

24. Notable here is the Human Rights Committee formed by A. Sakharov and others, which functioned between 1970 and 1973. Its work was extensively reported in the *Chronicle of Current Events.*

25. For example, the Working Commission to Investigate the Use of Psychiatry for Political Purposes, formed in Moscow and Leningrad in early 1977. See *Chronicle of Current Events* no. 44 *et seq.*

26. For example, the Action Group for the Defense of Human Rights in the USSR; see P. Reddaway, *supra* note 11, chap. 6.

27. See, for example, the annual reports of the Board for International Broadcasting, Washington, D.C. This board supervises the work of Radio Liberty and Radio Free Europe.

28. See T. Buergenthal and J. Torney, *International Human Rights and International Education* (Washington, D.C.: U.S. National Commission for UNESCO, 1976), p. 78; and V. Chalidze, *To Defend These Rights* (London: Collins/Harvill, 1975), chap. 2.

29. U.N. General Assembly, A/8991, January 4, 1973, quoted in V. Chalidze, *supra* note 28, p. 43 (amended translation).

30. Soviet Constitution of 1936 (replaced in 1977), Article 125.

31. See H. Berman and J. Spindler, *supra* note 5; also P. Reddaway, *supra* note 11, p. 11.

32. On all this see M. Bourdeaux, *supra* note 12, and *Patriarch and Prophets: Persecution of the Russian Orthodox Church Today* (London: Macmillan, 1969); also the English translations in booklet form of the *Chronicle of the Catholic Church in Lithuania* (6409 56th Road, Maspeth, New York 11378: L.R.C.P.L.A.) 1974 onwards.

33. These provisions of the Soviet Criminal Code provide for fines and

deprivation of freedom for violating laws on the separation of church and state and for religious proselytizing. See H. J. Berman and J. W. Spindler, *Soviet Criminal Law and Procedure*, 2d ed. (Cambridge, Mass.: Harvard University Press, 1972), pp. 169 and 192. See also Staff Study, *Christian Prisoners in the USSR 1977* (Kent, U.K.: Keston College, 1977).

34. See S. Bloch and P. Reddaway, *supra* note 7.

35. See *Prisoners of Conscience in the USSR: Their Treatment and Conditions* (London: Amnesty International, 1975).

36. See his *Sakharov Speaks* (London: Collins/Harvill, 1974).

37. For a penetrating firsthand account see A. Amalrik, *Involuntary Journey to Siberia* (London: Collins/Harvill, 1970).

38. See his *On Socialist Democracy* (New York: Knopf, 1975).

7: The Helsinki Agreement and Human Rights

A. H. ROBERTSON

THIS CHAPTER WILL CONSIDER THE PROVISIONS CONCERNING HUMAN rights in the Helsinki Agreement of 1975 and the developments to which they have given rise. In conclusion, the author will propose a few ideas about future action for the international protection of human rights, whether resulting from the Helsinki provisions or concerning the operation of the U.N. system.

I. The Final Act of the Helsinki Conference

The Conference on Security and Cooperation in Europe was formally opened at Helsinki on July 3, 1973; continued at Geneva from September 18, 1973, to July 21, 1975; and concluded at Helsinki on August 1, 1975. The 35 participants included all the states of Eastern and Western Europe, except Albania, and also the United States and Canada. The Holy See and the three "ministates" of Liechtenstein, Monaco, and San Marino participated on a basis of equality with the U.S. and the USSR.[1]

The final Helsinki session was attended by the heads of state or of government of nearly all the participating States including President Valéry Giscard d'Estaing, Chancellor Helmut Schmidt, Premier Leonid Brezhnev, Prime Minister Harold Wilson, and President Gerald Ford. The final agreement, which was signed on August 1, 1975, included four sections relating to questions of security in Europe; cooperation in the fields of economics, science and technology, and the environment; cooperation in humanitarian and other fields; and the "follow-up" to the conference.[2]

One should note at the outset that the final act of the conference is not a treaty, but a declaration of intentions. The Helsinki final act does not use the standard formulation for a treaty. Rather it states,

"The High Representatives of the participating States have solemnly adopted the following." It then continues, "The participating States will respect each other's sovereign equality . . . "; "The participating States regard as inviolable all one another's frontiers . . . "; "The participating States will respect the territorial integrity of each of the participating States"; and so on.

At first sight it may seem that there is little practical difference between an undertaking by states to do certain things and a statement that they will do certain things. One might think that the difference is no more than a lawyer's quibble, but to do so would be a mistake. There are at least two important differences between a legal undertaking and a declaration of intention. First, a treaty is not binding in most countries unless it is ratified by the legislature. However, because the Helsinki final act is not a treaty, it does not require ratification and consequently has not been submitted to the various national parliaments for this purpose. Second, while nonobservance of a treaty constitutes a breach of international law and, in many cases, can lead to proceedings before the International Court of Justice, no such consequences can result from the nonobservance of a declaration of intention.

The fact that it is not a treaty does not mean that the Helsinki final act is unimportant. But a failure to understand that it is something less than a treaty and does not establish legal obligations would lead to confusion—perhaps even to acrimony. Most people would agree that the final act sets out moral, and no doubt political, obligations of states, but these obligations are not binding in international law. As a result, it is inaccurate, from a legal point of view, to speak of the "Helsinki Agreement." But since this expression has come into common use and is more manageable than the "Final Act of the Conference on Security and Cooperation in Europe," there is no harm in adopting it, so long as it is understood that the word "Agreement" is used in its popular, not legal, sense.

The second point to be noted is that the final act is concerned principally with international security and relations between states. For various reasons it was impossible to conclude a peace treaty after the end of World War II. During the period of the Cold War it was evident that formulation of a mutually satisfactory definition of relations between East and West remained an impossibility. But after some years of "détente" and of the new "Ostpolitik" of Chancellor Willi Brandt, the agreement between the two Germanies and the admission of both to the United Nations, some new arrangements for "peaceful coexistence" between East and West finally seemed possible. For years the Soviet Union had been seeking recognition by the other powers of its western frontiers as established after the end of the war, and Brezhnev had made this recognition a central issue of his foreign policy. After much hesitation the Western powers agreed to the holding of a Conference on Security and Cooperation in Europe, even though many people in the West feared that, while the Soviet Union had much to gain from the recognition of its frontiers, there was little that the Western powers were likely to receive in return. They had no territorial claims to make (except for the Germans, who knew in advance that the reunification of Germany was not to be expected), and they recognized that any fundamental political changes in the Eastern countries in the direction of liberalization were to be excluded. Nonetheless, the Western nations tried to obtain certain modest concessions in regard to freedom of movement and of information between East and West. Such concessions, it was thought, might be the beginning of a gradual liberalization of authoritarian regimes.

The third preliminary point concerns the human rights provisions of the final act. Since the latter act deals with relations between and interests of states, the provisions concerning human rights do not seek to protect the individual as such. The interests of individuals are rather subordinated to reasons of state. The final act does not follow the method of the Universal Declaration or of the U.N. covenants in providing that "everyone has the right to" a number of fundamental rights and freedoms. Rather, it provides that "the participating States will respect human rights and fundamental freedoms." Thus, in accordance with the whole philosophy of the final act, it is the action of states which is envisaged rather than the situation or behavior of individuals as such.

The first three sections of the actual text of the final act are commonly known as three "baskets." It is widely believed that the third basket contains the provisions concerned with human rights, but this assumption is a mistake. More important to a consideration of human rights is Basket One, which begins with a "Declaration on Principles Guiding Relations Between Participating States." This declaration sets out ten fundamental principles:

1. Sovereign equality and respect for the rights inherent in sovereignty.
2. Refraining from the threat or use of force.
3. Inviolability of frontiers.
4. Territorial integrity of states.
5. Peaceful settlement of disputes.
6. Non-intervention in internal affairs.
7. Respect for human rights and fundamental freedoms, including freedom of thought, conscience, religion, or belief.

8. Equal rights and self-determination of peoples.
9. Cooperation among states.
10. Fulfilment in good faith of obligations under international law.

Each of these principles is explained in some detail in the final act. It is perhaps significant that the principle concerning human rights and fundamental freedoms has an eight-paragraph explanatory text. This text (see the appendix to this chapter) makes four principal points. First, "the participating States will respect human rights and fundamental freedoms"; freedom of thought, conscience, religion or belief are mentioned specifically. Second, the participating states promise to "promote and encourage the effective exercise of civil, political, economic, social, cultural, and other rights and freedoms." It is important to note that while this affirmative statement relates to human rights and fundamental freedoms in general, it does not specify expressly those rights and freedoms to which it applies, except for freedom of thought, conscience, religion or belief. It is significant that the very widely drawn reference to "civil, political, economic, social, cultural and other rights and freedoms" is preceded by the words "promote and encourage." Thus the participating states agree to a considerably weaker statement than would be a promise to "respect" these rights and freedoms. It recalls Articles 1 (3) and 55 of the U.N. Charter, which by speaking of "promoting and encouraging respect" for human rights and fundamental freedoms contain an expression of intention for the future without an immediate obligation.

The third principal point to note in the text is that it contains a statement that the participating states will respect the rights of national minorities; the text thus recalls Article 27 of the Covenant on Civil and Political Rights. The fourth point is that there are two references in the text to the human rights work of the United Nations. The sixth paragraph—which states that the participating states will endeavor "jointly and separately, including in cooperation with the United Nations, to promote universal and effective respect" for these rights and freedoms—substantially repeats Article 56 of the charter. Finally, in the eighth paragraph, the participating states assert that they "will act in accordance with the purposes and principles of the Charter of the United Nations and with the Universal Declaration of Human Rights." This paragraph refers specifically to the states' "*obligations* as set forth in the international declarations and agreements in this field, including *inter alia* the International Covenants on Human Rights, by which they may be bound."

To summarize, then, it is evident that the "Declaration on Principles Guiding Relations Between Participating States" includes respect for human rights among its basic principles, alongside such other principles as the inviolability of frontiers, the peaceful settlement of disputes, and refraining from the use or threat of force. The seventh principle in the final act is wide in scope, because its second paragraph refers to the effective exercise of all categories of rights and freedoms, but it is also limited in effect because (like the Charter itself) it contains expressions of intention to "promote" and "encourage" rather than affirmative statements of a determination to "respect" human rights. In addition, some of its provisions would appear to be tautologous, as reaffirming existing obligations. However, this is not a criticism, since the constant reaffirmation of the obligation to respect human rights may help to impress that obligation more indelibly in the conscience of both governments and the general public.

It is now time to examine the third basket. (It is not necessary for the purpose of this essay to consider Basket Two, which sets out a series of measures relating to commercial exchanges, industrial cooperation, science and technology, and the environment.) The contents of Basket Three can be summarized briefly. Entitled "Cooperation in Humanitarian and Other Fields," Basket Three contains four sections. The first relates to "human contacts" and deals *inter alia* with reunification of families, marriages between citizens of different states, travel, tourism, meetings of young people, and sports activities. The second section—which would be of great importance for the future if effectively implemented—concerns the free flow of information. The participating states "make it their aim to facilitate the freer and wider dissemination of information of all kinds" and set out a number of steps to be taken for this purpose relating severally to oral, printed, filmed and broadcast information. The steps to be taken include measures "to facilitate the improvement of the dissemination on their territory of newspapers and printed publications . . . from the other participating States" and measures "to improve the conditions under which journalists from one . . . State exercise their profession in another." Finally, Basket Three contains two short sections about cooperation and exchanges in the fields of culture and education.

II. Post-Helsinki Developments

The signature of the Final Act of the Conference on Security and Cooperation in Europe was much more widely acclaimed and its contents more widely publicized in the East than in the West. This fact is not surprising. The Soviet Union had a greater interest in the successful conclusion of the conference, because the final act constituted an official acceptance by the West of the territorial acquisitions of the USSR during World War II. What had been agreed by three powers at Yalta—and a good deal more than that—had now been accepted as permanent 30 years later by the whole of Europe, plus the United States and Canada. This was a real achievement for Soviet diplomacy.

One might have thought that this agreement would mark the beginning of a new era of détente and cooperation in Europe. Such hopes, however, have so far been disappointed. In fact, little has changed, and the old atmosphere of mutual suspicion seems to continue almost unabated. What has changed, however, is public opinion, at least in certain intellectual circles in Eastern Europe. The publicity given to the final act led many people to believe that its provisions on human rights would be implemented and that an era of liberalization was about to begin. The well informed knew that all the East European states also had ratified the U.N. covenants and thus accepted binding obligations in international law to respect human rights. With these two significant developments, it was hardly surprising that politically conscious individuals began to expect their governments to allow a freer flow of information and greater liberty of expression—even if they were not so foolhardy as to expect the right to form a political opposition.

The most striking example of this new spirit was in Czechoslovakia; there nearly 500 intellectuals and other subscribed early in 1977 to a human rights manifesto which they called "Charter 77." The manifesto takes as its point of departure the ratification by Czechoslovakia and the publication in the "Czechoslovak Register of Laws" on October 13, 1976, of the two U.N. Covenants on Human Rights and the reaffirmation of the covenants in the final act of the Helsinki Conference. "Charter 77" welcomes accession to those agreements but also continues: "Their publication, however, serves as a powerful reminder of the extent to which basic human rights in our country exist, regrettably, on paper alone." A series of examples are then given of various rights which have been proclaimed and protected by the covenants but, in fact, are systematically violated in Czechoslovakia. These rights include freedom of expression, freedom of information, freedom of religion, freedom of association, the right to form trade unions, the right to privacy, and the right to emigrate freely.[3]

"Charter 77" is not an organization and expressly states that it does not form the basis for a political opposition. Rather, its subscribers seek to conduct a constructive dialogue with the political and state authorities, just as many nongovernmental organizations do in democratic countries. The signatories authorized three of their number to act as spokesmen; the first of these was Jan Patocka.

The repressive measures taken against the signatories of "Charter 77" have been widely reported in the press.[4] Alexander Dubcek, head of the government responsible for the "Prague spring" in 1968, was prevented from signing the charter because of police supervision but indicated his support through an intermediary.[5] In March 1977, Max van der Stoel, the Dutch Foreign Minister and well-known champion of human rights, was in Prague on an official visit.[6] He accepted Patocka's request for a meeting. The Czech government responded by canceling van der Stoel's appointment with the president of the republic. Patocka died shortly after, having been subjected to prolonged interrogation; two other spokesmen for the group were arrested. Eleven signatories of the charter, all ousted members of the Central Committee of the Czechoslovak Communist Party, have appealed to other European communist parties to protest against this repression, insisting that the government's actions gravely discredit socialism not only in Czechoslovakia but in the whole of Europe.

"Charter 77" has, in fact, evoked considerable support in other Eastern European countries. In Yugoslavia, Milovan Djilas, a former leader of the Communist Party, has appealed to West European communist parties to support the charter and the movement for human rights not only in Czechoslovakia but also in his own country where, he says, on a proportional basis there are as many political prisoners as in the Soviet Union. Repercussions also have been observed in East Germany, in Poland, and in Roumania, where the writer Paul Goma, who led the movement for the observance of the Helsinki provision, was arrested.

But the most important reaction to the Helsinki Agreement was no doubt that in the Soviet Union itself. A committee under the chairmanship of Youri Orlov was established to supervise its application; the detention of Alexander Ginzberg has led to the signature of a manifesto by 248 supporters; and Andrei Sakharov, who formed the Soviet Committee on Human Rights nearly ten years ago, has continued his struggle in unprecedented fashion, including an American television interview, a personal letter to President Carter, and a letter to all the heads of State or of government who signed the final act. President Carter replied to Sakharov's letter, "You may be assured that the American people and our government will maintain their firm engagement to promote respect for human rights not only in our country but also abroad."[7] Vladimir Boukovski, who was exiled from the Soviet Union in December 1976 after serving 12 years in prison, in an exchange for the Chilean communist leader Luis Corvalan, was received by President Carter in February 1977 and testified to a Congressional committee that none of the human rights provisions of the Helsinki Agreement are being respected in the USSR. In February 1977, Andrei Amalrik, a dissident historian exiled in 1976, solicited an interview with President Giscard d'Estaing of France which was refused, but Amalrik spoke to the press in Paris as a representative of the committee on the application of the Helsinki Agreement.[8]

Similar developments continued in 1978. Youri Orlov, after a trial from which all Western observers and Andrei Sakharov were excluded, was condemned to seven years in a labor camp and five years' exile. This led to a protest from 500 nuclear physicists at the European Organization for Nuclear Research in Geneva, calling for a suspension of collaboration with the Soviet Union until he should be liberated. Another human rights worker, Anatoly Chtcharanski, suffered prolonged detention awaiting trial on a charge of treason, for which he risked the death penalty.

This brief—and necessarily incomplete—summary of recent and well-known developments paints the broad outlines of a picture of the contemporary scene and shows that the Helsinki Agreement—or, more specifically, its human rights provisions—have had an effect. In Eastern Europe the impact has surpassed the expectations of some of its authors; in the communist world, reaction to the agreement highlights the fact that its human rights principles remain largely a dead letter in those countries. What is new is that the Helsinki texts have been widely publicized in Eastern European countries and that this publicity has given new courage to those who are prepared to fight for their rights.

Still another new factor is the reaction to the agreement in the West, particularly that of the President of the United States. The Soviet Union has retorted that this Western reaction constitutes an improper interference in its internal affairs, which in itself is contrary to the Helsinki Agreement. An American proposal to the U.N. Commission on Human Rights requesting that the Soviet government provide information "about recent reports of arrest and detention in the U.S.S.R. of persons who have been active in the cause of promoting human rights"[9] had to be withdrawn in the face of a counter motion by Bulgaria not to discuss the American proposal.[10]

However, the Russian point of view cannot and should not be dismissed out of hand. The sixth principle in the "Declaration on

Principles Guiding Relations Between Participating States" (see the appendix) concerns non-intervention in internal affairs. This principle states in part:

> The participating States will refrain from any intervention, direct or indirect, individual or collective, in the internal or external affairs falling within the domestic jurisdiction of another participating State, regardless of their mutual relations.

Therefore, it is necessary to ask whether acts such as President Carter's letter to Andrei Sakharov, the testimony of Vladimir Boukovski before a Congressional committee, or the American proposal made to the U.N. Commission on Human Rights constitute an "intervention, direct or indirect... in the internal affairs falling within the domestic jurisdiction" of the Soviet Union. This evokes the question (mentioned in the first chapter) of the repeated attempts of Western and other states to introduce a procedure that would permit the U.N. Commission to consider complaints of violation of human rights and the equally repeated objection of the USSR that such action would violate Article 2, Paragraph 7, of the charter, which prohibits the United Nations from intervening "in matters which are essentially within the domestic jurisdiction of any State."

The problem of the meaning and effect of this provision of the U.N. Charter is as old as the United Nations itself. Since the same problem arises in relation to the Helsinki Agreement, it seems appropriate to summarize the issues involved at this point.[11] Of course, different governments have taken different positions at different times, depending on the political context. One of the more remarkable feats of U.N. diplomacy is the facility with which some delegates argue that it is outside the competence of the United Nations to discuss human rights situations in their own territory or that of their allies but quite proper to discuss alleged violations by their political opponents. For example, in 1946, Andre Vyshinsky of the Soviet Union argued that this provision did not prevent the United Nations from discussing the situation of Indians in South Africa.[12] On the other hand, in 1949, Santa Cruz of Chile insisted that "abuse of Article 2(7) of the Charter might paralyze the action of the United Nations," while in 1952 he insisted that "the international law created by conventions and agreements among countries removes a number of questions from the exclusive competence of States... since the adoption of the Charter, all fundamental human rights have formed part of international law since they are included in that multilateral treaty, the Charter."[13]

Among the texts of major importance to a discussion of Article 2, Paragraph 7, is the *1953 Report of the U.N. Commission on the Racial Situation in South Africa,* which discusses at length the meaning of Article 2(7) of the charter and cites the views of such eminent jurists as Lauterpacht, Cassin, and Kelsen. This report contains the following statement:

> ... the United Nations is unquestionably justified in deciding that a matter is outside the essentially domestic jurisdiction of a State when it involves systematic violation of the Charter's principles concerning human rights, and more especially that of non-discrimination, above all when such actions affect millions of human beings, and have provoked grave international alarm, and when the State concerned clearly displays an intention to aggravate the position.[14]

When this report was discussed in the General Assembly in 1953, South Africa introduced a draft resolution rejecting the report's conclusions and maintaining that the matters dealt with therein were "matters essentially within the domestic jurisdiction of a Member State" and therefore outside the competence of the United Nations; this draft was rejected by a vote of 42 to 7 with 7 abstentions. The same situation, of course, has arisen on many subsequent occasions, as illustrated by the *Second Report on the Racial Situation in South Africa,* by discussions in the Security Council in 1960 on the request of 29 states that the Council consider the Sharpeville massacre, by the discussions in the Security Council in 1963-1964 on the report of the Special Committee on the Policies of Apartheid, and by discussions in 1970 on the question of the arms embargo against South Africa. Henry Cabot Lodge stated the American position in regard to such discussions in 1960:

> We all recognize that every nation has a right to regulate its own internal affairs. This is a right acknowledged by Article 2, paragraph 7, of the Charter. At the same time, we must recognize the right—and the obligation—of the United Nations to be concerned with national policies insofar as they affect the world community. This is particularly so in cases where international obligations embodied in the Charter are concerned.[15]

Until 1945 international law considered that the manner in which a state treated its own nationals was, except in very unusual circumstances[16] when humanitarian intervention was permitted, a question within its own jurisdiction and competence and one with which other states had no right to intervene. To illustrate this attitude, the late

René Cassin often cited Goebbels's address to the Council of the League of Nations in which the latter asserted that the way in which the German government treated certain categories of German citizens was the concern of the German government alone. However morally reprehensible Goebbels's attitude may have been, it could be justified legally at the time.

Since that time, however, the legal position has changed. Matters in which states have accepted obligations in international law have ceased to be questions solely within their domestic jurisdiction. The unfettered rule of national sovereignty no longer applies. Other states that have accepted such obligations have a legitimate interest in seeing that the common undertakings are respected. The mere fact that these undertakings may relate to the maintenance by a state of the human rights of its own citizens does not justify a derogation from the fundamental rule of international law: *Pacta sunt servanda*. This reasoning provides the legal basis for President Carter's statement to the United Nations on March 17, 1977, in which he said:

> The search for peace and justice means also respect for human dignity. All the signatories of the U.N. Charter have pledged themselves to observe and respect basic human rights. Thus, no member of the United Nations can claim that mistreatment of its citizens is solely its own business. Equally, no member can avoid its responsibilities to react and to speak when torture or unwarranted deprivation of freedom occurs in any part of the world.

The same basic argument applies in relation to the final act of the Helsinki conference. Although this agreement is not a treaty enshrining obligations under international law, it does contain firm expressions of intention to which particular solemnity was attached in an essentially political context. Consequently, each participating state is entitled to expect that every other participant will honor its word.

The legal framework accepted by all members of the United Nations as the appropriate means of ensuring respect for human rights is that of the two U.N. covenants of 1966. Entry into force in 1976 of these covenants represented the fruition of 30 years' endeavor. The covenants contain legal obligations that are more detailed, more specific, and more stringent than the charter, the Universal Declaration, or the Helsinki Agreement. Consequently, any state that feels it necessary to reproach another for non-observance of human rights is in a much stronger position—both legally and morally—if it has itself accepted the international standards and commitments contained in the two covenants.

III. Some Reflections on the Future

The fourth basket of the Helsinki final act concerns the follow-up to the conference. It begins with a declaration by the participating states of their resolve "to pay due regard to and implement the provisions of the Final Act" unilaterally, bilaterally, and multilaterally. They then declare their intention of continuing the multilateral process begun at the conference through further exchanges of views on the implementation of the final act, of improving security, and of development cooperation and détente in Europe.

The first follow-up meeting took place in Belgrade from September 1977 to March 1978. It produced more acrimony than consensus; no progress was achieved in the field of human rights. A second such conference will be held in Madrid in 1980. Are there no possibilities of a meeting of minds in this domain between East and West?

Of the 35 participants in the Helsinki conference, by January 1978 nineteen had ratified the U.N. covenants on human rights. Could one not hope that one result of the next follow-up conference in Madrid would be a recommendation—or, even better, an agreement—that the other participants should take action to ratify the covenants and thus establish reciprocity of obligations about respect for human rights? Ideally, a separate "human rights committee" of the Conference on Security and Cooperation in Europe states would be established to supervise the application of the human rights provisions of the Helsinki Agreement. Even if it had no greater powers than the U.N. Human Rights Committee established under the covenants, such an organ would be an important step in the right direction. States which have ratified the covenants should, at least in theory, have no difficulty in accepting the establishment of such a committee, because it would not involve any more stringent obligations than those they have already accepted under the U.N. system of supervision. Though it would be unrealistic to expect such a development in the near future, the idea might be retained and explored for future negotiations.

Finally, if human rights are to be protected, the human rights machinery of the United Nations should be strengthened. In his March 17, 1977, speech to the United Nations, President Carter said: "We have allowed its [the U.N.'s] human rights machinery to be ignored and sometimes politicized. There is much that can be done to strengthen it." He then made three specific proposals: (1) that the Commission on Human Rights should meet more often and that all states should welcome its investigations, work with its officials, and act on its reports, (2) that the Human Rights Division should move back from Geneva to New York, and (3) that the proposal to appoint a U.N. high commissioner for human rights, made by Costa Rica 12 years ago, should be revived.

Even while recognizing the difficulties in implementing these proposals, one can only support them. One might entertain some doubts about the proposal relating to the location of the Human Rights Division. After nearly 30 years in New York, it was moved to Geneva in 1974, and the advantage of moving it back again now may be questioned. The most important thing, however, is to strengthen the standing and authority of the Commission on Human Rights.

Several suggestions to this effect have been made in recent years. The Assembly for Human Rights held in Montreal in March 1968, an unofficial conference of experts during International Human Rights Year, considered that the Commission has "a status which is not commensurate with the important responsibilities entrusted to it" and proposed that it should be given the same standing as the Economic and Social Council.[17] This suggestion has been repeated on several occasions, notably by representatives to the Commission such as Theo van Boven[18] and John Carey;[19] also by the present author in an earlier work.[20] Louis Sohn has even suggested the establishment of new machinery, including an organization for the promotion of human rights as a subordinate body of the United Nations with a human rights council as its main organ.[21] If this solution is adopted, the new body might be known simply as the U.N. Agency for Human Rights.

There are indeed several reasons why the status of the Commission on Human Rights should be reviewed. The first is that such a review would underline the increased concern for human rights that the United Nations has shown over the years and which many governments now wish to emphasize. Since the third aim of the United Nations set out in Article 1 of the charter is subdivided into the two objectives of "solving international problems of an economic, social, cultural or humanitarian character" and "promoting and encouraging respect for human rights," and since there is a council responsible for the first objective, it seems only logical to have another council responsible for the second.

Second, important new functions have been conferred on the Commission as a result of the adoption in 1970 by ECOSOC of Resolution 1503 (XLVIII) on the "Procedure for Dealing with Communications Relating to Violations of Human Rights and Fundamental Freedoms." These powers are important even if the results of the Commission's efforts have so far been disappointing. Third, the entry into force of the covenants will require the exercise by a U.N. organ of new functions which the Economic and Social Council does not appear particularly well qualified to discharge, if only on account of its many and varied other responsibilities. There is therefore much to be said for reinforcing the position of the Commission on Human Rights and promoting it to the status of a council.

If it is objected that with the three existing councils established under Article 7 of the Charter the machinery of the United Nations is already sufficient, it should be remembered that with the passage of time the responsibilities of the Trusteeship Council have considerably diminished because nearly all of the territories whose interests it was designed to protect have become independent members of the organization. A good case therefore can be made for transferring the remaining functions of the Trusteeship Council to a new council on human rights, all the more since the Trusteeship Council's duties in relation to the trust territories which remain are largely concerned with protecting the human rights of their inhabitants.

Of course, creating a council on human rights would not be easy, because it would entail amending the charter. But if the result would be to strengthen the effectiveness of the United Nations as an instrument for the protection of human rights, it would be worthwhile to make the attempt. As an alternative, if it is considered too difficult to amend the charter, then a U.N. agency for human rights could be created by resolution of the General Assembly.

A council or agency on human rights entrusted with these wider powers and responsibilities then could take over the tasks conferred on the Economic and Social Council by the two covenants. It thus would constitute an organ capable of discharging one of the principal functions of the United Nations with great authority and with all the necessary means at its disposal.

It is interesting to note that these proposals have recently been given new force through the support of several governments and nongovernmental organizations. In accordance with Resolution 3221 (XXIX) adopted by the General Assembly in 1974, the Secretary General presented a report to that body in 1975 on "Ways and Means in the Framework of the United Nations System for Improving the Effective Enjoyment of Human Rights and Fundamental Freedoms."[22] This report was based on information and opinions submitted by governments, the Specialized Agencies, and regional and nongovernmental organizations. In his report the Secretary General stated that several governments—particularly Italy, the Netherlands, and the Philippines—had suggested that the status of the Human Rights Commission be raised to that of a "Human Rights Council" which would report directly to the General Assembly.[23] Moreover, the Group of Experts on the Structure of the United Nations System has made certain similar suggestions, adding that a new council on human rights should replace the Trusteeship Council.[24] The proposal also has been supported by the Christian Democratic World Union and the International Commission of Jurists.[25]

Having considered this report during its thirtieth session in 1975, the General Assembly asked governments and organizations which had not yet sent in their views to do so without delay and decided to return to the matter at its thirty-second session in 1977 on the basis of an updated report by the Secretary General.[26] As a contribution to this study, a subcommittee of the NGO Committee on Human Rights in New York made its own examination of the problem and considered a paper which favors either the "upgrading" of the Human Rights Commission to the status of a council by means of the amendment of the charter or the alternative of creating a U.N. agency for human rights by resolution of the General Assembly.[27] Other useful suggestions for improving coordination in the human rights work of the United Nations have been made by Austria and Denmark.[28] Canada has proposed the establishment of two new subcommissions of the Commission on Human Rights with five members in each subcommission and with competence for the promotion of human rights and the protection of human rights, respectively.[29]

It is evident that new ideas are in the air[30] and that significant discussions may be expected at forthcoming sessions of the General Assembly in New York. President Carter's recent initiatives have been very timely. Our objective must be to strengthen the international machinery for the protection of human rights, whether in a pan-European or a worldwide framework, in order to ensure that (in an adaptation of Article 10 of the Covenant on Civil and Political Rights) "all persons... shall be treated with humanity and with respect for the inherent dignity of the human person." The last word may be left to the late Wilfred Jenks, director general of the International Labor Office and an ardent long-time champion of human rights: "In the last analysis there is no answer to Abraham Lincoln; it is no more possible internationally than nationally for a society to endure permanently half slave and half free."[31]

Appendix

Extract from the Final Act of the Conference on Security and Co-operation in Europe

DECLARATION ON PRINCIPLES GUIDING RELATIONS
BETWEEN PARTICIPATING STATES

VI. Non-Intervention in Internal Affairs

The participating States will refrain from any intervention, direct or indirect, individual or collective, in the internal or external affairs falling within the domestic jurisdiction of another participating State, regardless of their mutual relations.

They will accordingly refrain from any form of armed intervention or threat of such intervention against another participating State.

They will likewise in all circumstances refrain from any other act of military, or of political, economic or other coercion designed to subordinate to their own interest the exercise by another participating State of the rights inherent in its sovereignty and thus to secure advantages of any kind.

Accordingly, they will, inter alia, refrain from direct or indirect assistance to terrorist activities, or to subversive or other activities directed towards the violent overthrow of the regime of another participating State.

VII. Respect for human rights and fundamental freedoms, including the freedom of thought, conscience, religion or belief

The participating States will respect human rights and fundamental freedoms, including the freedom of thought, conscience, religion or belief, for all without distinction as to race, sex, language or religion.

They will promote and encourage the effective exercise of civil, political, economic, social, cultural and other rights and freedoms all of which derive from the inherent dignity of the human person and are essential for his free and full development.

Within this framework the participating States will recognize and respect the freedom of the individual to profess and practice, alone or in community with others, religion or belief acting in accordance with the dictates of his own conscience.

The participating States on whose territory national minorities exist will respect the rights of persons belonging to such minorities to equality before the law, will afford them the full opportunity for the actual enjoyment of human rights and fundamental freedoms and will, in this manner, protect their legitimate interests in this sphere.

The participating States recognize the universal significance of human rights and fundamental freedoms, respect for which is an essential factor for the peace, justice and well-being necessary to ensure the development of friendly relations and co-operation among themselves as among all States.

They will constantly respect these rights and freedoms in their mutual relations and will endeavour jointly and separately, including in co-operation with the United Nations, to promote universal and effective respect for them.

They confirm the right of the individual to know and act upon his rights and duties in this field.

In the field of human rights and fundamental freedoms, the participating States will act in conformity with the purposes and principles of the Charter of the United Nations and with the Universal Declaration of Human Rights. They will also fulfill their obligations as set forth in the international declarations and agreements in this field, including inter alia the International Covenants on Human Rights, by which they may be bound.

NOTES

1. In addition, statements were made to the conference by representatives of Algeria, Egypt, Israel, Morocco, Syria, and Tunisia. One section of the final act relates to "Security and Cooperation in the Mediterranean."
2. The full text of the final act may be found in various official publications. Extensive extracts are given in Keesing, 27 *Contemporary Archives* (1975): 301-308; and 23 *European Yearbook* (1975): 211 ff.
3. For the full text of "Charter 77," see *The Times* (London), February 11, 1977.
4. For example, *Le Monde,* January 29, 1977; *International Herald-Tribune,* March 18, 1977.
5. See *supra* note 3.
6. Van der Stoel was *rapporteur* of the Assembly of the Council of Europe for the question of human rights in Greece in 1968 and 1969. Later, he was president of the Parliamentary Conference on Human Rights held by the Council of Europe in Vienna in 1971.
7. *Daily Telegraph* (London), March 4, 1977; *The Times,* February 24, 1977.
8. *Le Figaro,* February 22, 1977.
9. *U.N. Doc.* E/CN.4/1352 (1977).
10. *U.N. Doc.* E/CN.4/1354 (1977).
11. A most useful collection of the relevant texts is assembled in L. Sohn and T. Buergenthal (eds.), *International Protection of Human Rights* (New York: Bobbs-Merrill, 1973), pp. 556-856, and a brief review of some of the issues is given in a review of that book by the present author in 8 *Human Rights Journal* (1975): 289, 293-296.
12. Sohn and Buergenthal, *supra* note 11.
13. *Ibid.,* pp. 623, 639.
14. *Ibid.,* p. 649.
15. *Ibid.,* p. 674.
16. *Ibid.,* pp. 137-211. The best known examples were intervention by the European powers in favor of the Christian minorities in the Ottoman Empire during the nineteenth century.
17. Montreal Statement of the Assembly for Human Rights, presented to the U.N. Conference on Human Rights in Teheran, 1968.
18. T. Van Boven, "The U.N. Commission on Human Rights and Violations of Human Rights," 15 *Nederlands Tidschrift* (1968). Van Boven is presently director of human rights in the United Nations.
19. J. Carey, *U.N. Protection of Civil and Political Rights* (1970), p. 175.
20. *Human Rights in the World* (1972), pp. 46-49, an extract from which is used in the text.
21. L. Sohn, "U.N. Machinery for Implementing Human Rights," 62 *American Journal of International Law* (1968): 909.
22. *U.N. Doc.* A/10.235 (1975).
23. *Ibid.,* at 116.
24. *U.N. Doc.* E/AC.62/9 at 62 (1975).
25. *U.N. Doc.* A/10.235, at 122 (1975).
26. General Assembly Resolution 3451 (XXX) of 1975.

27. Unpublished paper of September 28, 1976 by D. Lack, legal advisor of the World Jewish Congress, Geneva, to whom I am indebted for the information given in the text.

28. *U.N. Doc.* A/10.235, at 117 (1975).

29. *U.N. Doc.* E/CN.4/L.1324 (1976).

30. Another new project concerns new international measures for the suppression of torture. Largely as the result of initiatives by Amnesty International, the General Assembly adopted two texts on this subject in 1975, General Assembly Resolution 3452 (XXX) and 3453 (XXX). The Commission on Human Rights in 1977 and 1978 worked on the question of measures of implementation.

31. C. W. Jenks, *Human Rights and International Labour Standards* (1960), p. 46.

Bibliography

BAUMAN, S., "Soviet Jews, Human Rights, and the U.N.," 8 *Vista* (September–October 1972): 32.

BOURDEAUX, M., Debly H., and Voss, E. (eds.), *Religious Liberty in the Soviet Union* (Kent, 1976).

BOZEMAN, A. B., *The Human Factor in U.S.-Soviet Relations*, Proceedings of the National Security Affairs Conference (Washington, D.C., 1977).

———, "Understating the Communist Threat," 15 *Society* (November–December 1977): 92–96.

DAVY, R., "No Progress at Belgrade" *The World Today*, April 1978, pp. 128–135.

HALASZ, J., *Socialist Concept of Human Rights* (Budapest, 1966).

HIRSZOWICZ, M., "Human Rights in Perspective: The Marxist Approach," 18 *International Social Science Journal* (1966): 11–21.

KARTASHKIN, V. A., *International Defense of Human Rights* (Moscow, 1977).

LISHOFSKY, S., *Conference on Security and Cooperation in Europe: Report on Human Rights Provisions* (New York, 1976).

REDDAWAY, P., "Dissent in the Soviet Union," 23 *Dissent* (Spring 1976): 136–154.

REDDAWAY, P., and Bloch, S., *Psychiatric Terror: How Soviet Psychiatry is used to Suppress Dissent* (New York, 1977).

SHULMAN, M., "On Learning to Live with Authoritarian Regimes," 55 *Foreign Affairs* (January 1977): 325–338.

STERNBERG, H. A., "The Human Rights Movement in the U.S.S.R.," 25 *Problems of Communism* (May–June 1976): 82.

TEDIN, K. L., "Development of the Soviet Attitude Toward Implementing Human Rights Under the U.N. Charter," 5 *Human Rights Journal* (1972): 399–418.

TOLKES, R. C., *Dissent in the U.S.S.R.: Politics, Ideology and People* (Baltimore, 1976).

PART FIVE
International Monitoring Agencies

Introduction

THE INTERNATIONAL PROTECTION OF HUMAN RIGHTS DEPENDS UPON an efficient system for monitoring human rights violations. No such system currently exists. What does exist, in addition to the cumbersome machinery and inadequate reporting procedures of the United Nations, are diverse nongovernmental monitoring groups whose reports are marked by varying degrees of reliability. Nigel Rodley builds upon A. H. Robertson's general discussion in Chapter 1 by looking more closely at the procedures and processes designed to cope with complaints of human rights violations throughout the world. Laurie S. Wiseberg and Harry M. Scoble examine the nature and functions of nongovernmental groups (NGO's) concerned with human rights. Both chapters examine the role of monitoring in the international protection of human rights. The first finds the human rights work of U.N. agencies shackled by conflict between ideological blocs; the second sees many NGO's serving special interests and jockeying for a position of advantage in the making of an American human rights policy.

Before turning to Rodley's chapter, it might be helpful to identify those U.N. organs concerned with human rights. These include the Economic and Social Council (ECOSOC); the Commission on Human Rights; the Sub-Commission on Prevention of Discrimination and Protection of Minorities; the Commission on the Status of Women; the Trusteeship Council; the Divison of Human Rights within the Secretariat; the Office of the United Nations High Commissioner for Refugees (UNHCR); the International Labor Organization (ILO); the United Nations Educational, Scientific, and Cultural Organization (UNESCO); the General Assembly's Special Committee of Twenty-Four; the Council of Namibia; the Human Rights Committee (created by the Covenant on Civil and Political Rights), and the Committee for the Elimination of Racial Discrimination (created by the Convention on the Elimination of All Forms of Racial Discrimination). The last two committees are relatively recent creations and therefore limited in what they have been able to accomplish so far. Most of the remaining agencies are concerned with the formation of international public policy on human rights and not with the collection or monitoring of human rights violations under the Universal Declaration and other international instruments. Monitoring is mainly the responsibility of the Commission on Human Rights (an agency under ECOSOC) and the Sub-Commission on Prevention of Discrimination and Protection of Minorities (an agency under the commission), which is one reason for Rodley's preoccupation with these two bodies.

The most significant developments in the United Nations on the human rights front, in Rodley's view, have taken place since 1967. In that year the commission was empowered to investigate situations revealing "a consistent pattern of violations of human rights," which eventually led to inquiries by working groups appointed by the commission and subcommission into human rights violations in Southern Africa, Chile, Cyprus, and the occupied territories of the Middle East. Since 1976 most of the controversy about the U.N.'s human rights role has revolved around the activity of the subcommission, which has sought unsuccessfully to place certain items, such as atrocities alleged to have taken place in Uganda, on the commission's agenda and to draw attention to human rights violations in African countries other than those practicing apartheid.

Much of Rodley's paper centers on ECOSOC Resolution 1503, a precedent-breaking rule that allows the subcommission to consider communications from private persons as well as from governments and nongovernmental organizations. These communications are forwarded initially to the Secretary General. According to an authoritative source the Secretary General receives approximately 25,000 of these communications per year. But the subcommission has authority to consider only those complaints that reveal "a gross and consistent pattern of violations of human rights" and only after consultation with offending countries, in the absence of whose cooperation the matter cannot be properly investigated. The final decision actually to investigate is made by the commission itself after the matter has been placed formally on its agenda by the subcommission.

But commission and subcommission meet for only very short periods each year, resulting in wholesale inattention to the overwhelming majority of 1503 complaints. Moreover, the subcommission has been unable to get the commission to act on the few complaints it has placed on the latter's agenda. Still, Rodley notes, offending countries are frequently forced, albeit behind closed doors, to reply to 1503 charges brought to the attention of the subcommission by its members, all of whom, since they serve in their individual capacities, are free—except for members who yield to pressure by governments—to raise questions about the conduct of certain states.

At the present time, it is interesting to observe, the Soviet Union is leading an effort to abolish the 1503 procedure, although influential NGO's, such as the International Commission of Jurists, are fighting hard not only to retain the existing procedure, fragile as it is, but also to establish the general right of individuals, including prisoners, to have their complaints transmitted to and heard by the U.N. Human Rights Committee. It is worth noting, too, that in 1977 the ICJ's Committee on the Implementation of Human Rights recommended that the jurisdiction of the International Court of Justice also be expanded to allow NGO's to ask for advisory opinions from the court in human rights matters and to file *amici curiae* briefs and memoranda in cases pending before the court.*

Several interesting suggestions have been made concerning the improvement of U.N. procedures. Instead of meeting once a year, the subcommission and commission should have emergency ad hoc meetings and perhaps even permanent sessions if human rights complaints are to be handled expeditiously. Many are critical of the cloak of confidentiality with which the United Nations masks the handling of complaints and express the hope that the United States and other countries would seek to open U.N. human rights proceedings to public view or push for the establishment of a high commission on human rights empowered to hold public hearings on human rights violations. Barring that, they suggest that NGO's assume the initiative in setting up, as suggested in Chapter 3, a "shadow" model of what that machinery should be. That shadow model would be a commission with powers very similar to those of the U.S. Commission on Civil Rights.

Others fear that NGO pressure might actually jeopardize the few little measured steps (e.g., the 1503 procedure) adopted by the United Nations to serve the cause of human rights. Finally, many supporters of Resolution 1503 are concerned about the many thousands of communications that never reach the United Nations because of their seizure by governments, and they underscore the necessity of devising a process to ensure the delivery of such communications. Many also stress the importance of converting 1503 into an adversary proceeding between the complainant and the offending government.

---

*See International Commission of Jurists, *Report of Committee No. 1* (Vienna, April 19-27, 1977). Any such expansion of the court's jurisdiction, which is now confined to disputes between states, would require an amendment to the U.N. Charter, a most unlikely development.

The reluctance of the United Nations adequately to report and investigate human rights violations together with the failure of individual nations to cooperate in the effort has prompted the burgeoning growth in recent years of NGO's devoted to monitoring such violations. The chapter by Harry Scoble and Laurie Wiseberg is an analysis of the role of NGO's in this monitoring process and in shaping American human rights policy. (The U.S. government is a principal NGO target because of the global impact of American economic, trade, armaments, and development policies.) The authors set out first to describe the types and strategies of NGO's. Types range from those highly respected international groups long devoted to human rights (e.g., the International League for Human Rights, the International Commission of Jurists, Amnesty International, and the International Committee of the Red Cross) through recently established groups focusing on specific issues and problems to churches and professional associations that have lately experienced an emerging interest in human rights.

In addition to reports and public statements calculated to influence public opinion, NGO strategy includes direct lobbying before the United Nations, before regional associations such as the Organization of American States, and before world financial institutions. In the United States direct lobbying has frequently taken the form of seeking the ratification of international human rights treaties and pushing for human rights legislation. More recently, as Scoble and Wiseberg report, NGO's have started to consult with one another and to take steps that might eventually lead to a loose coalition or confederative arrangement reminiscent of the Leadership Conference on Civil Rights. The merger would be designed to strengthen the clout of NGO's disappointed by the failure of the U.S. government energetically to implement its own human rights policy.

The selective interests of many NGO's poses a serious difficulty of acquiring a complete picture of the kinds and volume of human rights violations in the world today. Perhaps a more fundamental difficulty, not discussed by Scoble and Wiseberg, is how U.S. foreign policy-makers can independently verify reports of human rights violations filed by NGO's. It would seem indiscrete or impolitic for the Department of State unquestioningly to accept at face value even the reports of reputable organizations such as Amnesty International, Freedom House, the International Commission of Jurists, or the National Council of Churches. Ordinarily such reports, even from several points of view, have to be carefully assessed within the foreign policy bureaucracy.

Recently the State Department has begun, with the aid of its field offices, to compile country-by-country human rights reports of its own. But these official reports have in turn come under attack by certain NGO's for their lack of objectivity and reliability. Still, State Department officials and members of Congress have taken note of the significant contribution of certain NGO's regarding human rights violations. But others insist that the U.S. government, given its vast intelligence capability, could be doing far more to uncover human rights violations around the world, although Scoble and Wiseberg seem to doubt the integrity of any governmental effort to monitor human rights violations.

To what extent are NGO's influencing American human rights policy? Scoble and Wiseberg describe the existing human rights "lobby" in Washington, D.C., as "an amorphous yet multifaceted aggregate with a core of as many as a hundred organized groups which identify themselves as acting with a human rights concern." How effective is this lobby? Writing as social scientists skeptical of the claims of quiet diplomacy, the authors raise questions about how influence on human rights policy is quantitatively to be measured. But in the end they fall back on their own intuitions in this matter and find the results very mixed. Their analysis concludes on a note of doubt as to what the future holds, in part because, as they read the political landscape, governmental elites are blunting the impact of the NGO's by co-opting their leaders and deluding them into the belief that political officials are behind the enforcement of a strong human rights policy, when in fact they are not.

At the end of World War II the United States started out in a position of leadership in the field of international human rights, but since the 1950's it has declined to play a prominent role in promoting human rights through the United Nations. Recently the Carter Administration reversed this course. New initiatives are needed, including the recognition of the significance of economic, social, and cultural rights. American adherence to the principal international conventions and covenants on human rights would demonstrate that the United States is serious about its devotion to human rights. The NGO community should encourage these developments and give the United Nations the attention and support it deserves. From these and other efforts might come eventually the development of an effective international system for the protection of human rights.

8: Monitoring Human Rights by the U.N. System and Nongovernmental Organizations

NIGEL S. RODLEY

Introduction and the Concept of Monitoring

Felix Ermacora, who has represented Austria on the U.N. Commission on Human Rights since 1959, has observed that "the U.N. has created step by step—sometimes backwards and sometimes forward—and year after year a certain case law in regard to the combat against violations of human rights."[1] Slow and frustrating as developments at the U.N. in this field have seemed to many involved in seeking to increase its effectiveness, it is well to remember that the corpus of practice that emerges reflects more steps forward than backwards.

It should be borne in mind that none of the intergovernmental organizations whose activities regarding human rights are discussed in this paper was established with the specific purpose of monitoring allegations of violations of human rights, although all these organizations were by their constitutions designed to play some role in promoting and protecting human rights at the international level. In no way, however, could this role be considered that of monitor so much as that of promoter, because these organizations function by exhorting the desirability of, and by legitimizing standards of behavior that conform to, agreed human rights norms rather than by testing specific state compliance with these norms.

The concept of monitoring itself requires some clarification. On the one hand, it can be simply the process of acquiring and amassing information with a view toward recording behavior. Alternatively,

The views and analysis contained in the chapter are those of the author alone and are not, accordingly, to be attributed to Amnesty International.

monitoring can involve an activist role whereby such behavior is the subject of continuing inquiry. Either of these courses could involve publishing information. For the purposes of this paper, all three roles—passively receiving information, actively seeking to acquire information, and publishing such information as is acquired—will be deemed to be within the concept of monitoring.

One feature both of potential and, indeed, of actual intergovernmental activity not included in the concept of monitoring is taking political action to secure compliance with human rights standards where the monitoring process already has suggested that noncompliance may have occurred. Insofar as such political action is not necessarily conducive to the public dissemination of information gleaned in the monitoring process or relating to such political action, it should be remembered that the publicizing aspect of monitoring is not a suitable means of bringing violations of human rights to an end in all cases. Sometimes the mere threat of publication can serve as a deterrent or indeed a remedy.

It is in the context of these considerations that I shall now proceed to discuss the pertinent work of various organizations. I shall start with the United Nations proper, the work of which will be dealt with under two broad sections: human rights activities through binding treaties and human rights activities undertaken with no special treaty power by various organs of the United Nations. The treaties in question are the International Covenant on Civil and Political Rights and the International Convention on the Elimination of All Forms of Racial Discrimination. The section on nontreaty activities will pay special attention to the Powers of the U.N. Commission on Human Rights to deal with "situations which appear to reveal a consistent pattern of gross and reliably attested violations of human rights." This section will conclude with a short reference to the new procedure established by the U.N. Sub-Commission on the Prevention of Discrimination and the Protection of Minorities to examine the problems of the human rights of all persons who are subject to any form of detention or imprisonment.

The work of the United Nations will be followed by a brief mention of the work of two of that organization's specialized agencies, UNESCO and the International Labor Organization.

U.N. Treaty Activities

Since the adoption of the Universal Declaration of Human Rights on December 10, 1948, the two major achievements of the United

Nations in the field of promotion of international human rights standards have been perhaps the adoption of the international covenants on human rights (i.e., the International Covenant on Economic, Social, and Cultural Rights, the International Covenant on Civil and Political Rights, and the optional protocol to the latter covenant) and the Convention on the Elimination of All Forms of Racial Discrimination.

The International Covenant on Civil and Political Rights, which covers *inter alia* those human rights which are known in the West as fundamental freedoms, entered into force on March 23, 1976, having been adopted by the U.N. General Assembly on December 16, 1966. The covenant operates in three ways.

First, all parties to the covenant—and there are as of May 1978 some 49 of these—are obliged to submit a report on the extent of their compliance with the standards set by the covenant within a year of their becoming bound by the treaty. Thereafter they are required to submit periodic reports at times fixed by the Human Rights Committee, a body which itself has been established by the covenant. The committee, composed of 18 members elected in their individual capacities as experts for four years, has the task of examining the report submitted by each member state and compiling its own report.

There is nothing in the covenant permitting the introduction of additional material external to that provided by the states. However, the committee has adopted flexible rules of procedure—similar to those of the Committee for the Elimination of Racial Discrimination—and a number of the members of the committee seem willing to pose informed pertinent questions to the states submitting reports. It would be surprising if members did not pose questions based on information they have acquired from external sources.

Second, once a state has made a declaration under Article 41 of the covenant, another state which has made a similar declaration with respect to itself may make a complaint alleging a violation of any of the articles of the covenant by the first state. So far six states have made such a declaration. Of these, five are members of the Council of Europe and parties to the European Convention on Human Rights; consequently, they have made reservations exempting from consideration cases that have been considered or are under consideration by some other international instance.

Third, there is the Optional Protocol to the International Covenant on Civil and Political Rights under which victims of human rights violations may petition the Secretary General of the United Nations to the effect that their rights under the covenant have been violated by a state party to both the covenant and the optional protocol of whom there are 19 as of May 1978. At this point it should be noted that only victims of alleged violations may make such a complaint and that no provision is made in the covenant for those victims who, for whatever reason (e.g., failure of the postal system to transmit the complaint or the fact that the person is being detained incommunicado), are unable to communicate with the United Nations. However, Rule 90, paragraph 1(b), of the Committee's provisional rules of procedure provides that the committee "may ... accept to consider a communication submitted on behalf of an alleged victim when it appears that he is unable to submit the communication himself."

A parenthetical word should be said here about the International Covenant on Economic, Social, and Cultural Rights, which has established only one mechanism—that of the submission by states parties to the covenant of reports on compliance with the rights guaranteed in the covenant. These reports are then considered by the Economic and Social Council (ECOSOC). Insofar as the rights in question are more of a programmatic than a peremptory nature, it might be expected that these reports and the examination of them would be less sensitive and controversial than would obtain with respect to the Covenant on Civil and Political Rights. Nevertheless, the ECOSOC has been slow to make arrangements for carrying out this function.

The 1965 Convention on the Elimination of All Forms of Racial Discrimination has now been ratified by a substantial majority of the members of the United Nations. It operates on lines similar to those of the Covenant on Civil and Political Rights, except that it includes no optional protocol. The convention has established the Committee on the Elimination of Racial Discrimination (CERD), which is charged with examining reports submitted by parties to the convention. In addition, without any special declaration, any state party to the convention may raise an allegation that another state is not complying with its obligations; the CERD is then empowered to examine such an allegation.

Under Article 14 states parties to the convention also may declare that they recognize the right of individual petition to CERD if the individual in question feels that his or her rights under the convention have been violated. This article has not received the required ten declarations to bring the procedure envisaged into force. Accordingly, most of the activity of the CERD in fact has been limited to dealing with the reports of states parties to the convention. The committee has established a practice of scrutinizing reports closely and posing probing questions to the state submitting them. CERD frequently will ask states to provide additional information and explanations and will even suggest measures to be taken to ensure full compliance with one article or another of the convention. It will come as no surprise, however, that the populations of South Africa, Namibia, and Rhodesia/Zimbabwe—the very people most in need of the protection of the convention—are deprived of it, because the governments that rule them are not parties to the convention.

Nontreaty Activities

The first task undertaken by the United Nations to protect human rights in the case of individual allegations of their violation was accomplished with respect to trusteeship and non-self-governing territories. Article 76 of the U.N. Charter provides that among the basic objectives of the trusteeship system is "to encourage respect for human rights and for fundamental freedoms for all without distinction as to race, sex, language or religion."[2] In addition, Article 87 of the charter provides that the "General Assembly and, under its authority, the Trusteeship Council, in carrying out their functions, may ... accept petitions and examine them in consultation with the administering authority."[3] There are very few trust territories left now, and their populations are very small, but it may be remarked ruefully that there are millions of inhabitants of sovereign independent states who could well benefit from this right that accrued to certain colonial subjects.

The work of the Committee on Decolonization—the so-called Committee of Twenty-Four—which was mandated to oversee the implementation of the famous declaration on the Granting of Independence to Colonial Countries and Peoples,[4] paid scrupulous attention to the human rights of the inhabitants of those non-self-governing territories which did not fall within the trusteeship system. Again, however, proportionate to the world's population, the number of people now affected by this committee's work is very small.

The role of the Trusteeship Council in supervising the human rights performance of trust territories, which at one time applied to the League of Nations mandate of South-West Africa, has been assumed by the Council for Namibia since the termination of that mandate. Under this council's authority the U.N. Commissioner for Namibia in recent years has grown particularly sensitive to the violations of human rights of individuals as well as of the population as a whole and has sought all means at his disposal to bring international pressure to bear to prevent or at least mitigate these violations.

It is remarkable to reflect that until only ten years ago *these* were the only systematic activities of the United Nations with regard to the monitoring and protection of individual human rights. It was only in 1967 that the Commission on Human Rights decided to set up an ad hoc working group of experts to investigate the human rights situation of trade unionists in southern Africa. Until this date the taboo against this sort of activity by the United Nations had been so pervasive that the commission decided to seek the authorization of ECOSOC to "examine information relevant to gross violations of human rights and fundamental freedoms" and to

> make a thorough study of situations which reveal a consistent pattern of violations of human rights, as exemplified by the policy of *apartheid* as practiced in the Republic of South Africa and the territory of South West Africa under the direct responsibility of the United Nations and now illegally occupied by the Government of South Africa, and racial discrimination as practiced notably in Southern Rhodesia, and report, with recommendations thereon, to the Economic and Social Council.[5]

Of this resolution and subsequent resolutions pertinent to it, more will be said later. Here it will suffice to note that the ad hoc working group of experts has continued to function on a mandate extended from year to year and has produced a series of thoroughly documented reports attesting to the institutionalized violations of human rights and fundamental freedoms perpetrated by the governments controlling these territories. The ad hoc working group has not been allowed to visit the territories in question but has sought information from all sources, including nongovernmental organizations, which have been in a position to contribute pertinent information to their work.

The same individuals who were members of the ad hoc working group of experts also became members of the special working group of experts that was set up in 1968 to examine the situation of human rights in the occupied territories of the Middle East. The establishment of the group, however, was only a temporary measure, pending the establishment by the president of the General Assembly of the special committee of three which had been authorized by the assembly to deal with this question. In addition, this committee was designed to consider the human rights situation in the occupied territories after the Six-Day War; there could be little doubt that this situation was not a question of domestic jurisdiction as would normally apply to internal situations.

The next development of a precedential nature involved the consideration by the United Nations of human rights conditions in Chile after the coup which overthrew President Salvadore Allende in September 1973. The first U.N. action was taken in March 1974 when the Commission on Human Rights decided to send a telegram to the new ruling junta in Chile calling upon it to respect human rights and fundamental freedoms, which it had been flagrantly disregarding through mass detentions, torture, and summary execution. Later that year, the twenty-seventh session of the Sub-Commission on Prevention of Discrimination and Protection of Minorities recommended that the Commission on Human Rights investigate the human rights situation in Chile. This recommendation was echoed at the intervening twenty-ninth session of the General Assembly, which, in Resolution 3219 (XXIX),[6] endorsed the subcommission's recommendation.

Finally, at its thirty-first session in 1975, the commission established a working group of its members to investigate the situation in Chile, empowering that committee to take testimony from all sources including sources within Chile on the basis of an in loco investigation. The working group has yet to be permitted to enter Chile, because the Chilean government has amassed a variety of procedural and technical reasons for failing to agree on the modalities of such an in loco investigation. Nevertheless, the working group did compile three reports to the General Assembly of 1975, 1976, and 1977 and three reports to the Commission on Human Rights of 1976, 1977 and 1978. These reports, following the example set by the ad hoc working group of experts on southern Africa, are well researched, thoroughly documented, and very respectable pieces of legal and factual analysis which cover the whole range of violations of human rights in Chile. The commission's thirty-fourth session in 1978 renewed the mandate of the working group.

It should be noted that none of these U.N. organs invoked any specific authority to justify their actions even though what they were doing constituted a radical departure from previous practice. Although it could be argued that the authority is provided by ECOSOC Resolution 1235 (XLII), discussed in connection with the establishment of the southern Africa investigation in 1967, it also could be argued that the actions were based on some sort of implicit authority of which the resolutions and decisions in question are merely the specific manifestations. It certainly can be argued that the General Assembly requires no prior authorization to take action and that Resolution 3219 (XXIX), constitutes the authority, if not for the sending of the earlier telegram by the commission, at least for the subsequent investigation.

In February 1976, at its thirty-second session, the Commission on Human Rights had before it the question of Cyprus. The member for that country drew attention to a variety of human rights violations in the zone of Cyprus occupied by Turkey, paying particular attention to the problem of refugees and displaced persons as well as to that of missing persons in Cyprus. Over the heated objections of the observer to Turkey, the commission adopted Resolution 4 (XXXII), which called upon the parties concerned to undertake "urgent measures to facilitate the voluntary return of all refugees and displaced persons to their homes in safety and to settle all other aspects of the refugee problem and requested the Secretary-General to continue and intensify his efforts... in respect of missing persons in Cyprus."[7] The commission also called upon the parties concerned to cooperate with the Secretary General in the fulfillment of his task.

Since this resolution clearly was aimed at Turkey, it could well be argued that it builds upon the precedent of concern for human rights in the occupied territories of the Middle East and as such constitutes an area of international concern that is not covered by domestic jurisdiction. The initiative taken in the Turkish situation therefore lacks precedential weight. But after the Chilean initiative of 1974, there could be said to be a consolidating practice of permitting issues to be discussed when they are raised by individual governments. The limits to this procedure—and they are crucial—are that the governments raising the issue have to be able to find the votes to translate the initiative into positive action by the commission.

Thus, the British government introduced a draft resolution at the thirty-fourth session of the commission, in 1978, whereby the commission, invoking ECOSOC Resolution 1235 (XLII), would appoint a special *rapporteur* to investigate reports of extensive violations of human rights. This draft resolution was not pressed to a vote, presumably because the required majority was not available, but the commission took action. By Decision 9 (XXXIV) of March 8, 1978, it requested the Secretary General to transmit to the Kampuchean government the commission documentation relating to the human rights situation in that country, to invite a response from the government and to transmit that response, "together with all the information that might be available about the situation," to the commission at its next (1979) session. Not only does this decision represent a step in the process of consolidation mentioned above, it also marks a new approach in permitting the Secretary General to seek to develop "all the information that might be available."[8]

The next development occurred in the autumn of 1976 when, at its twenty-ninth session, the Sub-Commission on Prevention of Discrimination and Protection of Minorities adopted Resolution 2 (XXIX) on a variety of situations.[9] This resolution expressed particular concern at the situation in Western Sahara, a matter which traditionally had been viewed as falling within the sphere of U.N. interest because it was a question of self-determination in a former colonial situation. The resolution also expressed concern over the situation in Argentina, with particular respect to the problem of persecution of refugees in that country. United Nations' concern for refugees is an accepted reality; indeed, the resolution referred for some of its evidence to a report of the U.N. High Commissioner for Refugees appealing to countries to take some of the refugees who were then in Argentina. However, the portion of the resolution referring to Uganda was completely new. Here the resolution specifically requested the Commission on Human Rights to initiate a thorough study of the human rights situation in that country. In one of its preambular paragraphs, it specifically invoked ECOSOC Resolution 1235 (XLII). Although this resolution had been adopted without any particular public discussion of the human rights situation in Uganda, it may be that in passing it the members had in mind information acquired during the subcommission's confidential session.

At this point, one should note two developments. The first is that when the commission next met early in 1977, it refused to consider the Uganda situation in public session, leaving it rather for consideration in its confidential closed session. The second is that the subcommission, which is composed of independent experts acting in their personal capacity, can be a serious forum for airing serious allegations of violations of human rights. What is required if the subcommission is to serve this function is that there be a member willing to raise the particular question. The chances of finding such members are clearly greater in the subcommission than in the commission, which is composed of representatives of member states. However, not all the members can be said to be truly independent; sometimes those that try to exert their independence find themselves under pressure from their governments, which in turn have come under pressure from countries which are of concern to the subcommission. Furthermore, initiatives are not necessarily undertaken on the basis of data that has been systematically acquired and examined. Apart from the Uganda episode, where the required information presumably reached the subcommission via its working group on communications, there is no established data base to permit the commission to act when the events become apparent.

Surprisingly, such a data base is provided by the thousands of communications from individuals and groups alleging violations of human rights received by the United Nations every year. When the United Nations came into being, many of those individuals who were not citizens or inhabitants of trust territories did not examine the

U.N. Charter to find that there was no provision for them to petition. Instead, if such individuals suffered an infringement of their human rights or perceived themselves to have suffered such an infringement, they simply wrote to the United Nations. Consequently, as early as 1947 the Commission on Human Rights first considered what it was to do with such communications and concluded that it had "no power to take any action in regard to any complaints concerning human rights."[10] This position was endorsed by the Economic and Social Council in Resolution 75 (V).

Resolution 454 (XIV) of 1952 established ECOSOC's position that nongovernmental organizations would have their communications on human rights violations handled in the same confidential way as was applied to other communications.[11] Otherwise NGOs would have the privilege under the normal rules of their consultative status to circulate information that states which were members of the United Nations might find distasteful. In 1959 the Economic and Social Council reaffirmed this position in Resolution 728F (XXVIII).[12] This resolution provides for the Secretary General to compile before each session of the Commission on Human Rights a confidential list containing a brief indication of the substance of communications alleging violations of human rights and to furnish that list to members of the commission in private meeting. Each member state receives a copy of any communication concerning human rights which refers explicitly to that state or to territories under its jurisdiction.

Governments sending replies to communications brought to their attention are then asked whether they wish their replies to be presented to the commission in summary form or in full. Meanwhile, individual authors of communications concerning human rights are merely informed that their communications will be handled in accordance with Resolution 728F and that the commission has no power to take any action in regard to any complaint concerning human rights.

Authoritative commentators have pointed out that when a government receives a communication transmitted by the Secretary General, it may feel called upon to reply, if only to counter the allegations contained in the communication. However, it may well be that such replies are more positive and more constructive than might be expected. One should not underestimate a government's desire to present itself in the best light. Nevertheless, apart from a possible request as to whether the author of a communication wishes his or her name to remain confidential, a single acknowledgment is the last the author of the communication will hear from the United Nations on the matter of his or her allegation.

A major development occurred on June 6, 1967, when the Economic and Social Council adopted Resolution 1235 (XLII).[13] It will be recalled that ECOSOC had authorized the Commission on Human Rights and the Sub-Commission on Prevention of Discrimination and Protection of Minorities "to examine information relevant to gross violations of human rights and fundamental freedoms." The information in question was to be that contained in the communications listed by the Secretary General pursuant to Economic and Social Council Resolution 728F (XXVIII) of July 30, 1959.

It further authorized the commission to "make a thorough study of situations which reveal a consistent pattern of violations of human rights." During that same year the Sub-Commission on the Prevention of Discrimination and the Protection of Minorities availed itself of its new powers to draw the attention of the commission to situations in the Republic of South Africa, South West Africa, Southern Rhodesia, Angola, Mozambique, Guinea Bissau, Greece, and Haiti. The commission acted separately on each of the countries and colonies of southern Africa and took no action with respect to Greece and Haiti. Indeed, the subcommission was roundly criticized by some members of the commission for even bringing up the nonsouthern African countries.

These developments, together with the early recognition by the subcommission that procedures for handling the authority conferred by Resolution 1235 (XLII) were required, led to the adoption by ECOSOC in May 1970 of Resolution 1503 (XLVIII), the Procedure for Dealing with Communications Relating to Violations of Human Rights and Fundamental Freedoms.[14] The resolution authorized the subcommission to appoint a working group of not more than five of its members, who would meet once a year for up to ten days in private meetings immediately before the regular session of the subcommission. The task of the group, which was to be appointed "with due regard to geographical distribution" (i.e., with one member from each of the U.N. politico-geographical groupings), was "to consider all communications, including replies of governments thereon" received by the Secretary General under council Resolution 728F (XXVIII) of July 30, 1959.

On the basis of such an examination, the group was to bring "to the attention of the Sub-Commission those communications, together with replies of governments, if any, which appeared to reveal a consistent pattern of gross and reliably attested violations of human rights and fundamental freedoms." The full subcommission was then requested by the resolution to consider in private meetings the communications forwarded to it by the working group and to decide whether or not to refer any particular situations to the Commission on

Human Rights. Any situation so referred would then be examined by the Commission on Human Rights with a view toward determining whether the commission should undertake a thorough study in accordance with the terms of ECOSOC Resolution 1235 (XLII) or whether the situation should be the subject of an investigation by an ad hoc committee to be appointed by the commission.

Such an investigation could only be undertaken with the express consent of the state concerned, conducted in constant cooperation with that state, and completed under conditions to be determined in agreement with the state. In addition, it could only be undertaken if "all available means at the national level have been resorted to and exhausted and [if] the situation does not relate to a matter which is being dealt with under other procedures prescribed in the constituent instruments of, or conventions adopted by, the United Nations and the specialized agencies, or in regional conventions, or which the state concerned wishes to submit to other procedures in accordance with general or special international agreements to which it is a party."[15] However, these restrictions do not apply to thorough studies undertaken pursuant to Resolution 1235 (XLII). Resolution 1503 sets down various rules regarding further conduct of such an ad hoc committee, including its obligation to "strive for friendly solutions before, during and even after the investigation" as well as its obligation to conduct its proceedings in private. All actions envisaged in the implementation of the resolution would remain confidential until such time as the commission might decide to make recommendations to the Economic and Social Council.

Resolution 1503 (XLVIII) itself provided that the first stage in its implementation would be action by the subcommission at its next session to "devise appropriate procedures for dealing with the question of admissibility of communications received by the Secretary-General under Council Resolution 728F (XXVIII) and in accordance with Council Resolution 1235 (XLII)." Because the subcommission was not able to discharge this task of devising procedures until the following year (1971), when it adopted Resolution 1 (XXIV), the actual implementation of the procedure could not get underway until the subcommission's twenty-fifth session in the autumn of 1972.[16]

Apart from a statement at its thirty-third session in 1977 by the chairman, Aleksandar Bozovic of Yugoslavia, to the effect that the commission had considered items under Resolution 1503 and had taken measures in accordance with its responsibilities, there had been no official documentation until 1978 to indicate whether any action had been taken by the subcommission or its working group or whether the commission itself had seen fit "to make recommendations to the Economic and Social Council." However, investigative reporting by the press, together with selective lapses from governments, permitted a picture of the operation of Resolution 1503 to be constructed. For example, it can be verified that in May 1972, Frank C. Newman of the University of California at Berkeley, acting as counsel for five nongovernmental organizations, filed a communication alleging a consistent pattern of gross violations of human rights in Greece. At its twenty-fifth session in the autumn of 1973 the subcommission was not reported to have forwarded any situations to the Commission on Human Rights.

According to a report in *The Times* (London) on September 24, 1973, at its twenty-sixth session in 1973 the subcommission forwarded eight cases to the Commission on Human Rights. Therefore, it can be supposed that these cases were before the Commission on Human Rights at its thirtieth session in 1974. However, *The Argus* reported on April 17, 1974, that the commission took no action on these cases. It did, however, set up a working group to examine these eight communications at its next session as well as others that might be submitted in the meantime by the subcommission. Then, the subcommission, meeting later in 1974 for its twenty-seventh session, indeed forwarded another three cases to the commission's 1975 session. This brought the total of cases before the commission at its thirty-first session to 11 (see London *Sunday Times* of March 14, 1976). It should be borne in mind that the subcommission had openly referred the situation in Chile to the commission with a suggestion that it investigate the situation in that country. At its thirty-first session in 1975 the commission acted favorably on the recommendation for an investigation of the situation of human rights in Chile on the basis of the public resolution that had been adopted by the subcommission and endorsed by the General Assembly in public session. According to the London *Sunday Times* of March 14, 1976, the remaining ten cases were recommended neither for thorough study nor for investigation. Of the ten, eight were dropped for one reason or another, while only two were retained for further consideration on the basis of information promised by the respective governments. When the subcommission met at its twenty-eighth session in 1975, it forwarded to the commission one more situation. Information relating to Chile, the occupied territories of the Middle East, and the countries of southern Africa were to be handled according to the separate agenda items that were now reserved for those situations.

Thus, when in 1976 the Commission on Human Rights met for its thirty-second session, it had before it the two cases left over from the previous year as well as a new case submitted by the subcommission at its intervening session. The commission appears to have taken no action on any of these cases.

At its twenty-ninth session the subcommission in 1976 forwarded five cases to the commission (London *Guardian,* August 20, 1976). These cases were before the commission in 1977 at its thirty-third session, which met in the wake of the highly publicized deaths of Archbishop Luwum and two cabinet ministers in Kampala, Uganda. While it retained these cases "under review" until 1978, the commission authorized neither a thorough study nor the creation of an ad hoc committee to investigate any of them (London *Daily Telegraph,* March 3, 1977).

On the basis of the public subcommission resolution on Uganda recommending that the commission undertake a thorough study of the situation in that country, the governments of Canada and the United Kingdom sought to open a public discussion of the situation with a view toward passing a resolution that would require an inquiry into the situation. However, the commission refused to discuss the question in public session and handled the matter together with the other cases in confidential session. It should be pointed out that the governments of all five countries whose situations had been referred to the commission have appeared before the commission ready to defend themselves against the charges contained in the communications.

At its following (thirtieth) session in 1977, the subcommission, according to the London *Guardian* of September 3, 1977, forwarded information on situations, including those of a further four countries, bringing to nine the number of cases before the commission at its thirty-fourth session in 1978. At this session of the commission, not only was there a statement by the chairman, Keba M'Baye of Senegal, announcing that the commission had taken "decisions" on the cases before it, he went further and named them.[17] The decisions were not specified. However, according to the *Guardian* of March 13, 1978, they included a "mission to Uganda."

This narrative may suggest that the bottle is more empty than full—after all, in the several years since the adoption of council Resolution 1503 the commission has only managed to find one case worthy of thorough study and none worthy of on-the-spot investigation under its procedures. However, there clearly is some liquid in the bottle. Governments do not like having what they consider to be their internal affairs subjected to international scrutiny. Consequently, they frequently have replied and, indeed, have appeared in order to defend themselves against the charges contained in the communications referred by the subcommission. There are few international pressures that can elicit even this measure of concern for international opinion. When the commission does decide to keep a situation under review, there remains the threat—albeit distant—of possible action the following year unless the situation improves demonstrably. Nonetheless, to remain credible a deterrent must carry the real threat of implementation.

In the case of Resolution 1503, unlike that of nuclear weaponry, this threat requires use sometimes against somebody if it is to remain viable. It also should be borne in mind that while Resolution 1503 may be inadequate, the scrapping of its procedures would only secure the objectives of those who from the beginning have opposed both its creation and its implementation. That they continue to oppose it suggests that it represents more than a fig leaf to mask U.N. inactivity.

Meanwhile the subcommission, frustrated by the limited and seemingly dilatory action of the commission and aware that many of the communications in question relate to situations of governmentally committed or at least governmentally sanctioned terror, arbitrary arrest, disappearances, and death, decided at its twenty-seventh session in 1974 to review annually the developments in the field of the human rights of persons who have been subjected to any form of detention or imprisonment. The resolution containing this decision also provided that the subcommission would take into account "any reliably attested information from governments, the specialized agencies, the regional inter-governmental organizations and the non-governmental organizations in consultative status.

Following the adoption of this resolution, a number of nongovernmental organizations submitted pertinent material. While this material was available to members of the subcommission, it was not circulated as an official U.N. document. Nevertheless, the information was such that it permitted the subcommission to single out a number of individual issues in the field that required particular attention, including long detention without trial, judicial investigation of illegal practices against detained persons, judicial control over arrest and detention practices, the role of secret police and paramilitary organizations, the problem of the family and relatives of arrested and detained persons, and the special problems relating to the human rights of women detained or imprisoned.

The subcommission, in Resolution 4 (XXVIII), requested the Secretary General to invite the bodies referred to in its resolution of the previous year to provide any reliably attested information relating to the particular problems mentioned above. However, while the Secretary General was asked to submit the information received from governments, specialized agencies, and regional intergovernmental organizations, he was asked to submit only "a synopsis of the material received from non-governmental organizations." Several non-governmental organizations had submitted material pertinent to these problems, identifying where human rights had been violated under these headings. However, the synopsis produced by the Secretary General contained this information without mentioning the names of the countries concerned or, for that matter, the specific nongovernmental organization making a particular allegation.

In some cases, though, the identities of the countries in question were very thinly camouflaged. An examination of this information led the subcommission to single out two areas of special concern. These are the effect of public emergencies or states of siege on the human rights of detained persons and the necessity of judicial and administrative supervision over arrest, interrogation, and detention practices of secret police, other civilian police, and local military authorities. Meanwhile, in the same resolution the subcommission recommended that the Commission on Human Rights request the Economic and Social Council to authorize the chairperson of the subcommission to appoint a group of five of its members to meet for not more than five working days prior to each session of the subcommission to analyze the materials received in connection with the subject and to prepare the subcommission's annual review of developments in the field.

By this point it has become clear that the subcommission was slowly edging toward providing an alternative mechanism for dealing with allegations of human rights violations in this particular area. It would not be rash to presume the Commission on Human Rights also felt the same way and that, consequently, it failed to adopt a resolution at its thirty-third session in 1977 that would have transmitted this resolution to ECOSOC. A draft resolution that would have granted the required authority for the establishment of the group was, in fact, introduced at the sixty-second session of ECOSOC in spring 1977, but it was withdrawn by its sponsors, who did not want to risk its defeat. The subcommission continued to deal with the item at its thirtieth session in 1977 and its examination led it to request two of its members to prepare an outline for a study on the effects of states of emergency on the protection of human rights. It remains to be seen whether the question of establishing a working group to prepare the annual review of the item will be taken up again in the future. The important point about the whole experiment is that the subcommission is by far the most independent U.N. organ dealing with human rights, and it should be in a position to determine on its own what it should do with the information it examines pursuant to its annual review in the field.

Special Agencies of the United Nations

International Labor Organization

The work of the ILO in monitoring compliance with standards under its concern has been fully documented by various authors.[18] The Governing Body Committee on Freedom of Association is the principal ILO group competent to examine complaints of infringement of trade union rights. Under the applicable procedure, complaints are receivable if they are submitted either by workers' or employers' organizations or by governments. In addition the ILO Committee on Application of Conventions and Recommendations literally monitors the extent of compliance by members of the ILO with their obligations under the ILO constitution or under ILO conventions that they have ratified. The special list compiled by this committee is one on which many governments find themselves from time to time and from which each state always wishes to be removed. Finally, the governing body of the ILO sometimes mandates full-scale commissions of inquiry into the situation of trade union rights in a particular country.

UNESCO

Until recently, UNESCO's powers to deal with violations of human rights within its field of concern was very limited. The basic position was that contained in Executive Board Resolution 77 EX/8.3, which was adopted in 1967.[19] By that resolution the board found "that UNESCO is not authorized under its constitution to take any measures in connection with complaints regarding human rights, which can be entertained only in accordance with the covenants and protocols subscribed to by member states." If this sounds similar to early U.N. practice, it will come as no surprise that the resolution went on to decide "that communications addressed to UNESCO in connection with individual cases alleging a violation of human rights in education, science and culture shall be handled by it in the same manner as is stipulated in the Economic and Social Council resolution 728."[20]

The body to which this resolution has assigned a role similar to that played by the U.N.'s Commission on Human Rights is the Special Committee on Discrimination in Education, which is now known as the Committee on Conventions and Recommendations in Education. It is ironic that the resolution in question was adopted the same year that ECOSOC adopted Resolution 1235 envisaging consideration of consistent patterns of gross violations of human rights. Nevertheless, this position was reaffirmed by the Executive Board in 1975 in decision 98 EX/9.6.[21] The restrictions imposed did not, however, prevent the Executive Board from reacting to the practices of the Chilean junta in the post-1973 period or from making provision for the Director General and the Committee on Conventions and Recommendatons in Education to follow the situation and report on it publicly.

This familiar pattern has recently been radically departed from. The General Conference of UNESCO, at its nineteenth session held in Nairobi from October 26 to November 30, 1976, adopted Resolution 12.1, which invited the Executive Board and the Director General "to study the procedures which should be followed in the examination of cases and questions which might be submitted to UNESCO concerning the exercise of human rights in the spheres to which its competence extends, in order to make its action more effective."[22] Pursuant to this mandate the Executive Board set up a working party to examine the question. The working party reported to the board's one hundred-and-fourth session[23] proposing a far-reaching revision of UNESCO's procedures for dealing with violations of human rights. The recommendations were adopted by the board at its one hundred-and-fourth session, spring 1978, in its decision 104EX/Decision 3.3.

The new procedure provides that communications concerning violations of human rights within UNESCO's competence shall, subject to certain procedural requirements, be transmitted by the Director General to the Committee on Conventions and Recommendations (as the decision renames the previous Committee for Conventions and Recommendations in Education). The committee is to examine such communications in private session. Government representatives "may attend meetings of the committee in order to provide additional information or to answer questions from members of the committee on either admissibility or the merits of the communication." It is not clear whether this right rests on the invitation of the committee, nor whether it applies to the full deliberations of the committee with respect to the country concerned or only with respect to a part of the committee's proceedings, as necessary. Certainly the author of the communication has no similar rights, though the committee may seek "additional information it may consider necessary for the disposition of the matter." Presumably the author would be one source of such additional information. In addition, the committee "may, in exceptional circumstances, request the Executive Board to authorize it under Rule 29 of the Rules of Procedure to take appropriate action."[24] This appears to mean that persons such as authors of communications or even witnesses called by them may be given special permission to testify before the committee.

The authors' rights are still significantly greater than those under the comparable U.N. non-treaty based procedures. The author is to be notified of the committee's decision on admissibility. Notification also takes place if the committee decides on the merits that no further action is warranted. When further consideration is warranted the committee is to seek to bring about "a friendly solution designed to advance the promotion of human rights falling within UNESCO's fields of competence."

The committee keeps the Executive Board informed of its work and its reports may make not only general recommendations but also specific ones "regarding the disposition of a communication under consideration." The board considers the reports in private session and may decide to take further action as necessary in accordance with Rule 28 of the Rules of Procedure.[25]

By the same decision the Executive Board also provided for the consideration of "questions of massive, systematic or flagrant violations of human rights and fundamental freedoms... falling within UNESCO's fields of competence" in public meetings of the board and the General Conference. The board can be seized of such a question where the committee transmits to it a communication which testifies to the existence of one.

This comprehensive procedure for dealing with general situations, in public, and specific cases, in private, can be set in motion by virtually anybody. Communications may, of course "originate from a person or a group of persons who, it can reasonably be presumed, are victims of an alleged violation." In addition, however, "any person, group of persons or non-governmental organization having reliable knowledge" of violations may also originate communications.

The mandate contained in the procedures comes surprisingly close to that of the ILO Governing Body Committee on Freedom of Association, but this time covering the whole field of human rights in the area of education, science and culture. It is to be hoped that those in a position to do so will ensure that the Director General receives the communications necessary to stimulate UNESCO's action in this area.

Role of Nongovernmental Organizations

It is clear that nongovernmental organizations (NGO's) are not subject to the restraint that are the normal lot of intergovernmental organizations. They can amass information from all quarters and—subject, presumably to the obligation not to act in a manner which might be detrimental to the interests of victims of violations of human rights—are free to disseminate the information as widely as they can, since protecting states or groups of states from embarrassment is of no concern to NGO's. On the other hand, they are relatively small and sometimes have very restricted mandates. Nonetheless, it is equally clear that the nongovernmental organizations are in a position to assist the intergovernmental organizations when the latter undertake measures for the protection of human rights.

The major U.N. treaties—namely, the Convention on the Elimination of All Forms of Racial Discrimination and the International Covenant on Civil and Political Rights—do not provide for any participatory role for NGO's. However, neither do they prevent NGO's from making information available to individual members of the respective committees established under the conventions. Similarly, it might be possible for NGO's to act as duly authorized representatives of individuals who claim that their rights have been violated. In this function their role would be essentially that of lawyer. This is a role which has already been undertaken by certain NGO's, both national and international, with respect to applicants before the European Commission on Human Rights which was set up under the European Convention for the Protection of Human Rights and Fundamental Freedoms. Indeed, the only convention which envisages a direct role for NGO's acting *sua sponte* is the American Convention on Human Rights of 1969. Article 44 of this convention provides that

> Any person or group of persons, or any nongovernmental entity legally recognized in one or more member states of the organization, may lodge petitions with the Commission containing denunciations or complaints of violation of this convention by a state party.

In July 1978, the American Convention on Human Rights entered into force having been ratified by eleven states.

All the U.N.'s nontreaty mechanisms and procedures, as well as that of UNESCO, envisage an information role for NGO's, and, indeed, many of the working groups and inquiries which have been discussed in this essay have actively sought the help of NGO's in compiling the information required for them to prepare their reports.

As far as the ILO is concerned, there is no particular role envisaged for NGO's for the Committee on Application of Conventions and Recommendations. Here, however, the remarks made above concerning the provision of information to members of CERD and of the human rights committee are applicable. It should also be borne in mind that, by virtue of the tripartite nature of the structure of the ILO, the committee is itself composed not only of state representatives but also of representatives of employers' and employees' organizations. As to the Governing Body Committee on Freedom of Association, one should remember that complaints are receivable only if they are submitted by workers' or employers' organizations or by governments. While this would restrict the activities of ordinary human rights organizations such as Amnesty International or the International Commission of Jurists, a sufficient number of organizations fall into the competent category that they would be able to avail themselves of relevant information in the hands of nongovernmental organizations that do not have such status.

The need for intergovernmental organizations to expand, intensify, and consolidate their work in the field of protection of human rights is likely to be matched by the continuing need for nongovernmental organizations to continue their own work and to contribute the product of their own work to that of the intergovernmental organizations wherever they can.

NOTES

1. F. Ermacora, "Procedure to Deal with Human Rights Violations: A Hopeful Start in the United Nations?" 7 *Human Rights Journal* (1974): 670-671.
2. L. Sohn and T. Buergenthal, *International Protection of Human Rights* (New York: Bobbs-Merrill, 1973), p. 527.
3. *Ibid.*, p. 528.
4. General Assembly Resolution 1514 (XV) of December 20, 1960.
5. *Ibid.*, pp. 800-801 (ECOSOC Resolution 1235 [XLII] of June 6, 1967).
6. *Index to the Proceedings of the General Assembly* (29th Session). This resolution concerning the reestablishment of basic human rights and fundamental freedoms in Chile was adopted by the General Assembly at its 2278th meeting.
7. Official Records of ECOSOC (60th Session), Supp. 3, *Commission on Human Rights, Reports on the 32nd Session*, February 2 to March 5, 1976 (Commission on Human Rights Resolution 4 [XXXII] of February 19, 1976).
8. Official Records of ECOSOC, 1978, Supp. 4, *Commission on Human Rights, Report on the 34th Session*, February 6 to March 10, 1978.
9. Official Records of ECOSOC (62d Session), Supp. 6, *Commission on*

Human Rights, Reports on the 33rd Session, February to March, 1977, p. 59 (a discussion concerning Resolution 2 [XXIX] of the Sub-Commission on the Prevention of Discrimination and Protection of Minorities).
10. L. Sohn and T. Buergenthal, *supra* note 1, pp. 748-750 ECOSOC Resolution 75 [V] of August 5, 1947).
11. *Ibid.*, p. 758 (ECOSOC Resolution 454 [XIV] of July 28, 1952).
12. *Ibid.*, pp. 771-772 (ECOSOC Resolution 728F [XXVIII] of July 30, 1959).
13. *Supra* note 3.
14. L. Sohn and T. Buergenthal, *supra* note 1, pp. 841-844 ECOSOC Resolution 1503 [XLVIII] of May 27, 1970).
15. *Ibid.*, p. 843.
16. *Ibid.*, pp. 852-853 (Sub-Commission on Prevention of Discrimination and Protection of Minorities Resolution 1 [XXIV] of August 14, 1971).
17. Bolivia, Equatorial Guinea, Ethiopia, Indonesia, Republic of Korea, Malawi, Paraguay, Uganda and Uruguay.
18. Authors who have documented ILO monitoring procedures are H. G. Bartholomei, *Protection Against Anti-Union Discrimination* (Geneva, 1976); J. N. Garcia-Nieto, *A Critical Analysis of the Right to Strike* (Geneva, 1967); E. B. Haas, *Human Rights and International Action—The Case of Freedom of Association* (Stanford, 1970); C. W. Jenks, *Human Rights, Social Justice, and Peace—The Broader Significance of the ILO Experience* (Geneva, 1967) and *Social Policy in a Changing World: The ILO Response* (Geneva, 1976); and G. von Potobsky, "Protection of Trade Union Rights: Twenty Years Work by the Committee of Freedom of Association," 105 *International Labour Law* (January 1972): 69.
19. "The 77th Session of the Executive Board," 13 *UNESCO Chronicle* (December 1967): 461-463 (Executive Board Resolution 77 Ex/8.3 of October-November 1967).
20. *Supra* note 9.
21. "The 98th Session of the Executive Board," 21 *UNESCO Chronicle* (December 1975): 341 (Executive Board Resolution 98 Ex/9.6 of September-October 1975).
22. "The 19th Session of the General Conference," 22 *UNESCO Chronicle* 363 (Resolution 12.1 of November 30, 1976).
23. UNESCO doc. 104 EX/3, March 3, 1978.
24. Rule 29 states, in pertinent part:

> 2. Observers of member states, non-member states, intergovernmental or non-governmental organizations and other qualified persons may be invited by the Board to address it on matters within their competence.

25. Rule 28 states, in pertinent part:

> 2. Any decision taken by the Board at a private meeting shall be announced at a subsequent public meeting.
> 3. At each private meeting the Board shall decide whether a report of its work at that meeting shall be published.

9: Monitoring Human Rights Violations: The Role of Nongovernmental Organizations

LAURIE S. WISEBERG
HARRY M. SCOBLE

Introduction

Because the cause of human rights has become the moral banner of the Carter Administration, it seems appropriate to begin this essay with a few remarks which might otherwise seem banal. First, one might note that the concern for human rights, both in the United States and in the world at large, antedates this particular American government. Even if one limits discussion to the recent past,[1] students of American politics know that the impulse and momentum behind current American concern for human rights violations by foreign governments preceded Jimmy Carter's inauguration and came, rather, from a few key Congressmen and Senators during the Nixon and Ford years.[2]

The benchmark of this reawakened consciousness for human rights was the hearings chaired by Representative Donald Fraser, chairman of the Subcommittee on International Organizations of the House Committee on International Relations—hearings which began in 1973 and are still continuing.[3] Moved, perhaps, by a sense of moral destitution resulting from American involvement in Vietnam and Chile, by the amorality of the Nixon-Kissinger-Ford administrations, and by a fear that the democracies were losing out to the Soviet Union and China in the ideological struggle over the Third World, Congress from 1973 on moved slowly but steadily to interject human rights into U.S. foreign policy considerations. Thus, in the 1973 Foreign Assistance Act, Section 32 declared the "Sense of Congress" that economic and military assistance should be denied foreign governments which imprison their citizens for political reasons; the 1974 Foreign Assistance Act added Section 502B which again declared a "Sense of Congress" that, except in extraordinary circumstances, the President should withhold security assistance from governments which are gross violators of human rights; in 1975 the Harkin Amendment to the International Development and Food Assistance Act prohibited outright economic assistance to gross violators of human rights unless it could be shown that the "assistance will directly benefit the needy people in such a country"; and, finally, Revised Section 502B of the International Security Assistance and Arms Export Control Act of 1976 made the promotion of human rights standards an explicit goal of U.S. foreign policy, instructed the President to formulate military and aid programs to promote human rights and to avoid identification with repressive regimes, provided for termination or restriction of security assistance to governments which consistently violate the human rights of their citizens, and made it mandatory for the State Department to file complete reports on the human rights situation in every country receiving security assistance.[4]

This Congressional concern did not, of course, manifest itself in a vacuum; rather, in this struggle to write human rights into the American foreign policy agenda, there were many groups—both American and international—solidly behind these initiatives. This fact leads to a second introductory point. Antedating Congress' recent concern with human rights has been the persistent concern and commitment with human rights of a variety of nongovernmental organizations—some based in the United States and some based abroad. These NGO's appear to act on the premise that there are substantial reasons for at least partially distrusting the policies and pronouncement of even the most open and honest governments in matters both of domestic and international human rights.

Evidence for this contention can be easily mustered. It seems a regrettable historical truth that few political elites are either willing or able to discriminate between legitimate internal opposition and outright "treason." Consequently, to make sure that democratic-professing elites do make such discrimination and act on the democratic values they allegedly have internalized, those out of power—notably nongovernmental human rights-oriented organizations—must constantly monitor their behavior. In the American context, this point can be underlined by citing the efforts—so far either delayed or unsuccessful—of the families of Mark Clark and Fred Hampton to seek justice through the federal court system. Historians of political repression in the United States would do well to take note that during the week in December 1969 when the Chicago police killed the two Illinois Black Panther Party leaders, FBI-inspired local police raids occurred simultaneously in Los Angeles, Oakland, and Cleveland. The then-retired chief of police of Seattle was quoted shortly thereafter in the *New York Times* to the effect that the FBI had importuned a raid on black militants' headquarters in that city as well.

In the external relations of democratic governments—especially those of the great powers—monitoring is equally critical. An example readily at hand of the need for monitoring is the coalition which has formed behind Senator Henry Jackson of Washington. Here one can see how readily the political elite (or a part of it) tends to become silent about political repression in South Korea, Iran, the Philippines, Indonesia, or southern Africa and to focus their criticism only on repression in the USSR and the "captive nations" of Eastern Europe. There is then a danger of a highly situational and partisan *selective* approach to human rights, and one cannot say that only the black African and Third World elites are selective in their approach to what should be universal principles.[5] The elites of the First and Second worlds can be, and often are, equally selective.[6]

It seems to be the implicit assumption of many NGO's that the role of the United States in world affairs so overshadows that of any other nation that this fact provides *the* critical leverage for change in the international human rights situation. In this view the underlying premise is that if the U.S. government were simply to cease certain activities and programs, this in itself would accomplish significant desired change.

One can readily find empirical data that make this assumption reasonable. First, no other nation is more heavily involved in arming and training the rest of the world militarily than the United States. American arms sales in fiscal year 1977 reached the level of $10 billion and constituted half of all known international arms transactions during that year.[7] The U.S. Army School of the Americas in the Panama Canal Zone is reported to have trained more than 30,000 Latin American military officers between its opening in 1949 and the end of 1976. The Agency for International Development (AID) estimates that more than a million foreign policemen have received some training or supplies through its "public safety" program—training not only in routine police matters but also in paramilitary and counterinsurgency techniques for dealing with civil unrest.[8] The role of U.S. public agencies and private corporations in "technology transfer" for political torture—to DINA of Chile, SAVAK of Iran, BOSS of South Africa, and the Korean CIA—is only now being specifically investigated through Freedom of Information Act suits and other means.[9]

Second, the United States plays a preponderant role both in bilateral and multilateral economic assistance programs. In fiscal year 1976 Third World nations received $24.9 billion in direct credits, government-guaranteed loans, government-insured investments, and official debt deferments under 15 different U.S. bilateral programs and U.S.-supported multilateral agency programs; all forms of U.S. military assistance made up $2.69 billion of this figure.[10] Some $4.7 billion went to the highly repressive regimes of South Korea, Chile, Indonesia, the Philippines, and South Africa.[11]

A recent study by Lars Schoultz indicates that there is a strong positive correlation between the amount of U.S. bilateral aid to Latin American governments and the propensity of those governments to torture their own citizens.[12] Moreover, in the last decade, as the Congress has exhibited a desire for a more active role in overseeing bilateral aid programs, the Executive Branch has deliberately shifted to an increased reliance on multilateral funding agencies as a means of avoiding Congressional scrutiny. Meanwhile, to indicate the potential leverage of the U.S. government through multilateralism, one might note that the U.S. share of stock and subscriptions in the World Bank is 25.3 percent; in the International Finance Corporation, 32.5 percent; in the International Development Association, 37.9 percent; and of the Inter-American Development Bank, 52.0 percent.[13]

A third example relates to the wide variety of federal programs that support and encourage U.S. multinational corporations, especially the major commercial banks, in their "private" activities in the highly repressive nations of the Third World. Credits extended by the Export-Import Bank and insurance against "political risks" by the Overseas Private Investment Corporation provide two concrete illustrations of such programs.[14]

Thus, if one properly should distrust all governments, if governments move affirmatively with regard to human rights issues largely because of the prodding of nongovernmental organizations, and if the role of the United States in world affairs is as significant as suggested by the above data, the part played by human rights NGO's in monitoring and shaping U.S. foreign policy requires analysis.

The Universe of Human Rights NGO's: Five Historical Trends

One must note at the outset that only recently have social scientists paid attention to the work of NGO's in the human rights field. In part because students of international politics have considered the subject of human rights to be more a matter of law and philosophy than politics and also as a result of a state-centric model of the international system (a model which *a priori* rules out any significant influence by nonstate actors),[15] the literature on NGO's has consisted for the most part of descriptive and episodic accounts of journalists or the activists themselves.[16] Therefore, as a starting point for the development of serious political analysis on the question of the effectiveness of such groups, two things were required: (1) political organizational biographies of the human rights NGO's and (2) a taxonomy that could permit a meaningful classification of these groups and the placement of them in a comparative framework with other political interest groups and transnational actors. After considering these preliminaries[17]—and we are only beginning to understand the nature of the groups involved—one could then pose the question of the "public policy" implications or conduct an "impact analysis" of these groups.

In examining the universe of relevant NGO's that impinge on the human rights dimensions of U.S. foreign policy, one can discern five broad interrelated historical trends in the short life of organized human rights activity. These trends are the proliferation and increasing diversity of private organizations concerned with some aspect of human rights; the increasing involvement of previously organized groups that were not exclusively devoted to human rights concerns; a continued functional specialization by, and increasing cooperation among, human rights NGO's; an evident tendency toward experimentation in tactics and strategies; and, finally, organized efforts to mobilize and recruit new types of members.

1. Proliferation and Increasing Diversity of NGO's

Until approximately 1972 there were very few nongovernmental organizations anywhere which identified themselves as primarily human rights NGO's. If the U.S. government paid any attention at all to such groups, it confined this attentiveness almost exclusively to the four best-known organizations: the International League for Human Rights (formerly the International League for the Rights of Man, founded in New York in 1942),[18] which is oriented primarily toward the drafting of international human rights standards in the U.N. arena; the International Commission of Jurists (a group of no more than 40 eminent jurists, established initially in 1952 to monitor abuses of justice in the Warsaw Pact nations), which is dedicated to the support and advancement of the rule of law worldwide; the London-based Amnesty International (founded in 1961), which is concerned with securing the release of prisoners of conscience and, in recent years, with the abolition of torture and capital punishment; and the International Committee of the Red Cross (created in Switzerland in 1863 and probably the oldest secular humanitarian organization), which is oriented toward upholding the laws of warfare and maintaining minimum standards for the treatment of prisoners of war and, in recent years, of political prisoners. By contrast to these groups, the human rights "lobby" in Washington, D.C., today is an amorphous yet multifaceted aggregate with a core of as many as a hundred organized groups which identify themselves as acting with a human rights concern.

Prominent examples of this human rights "explosion" may be found in the anti-apartheid coalition, the cooperative network of groups of South American political refugees and exiles, and the Human Rights Working Group of the Coalition for a New Foreign and Military Policy. (The Coalition represents the reconstitution of vital elements of the anti-Vietnam War movement and brings together 33 organizations concerned with a total reformulation of U.S. foreign policy. Its Human Rights Working Group—which focuses more specifically on bringing policy into line with international human rights standards—draws not only upon these coalition members but also upon many other organizations that are not formally affiliated.) Other indirect indicators of the proliferation of organized constituencies concerned with human rights are found in the growing number of seminars, conferences, and public forums on human rights all across the country;[19] the amount of newspaper space devoted to human rights stories;[20] the growth and development of law school and university courses focused on human rights;[21] and the interest shown by academics, activists, and policy-makers in a recently founded communications network—the Human Rights Internet.[22]

2. Increasing Involvement of Previously Nonexclusive Groups

The second trend concerns the increasing involvement in the human rights struggle of existing groups which, until recently, devoted only modest—if any—resources to the formulation and implementation of human rights standards. Churches, for example, allocated only minimal resources while scientific and professional associations usually ignored these issues entirely. To amplify, one might consider the revitalization of the Roman Catholic church associated with Vatican I and Vatican II which has led to the creation of the

Pontifical Commission on Justice and Peace and its American national counterpart.[23] The Geneva-based World Council of Churches, under the impact of the radicalization of Protestant missionaries working in repressive societies, the decolonialization of Third World church structures, and the growing consciousness of inequities in the international economic order, has moved human rights to a priority position on its agenda. In October 1974 the WCC held a major consultation on "Human Rights and Christian Responsibility" in St. Polten, Austria;[24] in 1975, in response to pleas from Chilean churches, it created a Human Rights Resources Office on Latin America;[25] and, since the Fifth Assembly of the WCC in Nairobi, in 1975, it has dedicated itself to the search for "a just, participatory, and sustainable society."[26] Concurrently, under the impact of the domestic civil rights movement and the "war on poverty," the American National Council of Churches of Christ has taken similar steps, including most recently the creation of a Human Rights Office in its Divison of Overseas Ministries.

As for scientific and professional associations, the year 1977 has witnessed a new activism by important organizations of physicists, mathematicians, psychiatrists, and medical doctors on behalf of occupational colleagues who have been imprisoned, "disappeared" or been tortured or killed by dictatorial regimes. By way of illustration one might cite the American Association for the Advancement of Science which in 1976 formed a new committee on scientific freedom and responsibility to function as "a human rights clearing house" for the 300 scientific and technical associations affiliated with the AAAS. At the same time the National Academy of Sciences formed a similar committee and took its first active steps with regard to scientists imprisoned for political reasons in Argentina, the Soviet Union, and Uruguay.[27]

3. Continued Functional Specialization and Increasing Cooperation

The third trend relates to continued functional specialization by and increasing cooperation among human rights NGO's. By and large, since NGO's in the human rights field cut into the problem from a variety of perspectives, they tend to specialize in certain kinds of problems or issues. There are a few NGO's whose stated purpose is the furtherance of all human rights and which can claim a universal approach to the problem. Thus, for example, the International League for Human Rights uses the International Bill of Rights (the Universal Declaration and the International Covenants) as its platform. Founded by American civil libertarian Roger Nash Baldwin as an international counterpart of the American Civil Liberties Union, the ILHR's interpretation of human rights tends to be a Euro-American one. However, its efforts recently have broadened the organization's perspective to include economic, social, and cultural rights. As stated in a 1970 ILHR newsletter:

> Whereas League concentration in the past has centered—and will continue—primarily on political and civil rights, new horizons have emerged in the area of economic, social and cultural rights and touching on such questions as the population explosion, the human environment and new technological and scientific invasions of privacy. Human rights must be protected. The League will respond to threats in any one of these areas.[28]

Notwithstanding this 1970 pronouncement, the league's resources remain limited and its affiliates and members largely Euro-American.[29] Consequently, as it has continued to respond to those human rights crises which the leadership considers to be most serious, this has meant a continued primary focus on such issues as the plight of Soviet dissidents and Soviet Jewry, the extermination of South American Indians, and the apartheid situation in southern Africa. The Paris-based International Federation for Human Rights,[30] which also subscribes to the entirety of the Universal Declaration and Covenants, is forced by limited resources to be selective in its range of activities. However, with a leadership and membership more open to socialist perspectives, it tends to focus on economic, social, and cultural rights and, thus, deemphasizes individual civil and political liberties.

The Geneva-based International Commission of Jurists, the Brussels-based International Association of Democratic Lawyers, and the Paris-based Movement of Catholic Lawyers are all concerned with the maintenance of the rule of law, with fair and open trials, and with the independence and integrity of the judiciary. Nevertheless, while there are occasions in which these groups are able to cooperate with fruitful results, each subscribes to a basic ideology that leads to an inevitable selectivity of cases.[31]

The functional specialization of other organizations is more explicit. Amnesty International concentrates on political prisoners; P.E.N. International campaigns on behalf of freedom of expression and takes up the cases of writers, artists, and allied intellectuals whose activities bring them into conflict with their governments;[32] the Lelio Basso International Foundation for the Rights and Liberation of Peoples (a new organization based in Rome which is an outgrowth of the Bertrand Russell Tribunal II, a meeting which focused on repression in Latin America) directs particular concern to the problems (e.g., economic dependency and cultural imperialism) of the peoples of the Third World;[33] and the London-based Anti-Slavery Society focuses on such problems as wage-slavery, white-slavery, prostitution, and the exploitation of aboriginal peoples.[34]

More specific to the American scene, functional specialization often has a geographic focus. Thus the Washington human rights "lobby" is made up of such issue-specific organizations as TAPOL (the Campaign for Indonesian Political Prisoners), the Washington Office on Africa (which tends to concentrate attention on southern Africa), the Washington Office on Latin America, the Chile Committee for Human Rights, the Argentine Commission for Human Rights, Non-Intervention in Nicaragua, the Committee for Artistic and Intellectual Freedom in Iran, and the Friends of the Filipino People.[35] One can find evidence of a functional specialization which is closer to the original Weberian meaning in the dichotomy between lobbying and research. For example, the International League, restricted from formal lobbying by its application for tax-exempt status, devotes most of its energy to primary research through field missions to repressive areas, the sending of observers to political trials, and the publishing of reports; the Inter-faith Corporate Responsibility Center (a research-oriented activity sponsored by the National Council of Churches) searches out church holdings in corporations engaged in business in repressive areas and seeks to mobilize this potential institutional leverage; and the Washington Office on Latin America and that on Africa are more legislator-oriented and are thus closer to the conventional definition of lobbying.

Thus, in some ways, the first two groups are research-gatherers, while the latter are research-users. However, this distinction is a very fuzzy one in that all of these groups do engage in research on their own. Moreover, even those which do not engage in formal lobbying necessarily are involved in indirect lobbying, because they testify when called upon to do so before Congressional committees (and sometimes initiate these hearings), they disseminate their reports to authoritative decision-makers in the hope of producing a policy-relevant response, they try to utilize the quality mass media to sensitize and build an informed public, and, where they possess consultative status with an international organization (e.g., ECOSOC, UNESCO, and the OAS), they recognize their formal lobbying function in these particular international arenas.

While specialization of interest and activity inevitably will continue, the last several years have witnessed increased informal coordination and cooperation among the proliferating groups. There is, for example, an informal but effective process of consultation on an almost daily basis among Martin Ennals, secretary general of Amnesty International; Naill MacDermot, secretary general of the ICJ; Ben Whitaker, director of the Minority Rights Group;[36] and Jerome Shestack, president of the International League.[37] The cooperation can have meaningful results. In the matter of sending observers to political trials, for instance, such consultation may result in a decision to send separate missions, a joint-sponsored mission, or a follow-up investigation area group in order to have a cumulative impact.

More recently these same principals have engaged in a discussion of the possibility of a joint training program for the lawyers and jurists sent on such missions.[38] In addition, cooperation and coordination in Washington clearly have been manifested in a new dimension by the formation of the Human Rights Working Group (HRWG) of the coalition. The HRWG meets at least once a month, has a prepared agenda, has established a series of subcommittees and task forces to probe specific problems or issues, and frequently sponsors briefings on particular crises. For example, the HRWG held a two-day conference for human rights activists to examine alternate tactics and strategies.[39] A similar but not as structured effort at cooperation and coordination was initiated in England in 1977. As a result of collaborative activities dating from the Human Rights Year 1968 and at the initiative of the Human Rights Committee of the United Nations Association of the United Kingdom, the network was set up as a mechanism to bring together some 50 British organizations in the human rights field at least twice a year. While there is no continuing official leadership or agenda, the network serves to inform member organizations of the activities of each and to isolate a small number of issues (e.g., the present campaign for a British bill of rights and for the establishment of a Parliamentary select committee on foreign policy/human rights) to which major efforts will be devoted.[40]

Such cooperation is a logical imperative in a situation of multiplying groups, each with a specific interest area and limited resources but also with interests which link up to general human rights concerns. To the extent that human rights remain high on the legislative agenda in the United States, one would expect to see these emerging forms of cooperation and coordination become more highly formalized, probably resulting in a collective effort similar to the Leadership Conference on Civil Rights which emerged during the legislative phase of the Civil Rights Movement in the early 1960's.[41] We do not mean to imply that we foresee a merger of all groups. Indeed, given the differences in ideology, culture, motivation, personality, and ambition among the groups, such a union would be utopian. As an illustration one might mention that in the summer of 1977 the presidents of the International League and the International Federation for Human Rights opened discussions aimed toward a possible confederation in which the affiliates of these two organizations would automatically each become the affiliate of the other.[42] However, the leadership of each group has reservations about the approach to human rights taken by its counterpart, and it remains to be seen whether even such a modest step toward aggregation will in fact occur. At the minimum, however, one can clearly expect coalition-building around specific issues to continue and to provide mechanisms and incentives for cooperation and common strategies.

4. Experimentation in Tactics and Strategies

The fourth trend concerns experimentation in the tactics and strategies of NGO's. This trend can, perhaps, be illustrated best by examining three transformations in activity—a movement away from an emphasis on drafting international human rights standards to one on implementing existing legislation, a transition from a humanitarian response to an ecumenical search for a just society, and a change by NGO's from the conventional targets of governments and intergovernmental arenas to a broad-scale focus on all centers of power. Additionally, as the NGO's have become reasonably successful in attaining some of their goals, they have generated a reaction by opposed forces and, consequently, have been forced to engage in certain defensive actions.

From the 1940's through most of the 1960's the established NGO's devoted themselves exclusively to human rights while their co-interest groups had one primary focus to their activities: the drafting and ratification of international human rights standards both within the U.N. forum and within regional organizations. A second and related activity was support for the process of decolonization. However, by the end of the 1960's these tasks essentially had been accomplished. By the late 1960's there existed a large body of international human rights law and almost all of the Third World had gained formal political independence. Nonetheless, there was a recognizable irony in these very successes, for the achievement of positive law had little effect on the behavior of political elites and decolonization had left most of the Third World nations in conditions of "dependencia." For these reasons it became evident to the human rights NGO's that while legislation is the beginning of political success, without effective implementation, legislation provides only hollow victories. Hence the prime question has now become one of finding the means to enforce international human rights standards in a world of national sovereignties.

This new orientation requires experimentation in order to explore both the utility of employing existing procedures and institutions of the international system and of inventing new procedures and international institutional structures. Therefore, the NGO's have used their consultative status with the ECOSOC to assume a dynamic role in the proceedings of the U.N. Human Rights Commission and its Subcommission on the Prevention of Discrimination and the Protection of Minorities (as well as in other relevant U.N. bodies, notably the International Labor Organization) and have taken it upon themselves to inform individuals and the NGO community at large about the technicalities involved in complying with formal procedures.[43] Furthermore, they have pressured both the agencies themselves and the member states whose delegations might be sympathetic to reform those procedures and institutions in order to make them more effective agents in the maintenance of human rights standards.

In the latter context the NGO's have been wrestling with classic bureaucratic problems of implementation of existing positive law; thus they have sought to create universal and regional international executive agencies with recognized jurisdiction, trained staffs, and adequate budgets to devote full time to what the NGO's perceive to be the human rights agenda. In a recent working paper, "On Strengthening the Role of the United Nations in the Field of Human Rights,"[44] the NGO's have pressured for such specific reforms as the revision of the U.N. procedures under ECOSOC Resolution 1503 (finally adopted in 1970), which requires a definitive disposition of the thousands of cases of alleged gross violations submitted annually by individuals and organizations and which currently remains in a "confidential" limbo; pressing for meetings to be held at least seminannually of the Human Rights Commission and its subcommission so that human rights matters may receive sustained consideration and gross violations may be handled as they occur rather than a year or two after the fact; greater use of genuinely independent individual experts to dilute the partisanship displayed by national sovereignties; and the creation of a new office of a U.N. High Commission for Human Rights, with a capacity to respond to crises and to serve as humanitarian protector for victims of repression.[45] In a like manner the NGO's have served as advocates of similar procedural and structural changes of the Inter-American Commission on Human Rights of the OAS and have supported efforts to create an African human rights commission.[46]

The trend away from a simple humanitarian response to disaster/crises and toward the creation of a just society is most notably characteristic of churches, both Protestant and Catholic. While there inevitably remains a continuing need to respond to the human misery resulting from natural disasters and political upheavals (e.g., disaster assistance, famine relief, and refugee aid), there has been a growing recognition among church leaders that "Christian charity" is inadequate unless it is accompanied by efforts at societal change and institutional transformation.

A concrete example of such thinking appears in action in Chile since 1973. In this instance it was impossible for the churches to provide any meaningful charity in the traditional mode without at the same time sustaining a highly repressive regime; consequently, effective response to the political situation clearly demanded an ecumenical effort (as manifested in the Vicariate of Solidarity) to provide legal assistance to the targets of Pinochet's repression, to publicize and denounce the crimes of the junta, and to join forces with those committed to the restoration of a more just society. Similarly, the situation in southern Africa has forced the Christian churches to abandon their conventional humanitarian mode of response and to experiment with alternatives of a political nature. Admittedly, such departures have not been without cost and have provoked considerable ferment within both church communities; nonetheless, while conservative elements have resisted these efforts—even to the point of secession—the new trends seem firmly established among a number of Christian churches.

Finally, the human rights NGO's have recognized the limitations of focusing all their energies solely on such traditional intergovernmental arenas as the United Nations, the EEC, the OAS, or on governmental authorities restrictively defined only as diplomats and State Department/Foreign Ministry personnel. It has become increasingly apparent to human rights NGO's—particularly in the light of the emphasis that has been placed on multilateral assistance since the U.N. Decade of Development—that significant decisions affecting human rights regimes are taken in the World Bank, the IMF, and the regional development banks and that these must be targeted as points of potential leverage. Equally clear is the fact that multinational corporations and private banks must be brought within the range of the NGO's activities if the nongovernmental organizations are to succeed in their objectives. The Human Rights Working Group of the Coalition has devoted considerable resources to documenting the role of commercial banks, multinational corporations, and multilateral lending agencies in buttressing dictatorial regimes.

A coordinated campaign has been launched by the anti-apartheid movement to boycott commercial banks that make loans to the South African government or government-controlled corporations.[47] At the same time, the movement in support of Namibian independence has made a concerted effort to publicize and denounce multinational corporations that exploit Namibia's natural resources and pay taxes to the South African government.[48] Moreover, in the American context, the human rights NGO's have become sophisticated enough to recognize the importance, for their interests, of decisions taken in the defense, treasury, commerce, and agriculture departments as well as in a host of other federal agencies.

However, as the NGO's have had some success in achieving their goals, they have become visible and visibly threatening not only to oppressors but also to those who want to conduct "business as usual" without allowing room on their agendas for human rights issues. To illustrate this point one might cite the frequency with which Amnesty International's reports and data are cited in Congressional hearings and State Department reports as both an indicator of Amnesty International's research effectiveness and legitimacy but, at the same time, this fact marks the organization as an obvious target for the counteractions of dictatorial regimes. As a result, Amnesty has become very concerned with the need to increase the security of its files which identify individual sources of allegations of gross violations, indicate cross-references for validation of such complaints, and document the names of the tortured and the torturers in its international headquarters. A further example is the threat posed by an unlikely coalition of Chile, Argentina, the USSR, the Ukraine, and probably Iran to revoke the consultative status of the most aggressive of the human rights NGO's—Amnesty International, the International Commission of Jurists, the International League for Human Rights, the Anti-Slavery Society, and the Minority Rights Group—when their cases came up for routine review by the ECOSOC in 1977[49] and in years to come.

5. Mobilization and Recruitment of New Kinds of Members

The fifth and final major trend we perceive in human rights NGO activities concerns the mobilization and recruitment of new kinds of members to the human rights movement. Although there has as yet been no definitive research on the social backgrounds of the members and leaders of human rights NGO's, one may hazard some informed guesses. In the 1940's and 1950's the human rights NGO's, especially those based in the United States, were characterized by limited membership essentially by invitation only of prestigious persons who operated through "old boy" networks and had a marked preference for "quiet diplomacy" as their technique of operation. In this early period mass membership was not viewed as a relevant organizational resource. It was the status of the individual member, which often gained "privileged access" to authoritative decision-makers, which counted.[50] Since 1960, by contrast, and with the growth of Amnesty International, one notes a mobilization—perhaps initially unintended—of a wider and more active constituency base. In particular, we note that the American civil rights movement and the anti-Vietnam War coalition have provided a reservoir of activists prepared to channel their energies into international human rights and increasingly willing to engage in overt political demonstrations, for example, the picketing of the White House in September 1977 against President Carter's invitation to General Pinochet, General Videla, General Geisel, and other Latin American military dictators to witness the signing of the Panama Canal Treaties; the sit-ins which took place in Washington, D.C., San Francisco, and other major American cities in June 1977 and 1978 in sympathy with the Santiago sit-in at the offices of the Economic Commission for Latin America by relatives of "the disappeared"; and the demonstrations in May 1977 by members of the American Center of P.E.N. at the Iranian Embassy in protest of the Shah's treatment of writers, artists, and intellectuals.[51]

The recent tentative steps taken by scientific and professional associations on behalf of the rights of occupational colleagues also are significant. In certain respects, what we see here seems a reactivation of the conscience of the scientific community similar to that which occurred following the invention and use of the atomic bomb or that which accompanied the use of biological and chemical warfare agents in Indochina. Additionally, one must mention the efforts being made to sensitize the medical/psychiatric community to the complicity of those professions in the administration of political torture and the incarceration of political dissidents in mental institutions.[52]

Parallel efforts have been made to attract the concern of young lawyers. The legal community is a natural human rights constituency that, until recently, has been exceedingly resistant to claims made upon it by NGO's. There are illustrations, however, of this situation changing. For example, the 1976 human rights internship program funded by the Ford Foundation and administered by the University of Minnesota Law School was aimed largely at providing relevant occupational experience for young lawyers.[53] An allied experiment has been carried out by the International League for Human Rights and the Council of New York Law Associates (an association of some 1,600 young "public interest" lawyers in the New York City area) in creating a new Lawyers' Committee on International Human Rights.[54] A less formal program to engage young lawyers has been carried out by Frank Newman of Boalt Hall, the University of California at Berkeley, for several years. In this program Newman has subsidized 10 to 12 students each year so that they could attend the meetings of the U.N. Subcommission on Human Rights. "Newman's mafia," as they have come to be known, have gone on to positions and careers in which human rights issues predominate. Young Americans are also being recruited by such organizations and programs as the summer session on human rights of the International Institute of Human Rights in Strasbourg, France.[55]

Apart from these specific illustrations, the phenomenal growth of Amnesty International both in the United States and abroad (it has over 100,000 members worldwide) provides hard evidence that a large pool of potential members exists to be tapped by human rights groups. More generally, with the growth of the college-educated population since World War II and with the concomitant decline in political party identification as the organizing basis for American politics, the potential reservoir upon which to draw for new members now numbers one or more million American adults.

The Effectiveness of NGO's in Monitoring Human Rights Violations

From the perspective of social scientists the key analytical problem in dealing with human rights concerns lies in assessing the impact of all the activities engaged in by human rights NGO's. To address this question we must first examine general problems entailed in evaluating effectiveness. Then we must place our examination in the specific context of the foreign policy of the United States and the Carter Administration; through such an analysis we can draw some tentative conclusions concerning the effectiveness of human rights NGO's in this country at this time.

1. General Problems of Evaluating Effectiveness

Despite the human rights honeymoon of the Carter Administration, we feel obligated as social scientists to call attention to several caveats drawn from the study of power and influence. First, activity is not influence. Activity is a necessary precondition for influence, but it is not the same thing as influence. For example, in our earlier publications we sought to draw a distinction between zero-order and first-order activities of political groups.[56] Zero-order activities are all of those organizational efforts which seek to recruit and expand membership, generate (in the Western World) a financial resource base, and so on. An organization may be very efficient at this level, which might be termed parapolitical, and yet evidence no measurable impact on public policy or the behavior of elites. Therefore, the spectacular increase in the membership of Amnesty International-U.S.A., the large number of legal-systems analyses published by the International Commission of Jurists, or the fund-raising drives successfully conducted by the International League for Human Rights are not in themselves indices of political impact. Of course, without such organizational activity, there can be no policy impact; but even with them, there only *may* be desired influence.

A second caveat derives from a social science point of view: that there is no necessary cause-effect relationship between a political event and the activities of a political actor intended to bring about the event. That is, in a multiactor situation, in a world in which we have no direct access to the motivations and cognition of political elites, we cannot prove that the activities of human rights organizations are the determining factor in bringing about change. By way of illustration, one might cite the recent "victory for human rights" in India: the curtailment of the state of emergency and the open elections which brought the defeat of Indira Gandhi and the Congress Party. In this case the human rights NGO's might claim credit, but no social scientist could prove this fact. (But this is the generic problem for all who try to establish the causal chain from political participation to public policy.)

Elsewhere in our publications we have expended considerable time and effort in describing and evaluating how the human rights organizations evaluate themselves and appraise their own activities. Here we wish to focus on the separable problem of how the independent political analyst can try to reach some reasoned judgment.

A first problem in judging effectiveness is that there is no material product that the organization sells in a market, the allegedly "hidden hand" of which sets a variable price that supposedly puts supply and demand into equilibrium. How is one to put a price on the value of human life? And there is no way to repay a person for years of wrongful imprisonment for political thought and association. Therefore, even if the World Council of Churches seems to be making an excessive budgetary expenditure to gain the release of a small number of political prisoners and even if it is *not* successful, nevertheless, the external publicity it receives may save those prisoners from summary execution, may prevent the secret police from engaging in the worst forms of torture, or may bring even a brief pause in the regime's systematic repression. And how does one qualify such results in terms of dollars and cents?[57]

While social scientists necessarily must pursue quantitative indicators of heightening or lessening repression over time (e.g., the number of political prisoners and number of prisoners-of-conscience released, budgetary changes regarding internal security forces, and political surveillance technology), the present state of the art is such that these indicators are only of ancillary use.

A second problem derives from the fact that while mankind is unitary, the institutional world is fragmented. That is, there is a vast array of institutions that can and do impinge upon human rights, and this fact necessarily means that there is a very wide array of strategies and tactics that may be efficient. Moreover, many of these strategies are being employed simultaneously, while many have yet to be employed at all. In such a situation, how is the analyst to judge that Strategy A is more effective than Strategy B or that Tactic I is more productive of the desired outcome than Tactic II with reference to Strategy A?

Of those strategies which we know have been employed, two major ones are "the power of pitiless publicity" (and Justice Brandeis's faith in sunshine as a political disinfectant) as against that of "quiet diplomacy." The latter is and has been the preferred approach both of the Foreign Service Officer careerists and of the International Committee of the Red Cross. According to the *New York Times,* Ambassador Richard L. Sneider, a career foreign service officer and then U.S. Ambassador in Seoul, South Korea, was reportedly "infuriated" when, in 1977, a four-man Congressional delegation insisted upon face-to-face meetings with some of the dissidents struggling against the human rights denials of the Park regime. Sneider had been in his post two and a half years, a period during which serious human rights violations had occurred in South Korea. One supposes that Sneider could argue in defense of his gentlemanly diplomacy that the situation would have been far worse without his quietly holding back the forces of evil. On the other hand, one suspects that the hearings Congressman Donald Fraser held on South Korea have had far more positive results.[58]

Or one might take the example of the International Committee of the Red Cross, which undoubtedly has an impressive public image, derived in part from its work on behalf of prisoners-of-war. Nonetheless, as Thomas Buergenthal has pointed out,[59] the ICRC permitted itself to be used—whether knowingly or not—by the Nazi regime during World War II. In Sachsenhausen, a concentration camp the ICRC was always permitted to visit, the Nazis had a model medical facility (where they cured patients only to kill them later); there also were actually two concentration camps by the name of Auschwitz located three miles apart—one which the Red Cross regularly inspected and the other, the real Auschwitz, which the ICRC never saw, where the Nazis gassed their victims. The ICRC, by not exposing or being aware of this deception, lent its respectability to Hitler's Third Reich. In general the ICRC's refusal to "go public"—its reports are publicized only if the regime investigated publishes them or if the regime significantly distorts the inspection team's private evaluation of the situation—permits repressive regimes to create an appearance of openness and, thus, to gain legitimacy.

As far as we know there are as yet no systematic research reports specifying the conditions under which quiet diplomacy succeeds. Undoubtedly, there are regimes that are sensitive and responsive to these kinds of external initiatives as well as governments that are prepared to moderate their policies in order to preclude a publicity campaign; perhaps quiet diplomacy is a logical phase in which human rights NGO's must participate before going public. One organization that seems willing to explore these potentialities is the ICJ, which has employed quiet diplomacy in its delicate negotiations with the Shah of Iran concerning a movement toward a rule-of-law system of justice.[60] Yet even if the ICJ attains some of its goals here, social scientists will have to examine the total context of that success. They may, in consequence, conclude that success is contingent upon the alternative and simultaneous strategy of publicity engaged in by such organizations as the Iranian Students Association, P.E.N. International, and others.[61] Therefore, while there is a large body of testimony of victims of repression which speaks to the vital importance and efficacy of public exposure of their condition, the social scientist is obligated to conduct further research on these two alternative major strategies.

Meanwhile, the hard issues of human rights in the real world confront the researcher both with multiple groups and multiple strategies. Consequently, it may be necessary and useful to assess the effectiveness of individual strategies and/or individual groups. However, the analysis must not stop here, because in isolation, a given group or strategy may appear ineffectual or unnecessarily "costly." Nonetheless, since we are concerned with a human rights movement and its goals as focused on a particular issue, particular groups and strategies have to be analyzed as part of this total complex. What is called for are systematic case studies of specific human rights crises—Chile, southern Africa, Argentina, and the Philippines—in order to examine the relative impact of interacting groups and interacting strategies.

A third and final general problem concerning effectiveness is, of course, the fact that no group acts in isolation from the system; a human rights organization or movement acts in and as a part of an ongoing political system. Thus the human rights organizations will act both in covert and open alliance with other groups dedicated to the same goal, they will act upon those with authority (legitimized power to control the behavior of others), and they will act against and to defeat known and unknown oppressors. In this process of conflict the human rights movement or organization may acquire more and new resources. Yet, if these resources are provided, there may be no net increase in effectiveness for the simple reason that the total system has changed. The system heats up with more people and other political resources mobilized, politicized, and polarized, both on the side of those struggling to enhance human rights and among those repressing human rights. A few examples can illustrate the point. Since 1960 Amnesty International can claim increasing numbers of adopted prisoners-of-conscience released, the International Commission of Jurists can document increasing numbers of political trials observed, and the anti-apartheid movement can show a dramatic increase in the amount of publicity given to repression in southern Africa. Yet in and of themselves, such quantitative data are meaningless. They must be placed in the context of a ratio—of the growth in the political prisoner population during that same period, of the increase in the number of political trials staged during those decades, and of the growth of political repression in southern Africa since Sharpeville.

In concluding this treatment of general problems of assessing the effectiveness of human rights NGO's, it seems crucial to underline the lack of viable theories of regime change both at the international and at the national levels. Students of human rights and activists who desire to change national governmental policy and to create a more humane world order currently work in isolation from the efforts of political scientists and international relations scholars to understand system change, especially those factors which prevent a transformation to an order that values human rights. Yet it is clear that without empirically based theory to inform us, both scholars and political activists must continue to operate on the basis of ill-formulated hypotheses and intuitive guesses.

2. Evaluating Effectiveness in the Context of the Current U.S. System

Despite the underdeveloped state of political theory relevant to human rights and despite the general problems of evaluating the policy impact of human rights NGO's, it is possible to arrive at some tentative conclusions concerning the meaning of the human rights "explosion" in the United States at this time. Given the dismal record of the Nixon-Ford administrations with respect to human rights, one must credit human rights NGO's, working with sympathetic allies in Congress, with helping to place human rights on the official agenda of the nation. This is not to say that there are no other interpretations of why the United States would stress human rights at this juncture of world history. Such an emphasis can distinguish the Carter Administration from its immediate predecessors, it can help to unify the diverse elements of the Democratic Party, and it can both restore the United States to a position of moral leadership in the wake of the Vietnam War desolation and provide a new moral lance in the ideological joustings with Soviet communism. However, from one perspective, motivations are largely irrelevant. What is significant is that human rights have been placed high on the U.S. foreign policy agenda and that the NGO's are making a determined effort to keep them there.

Nonetheless, it is appropriate to examine recent domestic political history with regard to both the civil rights movement and the War Against Poverty. The primary conclusion to be drawn is that the U.S. political system has a tremendous capacity for absorbing the energies of such citizens' movements by creating the appearance without the substance of change. Two techniques of the political elite evident in those domestic struggles and available today to treat with the human rights movement in a "least costly" fashion are symbolism and co-optation.

Symbolism is a technique by which the political elite arrogates for its own use the political slogans and "signs" of a challenging counter-elite. Thus the political rhetoric on the human rights of the Carter Administration, unless accompanied by substantive policy initiatives, may prove to be nothing more than symbolism. Consequently, as monitoring agencies the human rights NGO's must direct their attention to what the Carter Administration actually does and not merely what it says it is doing.

Co-optation frequently accompanies symbolism. In the street language of young black militants, the term for the same phenomenon was "tokenism." By this term one refers to the process by which the political elite selects one or a few prominent spokespersons to represent an excluded group or policy claim in order to attempt to restore legitimacy to a decision-making institution that has come under attack for being unrepresentative, unresponsive, and unaccountable. Carter's selection and support of Andrew Young, Allard Lowenstein, and Brady Tyson may lull the human rights NGO's into a belief that they now have a share of the power.

A related cosmetic approach to change may have manifested itself in the appointment of human rights officers to the area desks of the State Department and, more recently, to the embassies in the field. At the very least, the human rights NGO's must feel some disquiet at the fact that, in many instances, the human rights officer is little more than a new title tacked onto that of the previous labor officer. While this action may be deemed an improvement over the former bureaucratic void with respect to human rights, it remains to be demonstrated just how much power and influence these new subject-matter officers will exert. Even more disquieting were rumors circulating recently among members of the established human rights community that a number of the human rights officers at the embassy level are in fact former CIA personnel. While the basis of these rumors must be investigated, if there is any substance whatever to them, it would prove a devastating comment on the Machiavellian nature of the American political elite. Alternatively, if these rumors are utterly groundless and merely reflect the unwholesome paranoia still prevalent in American politics, there still remains a genuine political problem.

Assuming the sincerity of President Carter and his top aides, that problem is one of establishing their own credibility within the government when they publicly insist on the necessity that the members of an existing organization change their behavior. Bureaucracies such as the State Department have tremendous inertia. Careerist officers will change their behavior only when they perceive that the opportunity structure and institutional incentives will in fact reward them for acting in a pro human rights fashion and penalize them for not doing so. To date there is no evidence that State Department careers have been affected in any way by the new policy declared at the top.

To discuss the problem of co-optation from a slightly different perspective, one should see that the human rights NGO's will be made less effective if their key Congressional allies are subtly co-opted by a charismatic President who seems to share their values while simultaneously insisting on "flexibility," time to work out policy options, and the virtues of positive incentives. The lessons of the civil rights struggle again are apposite: When a Chief Executive who has publicly exhibited sympathy and responsiveness comes to office, it is time to increase Congressional pressure, not to relax it. Thus it is somewhat disturbing that in the 95th Congress, many of the key Congressional leaders in the human rights effort have deferred an offensive on U.S. participation in multilateral lending agencies (a delay which resulted in the defeat of the Badillo Amendment in the Senate) so as not to "tie the President's hands."[62] And indeed a number of the established human rights NGO's have been likewise charmed into quiescent acceptance of the Presidential initiative.

Co-optation manifests a further and even more threatening danger to the position of the human rights NGO's. Here the danger is that the issue of human rights can be preempted by one or both of two conservative coalitions in American politics—coalitions which have evidenced a marked resurgence since Watergate. The first group is composed of the traditional isolationists, who represent a utopian nineteenth-century philosophy and who would use the human rights issue to deny aid to all Third World nations. The Harkin Amendment type of legislation can be employed for this alternative agenda. The second threat originates in the thinking of such groups as the Committee on the Present Danger and the Moynihan Democrats, because these groups seem to want nothing more than to reignite the Cold War. These Cold Warriors would like to seize upon human rights as an ideological counteroffensive of the "free world" against both Soviet and Chinese communism. The seriousness of this resurgence was first evidenced during the summer of 1977 in the passage of an amendment in the House of Representatives to deny any bilateral or multilateral U.S. aid to Vietnam, Cambodia, Laos, and Cuba as well as in other attempts to deny aid to Angola and Mozambique.[63] It also surfaced in the eagerness with which many U.S.-based groups have flaunted any evidence they can uncover on human rights violations in Vietnam.[64]

Apart from the above considerations, there is the remaining problem that the human rights NGO's may inadvertently contribute to the potential of other groups and coalitions to monopolize the human rights issue. The human rights NGO's have exhibited a massive growth in organizational resources within the United States in the past several years. If such growth in membership and activities outruns the capacity of the NGO's to continue their central function of credible research with cross-verification and cumulative validation, then the NGO's run the risk of discrediting themselves.

There is a final threat to the effectiveness of the human rights movement in the United States at this time, one that is made clear in the fear of Europeans and people of the Third World that the Carter Administration's human rights emphasis (and by implication, the American human rights movement) is merely the latest manifestation of American imperialism. The United States may be perceived as once again acting out of the self-chosen role of "world policeman," and the human rights NGO's may be tainted by this same perception if American official concern with human rights is wholly external. This means that the human rights NGO's must monitor violations of human rights within the United States—with respect to the final act of Helsinki, for example—and maintain their distance from the incumbent administration if they are to preserve their credibility. They must uphold universal standards universally applied, not solely American standards applied exclusively yet selectively to others.

NOTES

1. For detailed treatment of past American concern for, and involvement in, human rights see V. Van Dyke, *Human Rights, the United States and the World Community* (New York: Oxford University Press, 1970); E. Luard, "The Origins of International Concern Over Human Rights," in E. Luard (ed.), *The International Protection of Human Rights* (New York: Praeger, 1967), pp. 7-21; T. Buergenthal and J. V. Torney, *International Human Rights and International Education* (Washington, D.C.: U.S. National Commission for UNESCO, 1976), chap. 5, pp. 86-101; J. Salzberg and D. D. Young, "The Parliamentary Role in Implementing International Human Rights: A U.S. Example," 12 *Texas International Law Journal* (Spring/Summer 1977): 251-278; and D. Weissbrodt, "Human Rights Legislation and United States Foreign Policy," 7 *Georgia Journal of International and Comparative Law* (1977): 231-287.
2. See, especially, J. Salzberg and D. Young, and D. Weissbrodt, *supra* note 1.
3. From August to December 1973, Donald Fraser's subcommittee held an initial series of 15 hearings which called on 45 witnesses—representatives of human rights NGO's, scholars, State Department officials, former U.S. representatives to U.N. bodies dealing with human rights—and which eventuated in a subcommittee report ("Human Rights in the World Community: A Call for U.S. Leadership," March 27, 1974) that developed a body of recommendations "for raising the priority given to human rights in U.S. foreign policy and strengthening the capacity of international organizations to insure protection of human rights." *International Protection of Human Rights: The Work of International Organizations and the Role of U.S. Foreign Policy,* hearings before the Subcommittee on International Organizations and Movements of the Committee on Foreign Affairs, U.S. House of Representatives, 93rd Congress, 1st Session, August 1 to December 7, 1973 (Washington, D.C.: U.S. Government Printing Office, 1974). The Fraser subcommittee has continued

these hearings and, as of the summer of 1977, there were a total of approximately 50 hearings dealing with human rights violations worldwide.

4. For a detailed discussion of these Congressional measures, see D. Weissbrodt, and J. Salzberg and D. Young, *supra* note 1.

5. On the selectivity of the Third World—and, in particular, African states—see L. S. Wiseberg, "Human Rights in Africa: Toward a Definition of the Problem of a Double Standard," 4 *Issue* (Winter 1976): 3-13; W. Weinstein, "Africa's Approach to Human Rights at the United Nations," 4 *Issue* (Winter 1976): 14-21; A. G. Mower, Jr., "Human Rights in Black Africa: A Double Standard?" 9 *Human Rights Journal* (January/March 1976): 39-70; and R. Emerson, "The Fate of Human Rights in the Third World," 27 *World Politics* (January 1975): 201-226.

6. Concerning the selective condemnation of human rights violations as a tool used by both the U.S. and the USSR in the Cold War, see R. B. Bilder, "Rethinking International Human Rights: Some Basic Questions," 2 *Human Rights Journal* (1969): 569-574. We shall have more to say about the selectivity of the United States in the concluding section of this paper. Concerning the selectivity of the Soviet Union, we would like to note the position expressed by Soviet scholar V. Kartashkin (senior researcher at the Institute of State and Law in Moscow) at the summer teaching session of the International Institute of Human Rights, Strasbourg, July 1977: that human rights violations are a matter exclusively within the domestic jurisdiction of states unless and until a U.N. body determines a consistent pattern of gross violations of internationally recognized human rights. That is, thus far, southern Africa, Chile, and Israel are the only cases where an expression of international concern is legitimate; in all other cases, condemning violations constitutes unwarranted interventions into the sovereign affairs of nations.

7. M. Klare, with the assistance of D. Volman, "Carter's Arms Policy: Business as Usual," 11 *NACLA's Latin America and Empire Report* (July/August 1977): 15.

8. J. Omang, "U.S. Militarized Latin America," *Washington Post*, April 11, 1977; N. Stein and M. Klare, "Police Aid for Tyrants," in S. Weissman and Members of the Pacific Studies Center and the North American Congress on Latin America, *The Trojan Horse* (San Francisco: Ramparts Press, 1974), p. 221.

9. In 1976, a new coalition of religious, educational, civil, and labor organizations—over 30 core members and some 15 cooperating organizations—formed itself into "The Campaign to Stop Government Spying" and is conducting research into the question of the transfer of U.S. technology for surveillance and political torture. The anti-apartheid movement has been very concerned with this question in connection with southern Africa, and Latin American-oriented groups have been investigating technology transfer to, and cooperation among, countries of the southern zone.

10. Center for International Policy, 3 *International Policy Report* (January 1977): 1 and 10.

11. *Ibid.*, pp. 1-2.

12. L. Schoultz, "United States Foreign Aid and Human Rights Violations in Latin America: An Empirical Assessment," June 1977, unpublished paper.

13. Center for International Policy, *Human Rights and U.S. Foreign Assis-*

tance Program, Fiscal Year 1978, Part 1—Latin America (Washington, D.C.: The Center, 1977), p. 9.

14. H. M. Scoble, "The Politics of the Overseas Private Investment Corporation (OPIC)," paper presented at the 18th annual meeting of the International Studies Association, March 1977, St. Louis, Missouri.

15. L. S. Wiseberg, "The International Politics of Relief: A Case Study of the Relief Operations Mounted During the Nigerian Civil War (1967–1970)," Ph.D. dissertation, University of California at Los Angeles, 1973, pp. 581–587.

16. Perhaps the best current bibliography of the literature on NGO's in the human rights field are the footnotes to D. Weissbrodt, "The Role of Nongovernmental Organizations in the Implementation of Human Rights," 12 *Texas International Law Journal* (Spring/Summer 1977): 293–320.

17. See, especially, L. S. Wiseberg and H. M. Scoble, "Human Rights and Amnesty International," 413 *The Annals* (May 1974): 11–26, and H. M. Scoble and L. S. Wiseberg, "Human Rights NGO's: Notes Toward Comparative Analysis," 9 *Human Rights Journal* (1976): 611–644.

18. L. S. Wiseberg and H. M. Scoble, "The International League for Human Rights: The Strategy of a Human Rights NGO," 7 *Georgia Journal of International and Comparative Law* (1977): 289–313.

19. Many of these conferences have been noted in the *Human Rights Internet Newsletter* which began publication in July 1976.

20. Until early 1978, a small selection of the numerous press stories on human rights were reprinted bimonthly in *Writing on Human Rights,* published by Clergy and Laity Concerned, Human Rights Co-ordinating Center.

21. Evidence of this also has been documented in the *Human Rights Internet Newsletter,* which reproduces syllabi of human rights courses, and in the panels on the teaching of human rights at a variety of professional associations' annual meetings.

22. From an initial membership of 30 concerned social scientists who set up this communications network in the winter of 1976, it grew in less than two years to a membership of close to 350 academics, activists, and policy-makers.

23. 3 *Human Rights Internet Newsletter* (September 1977): 12–13.

24. This consultation, on "Human Rights and Christian Responsibility," held in October 1974 in St. Polten, Austria, produced a variety of papers in preparation for the meeting as well as reports and papers subsequent to the meeting. Among them were *Human Rights and Christian Responsibility,* 2 vols., 1974; *Report of the Consultation, St. Polten, Austria, October 21–26, 1974;* and *CCIA Newsletter*—"Human Rights: Post-Assembly Follow-up," no. 4, 1976.

25. Interview with C. R. Harper, Jr., Human Rights Resources Office for Latin America, World Council of Churches, and with D. C. Epps, executive secretary, Commission of the Churches on International Affairs, World Council of Churches, Geneva, June 1977.

26. *Ibid.*

27. H. M. Scoble and L. S. Wiseberg, "The Policy Impact of Non-Governmental International Human Rights Organizations," paper presented at a conference on International Scientific and Professional Associations and the International System, University of Pennsylvania, November 1976, and revised for publication in a volume of conference proceedings; original reference to M. G. Scully, "U.S. Scholars Step Up Human Rights Drives," *Chronicle of Higher Education,* May 9, 1977, pp. 1 and 8.

28. The International League for Human Rights, *Bulletin*, September 1970, p. 3.

29. For a detailed analysis of the League affiliates, see L. Wiseberg and H. Scoble, *supra* note 18, pp. 297-299.

30. The French League for Human Rights created in 1902 is the parent organization of both the International Federation of Human Rights (based in Paris) and the International League for Human Rights (based in New York). The European Federation, forced to disband during World War II, reestablished itself in the United States during the Nazi occupation of Europe. When it moved back to France, at the war's end, the American-based International League continued as a separate organization with its own affiliates. For more detail, see L. Wiseberg and H. Scoble, *supra* note 18, pp. 292-294.

31. Interviews with N. MacDermot, secretary general, International Commission of Jurists, Geneva, and with N. Gérard, International Association of Democratic Lawyers, Brussels, June/July 1977.

32. 2 *Human Rights Internet Newsletter* (May 1977): 23-25.

33. 3 *Human Rights Internet Newsletter* (September 1977): 18; and interview with Lelio Basso, Rome, July 1977.

34. 1 *Human Rights Internet Newsletter* (December 1976): 19-20 and 3 (September 1977): 4; also, interview with Patrick Montgomery, secretary, Anti-Slavery Society, June 1977.

35. The activities of most of these organizations are discussed in issues of the *Human Rights Internet Newsletter*.

36. Interviews with Martin Ennals, Niall MacDermot, and Ben Whitaker, summer 1977, London and Geneva.

37. Interviews with Jerome Shestack, December 1976 and July 1977, New York and Strasbourg, France.

38. Interviews with Jerome Shestack and Frank C. Newman, July 1977, Strasbourg, France.

39. This conference took place October 1-2, 1977, in New York. 3 *Human Rights Internet Newsletter* (September 1977): 34-35.

40. Interview with Leah Levin, secretary, Human Rights Committee, United Nations Association (U.K.), June 1977, London.

41. Indeed, on October 6, 1977 a National Conference on Human Rights was called in New York City by Bayard Rustin on behalf of some 35 sponsors and funded by the Ford Foundation to explore the possibilities of establishing such a leadership conference—one that not only would link human rights NGO's that had an international focus, but that also would link the American human rights movement with the civil rights movement in the United States. What will eventuate from this meeting is not, however, clear at this time.

42. Interview with Jerome Shestack, July 1977, Strasbourg, France.

43. See, for example, the study supported by the Commission of the Churches on International Affairs of the World Council of Churches—G. da Fonseca, *How to File Complaints of Human Rights Violations: A Practical Guide to Inter-Governmental Procedures* (Geneva: World Council of Churches, 1975)—intended as a handbook for NGO's in their petitions to intergovernmental organizations.

44. "A NGO Working Paper on Strengthening the Role of the United Nations in the Field of Human Rights," prepared by a working group established by the NGO Committee on Human Rights (at headquarters) and circu-

lated as a relevant memorandum for the U.N. system in the name of the undersigned organizations in consultative status with the Economic and Social Council, mimeo, New York, January 1, 1977.

45. The proposal for a U.N. High Commissioner for Human Rights—similar to the Office of U.N. High Commissioner for Refugees—was first proposed by the government of Costa Rica 15 years ago, and the proposal has been on the General Assembly agenda and extensively studied by official and nonofficial groups for several years. The difficulties that the U.N. High Commissioner for Refugees had in trying to provide protection for refugees being brutalized by the Chilean junta, and the current insurmountable problems that office faces in providing protection for South American refugees—targets of the Argentinian military regime—underline the need for a Human Rights High Commissioner.

46. On proposals for an African Human Rights Commission, see B. G. Ramcharan, "Human Rights in Africa: Whither Now?" 12 *University of Ghana Law Journal* (1975): 88–105.

47. 2 *Human Rights Internet Newsletter* (April 1977): 8–10 and 3 (September 1977): 20–21.

48. United Nations resolutions prohibit multinational corporations from dealing with the government of South Africa as if it were still the *de jure* authority for Namibia; but this had not deterred many corporations from carrying on "business as usual" in Namibia.

49. For an expanded treatment of this question, see L. Wiseberg and H. Scoble, *supra* note 18, pp. 302–305, which provides the background against which the current threat is pending. In interviews with various NGO leaders as well as U.N. officials, we found different assessments of the likelihood that the coalition would actually move forcefully this year to try and disbar NGO's.

50. This was, particularly, the case with the International League for Human Rights. See L. Wiseberg and H. Scoble, *supra* note 18, pp. 296–297.

51. As reported in the *New York Times* at the time.

52. While bodies such as the World Congress of Psychiatrists have been, until recently, particularly resistent to taking what they argued were "political stands" on human rights issues (see, for example, D. Shaw and S. Block, "Another Dark Age of Psychiatry," *The Lancet* (February 24, 1973): 418–419), the medical community clearly has been forced to reassess its support for the status quo. Thus, in the summer of 1977, at its meeting in Honolulu, the World Congress of Psychiatrists came out with a very strong statement against psychiatric abuse of political dissidents.

53. While the program has not been aimed solely at lawyers, many of those who have been selected as interns have indeed been law students.

54. See L. Wiseberg and H. Scoble, *supra* note 18, pp. 308–309.

55. The International Institute of Human Rights, created by René Cassin and located in Strasbourg—the site of the European Commission on Human Rights—runs an annual four-week summer program in which many American graduate or law students participate.

56. H. Scoble and L. Wiseberg, *supra* note 17, pp. 19–20.

57. For an elaboration of this problem, see "Amnesty International: Evaluating Effectiveness in the Human Rights Arena," *Intellect* (September/October 1976): 79–82.

58. In this context one might note the remarks of Charles Runyon at the Notre Dame symposium, April 28, 1977, concerning the administration's ar-

gument to Congress: "that quiet diplomacy is better than speaking out and that both the facts about violations and about any efforts this government might make to promote human rights are better held in confidence from the legislative branch and the people. Of course, no one should deny that quietness, tact and indirectness can often be useful diplomatic tools. The trouble was that information was usually held back out of an excess of consideration for the states concerned and for day-to-day pleasant relations."

59. Addressing a panel at the International Studies Association annual meeting, St. Louis, Missouri, March 1977.

60. Precisely what the nature of these discussions are, and what will emerge from them, is not clear.

61. This may be illustrated more concretely by reference to the domestic civil rights struggle in the United States. That is, until his assassination in 1964, Malcolm X contributed—in ways unmeasurable with scientific precision yet real nonetheless—to whatever effectiveness Martin Luther King, Jr., and the Southern Christian Leadership Conference could claim. Malcolm X so contributed because he was viewed by white governmental leaders as a "least-liked" alternative—that is, as a credible competitor to King and the SCLC for leadership of the black masses in America and as one who was perceived both as more militant (concerning the timing of desired demanded changes) and especially as more extreme in the range and radical substance of such changes. Under such conditions the political elite will choose to "recognize" and seek to bargain with the leader/spokesperson most like themselves—most moderate.

62. The Badillo Amendment refers to the amendment offered by Representative Herman Badillo (Democrat, New York) to H.R. 5262—a bill authorizing $5.2 billion over three years for the U.S. participation in the World Bank, the African Development Bank, and the Asian Development Bank. It required that U.S. representatives to these international financial institutions vote against loans to governments that violate human rights unless the loans are for projects that directly address basic human needs. Defeated in the Banking Committee, Badillo took the amendment to the floor on April 6, 1977, where it passed by a voice vote. However, on May 5, 1977, the full Senate Foreign Relations Committee approved only a very mild human rights provision in their version of H.R. 5262—one which would not prohibit a U.S. representative to an international financial institution from casting a vote in favor of a loan to a repressive regime. Subsequently, in June 1977 Senators James Abourezk and Mark Hatfield introduced an amendment on the floor of the Senate to restore the Harkin language to this International Financial Institutions bill; but it was narrowly rejected on June 14, 1977, by a vote of 50 to 43. In 1977–1978, the pro-human rights legislators in the U.S. Congress—a tiny minority at most—suffered an almost unending succession of roll-call defeats: on the Transfer Amendment (on which the Coalition for a New Foreign and Military Policy lobbied much more effectively in the first session of the 95th Congress, in 1977), on the reauthorization (and expanded mandate) for the Overseas Private Development Corporation, on the Wittsveen Supplement (to the International Monetary Fund).

63. On June 14, 1977, the Senate adopted an amendment to the International Financial Institutions Bill offered by Senator Robert Dole requiring an automatic no vote on IFI loans to the socialist countries of Indochina. A week later the House passed similar amendments, this time to the Foreign Assis-

tance Appropriations Bill (H.R. 7797), that would bar U.S. funds for "direct and indirect" aid not only to Vietnam, Laos, and Cambodia, but also to Mozambique, Angola, Cuba, and Uganda. On all of these votes, human rights violations were cited as important factors. (The situation was slightly altered when, in the final act before the summer recess, the Senate deleted the House language from the Foreign Assistance Appropriations Bill that would bar U.S. funds for "indirect" aid to the above-mentioned seven countries; and, in another vote, an amendment by Senator Dick Clark was carried which allows the President, with Congressional approval, to waive the prohibition of direct aid to Angola and Mozambique.) Additionally, the Ashbrook Amendment to the Foreign Relations Authorization Bill (H.R. 6689) which passed in the House on May 4, 1977, prohibited even "negotiating reparations, aid or any other form of payment" to Vietnam, and was intended as a signal to the U.S. negotiators then talking with the Vietnamese in Paris. While in the Senate, the Glenn Amendment to the International Development Assistance Authorization Bill (H.R. 6714), which passed on June 15, 1977, barred the use of funds "for assistance to and or reparations for" Vietnam, Cambodia, or Laos.

64. The question of whether, and to what extent, there are gross violations of human rights in Vietnam has become a heated issue within the human rights movement in the United States. See, e.g., J. Finn, "Fighting Among the Doves," 20 *World View* no. 4 (April 1977): 4–9.

Bibliography

ABRAMS, M. B., "U.N. and Human Rights," *Foreign Affairs*, January, 1969, pp. 363-374.

BUERGENTHAL, T., "Implementing the UN Racial Convention," 12 *Texas International Law Journal* (1977): 187-221.

——, "International and Regional Human Rights Law and Institutions: Some Examples of their Interaction," 12 *Texas International Law Journal* (1977): 321-330.

CAREY, J., *United Nations Protection of Civil and Political Rights* (New York, 1970).

CLARK, R., *United Nations High Commissioner for Human Rights* (The Hague, 1972).

COMMISSION TO STUDY THE ORGANIZATION OF PEACE, *The United Nations and Human Rights* (New York, 1968).

FAWCETT, J. E. I., *The Application of the European Convention on Human Rights* (Oxford and New York, 1969).

FORSYTHE, D., *Humanitarian Politics: The International Committee of the Red Cross* (Baltimore, 1977).

GREEN, J. F., "Changing Approaches to Human Rights: The United Nations, 1954 and 1974," 12 *Texas International Law Journal* (1977): 223-237.

JACOBS, F. G., *The European Convention on Human Rights* (Oxford, 1975).

LILLICH, R. B., (ed.), *Humanitarian Intervention and the United Nations* (Charlottesville, 1973).

LUARD, D. E. T. (ed.), *International Protection of Human Rights* (New York, 1967).

ROBERTSON, A. H., *Human Rights in the World* (Manchester, 1972).

——, *Human Rights in Europe* (Manchester, 1977).

SCHROTH, P. W., *Racial Discrimination: the United States and the International Convention* (New York, 1973).

SCHWELB, E., "The International Measures of Implementation of the International Covenant on Civil and Political Rights and of the Optional Protocol," 12 *Texas International Law Journal* (1977): 141-186.

SOHN, L., "The Human Rights Law of the Charter," 12 *Texas International Law Journal* (1977): 129-140.

SOHN, L. B., and Buergenthal, T., *International Protection of Human Rights* (Indianapolis, 1973).

WEISSBRODT, D., "The Role of International Nongovernmental Organizations in the Implementation of Human Rights," 12 *Texas International Law Journal* (1977): 293-320.

WILLIAMS, A., "The European Convention on Human Rights: A New Use?" 12 *Texas International Law Journal* (1977): 279-292.

WORLD ASSOCIATION OF LAWYERS, COMMITTEE ON HUMAN RIGHTS, *The Ratification of International Human Rights Treaties* (Washington: World Association of Lawyers, 1976), p. 78.

PART SIX
American Foreign Policy and Human Rights

Introduction

ONE OF THE MOST PROMINENT FEATURES OF THE ADMINISTRATION OF Jimmy Carter has been the emphasis accorded to human rights. The President and the Secretary of State, Cyrus Vance, have given voice to the firm belief that human rights should be an important factor in the formulation and implementation of U.S. foreign policy. According to Carter and Vance, consideration for human rights should pervade bilateral relations with other nations and policy in such areas as arms transfer, foreign aid, and the North-South dialogue. In regard to human rights, then, the Carter foreign policy has represented a conscious shift away from that of former Secretary of State Henry Kissinger.

The negligible role played by the United States in promoting international human rights under previous administrations is well documented in the chapters by Roberta Cohen and Donald Fraser in this section, by Laurie Wiseberg and Harry Scoble in Part Five, and by Richard Lillich in Part Seven. Although Kissinger respected the principle of human rights, he felt that there were limits to human rights policy-making. For him, the responsibility of the policy-maker was to strike a "balance between what is desirable and what is possible." He believed that the United States must accommodate itself to a world in which four-fifths of the nation-states are controlled by some form of authoritarian regime. "Quiet but forceful diplomacy"—the code words for procrastination on humanitarian issues—was the best means to further respect for human rights in the international community.

But already in 1973, in reaction to Kissinger's *Realpolitik* and disinterest toward human rights concerns, both Congress and nongovernmental organizations were galvanized into specific action on the human rights front. Through a series of statutes linking foreign assistance or trade benefits to the status of human rights in foreign countries, Congress laid the basis for future human rights policy. Congress focused not only on security assistance and economic aid, but also enacted provisions aimed at particular foreign states. Both Cohen and Fraser as well as Wiseberg and Scoble and Lillich emphasize the importance of the Congressional initiative on human rights legislation during this period.

Of special merit is the report entitled *Human Rights and the World Community: A Call for U.S. Leadership,* which resulted from the original hearings on human rights and U.S. foreign policy held by Congressman Donald Fraser's House Subcommittee on International Organizations in 1974. This report contains recommendations for increasing the priority given to human rights in U.S. foreign policy and for strengthening the United Nations and other international organizations working in the field of human rights. Among the 29 recommendations they included in the report, the Fraser subcommittee urged the State Department to reorganize itself to ensure that human rights issues would receive a hearing at various policy-making levels. In 1975, in response to these recommendations, the State Department organized the Office of Coordinator for Humanitarian Affairs, appointed an assistant legal advisor for human rights, and assigned a human rights officer to each of the regional or geographic bureaus.

As both Cohen and Fraser make clear, the Carter Administration has enlarged and upgraded the Office of Coordinator of Human Rights and Humanitarian Affairs. Located on the all-important seventh floor of the State Department Building, the office has a relatively large staff of nearly 30 who have divided their responsibilities according to special issue areas: arms sales, the United Nations and its related agencies, international lending and financial institutions, the CSCE and the Helsinki declaration, nongovernmental organizations, country and regional matters, and refugee affairs.

The Coordinator of Human Rights reports directly to the Deputy Secretary of State. As human rights are a central concern of President Carter, the coordinator's office possesses considerable clout in the decision-making process. One of its primary functions is to make itself felt in the policy-making apparatus, in the planning and development of contingency courses, and in other areas of foreign policy where human rights input is relevant. This does not mean that human rights concerns are overriding in each case, but it does mean that they are considered and taken into account at the stages where policy is formulated. Thus, under the Carter Administration, an institutional structure has become effective which gives U.S. foreign policy-makers the opportunity to be informed about the human rights implications of their actions.

With the establishment of the Office of the Coordinator for Human Rights and Humanitarian Affairs and numerous other committees and subcommittees, human rights machinery has been set up in the Executive Branch to implement a human rights policy. The success of American human rights policy will depend in part on how effectively this machinery functions in devising and executing strategies. However, as Cohen points out, human rights concerns cut across many government agencies. While the State Department has responsibility for coordinating human rights policy, the decisions of other departments and agencies clearly affect the pursuit of human rights goals. For example, U.S. policies in trade, aid, finance, and technology transfer either promote or hinder social and economic rights of individuals in other countries.

A linkage also exists between arms sales and military training programs abroad and their effect on the human rights performance of aid-recipient countries. Cohen and other authors in this volume such as Wiseberg and Scoble suggest that the true depth of the U.S. commitment will be measured by how forcefully human rights objectives are pursued when advocates of that commitment are confronted with conflicting political, military, and economic priorities. Wiseberg also argues that the American government is still not adequately organized or oriented to fully implement human rights policy-making, and she calls for the formation of new institutions and instruments in the promotion of human rights. For example, Cohen, and Wiseberg and Scoble earlier in this volume, maintain that career foreign service officers are still resistant to placing human rights concerns high on the nation's foreign policy agenda.

Fraser's paper focuses on Congress's role in the making of human rights policy. One of the most interesting issues raised by Fraser is the tension that exists within Congress and also between Congress and the Executive Branch over human rights. Disconcerting alliances have formed within Congress between conservatives concerned with human rights violations in communist nations and liberals who are more upset by action in right-wing dictatorships. Liberals in Congress generally feel strongly about human rights and arms transfers, while conservatives look toward human rights policy as a means of cutting multilateral and bilateral development assistance. Conflicts between the Carter Administration and Congress have developed, particularly over the issue of punitive actions in the form of aid restrictions against countries which have openly violated human rights.

The principal issue for Congress is whether the Administration is serious about its commitment to human rights and will use aid cuts to back up its policy. The Administration, on the other hand, is concerned with whether Congress will yield the initiative in the human rights field and allow the Executive Branch to undertake initiatives on behalf of human rights short of aid cuts. Fraser supports a "low profile" Congressional policy giving President Carter an opportunity to work out a human rights policy and a reasonable period of time in which to achieve results. Earlier in this volume Wiseberg and Scoble argue that Congressional leaders are being co-opted by the President and that this is the time to increase Congressional pressure, not to relax it.

Both Cohen and Fraser agree that difficult decisions are required if the United States is to meet the challenge of its professed human rights policy. The authors underscore the importance of the Administration's preference for positive rather than punitive measures to promote human rights. Officials in the coordinator's office argue that punitive measures, such as cutting off military or economic aid or making public denunciations, tend to alienate governments and ultimately may prove to be counterproductive. They have suggested that the United States should use the carrot as well as the stick approach to encourage favorable trends in the protection of human rights. Among the positive enforcements that ought to be pursued are the offering of aid, credits, trading concessions, and favorable votes in multilateral institutions to states working to eliminate repression. The United States also might undertake efforts to ensure a more equitable distribution of economic benefits to the peoples of less-developed countries, to promote cultural and educational exchange with countries that generally are considered to be humane and democratic, and to avoid contact and identification with representatives of repressive governments.

Both Cohen and Fraser think that persuasion and negotiation are the instruments that the United States should employ in the implementation of its human rights policy. It is this theme along with the call for newly strengthened institutions and instruments for the promotion of human rights that characterize the chapters in Part Six.

10: Human Rights Decision-Making in the Executive Branch: Some Proposals for a Coordinated Strategy

ROBERTA COHEN

I. Introduction

This country's "commitment to human rights," President Jimmy Carter said at his inauguration, "must be absolute."[1] These words ushered in a new foreign policy which, for the first time in U.S. history, has made the international protection of human rights a "central concern"[2] of the Administration.

The impetus for this policy originated with Congress several years ago during the Nixon and Ford administrations. In reaction to the moral nadir to which the nation plummeted in the aftermath of the Vietnam War and the Watergate scandal, and in response to Henry Kissinger's *realpolitik*, members of Congress advocated a foreign policy true to America's traditional values, namely, respect for individual freedom and human rights. They argued that blatant U.S. support of unpopular police states had produced long-term negative results, while a policy intended to advance freedom internationally would serve the national interest.[3] Specifically, Congress enacted legislation prohibiting U.S. military[4] and economic[5] aid to governments brutalizing their populations. In the Congressional view, both practical politics and moral and legal imperatives dictated U.S. world leadership in the human rights area.

With President Carter's commitment to this view, the new Administration set out to define human rights, to find methods of implementing that definition in foreign policy, and to reconcile its objectives with conflicting governmental priorities. At the initiative of the President and Secretary of State Cyrus Vance, human rights machinery was established in the Executive Branch to institutionalize and implement this new undertaking.[6] Staff members in the White House and National Security Council were assigned to human rights issues. The President appointed the first Assistant Secretary of State for Human Rights. The Policy Planning Staff was directed to formulate "broad human rights policy," while geographic bureaus were instructed to develop strategy papers on the key human rights problems in their areas. An Interagency Committee on Human Rights and Foreign Assistance was created within the State Department, and the Office of Coordinator for Human Rights and Humanitarian Affairs was enlarged and upgraded. The Foreign Service Institute began its first human rights training course. Finally, human rights officers were dispatched to embassies abroad.

The complexity of this undertaking is becoming apparent. Rhetoric concerning human rights is one thing; operational policy is another. This paper will trace the origins and development of human rights machinery under the Nixon and Ford administrations, describe and assess the Carter Administration's human rights machinery, evaluate the obstacles confronting Carter's efforts, and make recommendations to ensure an effective and lasting impact on U.S. foreign policy.

II. Origins of Human Rights Machinery under the Nixon and Ford Administrations

The negligible role of the United States in promoting international human rights under the Nixon Administration has been well documented.[7] In his confirmation hearings before the Senate in 1973, Secretary of State Henry Kissinger rejected the inclusion of human rights objectives in American foreign policy:

> I believe it is dangerous for us to make the domestic policy of countries around the world a direct objective of American foreign policy.... The protection of basic human rights is a very sensitive aspect of the domestic jurisdiction of ... governments.[8]

During the Nixon-Ford years, consequently, the United States did not use its influence to prevent or ameliorate human rights violations abroad.[9] United States representatives seldom spoke out either in public or at the United Nations to condemn violations; they even appeared reluctant to advocate human rights objectives in quiet diplomacy. Countries that regularly violated human rights did not receive one less measure of United States aid. Nor did the United States play a prominent part in promoting human rights at the United Nations or the Organization of American States. The United States even failed to ratify the leading human rights conventions. And in its own State Department, it relegated human rights concerns to an obscure office with limited staff and virtually no influence.

The massive bureaucracy being created by the Carter Administration to advance human rights stands in stark contrast to the absence of such machinery in previous years. At the beginning of 1974 there was only one full-time human rights officer in the entire Executive Branch.[10] This lone occupant of the human rights desk sat in the State Department's Bureau of International Organization Affairs and was responsible for preparing U.S. government positions on human rights issues at the United Nations.

The Office of the Legal Advisor, which had responsibility in this area, had no staff person specifically assigned to the human rights area.[11] Although office memoranda frequently expressed the view that the United States had "a legal obligation to promote respect for human rights,"[12] this opinion carried no weight with Kissinger's State Department.

In the absence of leadership from the Executive Branch, Congressional pressure became the catalyst for the introduction of human rights machinery into the Executive Branch. In 1973 Congressman Donald Fraser, Chairman of the Subcommittee on International Organizations and Movements of the House Foreign Affairs Committee, held extensive hearings to examine the role of the U.S. government in the protection of international human rights.[13] The subcommittee summarized its findings as follows:

> The human rights factor is not accorded the high priority it deserves in our country's foreign policy.... The State Department... has taken the position that human rights is a domestic matter.... When charges of serious violations of human rights do occur, the most that the Department is likely to do is make private inquiries.... Unfortunately, the prevailing attitude has led the United States into embracing governments which practice torture and unabashedly violate almost every human rights guarantee pronounced by the world community.... A higher priority for human rights in foreign policy is both morally imperative and practically necessary.[14]

The subcommittee's report, entitled "Human Rights in the World Community: A Call for U.S. Leadership" (March 27, 1974), called upon the Department of State to upgrade the human rights component in foreign policy. In particular, it proposed human rights impact statements, forceful private diplomacy, public condemnations, raising of human rights issues at the United Nations and, finally, the suspension of military and economic aid to governments that persistently abuse the rights of their citizens.

To ensure that human rights issues would be treated as "a regular part" of policy-making, the subcommittee recommended the creation of an office for human rights within the State Department, the assignment of human rights officers to each regional bureau, and the appointment of an assistant legal advisor for human rights.[15]

Both houses of Congress initiated action in support of these recommendations. The House Foreign Affairs Committee introduced a "Sense of Congress" amendment to the Foreign Assistance Act which would prohibit military assistance to governments grossly violating human rights. By joint action of Congress this restriction was incorporated into the 1974 Foreign Assistance Act.[16] Additional bills and amendments were introduced in both houses urging the creation of a human rights office in the State Department.[17]

In response to this accelerating Congressional pressure, Deputy Secretary of State Robert Ingersoll submitted a memorandum to Secretary Kissinger in 1974[18] which noted that "violations of human rights abroad are becoming an increasingly urgent problem," primarily because "Congress is beginning to insist that military and economic aid be reduced when authoritarian regimes with which we are identified commit violations." It warned that "if the Department did not place itself ahead of the curve on this issue, Congress would take the matter out of the Department's hands."

As a result of Congressional pressure the State Department requested its embassies in countries receiving U.S. aid to prepare reports on human rights conditions in accordance with the terms of the Foreign Assistance Act.[19] In addition, it instructed its ambassadors to explain the new prohibitions to governments guilty of violations. It also set up rudimentary machinery to strengthen human rights organization in the department.[20] It promoted the lone occupant of the human rights desk to Deputy Director for Human Rights Affairs, assigned a second officer in the International Organizations Bureau to human rights issues, and appointed an Assistant Legal Advisor for Human Rights. And, most significantly, the department designated human rights officers in each regional or geographic bureau who were to be responsible for bilateral relations and in some functional bureaus, such as policy planning, security assistance, Congressional relations, and the Agency for International Development (AID). Finally, in 1975, the department created the Office of Coordinator for Humanitarian Affairs with overall responsibility for human rights and refugee matters.[21]

The impact of this new machinery on foreign policy turned out to be minimal. Two main obstacles impeded its influence. First, none of the human rights officers designated were senior level officers who could guarantee that human rights factors would be given adequate consideration in policy planning.[22] Second, the human rights officers designated in the regional bureaus and in the Humanitarian Affairs Office lacked training in or a real commitment to human rights, while those in the regional bureaus were not even expected to devote full time to human rights.[23] The department simply gave additional titles to foreign service officers who were already working in these bureaus and whose main instructions were geared to other foreign policy objectives and to maintaining amicable relations with the governments in their areas. Consequently, most human rights officers paid scant attention to human rights concerns.

In fact, when Congress called upon the Humanitarian Affairs Office or the regional bureaus to testify on human rights conditions in countries receiving U.S. military aid, the officers usually acted as apologists for the states concerned.[24] For example, in hearings on Paraguay in 1976 the Deputy Coordinator for Human Rights and the Deputy Assistant Secretary for InterAmerican Affairs both defended the Stroessner dictatorship by refusing to make a determination that it was consistently violating human rights.[25] Even in the face of evidence of egregious abuses, State Department officers continued to deny the existence of violations and to oppose any action that would impair bilateral relations.

Of course, the most powerful obstacle to the inclusion of human rights considerations in foreign policy was the low priority given human rights by the Secretary of State. A most dramatic example occurred when the secretary publicly rebuked the U.S. Ambassador to Chile for raising human rights issues in private military aid discussions with Chilean officials.[26] Another striking incident occurred when he advised President Ford not to meet with exiled Russian author Alexander Solzhenitzyn in the interests of détente.[27] The secretary's adamant discouragement of initiatives on behalf of human rights reverberated throughout the State Department and intimidated the human rights bureaucracy. It therefore was not surprising that the Office of Humanitarian Affairs, created to deal with human rights and refugee questions, for the most part sidestepped the issue of human rights and focused its attention almost exclusively on the Vietnam refugee problem.[28]

Policy planning staff proposals to promote human rights also were rejected by the secretary. Even when one study concluded that "the historic image of the United States as the supporter of freedom is being eroded by a counter-image of the United States as an ally of tyrannical regimes,"[29] Secretary Kissinger took no steps to disassociate the United States from such regimes. On the contrary, he disassociated the State Department from Congress, in particular, concerning Congressional decisions to reduce military and economic aid to countries violating human rights. This in fact became the subject of an unpublished memorandum by the Legal Office, which urged that "our diplomats should be firmly instructed never to place the 'blame' on the Congress," thereby implying that "although the Executive Branch understands why repression is necessary, the emotional Congress... may do something irresponsible."[30]

Henry Kissinger made clear throughout his term in office that he would counter any Congressional human rights initiatives which offended foreign governments. In 1975 the secretary forbade the release of a State Department-prepared report to Congress on human rights conditions in aid-recipient countries. Kissinger, in quashing the report's publication, affirmed that "neither the U.S. security interest nor the human rights cause would be served" by singling out individual states for "public obloquy."[31]

In 1976, when Congress compelled the department to submit reports under a new Foreign Assistance Act,[32] the department's description of human rights in five countries (Argentina, Haiti, Indonesia, Iran, and Peru) was clearly "censored" so as not to reveal the full extent of violations.[33]

During the Kissinger years the creation of human rights machinery in the State Department did not result in a fair hearing for human rights issues. Of course, some courageous voices did begin to be heard in the State Department on behalf of human rights, serving to exert some influence on foreign policy. For example, State Department testimony before Congress was notably candid on South Korea, and Congress subsequently reduced military aid;[34] the department did arrange the Bukovsky-Corvalan prisoner exchange;[35] private pressures were put on Chile and other governments with particularly egregious records;[36] and toward the end of his term, Secretary Kissinger did speak of a U.S. commitment to human rights at governmental conferences in Lusaka, London, and Santiago.[37] Nevertheless, the predominant initiatives for advancing human rights originated with and were carried out by Congress. It was the Congress which issued reports advocating a higher priority for human rights in U.S. foreign policy; it was Congress which recommended the creation of human rights machinery in the State Department; it was Congress which enacted laws curtailing U.S. economic and military aid to countries seriously violating human rights; it was Congress which held extensive hearings on human rights conditions in states receiving U.S.

aid; and it was Congress which reduced U.S. military assistance to Chile, Uruguay, and South Korea on human rights grounds.

III. The Carter Administration

President Carter distinguished himself immediately from his predecessors by making the human rights policy originated by Congress the most visible and vocal aspect of his foreign policy. His inaugural address signaled the beginnings of Executive Branch leadership in this area:

> Because we are free we can never be indifferent to the fate of freedom elsewhere. Our moral sense dictates a clearcut preference for those societies which share with us an abiding respect for individual human rights.... Our commitment to human rights must be absolute.[38]

Thereafter the President forcefully reiterated this pledge in almost all his public addresses and statements to the press.[39] At the same time he repudiated the arguments put forward by previous administrations to justify their nonaction on human rights issues. First, President Carter attacked the domestic jurisdiction obstacle utilized by his predecessors. He argued that the United States has both a "legal right" and responsibility, under the U.N. Charter and international law, to speak out against human rights violations.[40] He told the United Nations that "no member of the United Nations can claim that mistreatment of its citizens is solely its own business.... All the signatories of the United Nations Charter have pledged themselves to observe and to respect basic human rights." (The President further emphasized to the U.N. members that the U.S. obligation is embodied in its own law, because the 1976 Foreign Assistance Act requires the United States "to promote the increased observance of internationally recognized human rights by all countries.")

Second, the President rejected the famous Kissinger "linkage" argument which held that the promotion of international human rights would jeopardize other foreign policy objectives and thereby should not be pursued.[41] The President affirmed that his Administration would press for human rights goals simultaneously with and independent of efforts to meet political, economic, and military goals. The most striking manifestation of this new position was the President's human rights offensive against the USSR while preparations were in progress for U.S.-Soviet talks on strategic arms limitations.[42]

Third, the President made it clear that even if the human rights commitment strains bilateral relations, the United States will not "back down" on its pledge.[43] He asserted: "If we stand for something we ought to be forceful about it. We might win some and lose some in relationships with other countries."[44]

Fourth, the President rejected the position that U.S. efforts to arouse the consciousness of the world about basic human rights will lead to increased repression. "In the long run," he asserted, "this emphasis on human rights will be beneficial for those who desire free speech and an enhancement of their own human freedoms."[45] "Détente," in his view, is not the only means of achieving human rights progress: U.S. pressure also will compel change. He noted, "It is a mistake to undervalue the power of words and of the ideas that words embody."[46]

Finally, the President asserted that a foreign policy based on fundamental American values will serve the U.S. national interest. At Notre Dame he spoke of the importance to America's future of expanding democracy and freedom throughout the world and of regaining America's lost "moral stature."[47] In his first public address as Secretary of State, Cyrus Vance expanded upon this theme:

> We seek these goals because... we too will benefit. Our own well-being, and even our security, are enhanced in a world that shares common freedoms.... Let us remember that we always risk paying a serious price when we become identified with repression.[48]

Implicit in these statements is a growing ideological commitment to the view that standing for something compatible with America's own best traditions will be beneficial to the United States as a nation and to its place in the world.

The conceptual base established by the President to support and sustain the new policy was translated into action almost immediately. In an abrupt departure from the past the State Department denounced the communist government in Czechoslovakia for harassing intellectuals agitating for liberal reforms.[49] It also sent a series of sharp protests to Moscow on behalf of Soviet dissidents.[50] The President himself sent an open letter to Soviet physicist Andrei Sakharov promising to "use our good offices to seek the release of prisoners of conscience."[51] And in sharp contrast to President Ford's refusal to meet Alexander Solzhenitsyn, former Soviet prisoner Vladimir Bukovsky was invited to the White House.[52] The President and Secretary of State publicly condemned human rights abuses in Cuba, the USSR, Uganda, and South Korea.[53]

In an unprecedented move the Administration announced military aid cuts to Argentina, Uruguay, and Ethiopia on human rights grounds.[54] It secured Congressional repeal of the Byrd Amendment, thereby permitting the prohibition of the importation of chrome from Rhodesia.[55]

Vigorous efforts to promote human rights by quiet diplomacy were undertaken in numerous countries.[56] The State Department released surprisingly candid human rights reports on 82 countries receiving U.S. military aid.[57] Finally, the President announced his intention to seek Senate ratification of U.N. and OAS human rights treaties and made proposals before each body to further human rights.[58]

This revolution in American diplomacy naturally provoked strong reaction both at home and abroad. Initially, America was applauded for championing human rights.[59] The policy was hailed for raising the world's level of consciousness, for instilling hope in millions of people, and for giving powerful impetus to human rights movements aboard. Heartening reports were forthcoming from a number of countries indicating that repressive practices had been eased in response to the U.S. campaign; significant numbers of political prisoners were reported to have been released and long overdue judicial reforms enacted.[60]

At the same time many troubling questions were raised about the new policy. Critics favoring stronger action characterized the policy as mere "rhetoric" with few punitive measures to back it up.[61] Others described the policy as politically selective and conveniently focused on the USSR and other communist countries.[62] Still others pointed to what appeared to be a double standard, one for countries of strategic importance to the United States and the other for countries of more marginal interest.[63] These critics would note that while the United States has cut aid to Argentina, Uruguay, and Ethiopia, it has not recommended reductions for South Korea, the Philippines, or Iran, all countries where strategic interests conflicted with human rights concerns. As one critic warned:

> The Carter Administration runs the risk of dividing the world into two categories: countries unimportant enough to be hectored about human rights and countries important enough to get away with murder.[64]

Doubts also were raised as to whether the positive changes reported were real improvements or temporary facades to ensure continued U.S. military and economic support.[65]

In addition, strong objections were voiced by those governments against whom the policy was directed. When some such nations even took punitive action against the United States,[66] the question arose as to whether United States policy was proving counterproductive. Clearly there are many difficulties in translating moral principles into operational policy. And the setbacks encountered by the new Administration did prove greater than anticipated. Brazil, for example, canceled its mutual defense agreement with the United States, while other Latin American countries repudiated future United States military aid. The USSR warned that continued human rights criticism would jeopardize the SALT talks. Uganda threatened the safety of resident Americans after the United States condemned Ugandan human rights practices.

While moral principles tended to sound absolute when enunciated, there are definite limits to what a policy based on them can accomplish. Whereas in some instances there would be significant progress, in others the obstacles would render the policy futile or even harmful. Consequently, the President has warned against fashioning policy out of "rigid moral maxims."[67]

It was apparent that Presidential rhetoric and the sequence of actions that followed were but the rudimentary beginnings of what could be termed a human rights policy. Trial and error on an ad hoc basis was a more apt description of the Carter Administration's early efforts. The numerous clarifications issued by the President and Secretary of State in explanation of U.S. actions underscored this unsettled situation. Secretary Vance, for example, asserted in April 1977, after several months of human rights initiatives, that "a sure formula for defeat of our goals would be a rigid, hubristic attempt to impose our values on others."[68] He then emphasized that no simple formulas could solve the complex problem of human rights rapidly. Improving conditions around the world would require thoughtful long-term solutions.

While the failure of human rights policy under the Nixon and Ford administrations was due primarily to Executive sabotage of human rights initiatives, it became evident that the success of human rights initiatives would *now* depend on carefully designed efforts of those in the bureaucracy assigned to formulate and execute this new undertaking. It would be the responsibility of these officials to grapple with the thorny issues that was rendering the policy's application difficult. While Presidential support hopefully would remain behind human rights efforts, it would be up to those in the bureaucracy to define the goals and limits of the new policy, find appropriate methods for carrying it out, and reconcile its objectives with other foreign policy priorities. The effectiveness of the undertaking would depend ultimately on the adequacy of the human rights machinery created in the Executive Branch to accomplish this awesome task and the acceptability and support given this machinery by the rest of the government.

IV. Development of Human Rights Machinery under the New Administration

The Administration moved quickly to expand the human rights machinery of earlier years in order to build the institutional base necessary for a long-term human rights policy. In comparison with that existing during the Kissinger years, a massive human rights bureaucracy was created. While it is too early to evaluate this bureaucracy's impact, it is important and timely to study the structure and functions of the new machinery, to assess its limitations and strengths, and to make recommendations to guarantee its powerful and lasting influence on foreign policy planning. This section will examine and comment on the new machinery, devoting special attention to the policy planning staff, the regional bureaus, and the Bureau of Human Rights and Humanitarian Affairs in the Department of State. In the final analysis the success of the new policy will depend on how effectively this machinery functions in devising and executing strategies to achieve improvements in human rights internationally.

A. *The National Security Council and White House*

For the first time the National Security Council and White House have been assigned to human rights issues.[69] National Security Advisor Zbigniew Brzezinski has directed a staff member in the council's office of "global issues" to focus on human rights. In the White House a public relations officer has been appointed as liaison with non-governmental groups and the public. However significant these designations may prove, though, they are not adequate to the momentous task of human rights policy coordination required in the Executive Branch. While the State Department has responsibility for coordinating human rights policy and foreign policy decisions, the decisions of other departments and agencies might adversely affect the pursuit of human rights goals. Therefore, consideration should be given to the appointment of a special assistant in the White House to coordinate the human rights decisions of all federal agencies whose policies affect human rights.[70] The assistant would assess the impact of trade aggreements, weapons sales, grants-in-aid, and other decisions on human rights concerns and would work closely with the assistant secretary for human rights in the State Department who performs a coordinating role in that agency.

The designation of a special assistant in the White House would ensure a fair hearing for human rights in the decision-making of all government departments and agencies and would provide the broad overview necessary for the full integration of human rights objectives in foreign policy.

B. The Department of State

1. Policy Planners

Secretary Vance, at the beginning of the Carter Administration, directed the policy planning staff to "formulate broad human rights policy."[71] If concepts of human rights are to become "as integral to American foreign policy as is Marxism-Leninism to Soviet... operations and planning,"[72] then many complex questions will have to be grappled with and resolved to the advantage of human rights. Some of the thornier issues requiring attention by policy-planners are outlined below.

a. Definition of human rights. To begin with, policy-planners must define what is meant by human rights. In traditional U.S. usage, human rights has meant civil and political liberties. The Foreign Assistance Act of 1976 defines "internationally recognized human rights" in civil and political terms; in particular, it specifies denial of the right to life, systematic use of torture, and prolonged detention without trial.[73] State Department reports to Congress under this act are similarly framed in civil and political terms, and aid cutoffs are mandated on the basis of consistent abuse of civil and political rights.

However, policies based narrowly on Western concepts of political freedom are likely to neglect the vast range of economic and social rights that are guaranteed in international human rights agreements[74] and the fulfillment of which is crucial to the majority of the world's population. Secretary Vance has described the problem for U.S. policy: "If, for instance, we reduce aid to a government which violates the political rights of its citizens, do we not risk penalizing the hungry and poor" whose economic and social rights also deserve fulfillment?"[75]

In an effort to resolve this dilemma the secretary has announced that the United States will seek to promote three categories of rights: the right to be free from "governmental violation of the integrity of the person," the right to enjoy civil and political liberties, and the right to "such vital needs as food, shelter, health care, and education."[76] This all-encompassing definition has established the foundation for U.S. policy to further economic and social as well as civil and political rights. It is to be hoped that this definition will help to bridge the gap between Western and Third World concepts of human rights and also to spur development of strategies to promote both categories of rights.

b. Promotion of economic rights. To foster basic economic rights, planners must be willing to advocate measures which, at times, will run counter to U.S. economic interests at home and abroad. For example, they will have to propose cutting aid and credits to governments which fail to promote economic and social justice for their people. They will have to ensure that assistance programs eliminate the inequity frequently associated with past programs which benefited the rich more than the needy.[77] They will have to ensure U.S. commitment to and constructive participation in economic and trade discussions involved in creating a more humane international economic order.[78] "A peaceful world cannot long exist one-third rich and two-thirds hungry," the President has warned.[79] Furthermore, planners will have to study the effects of U.S. trade and investment abroad, particularly if they have adverse consequences for economic well-being. In South Africa, for example, policies should be revamped to link investments to the promotion of racial justice.[80] Finally, economic aid will have to be increased to help the world's poorest people.

c. Balancing rights priorities. At the same time, a balance should be struck between the promotion of economic and social and civil and political rights. If economic assistance is to be granted to a repressive regime, it also should be used as leverage to improve political rights. A road project to help farmers bring their produce to markets should be screened to ensure that the main purpose of the road is not to serve police or military forces. In multilateral development agencies, the United States also should promote discussion of civil and political abuses in the context of development programs. The United States could propose the inclusion of human rights considerations in reports on conditions of development lending. Finally, the United States could further exert its influence to encourage loans to countries observing both categories of rights.[81]

d. Human rights and national security. The relationship, which has long been ignored, between national security interests and human rights should be redefined. National security interests often have been given as the basis for supporting repressive regimes. This rationale may not withstand analysis. Planners may well find that national security is better served through promotion of human rights values. For example, improving human rights conditions in South Korea will, in fact, strengthen the U.S. security position. Conversely, continued repression will make it increasingly difficult for South Korea to rally its people in the event of an attack from the North. Similarly, support of majority rule in southern Africa may promote U.S. security interests far better than bolstering unpopular white minority regimes. In the case of Iran, planners should seriously question whether U.S. security interests will be served by the provision of massive weapons to a "one-bullet" dictatorship in which domestic opposition is growing. Short-run gains arising from association with repressive regimes should be appraised constantly in light of long-term losses from such association. Whatever the outcome, it is clear that practical politics mandate inclusion of human rights considerations in national security deliberations.[82]

Awareness by the United States that its military aid programs have bolstered repressive, unstable regimes has prompted some new policies to reduce arms sales, restrict the transfer of advanced weaponry, and reduce co-production arrangements with foreign states.[83] However, because the United States is the world's largest arms supplier, planners will have to counter the Pentagon's frequent overstatements of the military security argument. A *New York Times* editorial pointed out in challenging military aid to the Philippines that U.S. bases are *not* the only means to maintain an American presence in the Pacific and Indian oceans.[84] "The Pentagon," it concluded, "too often puts strategic arguments in absolute terms," causing the United States to "overlook brutal violations of human rights." Planners should carefully assess whether military alternatives do exist that would protect both human rights and strategic interests.

In cases where security interests justify military aid, planners should develop strategies to employ support as leverage to promote human rights. Planners should keep in mind that dictators frequently have no real alternative to their reliance on the United States.

e. Global applications. Crucial to an effective human rights policy is the development of effective strategies for its implementation in all countries. Failure to apply the policy globally would lend credence to charges of selectivity, political hypocrisy, and insensitivity to gross violations.[85] Hence, if the Administration's human rights commitment is to be credible, it must strive for universal application despite any other seemingly contradictory foreign policy goals.

At the same time, the strategies devised should vary from country to country, depending on differing historical, political, social, and economic realities.[86] The same measures cannot be applied to newly independent nations as can be to long-standing parliamentary democracies or to countries in which armed insurgents or national emergency justify some repressive acts. Moreover, measures effective in one country may prove harmful or ineffective in another. Public pronouncements about Chile resulted in political amnesties, whereas similar statements about Uganda led to threats against Americans resident in that country. Consequently, each situation should be judged on its own merits, with planners weighing and measuring the most appropriate course of action for the country under consideration.

Secretary Vance, in a speech in Georgia in April 1977, set forth criteria which would shape U.S. action "to the case at hand."[87] He said that U.S. efforts would range from quiet diplomacy to public pronouncements to withholding of assistance, depending on which action proved the most appropriate or forceful in the given situation. In deciding "how to act," consideration would be given to the nature and extent of the violation, available U.S. leverage, whether U.S. action would improve matters or make them worse, and whether both economic and political rights would be promoted.

Because U.S. action will differ from country to country, policy-planners will be left open to the charge of selective application. However, taking a pragmatic approach will enable the U.S. to select priorities in accordance with what it can do, if anything, to promote respect for human rights. Without a doubt this approach has the potential of proving to be the most meaningful for the promotion of international human rights.

f. Measuring human rights progress. In measuring human rights progress planners should draw distinctions between "cosmetic" changes aimed at pleasing and possibly duping the new Administration and long-term institutional changes which render real improvement. Nothing less than deep-rooted, enduring change accomplished by law should be the goal of U.S. policy-planners. Otherwise there will be no assurance that political amnesties, improved prison conditions, or other positive steps will not be followed by equally arbitrary arrests, torture, and other egregious abuses.[88] Attention also should be paid to the adoption of preventive human rights measures, particularly in countries where conditions are beginning to deteriorate. These measures ultimately can prove more effective than "reactive" strategies from the outside.

2. The Regional Bureaus

In February 1977 Secretary of State Vance requested that the regional or geographic bureaus develop strategy papers on "key human rights problems" in their areas "and tactics for dealing with them."[89] However, despite such a request considerable pressure by the secretary will be required to promote human rights action by these bureaus, because resistance to and ignorance of the human rights factor persists. Regional officers have no commitment to human rights. The reluctance of previous administrations to advance human rights was in considerable measure due to the advice of such officers. Their predominant concern has been the protection of their foreign "clients." Hence they have viewed human rights policy as expendable if its promotion was likely to offend the governments with which they had to deal.

This attitude has surfaced again under the Carter Administration. In testimony before Congress in April 1977, following U.S. aid cuts to Argentina and Uruguay, the Assistant Secretary of State for Inter-American Affairs insisted: "Such an abrupt approach now, after maintaining political-military relationships with these governments dating back to and beyond the Second World War, would produce widespread resentment and alienation."[90] In another incident the Bureau of Near Eastern Affairs displayed a singular lack of concern for human rights in allowing an Iraqi delegation entry into the United States to threaten Kurdish refugees in order to coerce them to return home.[91] In April an East European desk officer responded to an inquiry of the International League for Human Rights by stating that U.S. action on behalf of an arrested dissident would constitute "interference" in that country's internal affairs and that any restrictions on aid or credits would be "blackmail."[92]

To overcome the Kissinger legacy in the bureaucracy, several steps must be taken. First, it is vitally important that sustained leadership be exerted by the Secretary of State and his deputies to ensure human rights input in decision-making. This was the case in June 1977 when Deputy Secretary Warren Christopher decided to postpone an economic assistance project to Chile over the strenuous objections of the Inter-American Bureau.[93] Secretary Vance's forcefulness also was reflected in the decision to cut military aid to Uruguay, Ethiopia, and Argentina.[94] More such initiatives will have to be taken to overcome the strong resistance of the regional bureaus.

Second, career advancement should be utilized as an incentive to create affirmative service attitudes toward human rights. It has been said in the past that no one who advocates human rights at the State Department advances his or her career by doing so. Efforts should be undertaken to reverse this unfortunate pattern and to ensure that a human rights commitment is regarded as an important criterion for promotion in the department.

In this connection senior-level positions in the regional bureaus should be filled by persons committed to human rights, thus guaranteeing more favorable consideration at lower levels as well. In addition, full-time human rights officers should be assigned to all regional bureaus; to date, human rights is often a part-time assignment. The Secretary of State also might consider delegating to officers assigned to regional bureaus and to Ambassadors the authority to enunciate human rights policy. Such advocacy supported at the highest level of the Administration will strengthen the human rights commitment.

Finally, educational programs should be undertaken to shape new foreign service attitudes. To this end the Foreign Service Institute undertook its first human rights training program in Annapolis in June 1977.[95] Lectures were given on the political, legal, and philosophical bases for the new policy, how it could serve the U.S. national interest, and the precise steps the United States could take to improve human rights conditions worldwide. The seminar also offered case studies of countries whose human rights practices posed special problems for the United States. This impressive program should be expanded into a regular monthly or bimonthly series slated to reach large numbers of foreign service officers. The need for extensive course work was emphasized by the attitudes of officers in attendance. Not all were receptive to the new policy. Some dubbed it "moral imperialism"; others considered it "harmful" to the pursuit of more important foreign policy goals. As one department official indicated, "The battle for human rights will be won or lost over the long, hard pull." Sustained reeducation of the department will be needed to overcome deep-rooted resistance to the integration of human rights in foreign policy.

3. Human Rights Officers in Embassies

The Department of State recently designated human rights officers in most embassies abroad.[96]

The accuracy of the information these officers provide will determine the ability of the department to formulate effective and intelligent policies to promote human rights. These officers should therefore be required to prepare "candid" reports of human rights conditions regardless of the interests or sensibilities of their host country. They also should be instructed to recommend measures to improve human rights conditions and to evaluate the effectiveness of steps taken by the United States. In order to demonstrate support of their work, the United States should make host countries aware of the reporting requirements of embassies and of the importance it attaches to this effort. The work of the human rights officers also should be integrated with the embassy's other activities in order to emphasize that human rights concerns are shared and strongly supported by all elements in the Embassy.

4. Bureau of Human Rights and Humanitarian Affairs

The Carter Administration has enlarged, upgraded, and broadened the functions of the Human Rights Office, which was created in 1975 with the title of Office of Coordinator for Human Rights and Humanitarian Affairs.[97] Patricia Derian, the officer in charge, was sworn in by President Carter in August 1977 as the first Assistant Secretary of State for Human Rights and Humanitarian Affairs. This bureau is the focal point of State Department human rights activity and advocacy. Its staff has been increased to over 30, as many as 10 of whom concentrate exclusively on human rights questions while the remainder deal with refugee problems and missing-in-action or prisoner-of-war cases.

To facilitate the coordination and supervision of human rights policy-making in the Department of State, an Interagency Committee on Human Rights and Foreign Assistance was created.[98] Responsible to the deputy Secretary of State, it consists of representatives at the deputy assistant secretary level from all regional and functional bureaus whose work relates to human rights. The committee examines the human rights aspects of all AID budgetary program decisions and the U.S. position on loans awaiting action in the international financial institutions. A working group co-chaired by the Deputy Assistant Secretary for Human Rights reports to this committee. The Bureau also participates in the work of the Arms Export Control Board, which makes recommendations on security assistance overseas.

To guarantee that human rights concerns are incorporated in the decision-making of these interagency bodies, the Human Rights

Bureau will require forthright advocates. They will have to persuade and convince regional and functional officers to integrate human rights into their planned strategies. Frequently they will need the backing of the Secretary of State. This was the case when the deputy secretary ruled in their favor to delay economic aid to Chile over the strenuous objections of the Inter-American Affairs Bureau and AID.[99]

Another area in which the Human Rights bureau will have to struggle to make its voice heard is in the preparation of human rights reports to Congress. Under the 1976 Foreign Assistance Act, the office was given responsibility for these reports.[100] However, the information upon which the reports are based is provided by the regional bureaus. Hence it will be up to the office to guarantee that the information is candid. Its human rights officers will have to screen the data, check that it accords with press and nongovernmental accounts, and forcefully challenge the bureaus when essential facts are held back. The recent visit of the Assistant Secretary to Argentina was a positive sign that this office does not intend to leave all fact-finding to the regional bureaus.[101]

Patricia Derian expressed her preference for positive rather than punitive measures to promote human rights. She asserted before Congress that resorting to "aid cuts, public denunciations, and other ... more negative approaches" is an indication that "we have failed."[102] The Human Rights Bureau therefore must be vigorous in ensuring that positive actions are pursued by the State Department. However, if and when such efforts do fail, this Bureau should be prepared to advocate punitive measures. Among the measures the Human Rights Bureau might recommend are direct diplomatic approaches in individual cases; formal demarches about general conditions; attendance at human rights trials; affording of refuge in the U.S. Embassy in urgent cases; expediting applications for asylum; support of local institutions and groups; extension of aid, credits, and trade concessions as inducements to improve conditions; acts of disassociation; elimination of military and economic aid to countries seriously violating human rights; cooperation with other states and with international nongovernmental organizations working to further human rights; and support of initiatives at the U.N. or OAS to correct abuses.

Finally, the Human Rights Bureau must develop a staff of experts with the independence of mind, the commitment, and the advocacy necessary for the promotion of human rights in foreign policy. Education should be an important undertaking of the office. It should be incumbent upon its staff to provide training and information of the highest quality to all those in government who become engaged in human rights problems. The fact that the assistant secretary and deputy assistant secretary previously worked in the human rights field and are not career officers bodes well for this office's forthrightness in injecting human rights concerns into the rest of the department.

5. Other Bureaus in the Department of State

Many other bureaus and offices in the State Department lack human rights programs and should be instructed to undertake establishing them. The Bureau of Educational and Cultural Affairs is a case in point. In the past, under the agency's visitor's program, known perpetrators of human rights violations have been invited as guests of the United States.[103] Clearly, those in charge of the program should be instructed to strengthen ties with groups overseas that support human rights. Other cultural and exchange programs also should be brought into line with these objectives.[104]

Another serious deficiency in the department is that key offices are insufficiently staffed with human rights personnel. The Office of Legal Affairs, for example, has only one legal advisor for human rights. Additional human rights staff should be appointed, thus enabling the office to keep pace with the myriad of legal issues arising in response to the new policy.

C. Other Executive Branch Departments and Agencies

To be effective, human rights policy must extend beyond the State Department to encompass the entire Executive Branch. A coordinated strategy should guarantee that all departments and agencies give emphasis to human rights in their decision-making and that the policies of one department not thwart the human rights initiatives of another. For example, the arms sales and military training programs of the Department of Defense should be reconciled with the policies of the State Department in order to reduce security assistance to repressive regimes.[105] The covert activities of the CIA also should be regulated to prevent harm to human lives and freedom abroad. It should be regarded as unacceptable for CIA officials to assert that "covert activity should not be confused with missionary work."[106] CIA arrangements with foreign intelligence agencies in the United States should be controlled in order to curb the frequent persecution of foreign dissident nationals residing here.[107] In addition, the policies of the Justice Department toward refugees and aliens[108] and of the Treasury Department toward multinational lending institutions and private corporations[109] should be brought into line with human rights objectives.

To accomplish the needed coordination the President should direct government departments and agencies engaged in international activities to file human rights reports with the National Security Council. In particular, they should be called upon to identify any actions or policies that jeopardize or diminish respect for human rights, to provide justification for these measures, and to recommend alternative approaches in the future. Each department and agency also should be required to make available to the State Department its human rights information for inclusion in reports to Congress and for use in overall planning. Finally, consideration should be given to the appointment of senior-level human rights advisors in these departments to integrate human rights concerns in their programs.

V. Relations with Congress

The Department of State, together with Congress, could constitute a powerful alliance to foster promotion of international human rights.[110] To this end the department should reverse its previous adversary relationship with Congress and strive to develop shared initiatives in the human rights field. In particular, the department should make forthright reports to Congress about conditions of human rights and should initiate joint action with Congress to liberalize discriminatory immigration laws.[111] It should work with the Senate to secure ratification of human rights treaties adopted by the U.N. and OAS. It should cooperate with the Congressional commission monitoring the Helsinki accords to enable it to compile well-documented violations of the Final Act both here and abroad. Most significantly, the department should persuade Congress of the seriousness of its intentions to advance human rights. Since this policy originated with Congress and not the Executive Branch, it is understandable that members of Congress are reluctant to yield their hard-earned initiative. They will need firm assurances from the new Administration that it will pursue its commitment to human rights rigorously. Mere espousal by the President of human rights principles will not be a sufficient guarantee. As Senator James Abourezk has stated: "While the President's words sound very beautiful, after the announcements nothing really happens."[112]

Congressional distrust of Executive intentions flared up early in the Carter Administration over U.S. military and economic aid policies toward repressive regimes. The House of Representatives, over the objection of the Executive Branch, voted to compel U.S. representatives in the World Bank to oppose loans to repressive regimes automatically unless such loans clearly benefited the poor.[113] The assumption here was that the Executive Branch would otherwise take no measures to improve human rights conditions in the offending countries unless pushed by Congress. President Carter, in disagreement, appealed to Senator Hubert Humphrey to mobilize the Senate to overturn this decision on the grounds that the proposed strictures

> ... would handicap our efforts to encourage human rights improvements.... There may well be times when we can bargain with prospective borrowers to release prisoners or stop other offensive practices if we have our vote as leverage. We need this flexibility if we expect to influence borrower countries or the overall programs of the banks.[114]

The Senate, in response, backed the Administration, although the vote was a close 50 to 43. The Senators supported a formulation that mandated U.S. representatives to use their voice and vote to channel loans to countries that adhere to human rights standards.[115] This was eventually agreed to by the House.

In the meantime a similar controversy has developed over bilateral aid. The House Appropriations Committee voted in the spring of 1977 to cut military aid to Nicaragua over State Department objections.[116] The Administration, urging flexibility, lobbied successfully to reverse this decision on the House floor. Similar amendments have been introduced in House and Senate committees with respect to other repressive regimes.

In order to gain Congressional confidence the Administration should fully justify why it might be in the interests of the United States to maintain assistance to particular governments. In such cases it should inform Congress of the measures short of aid cuts it plans to take to advance human rights. It should evaluate the effect of its policies and be willing to take punitive action when positive measures fail. The Administration, on its own initiative, did cut aid to Argentina, Uruguay, and Ethiopia, but it continued or increased military aid to other repressive countries on "national security" grounds. Unless acceptable explanations for these latter decisions are forthcoming, questions will arise about the depth of the U.S. commitment to human rights.[117]

Of course, if Congress does gain confidence in the Administration's good faith, it may be willing to relax some of the restrictive procedures it has imposed—procedures which in particular cases may prove less effective than the positive steps backed by the Administration. At the same time the Administration must avoid giving the impression that Congressional human rights activity is opposed by the Executive Branch. It should welcome Congressional hearings and proposals to strengthen State Department organization in the human rights field. It should utilize Congressional initiatives to advantage in discussions with foreign governments. Congressional support also will bolster the position of human rights advocates in the State Department and serve to sustain the momentum necessary to the success of the human rights policy.

VI. Relations with Nongovernmental Organizations (NGO's)

Public support, too, is critical to the maintenance of the human rights offensive. The Department of State should cultivate closer contacts with private groups in the United States devoted to the promotion of human rights and support their efforts to bring this issue to the attention of broad sectors of the body politic. An electorate educated in the imperatives of human rights will prove essential to the continuation of the policy. In this connection the creation of an NGO advisory committee on human rights has been proposed to promote closer NGO-governmental ties.[118] Moreover, Congressman Donald Fraser has urged the establishment of a National Endowment for Human Rights to fund promising undertakings by private organizations.[119]

In the international sphere it is imperative that government action complement NGO activity. There are numerous instances, such as dispatching investigatory missions abroad or publishing condemnatory reports, when NGO's are the more suitable body to take needed steps on behalf of human rights. The United States should lend support to these efforts. In doing so it also should scrupulously respect the independence crucial to NGO reputation and effectiveness. Concerted government cooperation with NGO's, both national and international, will contribute to consistent and long-term public support for human rights, vital to the success of the new policy.

VII. Independent Public Oversight

The creation of an independent public oversight commission is needed to spur implementation by the Executive Branch of its human rights commitment. Father Theodore Hesburgh has proposed that the U.S. Civil Rights Commission perform this function.[120] The commission would assess the performance of the Executive Branch, evaluate the adequacy or inadequacy of particular programs, and make recommendations to improve overall government strategies and tactics. By virtue of its statute and impartiality, it would serve as a powerful influence to ensure that human rights considerations weigh heavily in decision-making. The expansion of the Civil Rights Commission's jurisdiction to include international human rights also would demonstrate the commitment of the United States to promoting both domestic and international human rights.

VIII. Conclusion

The institutionalization of human rights in the Executive Branch is a revolutionary first step toward making human rights concerns a permanent feature of American foreign policy. However, the strength of the campaign will depend on sustained Executive leadership and the dynamism of the machinery set up to carry it forward.

Because the initiative is without precedent in American diplomatic history, a long and arduous process lies ahead. The machinery created will have to be strengthened and enlarged to encompass the entire Executive Branch. Rooted resistance within the government will have to be overcome. As Senator Daniel Patrick Moynihan warned, unless the Kissinger legacy is dealt with, a state of nonaction on human rights could recur:

> What needs to be explained is how those years of silence came about, and what they signify. For there were reasons, and deep ones, and they could reassert themselves far more readily than any—perhaps especially the President—might suppose.[121]

President Carter has broken the conspiracy of silence that so long dominated U.S. policy toward international human rights questions. The difficulty now arises in translating the vision into effective action. The true depth of the U.S. commitment will be measured by how forcefully human rights objectives are pursued when advocates of that commitment are confronted with conflicting political, military, and economic priorities. If the application of professed principles is to be meaningful, the United States will have to make sacrifices. When domestic prosperity and development abroad seem at odds, the United States will have to bring its trade and aid more into line with economic justice. Policies designed solely to protect bases or investments in nations with repressive regimes will have to undergo radical change. In short, if initiatives on behalf of human rights abruptly end where national security considerations and economic interests begin, the United States will run the risk of discrediting its own policy and of inflicting damage on the entire human rights movement.

The complexity of this undertaking has been wisely recognized by the President and Secretary of State. They have stressed that human rights advocacy will mean involvement in a long and treacherous struggle:

> We have no illusions that the process will be quick or that change will come easily. But we are confident that if we do not abandon the struggle, the cause of personal freedom and human dignity will be enhanced.[122]

Implicit in their statements is the recognition that human rights work is neither glamorous nor chic. Striving to rid the world of torture and brutality and to promote respect for human freedom will be a grueling and painstaking effort requiring persistence and perseverance. Carefully framed policies and thoughtfully executed initiatives for all countries will be needed to improve egregious conditions and to prevent their further deterioration.

Continued Presidential emphasis on the interrelationship of human rights advancement and U.S. national interest and survival will be needed to generate the support necessary to sustain the policy's momentum. With expectation levels sufficiently aroused and support forthcoming from other nations, it is incumbent on the Executive Branch to exhibit the determination necessary to see the policy through.

NOTES

1. President Carter's Inaugural Address, January 20, 1977, *New York Times*, January 21, 1977.
2. Letter of President Carter to Andrei D. Sakharov, February 5, 1977, *New York Times*, February 18, 1977.
3. See *Human Rights in the World Community: A Call for U.S. Leadership*, Report of the Subcommittee on International Organizations and Movements of the Committee on Foreign Affairs, House of Representatives, 93rd Congress, 2d Session (Washington, D.C., 1974).
4. International Security Assistance and Arms Export Control Act of 1976, Section 502B, 22 USC 2151, Public Law 94-329, 94th Congress, H.R. 13680, June 30, 1976, 90 Stat. 729.
5. International Development and Food Assistance Act of 1975, Section

116, 22 USC 2151, Public Law 94-161, 94th Congress, H.R. 9005, December 20, 1975, 89 Stat. 849.

6. Memorandum for All Assistant Secretaries on Human Rights from Cyrus Vance, Secretary of State, Department of State, Washington, D.C., February 11, 1977. Report of the Secretary of State to the Congress of the U.S. Regarding the Operations and Mandate of the Bureau of Human Rights and Humanitarian Affairs, *Congressional Record* (95th Congress, 2d Session) Vol. 124, no. 12, February 6, 1978.

7. See J. J. Shestack and R. Cohen, "International Human Rights: A Role for the United States," 14 *Virginia Journal of International Law* (Summer 1974): 673–701. See also *Human Rights in the World Community, supra* note 3.

8. *International Protection of Human Rights, The Work of International Organizations and the Role of U.S. Foreign Policy,* hearings before the Subcommittee on International Organizations and Movements of the Committee on Foreign Affairs, House of Representatives, 93rd Congress, 1st Session (Washington, D.C., 1973), p. 507.

9. See *supra* note 7.

10. See J. Salzberg and D. D. Young, "The Parliamentary Role in Implementing International Human Rights: A U.S. Example," 12 *Texas International Law Journal* (Spring/Summer 1977): 274–278. See also *Human Rights in the World Community, supra* note 3, at 12.

11. *Human Rights in the World Community, supra* note 3, at 13.

12. *International Protection of Human Rights, supra* note 8, at 67–68.

13. *Ibid.*

14. *Human Rights in the World Community, supra* note 3, at 9–10.

15. *Ibid.,* at 13.

16. The 1974 Foreign Assistance Act, 88 Stat. 1815 (1974).

17. *International Protection of Human Rights, supra* note 8, at 223 and 594.

18. P. Breslin, "Human Rights: Rhetoric or Action?" *Washington Post Outlook,* February 27, 1977.

19. See J. Salzberg and D. Young, *supra* note 10, p. 270.

20. *Ibid.,* pp. 275–277.

21. Foreign Affairs Manual Circular, *Organizations and Functions, Coordinator for Humanitarian Affairs* (C/HA), Vol. 1, FAMC No. 700, June 24, 1975.

22. See J. Salzberg and D. Young, *supra* note 10, p. 276.

23. D. Fraser, "Freedom and Foreign Policy," *Foreign Policy* no. 2 (Spring 1977).

24. See Hearings on Human Rights in Chile, Iran, Indonesia, the Philippines, Uruguay, and Paraguay, before the Subcommittee on International Organizations and Movements of the Committee on Foreign Affairs, 93rd Congress and 94th Congress, 1974–1976.

25. *Human Rights in Uruguay and Paraguay,* hearings before the Subcommittee on International Organizations of the Committee on International Relations, House of Representatives, 94th Congress, 2d Session (Washington, 1976), at 114–116.

26. *New York Times,* September 27, 1974.

27. *New York Times,* February 14, 1974.

28. See P. Breslin, *supra* note 18; see also E. Drew, "Human Rights," *The New Yorker,* July 18, 1977, p. 36; and L. Howell, "Human Rights: Real Commitment or Seasonal Fad?" *Christianity and Crisis* April 18, 1977, p. 76.

29. See P. Breslin, *supra* note 18.

30. *Ibid.*
31. *New York Times*, November 19, 1975, p. 1.
32. See *supra* note 4.
33. The report in Iran, for example, did not admit that political prisoners were tortured, despite abundant supporting evidence. A similar lack of candor marked the other reports. See *Human Rights and U.S. Policy: Argentina, Haiti, Indonesia, Iran, Peru, and the Philippines,* reports submitted to the Committee on International Relations, U.S. House of Representatives, by the Department of State, December 31, 1976. See also Coalition for a New Foreign and Military Policy, *A Response by Non-Governmental Organizations to the State Department Reports* (Washington, D.C., January 14, 1977).
34. *Human Rights in Korea: Implications for U.S. Policy,* joint hearings before the Subcommittee on International Organizations and Movements and the Subcommittee on Asian and Pacific Affairs, of the Committee on Foreign Affairs, House of Representatives, 93rd Congress, 2d Session (Washington, D.C., 1974). See also J. Salzberg and D. Young, *supra* note 10, pp. 267-268.
35. *New York Times*, December 18, 1976, p. 1.
36. "U.S. Role Hinted in Chile's Decision to Release Political Prisoners," *New York Times*, November 18, 1976, p. 10. See also *New York Times*, September 20, 1977, p. 6; and J. Salzberg and D. Young, *supra* note 10, pp. 265-266.
37. E. P. Spiro, "A Paradigm Shift in American Foreign Policy," *Worldview*, January/February 1977, p. 42. See also *New York Times*, June 9, 1976, p. 1.
38. See *supra* note 1.
39. See *supra* note 2. See also Press Conferences of President Carter, reported in *New York Times*, February 24, March 10, and July 1, 1977; the President's statement over European TV, *New York Times*, May 3, 1977; the text of the President's Commencement Address at the University of Notre Dame, *New York Times*, May 23, 1977, p. 12; and the President's Address to the Southern Legislative Conference, *New York Times*, July 22, 1977, p. A4.
40. Transcript of President Carter's Address at the United Nations, *New York Times*, March 18, 1977, p. A10.
41. Press Conference of President Carter, *New York Times*, February 9, 1977.
42. *New York Times*, February 2, 1977; Press Conference of President Carter, *New York Times*, February 9, 1977; T. Wicker, "Holding Freedom's Standard," *New York Times*, February 15, 1977; and *New York Times*, March 23, 1977.
43. *New York Times*, February 2, 1977.
44. Statement of President Carter to Magazine Publishers Association, *New York Times*, June 12, 1977, p. 1.
45. Press Conference of President Carter, *New York Times*, July 1, 1977, p. A10.
46. Text of the President's Commencement Address at the University of Notre Dame, *New York Times*, May 23, 1977, p. 12.
47. *Ibid.*
48. Speech of Secretary Cyrus R. Vance on Law Day before the University of Georgia's Law School, April 30, 1977, Athens, Ga., reprinted by the Bureau of Public Affairs, Office of Media Services, Department of State, PR 194.

49. *New York Times,* January 27, 1977.
50. *New York Times,* January 28, February 8 and 12, and March 23, 1977.
51. See *supra* note 2.
52. *New York Times,* February 24, 1977.
53. *New York Times,* January 28, 1977; Press Conference of President Carter, *New York Times,* February 24, 1977.
54. *New York Times,* February 25, 1977.
55. See *supra* note 48.
56. See E. Drew, "Human Rights," *The New Yorker,* July 18, 1977, p. 59; A. Lewis, "A Question of Humanity," *New York Times,* February 28, 1977; "The Push for Human Rights," *Newsweek,* June 20, 1977, p. 53; and *New York Times,* June 1, 1977, p. A12.
57. Human Rights Reports prepared by the Department of State, submitted to the Subcommittee on Foreign Assistance of the Committee on Foreign Relations, U.S. Senate, 95th Congress, 1st Session, March 1977.
58. See *supra* note 40, and text of President Carter's Address to the Permanent Council of the Organization of American States, *New York Times,* April 15, 1977, p. A10.
59. See E. Drew, *supra* note 56, p. 61; "The Push for Human Rights," *supra* note 56, p. 46; "Poll Shows Majority Supports Carter's Human Rights Stand," *New York Times,* March 27, 1977; "Democratic Group Backs Carter," *New York Times,* May 14, 1977; A. Lewis, "Raising a Standard," *New York Times,* June 23, 1977; and L. Howell, *supra* note 28, p. 74.
60. See *supra* note 56.
61. See P. Breslin, *supra* note 18; see also "Human Rights: Deeds as well as Words," editorial, *New York Times,* February 27, 1977; "The Limits of an Activist U.S. Approach to Promoting Respect for Human Rights Abroad," *New York Times,* May 18, 1977, p. A14.
62. See R. J. Barnet, "U.S. Needs Modest, Uniform Standard on Human Rights," *Los Angeles Times,* March 12, 1977; see also L. Howell, *supra* note 28.
63. See "Carter's Morality Play," *Time,* March 7, 1977; see also R. Steel "Motherhood, Apple Pie and Human Rights," *The New Republic,* June 4, 1977, p. 15; "Position Paper of the New York Human Rights Coalition" (New York, 1977); B. Gwertzman, "Human Rights: It's Harder to Admonish Allies," *New York Times,* February 6, 1977; "Business and Human Rights," editorial, *Wall Street Journal,* July 7, 1977; and M. Reisman, "The Pragmatism of Human Rights," *The Nation,* May 7, 1977, p. 557.
64. R. Barnet, *supra* note 62.
65. See *supra* note 56.
66. See "The Limits of an Activist U.S. Approach," *supra* note 61; E. Drew, *supra* note 56, pp. 42 and 52; "The Push for Human Rights," *supra* note 56, pp. 47 and 53; "Argentine Paper Critical of Carter," *New York Times,* March 13, 1977; J. de Onis, "Latin View on Rights Is That Carter Doesn't Understand," *New York Times,* March 13, 1977; J. Reston, "A View from Bonn," *New York Times,* June 15, 1977; and "Pravda Cautions U.S. on Rights Criticism," *New York Times,* March 14, 1977.
67. See *supra* note 46.
68. See *supra* note 48.
69. *The Interdependent,* April 1977.
70. Congressman Donald Fraser has proposed the creation of a commission on international human rights in the White House to coordinate human

rights-foreign policy issues: see "Freedom and Foreign Policy," *Foreign Policy,* Spring 1977.

71. See *supra* note 6,

72. D. P. Moynihan, "The Politics of Human Rights," 64 *Commentary* (August 1977).

73. The Act states: "The term 'gross violations of internationally recognized human rights' includes torture or cruel, inhuman, or degrading treatment or punishment, prolonged detention without charges and trial, and other flagrant denial of the right to life, liberty, or the security of person"; see *supra* note 4.

74. See the Universal Declaration of Human Rights and the International Covenant on Economic, Social, and Cultural Rights, adopted by the United Nations.

75. See *supra* note 48.

76. *Ibid.*

77. See K. Bird and S. Goldmark, "Food Aid vs. Development," *Worldview,* January/February 1977, p. 38; "World Bank Alters Strategy to Focus on Aid to Very Poor," the *New York Times,* June 6, 1977, p. 45; and "Human Rights and the Single Standard," editorial, *New York Times,* January 11, 1977.

78. To "meet the most acute needs of the world's poorest nations," the Carter Administration proposed an expanded AID program, a 20 percent increase in foreign economic aid for 1978, and an emergency increase of $375 million in 1977; see *supra* note 48 and *New York Times,* May 31, 1977, p. 1. See also O. E. Clubb, "Morality, Law, and the New World Order," 20 *Worldview* (September 1977): 39.

79. See *supra* note 46.

80. See "The U.S. Search for a Policy in Africa," *New York Times,* March 27, 1977; and S. Karnow, "Carter and Human Rights," *Saturday Review,* March 2, 1977, p. 10.

81. See International League for Human Rights, *Report of the Conference on Implementing a Human Rights Commitment in United States Foreign Policy* (March 4, 1977), pp. 73-75.

82. See, generally, *ibid.,* pp. 8 and 17-18; and S. Karnow, *supra* note 80, pp. 7-11.

83. See *supra* note 46.

84. *New York Times,* editorial, February 27, 1977.

85. See *supra* note 63.

86. See N. MacDermot, "The Human Rights Explosion," an address to the Netherlands Society for International Affairs, May 23, 1977, pp. 6-7; "Human Rights and the 'Single Standard,'" editorial, *New York Times,* January 11, 1977; and E. Drew, *supra* note 56, pp. 57-58.

87. See *supra* note 48.

88. See E. Drew, *supra* note 56, p. 59.

89. See *supra* note 6.

90. "Congress Asked to Aid Latins Despite Rights Curb," *New York Times,* April 6, 1977.

91. J. Anderson, "A Toll of Dirty Tricks," *Washington Post,* April 24, 1977. Supporting evidence also is contained in letters at the office of the International League for Human Rights, New York.

92. Private conversation of the author with a desk officer in the Department of State.
93. *New York Times,* June 24, 1977; and E. Drew, *supra* note 56, p. 60.
94. E. Drew, *supra* note 56, p. 42.
95. Seminar on Human Rights, Foreign Service Institute, Department of State, Annapolis, May 31 to June 3, 1977. See also *Department of State Newsletter,* July 1977.
96. The author was informed of this by officials in the Department of State.
97. Amendment no. 472 to the Foreign Relations Authorizations Act, 1978, reproduced at 123 *Congressional Record* S9993, daily ed., June 16, 1977. See also *Washington Post,* August 11, 1977, p. B1.
98. See *supra* note 6; and statement of Mark Schneider before the Seminar on Human Rights, Foreign Service Institute, Annapolis, June 2, 1977.
99. See *supra* note 93.
100. See *supra* note 4.
101. *New York Times,* April 3, 1977.
102. Statement of Patricia Derian before the Subcommittee on Foreign Assistance of the House Appropriations Committee, April 5, 1977.
103. *New York Times,* January 30, 1977. Other examples are available in the files of the International League for Human Rights.
104. Secretary Vance did announce that the Cultural Affairs Bureau and the USIA would be asked to undertake human rights programs; see *supra* note 48.
105. See M. T. Klare, "Pointing Fingers," *New York Times,* August 10, 1977; see also Washington Office on Latin America, "U.S. Military Assistance Programs for Latin America," (March/April 1977); statement by Congressman Edward Koch, reproduced in *Congressional Record* H 759, February 1, 1977; "Arms Sales: Another Wobbling Promise," editorial, *New York Times,* May 8, 1977; and R. J. Barnet, *supra* note 62.
106. "The Pike Papers: House Select Committee on Intelligence CIA Report," *The Village Voice,* Special Supplement 1976, p. 27.
107. *Ibid.,* p. 31; see also *New York Times,* November 10, 1976.
108. President Carter proposed legislation to improve the legal position of aliens in the United States; see *New York Times,* July 21, 1977. The President also took steps to ease visa restrictions on visiting communists. Efforts should be undertaken to amend the 1965 Immigration Act, which discriminates against refugees from particular areas; see *supra* note 81, p. 44, and "Broader Refugee Policy Sought in Congress," *Christian Science Monitor,* December 10, 1976, p. 3.
109. The Department of the Treasury has immediate responsibility for directing U.S. representatives in the World Bank and other international lending institutions; see *supra* note 81. It also can exert control over multinational corporations, for example, in Namibia, through restrictions on tax credits. See "Carter, Human Rights and World Bank," *International Bulletin,* April 11, 1977, p. 4.
110. An example of Congressional support was the letter from 58 Senators endorsing President Carter's human rights stand prior to Secretary Vance's trip to Moscow; see *New York Times,* March 26, 1977, p. 1.
111. See *supra* note 108.

112. See E. Drew, *supra* note 56, p. 52.
113. *Wall Street Journal,* April 7, 1977. This restriction is already binding upon U.S. representatives in the Inter-American Development Bank and the African Development Fund, see Public Law 94-302, 94th Congress, H.R. 9721, May 31, 1976.
114. *New York Times,* April 20, 1977.
115. *New York Times,* June 15, 1977.
116. See E. Drew, *supra* note 56, p. 52.
117. See Center for International Policy, *Human Rights and the U.S. Foreign Assistance Program, Fiscal Year 1978, Parts I and II* (Washington, D.C., 1977).
118. See *Human Rights in the World Community, supra* note 3, at 13.
119. See D. Fraser, *supra* note 23.
120. *International Protection of Human Rights, supra* note 8, at 321-322.
121. See D. P. Moynihan, *supra* note 72.
122. Excerpts from President Carter's Address to the Southern Legislative Conference, *New York Times,* July 22, 1977, pp. A4 and 6.

11: Congress's Role in the Making of International Human Rights Policy

DONALD M. FRASER

THE CARTER ADMINISTRATION IS DEVELOPING A NEW POLICY FOR the human rights field.

This paper attempts to answer four questions. *First, what is Congress's role in monitoring the impact of American foreign policy on human rights abroad and developing legislative guidelines for such a policy?*

Congress has an important role to play in this matter. First, through public discussion of issues, particularly through hearings as well as on the floor of the House, Congress can very effectively draw attention to human rights problems abroad and thereby increase public concern and the receptivity of foreign governments to ameliorate their practices. Second, it establishes through law the standards upon which the Executive Branch uses the various assistance programs for leverage in the promotion of human rights.

Hearings have been a principal means by which the Congress has monitored foreign policy and sought to influence its direction. An important example of such a forum is the Fascell Commission—a joint Congressional-Executive Branch commission specifically designed to monitor compliance with the final act of the Helsinki Agreement. Over the last few years my own subcommittee has held more than 80 hearings on the subject of human rights and foreign policy. Nongovernmental witnesses have proved an invaluable resource in providing us with information with which to compare Department of State testimony. By listening to and questioning departmental testimony, we believe we have influenced the conduct of policy at least a little. If nothing else, the hearings have required the Department of State to place matters on the record that otherwise might not have been disclosed publicly. Also, from my own personal experience with respect to our subcommittee's hearings, I am certain that the hearings are taken very seriously by most foreign governments. They make every effort to indicate that their performance conforms with international human rights standards.

Congress also has enacted legislation in the field of human rights and foreign policy. Specific examples include Sections 502B (human rights and security assistance) and 116 (human rights and development assistance) of the Foreign Assistance Act as well as the human rights amendments aimed at the multilateral banks.

Both Sections 502B and 116 provide the Executive with a general framework within which the Administration is expected to shape its security and development assistance programs. However, neither law dictates specific decisions; rather, each allows flexibility for action in individual circumstances. For example, Section 502B prohibits, except under extraordinary circumstances, military aid or sale of military equipment to governments with a consistent pattern of gross violations of internationally recognized human rights. Congress has placed especially stringent standards on military aid because of the symbolic and sometimes practical importance of such assistance in carrying out repressive policy in numerous countries.

The relationship between human rights and development aid poses a more complicated question. Because we do not want to penalize the poor, Section 116 prohibits bilateral development aid to a repressive government only if that aid is not directly beneficial to needy people. Congress enacted this legislation under the Nixon and Ford administrations because of our belief that in certain nations, particularly Chile and South Korea, the Administration was using economic aid to prolong the staying power of regimes more than to provide help for needy people.

At this session one important human rights provision was inserted in the international financial institution act (PL 95-118). The U.S. delegates to the various international financial institutions are instructed to oppose any loan to a government engaged in a consistent pattern of gross violations of internationally recognized human rights unless the loan will provide for basic human needs of citizens of that country. The amendment was a compromise between those who wanted certain automatic negative votes by the U.S. delegate to repressive governments unless the aid was directly beneficial to needy people and those who wanted to provide greater flexibility to the Administration and not require negative voting.

I think the spirit of the amendment suggests that the United States should work with other delegations in the international financial institutions, particularly the donor governments, to press these institutions to give priority to those governments that are respecting human rights and are seeking to provide an equitable distribution of income and wealth in their countries. By such a positive approach it is certain that those governments that are repressive will receive less and less of the financial resources of international financial institutions. By emphasizing multilateral consultation and cooperative joint initiatives, I think our efforts will be more effective and more consonant with the spirit of multilateral decision-making.

Congress also has enacted legislation concerning specific countries. Such legislation was enacted during the Ford Administration and has continued during the Carter Administration. In 1975 a one-year ceiling was placed on military aid to South Korea. This amendment was proposed because of the severe restrictions on freedom of the press and other civil liberties in South Korea and the detention and trial of a number of Korean dissidents who sought to exercise these rights. With respect to Chile since 1975, ceilings have been placed on economic aid and military aid has been prohibited. These limitations were placed on Chile because of the junta's detention and severe treatment of political prisoners. Many were executed without trial; others were brutally tortured, and many have disappeared. In addition, the Ford Administration provided inordinate amounts of economic aid in the form of PL 480 of Title I (food aid at low interest loans), housing loan guarantees, and other forms of assistance to Chile.

In 1976 military aid was prohibited to Uruguay. Amnesty International has cited Uruguay as perhaps the most repressive country in terms of treatment of political prisoners. With respect to all the above-mentioned countries, the Subcommittee on International Organizations held hearings in the course of the Congressional decisions to apply sanctions.

Ironically, during the Carter Administration, an even greater number of specific country legislative prohibitions or limitations on military aid were enacted as compared with the Ford Administration. Many members of Congress are not as patient as the Administration in terms of encouraging repressive regimes to change their practices. They believe that many of these regimes have had a long enough time to mend their practices. They do not favor compromising the legislative principle that repressive regimes, except in extraordinary circumstances, should be disqualified from receiving military assistance. They favor a policy of frankness, of public opprobrium, and of a straightforward disassociation of the United States with the repressive regime through termination of military aid.

Pursuant to this line of thinking Congress prohibited all forms of military aid, including military training, to Argentina during the early period of the Carter Administration. However, it should be noted that the Executive Branch, in submitting its requests, had already cut military aid to Argentina as compared with the amount the Administration had originally intended to request. Three other countries in addition to Argentina were prohibited from receiving military aid by the Congress following their government's decision to renounce military aid: Guatemala, El Salvador, and Brazil. These countries renounced our military aid following the release of the State Department's reports on those countries submitted to Congress pursuant to the human rights and security assistance provision to the Foreign Assistance Act (Section 502B). The governments of these countries objected to the criticisms of their countries' practices contained in these reports.

Congress also cut back the military grant aid intended for the Philippines. This was certainly a significant decision in the light of the importance the U.S. government places on the air and naval bases in the Philippines. Congress also made an unsuccessful effort to prohibit military aid to Nicaragua. The Administration had requested $2.5 million for military sales credits. The House Appropriations Committee prohibited the aid; however, on the floor of the House, with support from the Administration, the ban was lifted. Nevertheless, the Administration indicated that it would not go forward with the military aid to Nicaragua unless there were improvements in human rights.

The second question is what tensions exist between Congress and the Executive? As the conflict over specific country legislation and legislation affecting the international institutions indicates, Congress has not accepted as fully bona fide the Administration's commitment to human rights. Tensions do exist; perhaps they are inevitable and desirable—even when the same party controls both the White House and Congress. Even if Congress had complete faith in the Administration's commitment, disagreement might remain over its implementation. There are many forces militating against a strong human rights element in foreign policy. The Executive Branch needs Congressional support, and in some instances this may mean that the Congress will take the lead on human rights initiatives or principles in human rights policy. Particularly since the Carter Administration took office, my preference has been for a "low-profile" Congressional policy giving the Executive an opportunity to work out a human rights policy and a reasonable period of time in which to achieve results. However, some members of Congress may be impatient and wish to see the Executive demonstrate in a public and concrete way its moral indignation at the repression that exists in many countries of the world. With respect to some countries, Congress believes that the repression is so blatant that we should disassociate ourselves immediately from it through termination of assistance programs.

The promotion of human rights is a complicated and difficult task. National pride makes other governments extremely sensitive to foreign criticism. The Executive Branch, as compared with Congress, has more tools and instruments at its disposal for bringing its concern regarding human rights to the attention of other governments. It can act with greater subtlety. It can take firm measures, including sanctions, without introducing these sanctions into the public arena. Consequently, an Administration willing to exert itself can have more effectiveness in this field than can Congress.

The instruments at the disposal of the Executive Branch are many. Initially, the Executive Branch through quiet, diplomatic means can bring to the attention of another government its concern about human rights violations and the possibility that such violations could damage relations with the United States and possibly cause a diminishing of assistance or some other problem with the United States. Should these quiet diplomatic initiatives fail to produce results, the Executive Branch can introduce sanctions in the form of bilateral or multilateral assistance. Such sanctions are many, including military assistance and bilateral development assistance. Through our considerable influence in the multilateral financial institutions, the Administration has already held up a number of loans to countries that are seriously violating human rights. Most of these initiatives have been taken privately, although in some cases they became public knowledge in due course.

The third question is how effective is the Congressional role? Despite the confrontational relationship that has existed between the executive and legislative branches in recent years, the Congress has achieved some positive results. In effect, Congress has laid a basis for the new Administration's human rights policy. Congressional initiatives have included the following:
1. The establishment of the human rights performance of the recipient government as a basic factor in decisions regarding military and economic assistance.
2. The creation of the Office of Coordinator for Human Rights and Humanitarian Affairs in the State Department and the suggestion that human rights officers in the regional bureaus be appointed. This suggestion has been accepted, and the coordinator has been elevated to the rank of assistant secretary.
3. The establishment of human rights reporting as a regular function of the embassies and of public reporting on proposed recipients of security and development assistance.

4. Pressure on the State Department to make human rights representations to foreign governments.
5. Pressure on the State Department in public hearings to take positions on human rights situations in individual countries.

All these activities have had the effect of raising the consciousness of foreign service officers regarding the relevance of human rights to foreign policy. Despite Secretary Henry Kissinger's generally unsympathetic concern during the previous Administration, many officers did become convinced that human rights could no longer be neglected.

It is too early to reach any firm conclusions on the effectiveness of the Congressional role in the Carter Administration. As I indicated earlier, the Congressional view of its role has been splintered between those who seek quick results and those who wish to give the Administration more time and flexibility.

The fourth question is how can Congress play a more effective role? The Congressional role as a partner, rather than as an adversary, in the formulation of foreign policy will be enhanced if the Executive maintains a steady dialogue with the Congress. The new Administration has made constructive efforts in this regard.

Congress needs to think creatively rather than to merely react belatedly to situations. Congress has often been reactive because it has lacked the resources—particularly information—upon which to foretell developments. Perhaps Congress needs its own independent source of information apart from the services already provided by the Congressional Research Service. One suggestion—made in fact by Father Theodore Hesburgh at one of my subcommittee hearings—has been for the U.S. Civil Rights Commission to prepare reports on international human rights issues.

Section 111(e) of the International Development and Food Assistance Act of 1977 contains a provision that at least $750,000 be spent on studies to identify and to carry out programs to encourage increased adherence to civil and political rights in countries eligible for U.S. assistance. I introduced this provision because I thought it would be desirable for AID to spend a small portion of its funds in the civil and political rights area. Notwithstanding the political sensitivity of such activities, it is hoped that AID will develop some creative initiatives from this provision.

Clearly, not enough is known of the initiatives taken by the foreign governments, parliaments, and political parties around the world with respect to human rights issues. Congress can encourage international parliamentary efforts in defense of human rights. Concerting international responses to human rights violations may be one of the effective means open to outsiders seeking to influence another government's actions. The European Parliament has set up a working group on human rights within the framework of an ongoing parliamentary exchange between the U.S. Congress and itself. In early 1977 before the Belgrade Conference, the Council of Europe Assembly in Strasbourg spent several days of debate on the final act of Helsinki. Much attention was devoted to the third basket relating to human rights. The Council of Europe and the Commission and Court established under the European Convention on Human Rights have played a significant role in giving international protection to human rights.

Representatives of international political movements—specifically the World Union of Christian Democrats, the Liberal International, and the Socialist International—are now examining the possibility of joining forces in international human rights efforts. Were the three international democratic political parties able to work together, this would certainly facilitate the exchange of information and joint cooperative initiatives. Obviously, in everyday political life these parties are competing against each other for political power and control. For this reason particularly it has been difficult to obtain agreement of the three parties to agree to work together even in terms of exchanging information and possibly of holding joint conferences. However, human rights should be one area where political parties make an exception to the general rule of maintaining a competitive relationship with each other. The internationals have agreed to meet together and continue to discuss the question of cooperation in the human rights field.

Congress, of course, must ratify more of the human rights conventions. The United States lags badly behind most countries in the numbers of such conventions it has ratified. President Carter has urged the Senate to act on at least four of these conventions—specifically, those dealing with racial discrimination, genocide, civil and political rights, and social, economic, and cultural rights.

But above all Congress needs to inform itself of the complexities inherent in a more forceful stance on human rights. It must recognize the limits on its ability to influence the course of events in other nations and the risks entailed in trying to do so. It should be prepared to look at situations and circumstances from more than one point of view. And it must accept the need for patience. Only long-term, sustained attention to the issues raised by human rights violations is likely to produce the constructive effects. And Congress also must recognize that the sheer weight of poverty can crush the human rights issues.

In short, Congress needs to gain the wisdom and maturity that will increase the value of its contribution to improving the lot of men and women everywhere. This is the challenge before those of us who serve in the U.S. Congress—and one I hope we shall meet.

Bibliography

BILDER, R. B., "Human Rights and U.S. Foreign Policy: Short-Term Prospects," 14 *Virginia Journal of International Law* (1974): 597–609.

BUERGENTHAL, T., and Torney, J., *International Human Rights and International Education*, U.S. National Commission for UNESCO, Department of State (Washington, D.C., 1976).

COHEN, R., and Shestack, J. J., "International Human Rights: A Role for the United States," 14 *Virginia Journal of International Law* 1974): 673, 701.

DREW, E., "Human Rights," *New Yorker*, July 16, 1977, pp. 36–38, 40–42, 44, 46, 51–52, 54–62.

FRASER, D. M., "Freedom and Foreign Policy," *Foreign Policy* (Spring 1977): 140–156.

GOULET, D., "Thinking About Human Rights," 37 *Christianity and Crisis* (May 16, 1977): 100–104.

HENKINS, L., "United States and the Crisis in Human Rights," 14 *Virginia Journal of International Law* (1974): 653–671.

LOESCHER, G. D., "U.S. Human Rights Policy and International Financial Institutions," 33 *The World Today* (December 1977): 453–463.

SALZBERG, J., and Young D., "The Parliamentary Role in Implementing International Human Rights: A U.S. Example," 12 *Texas International Law Journal* (1977): 251–278.

UNITED STATES HOUSE COMMITTEE ON FOREIGN AFFAIRS, *Human Rights in the World Community: A Call for U.S. Leadership* (Washington, D.C., March 27, 1974).

VAN DYKE, V., *Human Rights, the United States, and the World Community* (New York, 1970).

WEISSBRODT, D., "Human Rights Legislation and U.S. Foreign Policy," 7 *Georgia Journal of International and Comparative Law* (1977): 231–287.

PART SEVEN
Human Rights and Priorities in American Foreign Policy

Introduction

THE UNITED STATES IS COMMITTED UNDER THE U.N. CHARTER TO observe, respect, and promote human rights and fundamental freedoms for all peoples. But historically human rights have played only a marginal role in shaping American foreign policy. Not until Jimmy Carter's Presidency were human rights elevated to first rank on the foreign policy agenda of an American Administration. The priority accorded to human rights as a policy issue was underscored in the President's inaugural address, in his speech on March 17, 1977, before the United Nations, and in his remarks on May 22, 1977, at the University of Notre Dame where, in a major address, he proclaimed human rights "as a fundamental tenet of our foreign policy." The "new American foreign policy," said the President, would "no longer separate the traditional issues of war and peace from the new global questions of justice, equity, and human rights." It would be a foreign policy reflecting "our belief that dignity and freedom are fundamental spiritual requirements" in a complex and confused world.

In the introduction to Part Six we spoke of the conflicts that have emerged between the Executive Branch and Congress over the administration of human rights policy. In handling its own human rights policy, the Executive Branch has been vitally concerned with the security interests of the United States. Indeed, in its bilateral relationship with certain nations (e.g., South Korea and Iran) security interests, both military and economic, appear to prevail over human rights concerns. But there is also the perspective of Secretary of State Cyrus Vance, who, in his April 30, 1977, Law Day speech at the University of Georgia, admonished that a balanced view of human rights requires us to be "sensitive to genuine security interests, realizing that outbreaks of armed conflict or terrorism could itself pose a serious threat to human rights."

The issue of human rights versus security interests seems to arise mainly in our relationship to Third World countries beset with severe problems of social and economic development. These problems are often at the center of the political struggle between leftists and rightists within those countries. And, more often than not, the United States finds itself allied with Third World right-wing regimes (mainly in Asia and Latin America) guilty of gross human rights violations or in support of counterinsurgency groups conspiring to overthrow leftist regimes. The thesis advanced in the first essay of Part Seven is that the deeply ingrained antiradical bias of American foreign policymakers in Congress and the Executive Branch militates against the effective implementation of a human rights policy in Third World countries.

Tom J. Farer challenges the notion that Marxist regimes or radical movements in the Third World are a universal threat to American military or economic security. In arguing his case, he emphatically rejects the view, promoted in some official circles, that U.S. support for rightist regimes is "a purely defensive response to the hegemonic ambitions of the Soviet Union." Revolutionary victories in places like Cuba, Chile, Indo-China, and Angola—where the United States was allied, covertly or openly, with counterinsurgency forces—represent, in his opinion, more of a radical ideology of development than a manifestation of Soviet imperialism. The author feels that in the light of the Soviet Union's problems at home and abroad, not to mention that country's own precarious relationship to the Third World, American strategic interests would be better served by relaxing "our rigid definition of the enemy" and by maintaining a posture of neutrality with respect to internal political struggles in those situations where our military security is not seriously affected. With regard to economic security, he also disputes the widely accepted notion that American investments, property, and trade are less threatened in right-wing than in left-wing regimes.

Finally, Farer seeks to demolish what he calls the "moral case for sustaining the popular, congressional, and to a considerable extent bureaucratic bias in favor of right-wing regimes faced with actual or latent opposition from the left." He rejects the implicit assumption on the part of many observers that right-wing "authoritarian" regimes afford to citizens and groups a larger measure of freedom than do left-wing "totalitarian" regimes. Farer is not suggesting that the governments of Cuba, Chile, Angola, Vietnam, Cambodia, and Laos are innocent of gross violations of human rights or that the United States should not use its influence to protect human rights in such regimes as these. Rather his purpose has been to rebut the "presumptive attribution of superior moral features to regimes of the right" that have *uniformly* prompted the United States into supporting counterinsurgency forces and dulled her capacity to assess, on a case-by-case basis, what strategies would really serve American interests and human rights in given areas of the world.

Richard B. Lillich, who shares the concern for the false dichotomy that Farer sees between security interests and human rights, underscores the importance of constructing a coherent policy framework "to replace the prior unsatisfactory ad hoc approach" to human rights policy-making. He proposes a number of offensive stratagems and initiatives that would justify, on humanitarian grounds, "interference" in the affairs of other countries.

Lillich distinguishes between the processes of "intercession" and "intervention." A coherent policy of intercession on behalf of human rights, ranging from low-level (and largely symbolic) maneuvers to more serious "intrusions," would include (1) quiet diplomatic actions signaling disapproval of a country's human rights record, (2) open expressions of sympathy or support for oppressed individuals, including public criticism of a country's human rights violations, (3) formal protests by the President, ambassadors, and State Department officials, (4) systematic use of international forums and their judicial or quasi-judicial enforcement agencies on behalf of human rights, and (5) the uniform and consistent application of economic sanctions already embodied in Congressional statutes such as the Foreign Assistance Act, the Trade Reform Act (Jackson-Vanik Amendment), the International Development and Food Assistance Act, and the International Security Assistance and Arms Export Control Act.

The most extreme form of interference in the affairs of a nation is actual intervention involving the use of force. Here the concern of Lillich is not rescue operations—such as at Entebbe, where a nation sought to liberate its own from unlawful detention—but rather those *seemingly* less justifiable interventions to protect persons against the excessive cruelty or injustices of their own governments. Lillich favors the use of such interventions as "one part . . . of a long continuum of possible strategies for influencing other states for human rights purposes." International law, in his view, sanctions humanitarian interventions. On the other hand, the U.N. Charter contains a provision that a state is not to interfere in another state with respect to its territorial independence or its political integrity. Whether this provision negates the right of one state to exercise control over the acts of another to protect the latter's inhabitants against violations of their fundamental rights is the subject of fervid dispute among human rights scholars and diplomats alike.

It has been pointed out that because there is a broad consensus in the United Nations against forced intervention—as manifested, for example, in the General Assembly debate over Indian intervention in Bangladesh—the United States should be extremely cautious about moving to intervene in any nation independent of that consensus. There has been some suggestion that this consensus may have the force of law. But the weight of authority, both classical and modern, according to Lillich, is on the side of intervention. And in the absence of an international peace-keeping force that is responsive to gross human rights violations, the United States should insist upon the legality of and reserve the residual right to develop a policy of humanitarian intervention.

A central question is the extent to which certain rights should be given priority in American foreign policy. The official American commitment, as defined by statute, is "to promote human rights and fundamental freedoms." The U.S. position is that the Universal Declaration of Human Rights constitutes, as a matter of law, an authoritative guide to the Department of State in directing its attention to human rights problems throughout the world. Secretary of State Vance, in his University of Georgia address, defined human rights as (1) "the right to be free from governmental violation of the integrity of the person," (2) "the right to the fulfillment of such vital needs as food, shelter, health care, and education," and (3) "the right to enjoy civil and political liberties."

It has been suggested by some that as a matter of our international interest American foreign policy might be directed toward promoting liberal democracy throughout the world. The majority of policy-makers maintain that such a goal is unrealistic and beyond the capacity of American foreign policy. They are of the opinion that the United States should pursue the more modest goal of preventing human degradation wherever it may occur and argue that U.S. foreign policy would be more effective by concentrating on the most flagrant violations of human rights, namely, torture, summary execution, and prolonged detention without trial.

We conclude this introduction by noting that the Carter Administration initially employed publicized approaches and statements to advance the cause of international human rights. However, the necessity to achieve cooperative relationships, abide by long-standing commitments, or secure other goals has, in particular cases, limited the means available to pursue human rights objectives. The Administration now seems to favor the use of quiet diplomacy to promote the cause of human rights abroad. The United States is conscious of the need to calculate the potential consequences of American actions and in many instances now accepts the view that long-term improvement in human rights may be best fostered through increased contacts, economic relations, and the exchange of ideas. It is current Administration policy to employ quiet diplomacy before public statements are made or substantive actions are taken. It is believed that quiet diplomacy has the important virtue of allowing a government to respond to intercessions without seeming to yield to outside pressure.

Quiet diplomacy is not viewed by the Administration as minimal action or no action at all. A wide range of options exists within the realm of quiet diplomacy. However, there is as yet no systematic research specifying the conditions under which quiet diplomacy in fact succeeds. Undoubtedly there are regimes that are sensitive and responsive to quiet but forceful external initiatives and governments that are prepared to moderate their policies to preclude a publicity campaign, but social scientists should examine the relative success and failure of these options for more informed policy-making in the future.

12: On a Collision Course: The American Campaign for Human Rights and the Antiradical Bias in the Third World

TOM J. FARER

FROM THE REVOLUTIONARY WAR OF INDEPENDENCE TO THIS DAY, concern for human rights has been a prominent theme in the rhetoric of American foreign policy.[1] From time to time it probably has affected the reality as well.

The decades of the Cold War were no exception. Ostensibly we opposed the spread of Soviet and Chinese power not only for amoral reasons of state, but also, as we constantly reiterated, to defend the reality and expand the possibility of human freedom.[2] Why, then, are we flattered or agitated, as the individual case may be, by the sense of a new departure? In part, of course, because during the Kissinger years the theme of moral conflict was consciously muted. In equal or larger part because for the first time since the end of the World War II the Executive Branch seems broadly willing to recognize violations of human rights in states ruled by anticommunist regimes. The conspiracy of silence about the more nauseating participants in the "Free World Coalition" has collapsed. In the wake of its collapse we have witnessed some tentative steps, reminiscent of the first fearful locomotions of the long bedridden invalid, to translate candor into effective action.

Permanent Enemies and Bad Friends

Of the varied obstacles to effective action few are more intimidating than our visceral hostility to Third World movements whose leaders profess or at least are alleged to profess inspiration from some variant of the Marxist faith. Our determined opposition to such radical movements[3] is reiterated in the daily gestures of the national mind. Liberal journalists and politicians urge support for black aspirations in southern Africa lest the blacks turn to "radical" or "pro-communist" leaders. Their conservative counterparts urge opposite policies to achieve the same end of "saving southern Africa for the West." The disagreement is only on means.

Our fear and loathing of Marxist movements has helped to propel us into indiscriminate support of right-wing regimes including many whose behavior is characterized by persistent and gross violation of human rights. In the past, proposals to disengage from the more atrocious governments, much less to punish and thus in some cases incidentally destabilize them, have often been aborted by fears that diminished U.S. support might lead to their replacement by regimes of the left. This fear continues, albeit less openly and with somewhat less effect[4] to influence the debate over *means* for curbing violations of human rights. The putative Marxist threat is certain to remain a salient concern in this respect because right-wing, Third World regimes are the most susceptible to the sanctions and incentives we are able to deploy on behalf of human rights.

Antagonism to Marxist movements in the Third World rests both on moral and material or, in the broadest sense of the word, "strategic" grounds. Strategic concerns are focused upon the protection of investments and markets, access to raw materials, the protection of friendly states, competitive access to sites for military facilities and, most profoundly, upon direct threats to the institutions of our society whether executed through propaganda or covert physical intervention. I propose to defend three modest propositions: (1) that our strategic fears are exaggerated, (2) that indiscriminate support of vicious right-wing governments itself constitutes a threat to U.S. strategic interests, and (3) that there is no persuasive moral case for sustaining the popular, Congressional, and to a considerable extent bureaucratic bias in favor of right-wing regimes faced with actual or latent opposition from the left.

Before turning to the defense of those propositions I should note that my assumption that an antiradical bias has powerfully influenced the shape of U.S. foreign policy is not wholly uncontroversial. It has encountered two centers of resistance. One marshals such acts as our post-1948 entente with Marshal Tito and our brief flirtation with Kwame Nkrumah as decisive evidence of our freedom from any dogmatic antagonism to leftist regimes. The other insists that our support of rightist governments stems primarily from U.S. efforts to contain the aggressive thrust of the Soviet Union rather than from a profound ideological bias against Marxist movements however free of Soviet domination. Obviously, I have found both arguments unpersuasive. Let me explain why.

All the cases cited to demonstrate a shrewd, flexible discrimination are instances of pragmatic relations with *established governments*. Wherever we had a choice among competitors for power—as we did in the Belgian Congo, Angola, Guyana, Indo-China, and the Dominican Republic—we sought with varying degrees of effort to block the accession of leaders who identified themselves as leftists. Moreover, where leftists formed governments but, as in Guatemala and more recently in Chile, seemed vulnerable to rightest[5] opponents, we have been inclined to conspire with the latter to destroy the former.

Only by substituting faith for reason can we construe U.S. behavior as a purely defensive response to the hegemonic ambitions of the Soviet Union. I assume that fear of Soviet expansion was genuinely experienced by senior figures in the national security establishment. I will accept the proposition that in terms of those fears we may explain aid to a right-wing Greek government, raised to legitimacy on British bayonets and liberally staffed with Nazi collaborators. Although the communist insurgents were undeniably indigenous and received far less external assistance than that which the British and we delivered to their opponents, the proximity of Soviet power and the example of Poland and the other satellites threatened a loss of autonomy if the Greek communists won.

But they explain rather less well our reenthronement of the Iranian shah in 1954 following his resignation and flight. Why was the shah a clearly better guarantor of Iranian independence than the nationalist politician Mossadegh? Did we maneuver Mossadegh's ouster, after he had nationalized the Anglo-Iranian Oil Company, to thwart the Soviet Union or to penalize a government that had humbled a major ally while violating the sanctity of an investment agreement by nationalizing the Anglo-Iranian Oil Company? Or was it some combination of the two—our fearing that Mossadegh would require the support of the local communists and being convinced that they would be instruments of the Soviet Union?

The Russia-centered explanation of U.S. foreign policy becomes still less satisfactory when we turn to the whole counterinsurgency phenomenon. Counterinsurgency was always more than a set of tactics. It was inspired by an ideology, a world view in which apostles of open and closed economic systems, of consumer-oriented and demand economies, were locked in global combat. What was at stake, the ideologues of counterinsurgency argued, were two ways of life, two forms of political and economic development, and two visions of global order. Walter Rostow placed Vietnam in this larger context when he spoke exultantly of Ho Chi Minh as the last of the romantic revolutionaries. Victory for the United States in Vietnam would turn prophesy into reality and push reform into incremental, technocratic channels. Conversely, a victory for Ho would energize other revolutionaries. To the counterinsurgency zealots, aggression launched from China or the USSR no longer seemed the central threat to Western interests. Ho Chi Minh was not a proxy for the communist giants; rather he was the expression of an ideology of development which it was in our interest to obstruct.

Why? That, it seems to me, was always less clear. Different advocates had different theories. Some invoked security needs, but the reference was often circular, since prominent among the needs in question were those of the incumbents whom the theory itself assumed we had to protect. Others spoke of access to raw materials, the security of and opportunities for U.S. investors, and the availability of markets for our exports. But these latter themes, so pronounced in U.S. policy for over a half-century before World War II, were curiously muted. In the face of the Leninist claim that economic interests determine foreign policy in capitalist countries, American statesmen suddenly seemed diffident about declaring publicly the salience of such interests. Hence the determined effort to force the great bulk of U.S. coercive activity under a classic, balance-of-power blanket.

Arguably inadequate as a wrap for all our policies on the periphery of China and the Soviet Union, in Latin America the security rationale seems no larger than a loincloth, covering some vital parts, no doubt, but leaving others prominently exposed. It may not even cover Cuba very well, the case most frequently cited to support the proposition that revolutionary regimes have an almost irresistible impulse for military cooperation with the Soviet Union. What advocates of this proposition normally fail to note is that to a revolutionary like Castro, secretly determined on the radical transformation of his society, there were ample reasons to expect the worse from the United States once his intentions became clear.

There was not only the history of repeated interventions in Cuban affairs on behalf of American investors. In 1954 we had confirmed the continuity of American policy toward Latin America by subverting a democratically elected government in Guatemala where our historical ties were more tenuous and our vested economic interests less luxuriant than in Cuba.[6] Thus, even without the added stimulus of incipient covert operations against his government plus crescendoing hostility in the U.S. media and Congress, Castro might rationally have concluded that his only hope of survival lay in jumping under the Soviet umbrella.

Military Security

Given what we have learned in the two decades since the Green Berets marched into Vietnam, what can reasonably be said now about the security implications of a multiplication of regimes trying to adapt Chinese, Cuban, or Russian development models to their own national conditions? In the first place, let us reaffirm the circularity of one segment of the security argument: In order to preserve right-wing governments almost everywhere, we have opposed the triumph of a radical movement almost anywhere. Thus, if we relax our rigid definition of the enemy, a significant chunk of the security problem slides away.

The other principal dimension of the problem has been governed by military requirements flowing directly from our competitive relations with the Soviet Union and China. In the Third World we have sought to acquire bases for ourselves while denying them to our adversaries. The abatement of our Chinaphobia combined with dramatic changes in military technology have vastly diminished our need for overseas bases. Technology also has reduced the potential benefit of such bases to the Soviet Union except in connection with its expanded naval operations. For a number of reasons, including reliance on land-based air power and small service forces, base rights are in fact more important to the Russian navy than to ours.[7]

Soviet failure to acquire base rights in Mozambique or Angola should discourage any facile equation of a radical triumph in a Third World state with the promotion of Soviet security interests. We, of course, retain the capability to drive regimes under a Soviet security blanket, whether by directly threatening their political independence (as we did in the case of Cuba) or by overarming their enemies (as we may be doing in parts of the Middle East and Asia) or by refusing to deter aggressive neighbors when it is in our power to do so (as may yet happen in the case of Mozambique and other neighbors of Rhodesia and South Africa). We have at our disposal ample incentives to secure the neutrality of even radical regimes. For without wishing to taunt the Bear, let us be frank. It labors under severe handicaps: a dwarf economy in comparison to the West, second-rate technology, barely enough food to feed itself, and a stodgy, still rather provincial leadership. Clearly, we have much more to offer than our principal competitor.

It does not follow that considerations of military security can never justify a preference for one domestic political faction over another. Where one faction is more likely to threaten a neighbor whose security remains somehow linked to our own, we should prefer and in modest ways encourage the other. And in the unlikely event of a faction genuinely determined to submit to Soviet discipline even after it acquires the rudder of state, we should again naturally prefer its opponent. But in the overwhelming majority of internal conflicts, security factors do not justify our involvement even as cheerleaders.

Economic Security

Military security has not, of course, been the exclusive justification for the powerful American bias against radical movements in the Third World. Other considerations of state have buttressed it. Economic interests may appear a little crass, even slightly embarrassing; but it would be fatuous to suggest that they are negligible factors in shaping the attitudes which dominate day-to-day American diplomacy.

Wherein lies the radical threat? Are radical regimes more likely to nationalize existing American investments? less likely to compensate adequately? less likely to encourage new capital investment? less open to foreign trade? And does it really matter very much?

Concern over the safety of existing investment rests on the following assumptions: that radicals are more likely to expropriate U.S. holdings and less likely to pay adequate compensation and that the resulting costs to the American people are not inconsequential. What are the facts?

Both moderate and conservative Third World governments, driven like their radical counterparts by a passion for autonomy, have themselves demonstrated a lusty appetite for national ownership of important industrial and natural resources. Nationalization of our most valuable investments, the oil concessions, proceeds in impeccably conservative as well as radical states. There is in fact no evident correlation between the pace and extent of nationalization in a given oil producer and the ideological bent of its rulers. The Kuwaitis, for instance, are now effecting the total displacement of foreign ownership while the presumably radical Libyans apparently prefer to retain several Western companies as concessionaires.

While conservative governments prove themselves susceptible to the virus of nationalization, certain left-wing governments preserve or solicit foreign investments. The Angolan government, for instance, uses Cuban troops to help protect Gulf Oil Company facilities in

Cabinda. Vietnam has declared its receptivity to Western, apparently including American, oil investments.

The pattern of compensation for nationalized investments also is rather more diverse than many American business people probably imagine. Though few, if any, countries satisfy the official American preference for "going business value" payable immediately in hard currency or its equivalent, moderate-to-conservative governments, encouraged by a continuing need for capital, technical assistance, and access to Western markets, generally have negotiated very large settlements with individual investors. The same constraints doubtlessly influence radical regimes as well, but with less compelling force. Clearly they did not suffice in Chile and Cuba.

It is, however, unclear how much freight those precedents will carry. Through their dominant role in the Chilean economy over many decades, the American copper companies had acquired an enormous symbolic importance in local politics. Moreover, Chilean leftists found the United States and one or more of the major American investors active participants in the domestic political struggle against their electoral triumph. Cuban nationalization of American investments, coincident with an illusory offer of compensation, was an explicit response to Eisenhower's elimination of the Cuban sugar quota, a step which threatened the economic strangulation of Castro's nascent regime. Other foreign property was subsequently expropriated, but Castro nogotiated compensation settlements with the concerned European governments.

More important, perhaps, than the peculiarities of each case was the environment in which they arose, an environment characterized by U.S. hostility to radicals and a tradition of American intervention often encouraged and sometimes facilitated by U.S. corporations.

Recently the Cuban government has indicated willingness to negotiate a settlement of compensation claims. A lump-sum settlement would follow the precedents we have established with Eastern European governments. Whatever their theory about the right of the state to expropriate without compensation, in practice communist governments, once they detect U.S. willingness to accept their existence, seem prepared to pay substantial compensation as a precondition of full-scale normalization of relations.

Compensation paid by conservative governments is, nevertheless, likely to be fuller and more prompt. Their development strategies are more dependent on access to American markets and capital. Expropriation unaccompanied by reasonable compensation frightens private capital and activates the sanctioning machinery of the World Bank and other public lenders. Conservatives are, in addition, somewhat freer from political inhibitions on making adequate compensation.

Radicals must offer a secular explanation of the misery, humiliation, and felt injustice which goad their potential supporters. Marxism locates the source of popular dissatisfaction in the institutions of capitalism. The labor theory of value conveniently converts profits into theft. How, then, after the revolution can compensation be justified by a pragmatic elite? Where party discipline is strong and the elite is secure, perhaps the problem of explanation can be readily finessed. But the more genuinely egalitarian the radical movement, the narrower its room for pragmatic maneuver. Thus one would expect a radical movement that achieves power democratically to be least capable of compromising with the demands for adequate compensation.

Assuming that an elite's radical credentials will affect the incidence of expropriation and the magnitude of compensation, are the sums involved sufficient to impact significantly on the overall U.S. national interest? In 1974 our total direct investment in the developing countries was $28.5 billion, 24 percent of our global total, equivalent in value to about 2 percent of gross national product for that one year. Over $8 billion of that $28 billion represented petroleum investment, much of which has since been nationalized by conservative regimes. If we exclude petroleum's extraordinary and arguably transient profits from the calculation, the 1974 income earned by our Third World investments was less than $3 billion, roughly one-quarter of 1 percent of one year's national income. To put the matter still further into perspective, our investments are concentrated in relatively few developing countries. The issue, after all, is not whether the United States should be indifferent to the fate of all repressive conservative regimes, but whether we should exercise a powerful presumption on their behalf.

The putative threat to U.S. exports seems still less consequential. Autonomous communist governments outside Eastern Europe have shown no inclination toward economic integration with the Soviet Union. The problem, such as it may be, consists rather in the possible reduction of imports occasioned by the pursuit of egalitarian goals. Radical governments should, in theory, dam the flow of consumer luxuries—cars, television, stereos, and so on—in which high technology states still enjoy some comparative advantage. Though this may occur, the prospect is not terribly daunting. The greater part of our exports go to other developed states. The bulk of the remainder consists largely of agricultural products, arms, capital goods, and associated knowhow and is, moreover, concentrated in a very few trading partners. For example, in 1975 over two-thirds of our $15.6 billion worth of exports to Latin America were absorbed by three countries: Mexico ($5.1 billion), Brazil ($3.1 billion), and Venezuela ($2.2 billion). The next ranking country was Colombia at $.64 billion. So we find here little basis for objecting to a very much more selective approach to defining the enemy.

The size of Third World debt owed by certain right-wing governments to private financial institutions in the United States also may influence the prevailing view of radical movements. In this case too, however, the concentration of U.S. interests among other factors, should induce a more relaxed and discriminating response. Today a mere six countries account for two-thirds of all the non-oil-exporting developing countries' obligations to banks. There is, moreover, serious doubt about the net advantage to the American economy of encouraging the export of capital at this time. Some authorities have argued that we are already experiencing a serious capital shortage.

Unbending opponents of Third World radical movements often invoke access to raw materials as one basis for their antipathy. Imports supply a significant percentage of total U.S. demand for a great variety of minerals, in part because, though there may be domestic sources or substitutes, they are more expensive. We import virtually 100 percent of our platinum, mica, chromium, strontium, cobalt, tantalum, columbium and manganese; over 75 percent of such essential minerals as asbestos, aluminum, tin, and nickel; and though the percentage is a good deal lower, the significance of imports is still very great in the case of tungsten, petroleum, iron, and vanadium, among others on the list of 41 prepared by the Joint Economic Committee of the Congress.

One is struck, however, both by the great diversity of suppliers and the number of them that are developed states. Unless one envisions radical revolution as a torrent restrained only by the dam of U.S. power from engulfing the entire southern hemisphere, this variety of sources should by itself suggest that the dimensions of the threat are rather less than we are sometimes urged to believe. Skeptics also should ask the tocsin ringers why we should doubt that in the generality of cases, radical governments will be as anxious as conservative ones to sell their products at the best available price.

As far as price is concerned, ideology seems irrelevant. Different attitudes toward inflating the price of oil, for example, are governed by differences in reserve capacity and current revenue needs. Within OPEC a common conservatism has hardly produced a common front on prices between Saudis and Iranians. Nor, as we discovered, is an anti-Western embargo a weapon likely to recommend itself exclusively to Marxists.

While exaggerating the costs to our national interests arising from a proliferation of Marxist regimes, we have failed conversely to appreciate the full costs and risks of intimate indiscriminate association with the right. The cost most generally recognized is that incurred from the impulse to bail out ideologically impeccable losers. Losers are those who, as a consequence of incompetence and/or social forces beyond their control, cannot hack it on their own.

Our past efforts to rectify the natural balance of forces have incurred vast diplomatic, financial, moral, and human losses. The easy answer to this concern—that nothing in our generalized embrace of the right and hostility to the left prevents us from cutting our losses—ignores the domestic politics of foreign policy. Without the compelling force of a Manichaean view of international relations, the American electorate probably will not bear the costs of a global commitment to establish and sustain anti-Marxist governments. In order to nourish that view of the world, the national security bureaucracy and its political principals, buttressed by a complaisant mass media, have until very recently winked at the abuse of human rights in conservative states while trumpeting news of comparable delinquencies committed by Marxist regimes. Once having stirred up an electorate always seething with evangelical emotions, elite attempts at the prudent pruning of losers encounter formidable political obstacles.

Given the electorate's current agnosticism, my concern may seem obsolete. But that conclusion fails to take into account the residual strength of a visceral anticommunism which, after all, has for three decades serviced a luxurious variety of material, social, and psychic needs. A sustained and evenhanded effort to promote human rights will progressively inoculate the American public against the Manichaean virus. And thus it will facilitate the practice of a shrewd and flexible, and possibly of a more consistently moral, diplomacy.

There arises from our insufficiently discriminating embrace of the right a far more serious yet hardly noticed peril. It is a threat not to the United States as a participant in the game of nations, but rather to the relatively free and humane character of its society.

Ideas are contagious. Most societies—whether of the First, Second or Third Worlds—face comparable problems of alienation, class conflict, crime, ethnic tension, inflation, and unemployment. The temptation to resolve contradictions by suppressing them, to eliminate social tensions by annihilating one side of the dialogue, lurks in every nation.

Any nation's commitment to an open political process rooted in the egalitarian distribution of fundamental political and civil rights needs constant reaffirmation. The nation's commitment weakens if its government celebrates human rights at home while plainly assisting those who assault them abroad, even hailing the delinquents' achievement of domestic "order" and economic progress.

The potentially erosive influence on our own democratic process comes primarily from the rightist authoritarians who solicit our support and collaboration rather than from their left-wing enemies. The latter offer solutions to the problems of modern society which rub against the grain of our national ethos and challenge an overwhelming phalanx of vested interests. The former, on the other hand, being zealously committed to traditional capitalist institutions and economic formulas, offer solutions to contemporary societal ills which promise to reenforce existing hierarchies in the name of private enterprise and individual initiative. Thus they appeal to the self-interest of the upper, and even arguably the middle, classes and to the belief structure of the overwhelming majority of Americans. Moreover, having themselves chosen avenues of development which require a warm and intimate relationship with American investors and a continual flow-through of American managerial and technical personnel, they have channels for the projection of influence unavailable to regimes of the left which are more circumspect in their dealings with American capital and more autarkic in their approach to development.

During the 1930's, under conditions of economic recession, rapid social change, and a perceived crisis of law and order, liberal capitalism yielded in several European countries to its fascist deformity. Italy and Germany then, like a number of Third World countries now, exemplified the dissoluble character of the marriage between capitalism and democracy. There are few countries that can claim immunity to the risk of divorce.

The problem is not simply one of a contagion of ideas among elites. Just as the defenders of freedom feel threatened by powerful foreign enemies of the open society, so the authoritarians who rely on our goodwill are threatened by the existence of a liberal and democratic America which will shelter their enemies, condemn their barbarities and, by its very existence, challenge their view that capitalism requires the suspension of freedom. Hence they are bound to support forces and trends in our own society infirmly committed to democratic institutions.

Ideology and Human Rights: The Illusory-Pluralism Trap

The moral case for the anti-Marxist tilt in our relations with the Third World rests on a distorted version of the useful distinction between merely authoritarian regimes, on the one hand, and totalitarian ones on the other. In this respect *The Economist* is illustrative. Having concluded, in September 1974, that the "alternative to the Pinochet regime [in Chile] was the imposition of a totalitarianism of the left ... ," it proceeded to reject the suggestion that Pinochet in turn represented the totalitarian right:

> The word totalitarian was coined to apply to those governments—most notably the communist ones—which set out to bring almost every aspect of life under the control of the ruling party. The junta in Chile is not quite like that. Its government is an authoritarian one, and a very tough specimen of the breed, but it has not sought to impose its ideas on the totality of public life. Politics have been abolished, but men can still pursue their economic activities with a certain degree of independence; there remains a good deal of freedom in the world of culture and religion; people still have the right to travel in and out of the country. These things matter, because they mean that some centres of power and influence and independent opinion can still exist outside the reach of the government's arm. Such a country is not a totalitarian one, because the rudiments of pluralism survive.
>
> The distinction is important for Chile. The corners of freedom that can still be found even within an authoritarian state give men the possibility to recover the other freedoms they have lost. These fragments of freedom tend to expand as the regime gains more confidence in itself; there is less intrusion into people's lives in Spain today than there was 20 years ago—or than there is in Chile now.[8]

Does the putative distinction between right and left enjoy much intellectual merit? To begin with, one may reasonably doubt that the generality of right-wing autocrats has an inclination to restore freedom "as the regime gains more confidence in itself." "Confidence about what?" one may ask. Presumably about its success in so mutilating and intimidating the human beings and institutions of the left—as well as those liberals and moderate conservatives who will defend human rights and unexpurgated democracy—that the desired repressive social order can be maintained with reduced public order expenditures and less offense to humanitarian constituencies in the Western democracies.

Even if such regimes could acquire the necessary confidence, despite their pursuit of harshly inegalitarian ends which tend today to generate opposition, the result would hardly be anything we might call freedom. Anyone who bothers to listen to what Pinochet or the Brazil "hard-liners" or other of this breed say and write cannot avoid discovering a contempt for democracy indistinguishable from the views of the most hardened Stalinist.

The Spanish precedent is hardly felicitous. In the first place, the regime built its confidence like a vampire. One hundred thousand would be a conservative estimate of the persons massacred by Franco *following* his absolute triumph. This on top of the hundreds of thousands in exile and the vast number of potential enemies—republicans, anarchists, socialists, communists, liberals, and regional nationalists—killed in the course of the civil war. What Spain illustrates, then, is the degree of inhumanity required to infuse a regime with confidence when it is driven by ideological zeal and is determined to impose policies antagonistic to the interests of a large segment of the population.

Nor does Spain nicely exemplify a progressive slackening of the fascist impulse. The impulse survived over three decades; time simply decimated the ranks of those it possessed. Gradually they lost the power to impose the brutal regimen which they continued to prefer. The tenacity of fascism was impressive. Thirty-five years after Franco crushed the last vestige of resistance in a country of Western Europe directly exposed to the currents of liberalism and the pressure of neighboring democracies, political parties even of the center-right were still outlawed.

Compare Czechoslovakia in 1968 just before the Russian invasion braked the gathering momentum of self-liberation. Far more insulated by geography and international politics from the liberalizing influence of the West, that country seemed as close as Spain at Franco's death to the threshold of a free society.

There is simply no persuasive historical basis for the conclusion that right-wing autocracies are less tenacious and more subject to erosion by the yearning for freedom than those of the left. Nor is there a persuasive theoretical case.

A private sector within the economy does not necessarily represent a center "of power and influence and independent opinion ... outside the reach of the government's arm." In fact, the government may be little more than the militarized arm of the private sector. Or the two may be so intensely intertwined by mutual interest that no important differences of opinion can emerge. Or businessmen may exist purely at the sufferance of a military caste, Mamluks who prefer to leave economic activity to carefully screened and cowed civilians made malleable as well by the guarantee of liberal profits. Nor is it inevitable that cultural associations serve as independent centers of power. For they, too, can be participants in the regime or its docile servants.

Just as the presence of ostensibly nongovernmental institutions does not guarantee the existence of pluralism, so their absence does not necessarily assure monolithic control. However strong its aspiration to centrally directed uniformity, a Marxist party cannot annul the social, economic, political, and in some cases cultural contradictions that promote division within its ranks and encourage appeals for support to constituencies outside the elite structure. Who after witnessing the last decade's profound struggles within China will any longer speak of the "blue ants."

Neither in precedent, such as it is, nor in theory do I find a basis for the presumptive attribution of superior moral features to regimes of the right. What makes some regimes more tenacious and vicious than others is a function of national history, the domestic environment, the international context and, perhaps, the personality of leading figures. Ideology can make a regime more brutal where its application is peculiarly inappropriate to the particular society. If, for instance, a modern, highly secularized nation fell under the thrall of a band of Puritan fascists determined to reconstruct society along theological lines, there would be no alternative to an unending murderous repression.

Thus ideology needs to be taken into account as one of several factors that help us to anticipate the humanitarian dimensions of a particular movement's political triumph. But like the other factors, it does not in the abstract justify a powerful presumption in favor of fascists, caudillos, and other assorted horsemen of the right. In the moral realm, as in the practical, there is no satisfactory alternative to considering each case on its complicated and often precarious merits. Until this modest proposition is generally accepted by Congress and the national security bureaucracy, the antiradical bias will continue to constrain U.S. efforts to defend and promote human rights.

NOTES

1. See, for instance, the Joint Congressional Resolution declaring war on Spain in 1898 which, in its justificatory preamble, invokes "the abhorrent conditions which have existed for more than three years in the Island of Cuba [and which] have shocked the moral sense of the people of the United States." Preamble to the Joint Resolution of Congress of April 20, 1898, 30 Stat. 738 (1899).

2. See, for instance, President Kennedy's speech to the Latin American diplomatic corps on March 13, 1961, announcing the Alliance for Progress, quoted in A. Schlesinger, *A Thousand Days* (Houghton Mifflin, 1965), pp. 204-205.

3. In popular political and journalistic discourse, "leftist," "Marxist," "radical" and "revolutionary" are generally used interchangeably and applied

indiscriminately to regimes and movements with different roots, clientele, patrons, and programs. Their differences are frequently discounted or entirely ignored either because they are not observed or because they are deemed inconsequential in comparison to the characteristics shared by political movements that fall under these labels. The salient shared characteristics that tend to antagonize Americans are hostility to the market economy, a declared suspicion of foreign investment, an at least rhetorical commitment to the support of revolutions wherever they may be attempted, insistence on the inevitability of class exploitation and conflict and a coincident emphasis on the need to redistribute wealth and to eliminate party politics (which are assumed to be class-based), the unqualified subordination of property rights to collective interests, efforts to mobilize the lower classes for political and economic ends, and readiness to accept economic and military assistance from communist states, particularly from the Soviet Union. Perhaps most important of all as a cause of their negative image, they share the characteristic of having replaced or being engaged in the attempt to replace governments anxious to ally themselves with the United States. My object is to demonstrate the moral and strategic misconceptions that encourage an indiscriminate equation of governments or movements possessing the enumerated characteristics with "the enemy." In pursuing that object, while I will follow the popular custom of using "Marxist," "radical," and the like interchangeably, it must be apparent that for any purpose other than alluding to a popular prejudice I think all of these labels dangerously imprecise.

4. There clearly has been a fundamental change of perspective in the White House and the highest reaches of the State Department, a change exemplified by Ambassador Young, who has stated unequivocally that a repressive, right-wing regime's invocation of the Marxist threat will no longer suffice to attract U.S. support. But the House of Representatives' vote to bar aid to Mozambique and Angola illustrates the continued strength of the traditional mind-set.

5. That is to say, regimes that generally side with the United States on East-West issues, encourage foreign investment, perpetuate or intensify income inequality, and employ capitalist rhetoric to justify the social and economic order over which they preside.

6. See, for example, R. Steel, *Pax Americana* (New York: Viking Press, 1967), p. 202.

7. T. J. Farer, *War Clouds on the Horn of Africa: A Crisis for Détente* (New York: Carnegie Endowment, 1976), pp. 110–111.

8. "The Pinochet Way," 252 *The Economist* (September 14, 1974): 17.

13: A United States Policy of Humanitarian Intervention and Intercession

RICHARD B. LILLICH

"NEVER CONFUSE MOVEMENT WITH ACTION," ERNEST HEMINGWAY supposedly said.[1] This wise admonition should be kept in mind when surveying the Carter Administration's initial preachments on international human rights. Nonetheless, on balance, the movement to stress human rights concerns in the foreign policy process has been followed up by affirmative action; deeds have backed up rhetoric, as the repeal of the Byrd Amendment and the termination of military assistance to various Latin American juntas make clear. The United States undeniably has come a long way in a relatively short time. Just five years ago, for instance, this writer, in an introductory essay to a Symposium on Human Rights and United States Foreign Policy, seconded Tom Farer's apt observation that "[h]uman rights are the stepchildren of United States foreign policy"[2] and duly noted Richard Bilder's even more pessimistic contention that "human rights considerations seem likely to play only a relatively low role in U.S. foreign policy during the next few years."[3] How pleased the latter must feel now that events have proven his worst fears wrong!

Granted that—as President Carter observed in his commencement address at Notre Dame—the United States' "[foreign] policy should reflect our people's basic commitment to promote the cause of human rights,"[4] what strategies and techniques are most likely to achieve this objective while minimizing the risk of proving counterproductive? This problem is a relatively new one, if only because in the past national security rhetoric usually has been invoked to justify decisions which have ignored or overridden human rights concerns.

Copyright by The Procedural Aspects of International Law Institute, Inc., 1978. The author completed this chapter in June 1977.

One only need recall that in 1972 President Richard Nixon, having studiously avoided commenting on the brutal atrocities committed by the Pakistani army in what is now Bangladesh, had the further callousness to distinguish between "the political side" of the crisis and what he regarded as "the humanitarian *side issue*."[5] Now that humanitarian concerns have moved from the wings to center stage in the foreign policy decision-making process,[6] the need to construct some sort of policy framework to replace the prior unsatisfactory ad hoc approach is apparent. The present essay, which focuses on various humanitarian intervention and intercession options available to the United States, is a modest contribution to one aspect of this task of construction.[7]

Before proceeding, it is best to clarify exactly what is meant by the terms "intervention" and "intercession." The first term is used frequently, and often inaccurately; the second term, unfortunately, is rarely used at all. In spite of attempts to broaden the meaning of intervention to include everything from the landing of marines to an off-the-cuff response by Ambassador Andrew Young during an impromptu news conference, the term has been defined since the days of Lassa Oppenheim to mean a "dictatorial interference by a State in the affairs of another State for the purpose of maintaining or altering the actual condition of things."[8] This "dictatorial interference" usually involves the use of or the threat of the use of force. Intercession, on the other hand, has been defined as "interference consisting in friendly advice given or friendly offers made with regard to the domestic affairs of another State."[9] In diplomatic parlance, it should be noted, the word "friendly" is used to characterize almost any relationship—short of armed conflict—between sovereign states.[10] Thus, while both intervention and intercession are forms of interference in the internal affairs of other states, the distinction between the two lies in the fact that intervention is dictatorial and often forceful, while intercession includes a wide range of nominally friendly acts ranging from expressions of sympathy for oppressed persons in another state to economic or political sanctions, stopping short only of the actual use of force.

Humanitarian intervention, which occurs frequently and is the logical end of a long continuum of intercessionary-interventionary acts, has received considerable scholarly attention during the past decade.[11] It also is a matter of considerable concern to the U.S. government, which has relied on the doctrine to justify forcible measures it has undertaken on several occasions since World War II—most recently in the evacuation of both foreigners and U.S. nationals from Cambodia and South Vietnam in April 1975.[12] Rather than begin a discussion with this act of last resort, however, it is more profitable to start with an examination of various intercessionary acts which the United States might take in its day-to-day efforts to promote human rights in states with which it has relations. After considering what can be done at "six, eight, and ten o'clock," this essay will survey briefly the "five minutes to midnight" sanction of humanitarian intervention.[13]

I. Humanitarian Intercession

Intercessionary actions that the United States can initiate unilaterally, collectively with other States, or through regional or international organizations range along a continuum from the most innocuous acts to actions which approach the use of force. Five different clusters of acts along the continuum have been chosen—somewhat arbitrarily—to exemplify intercession. In no way should this choice imply that there are only five types of humanitarian intercession. There are actually as many different types as the imaginations of government officials and international human rights lawyers can devise. The purpose of focusing on just five is not to chisel in marble a fixed number of definitive categories but, rather, to call attention to several levels of intercessionary options so that they can be analyzed, developed, and refined for future use.

Initially one might note that, while the United States should make a studious effort to follow the niceties of diplomatic practice in its relations with those repressive regimes with which it has to deal, it need go only this far and not one pace farther. Why allow Vice-President Spiro Agnew to make an ostensibly sentimental journey back to the land of his forebears when even the most naive observer could see that the trip was little more than a supportive mission to prop up a corrupt junta of Greek colonels?[14] Why permit Secretary of State Henry Kissinger, during the one tour he made of Latin America while in office, to lavish praise—praise so fawning as to sicken any human rights observer—upon Brazil's military dictator?[15] More recently, why, especially considering the change of administrations, was Ambassador Richard L. Sneider not brought home from South Korea when it is abundantly clear that his close association with General Park's regime over the past four and a half years has compromised his credibility when protesting current human rights deprivations in South Korea?[16] And why name William Sullivan—who thinks so little of legal restraints upon executive power that he once justified President Nixon's illegal bombing of Cambodia by citing the 1972 election returns[17]—to be ambassador to Iran, which is surely one post where sensitivity to human rights should be the key quality required for appointment?[18] Scratching an unnecessary Vice-Presidential trip, avoiding a compromising dictatorial embrace, and selecting ambassadors who in the past have evidenced some concern for human rights would have conveyed an entirely different attitude toward the importance of human rights and would have sent an entirely different message to authoritarian regimes involved in the above cases. Moreover, such actions, while so low level that technically they might not even reach the threshold of "intercession," nevertheless would have significant symbolic impact.

Moving along the continuum, one comes to a second cluster of low-level actions that the United States can take to further human rights abroad. Among literally dozens of such actions are the following: inquiring of foreign offices and Washington embassies about particular human rights situations, supporting a proposed investigation in the U.N. Human Rights Commission, sending government personnel to observe human rights trials (or assisting U.S. and international NGO's, such as the International Commission of Jurists, to send observers), responding vigorously to any violations or threatened violations of the rights of U.S. nationals abroad, and making necessary arrangements to facilitate safe haven in the United States or in friendly countries for persons who may be in jeopardy in their own states. More public but equally low-level actions include expressions of sympathy and support for oppressed individuals and groups in foreign states. President Carter's reply to Andrei Sakharov's letter in early 1977 is an example of such action.[19] At the same level, one might include even such outspoken criticism of human rights deprivations as Daniel Patrick Moynihan's forthright condemnation of Uganda's General Amin as a "racist murderer" four years ago.[20]

Again, one should note that this type of action is so low level that it is questionable whether it even constitutes "interference," which is the key element in the definition of "intercession."[21] After all, did President Carter, by writing a personal letter to a Soviet citizen, really interfere in the internal affairs of the Soviet Union? Nonetheless—perhaps not surprisingly—Chairman Brezhnev did accuse the President of just such interference: "Washington's claims to teach others how to live... cannot be accepted by any sovereign state," he warned.[22]

President Carter actually had given a short and irrefutable answer to this accusation several days earlier in an address to the United Nations: "All the signatories of the United Nations Charter have pledged themselves to observe and respect basic human rights. Thus, no member of the United Nations can claim that mistreatment of its citizens is solely its own business."[23] A contemporaneous conference sponsored by the International League for Human Rights, in noting that "the Universal Declaration of Human Rights, as well as various human rights treaties, [also] establish[es] international standards and commitments by nations of the U.N.," correctly concluded that "calling upon a nation to respect those standards must not be seen as inappropriate interference in its internal affairs but as furthering compliance with international standards and world order and promoting the specific objectives of the United Nations Charter."[24] Similarly, U.S. appeals to the principles of the Helsinki Accords are perfectly proper. "To the protests of interference," the *New York Times* observed, the Carter Administration should reply "that calls for the observance of the 1975 Final Act of Helsinki are not part of any American policy to undermine the Communist social and economic systems. The act . . . requires [its signers] to 'respect human rights and fundamental freedoms.'"[25]

Proceeding farther along the intercessionary-interventionary continuum, one comes to a third cluster of actions that are slightly more coercive, if not forceful, than the low-level approaches previously mentioned. In building upon such official but informal protests as inquiring of foreign offices and Washington embassies about particular human rights situations, the United States should move through various stages of protest—informal to formal, oral to written, and low level to the very highest level. Since, as the International League for Human Rights has pointed out, the President and the Secretary of State can be expected to speak out only on selected occasions, ambassadors and other Department of State officials should be allowed to make statements on human rights issues where they deem such appropriate.[26]

As part of this process, serious attention should be given to regularizing the use of the diplomatic note as a method of expressing U.S. concern for human rights violations and as a means of requesting clarification of foreign government practices which are thought to violate human rights norms. Although the unselective use of the diplomatic note has been rare in recent years, the making of diplomatic representations for human rights purposes has a long history. Somewhat ironically, the textbook example of this practice occurred in the early 1890's, when the United States lodged official protests with the Russian government about the treatment of Russian Jews.[27]

The use of the diplomatic note—or the making of a statement, which is its rough equivalent on the multilateral level and is frequently employed for the purpose of explaining a U.S. vote on a resolution in the United Nations, the OAS, or some other international organization—should occur only in cases where there is substantial evidence that serious violations of human rights have occurred or are occurring in the foreign country involved. The note or statement should not be overly accusatory or strident in tone but, rather, should be couched in terms of factual representation and legal argument that the foreign country would be free to deny or explain. Both techniques would serve to manifest U.S. concern, but the diplomatic note would be a private gesture which would not necessarily elicit a public, much less a nationalistic, response—unless, of course, the foreign country wanted to bring the allegation into the open and thereby make public (and, presumably, also defend) its practices. Such notes and statements naturally cannot guarantee the cessation of human rights deprivations, but they might prove very helpful in individual cases; therefore, their use should be encouraged.

A fourth cluster of intercessionary acts involves the use of judicial or quasi-judicial procedures to advance human rights. The United States should take the initiative or, where it cannot do so for lack of standing (e.g., under the Civil and Political Covenant or the Racial Discrimination Convention), support the initiatives of other states in securing speedy resolutions of questions of law and fact in the human rights area. Because international litigation need not be an unfriendly act, seeking to promote and protect human rights by "going public" in this way certainly constitutes a permissible act of intercession. Past attempts to take this route have met with varied success. The initial attempt by the Western Allies to guarantee the protection of human rights in the former Axis states of Bulgaria, Hungary, and Rumania by resorting to the arbitration procedures set out in the Peace Treaties of 1947[28] came to naught when the International Court of Justice, in an advisory opinion requested by the U.N. General Assembly,[29] held that the U.N. Secretary General did not have the authority to appoint the third member of commissions established under the treaties without whose appointment (the three states having failed to appoint commissioners of their own) the arbitration process could not go forward.[30] However, subsequently, in the Namibia case,[31] another advisory opinion requested by the General Assembly, the ICJ ruled that South Africa's continued presence in the territory of Namibia constituted a denial of fundamental human rights in "flagrant violation of the purposes and principles of the [U.N.] Charter."[32] This opinion has had considerable effect in loosening South Africa's claim to—if not actual hold over—Namibia and suggests that resort should be made to the ICJ or other tribunals whenever feasible.

Although the United States at present has no standing to initiate proceedings under the Civil and Political Covenant or the Racial Discrimination Convention, other international procedures are open. Within the United Nations, for instance, it should raise questions, seek investigations, and request action with respect to human rights situations, focusing upon the Human Rights Commission as a forum for such actions. The fact that the commission "has the poorest track record of all,"[33] according to Congressman Donald Fraser, should not deter the United States from pressing for affirmative action in all cases where grievous violations of human rights can be shown to exist.

The commission is not without its successes; the excellent work it has done with respect to Chile[34] stands in marked contrast with its long-standing failure to take up the matter of Uganda.[35] In addition, the United States should take advantage of ECOSOC Resolution 1503, which authorizes the Sub-Commission on Prevention of Discrimination and Protection of Minorities to consider all "communications, together with replies of Governments, if any, which appear to reveal a consistent pattern of gross and reliably attested violations of human rights and fundamental freedoms."[36] Finally, on a regional level, the United States should utilize the Inter-American Commission on Human Rights of the OAS, which has performed admirably within its jurisdictional limits in the past but which can become a truly effective implementation device only with strong U.S. support.[37] The American Convention on Human Rights, should it come into force with U.S. ratification, would help bring into play several useful enforcement techniques, including a strengthened Inter-American Commission and a new Inter-American Court of Human Rights designed to protect and enforce the convention's guarantees.[38] Thus, both existing and potential judicial and quasi-judicial procedures offer attractive remedial routes for the enforcement of human rights and warrant invocation and development wherever possible.

The fifth and final cluster of intercessionary acts involves economic sanctions, either applied internationally, as in the case of U.N. sanctions against Rhodesia,[39] or regionally, as in the case of OAS sanctions against Cuba,[40] or unilaterally, as the United States under Congressional prodding has done of late. With the repeal of the Byrd Amendment,[41] which brings the United States back into line with U.N. sanctions policy, and the termination of sanctions against Cuba by the OAS,[42] which leaves the United States all alone in maintaining an embargo against Cuba, there is little new to be said about international economic sanctions. Given the great power which economic sanctions—especially when applied by a major power—can have in today's interdependent world, it is somewhat surprising that they have been invoked so infrequently by the United States in the human rights context. Only recently has this situation begun to change.

Beginning with a "sense-of-the-Congress" provision in 1973 to the effect that "the President should deny any economic or military assistance to the government of any foreign country which practices the internment or imprisonment of that country's citizens for political purposes,"[43] Congress has enacted a series of statutes linking foreign assistance or trade benefits to the status of human rights in foreign countries. One of the earliest and most-noted instances was the Jackson-Vanik Amendment to the Trade Reform Act of 1974[44] which prohibits, *inter alia,* the granting of most-favored-nation treatment to nonmarket economy countries that deny or restrict the right of their citizens to emigrate.[45] Although widely viewed as being unsuccessful in the case of the Soviet Union, the amendment apparently has been relatively helpful in the case of Rumania, in which President Ford took advantage of the discretion granted him by the amendment to waive its conditions in return for Rumania's tacit agreement to liberalize its emigration policies.[46]

Also enacted in 1974 was a new Section 502B to the Foreign Assistance Act of 1961;[47] this "sense-of-the-Congress" provision states that, "except in extraordinary circumstances, the President shall substantially reduce or terminate security assistance to any government which engages in a consistent pattern of gross violations of internationally recognized human rights." Two years later Congress eliminated the "sense-of-the-Congress" language and mandated the President to terminate or restrict aid to countries so violating human rights *unless* "extraordinary circumstances" existed which made it in the "national interest" to continue such military aid.[48] This discretionary clause—which was invoked by President Ford in late 1976 in connection with Argentina, Haiti, Indonesia, Iran, Peru, and the Philippines[49]—is subject to Congress's reserved power to terminate, restrict, or continue such aid by joint resolution. For reasons mentioned below, Section 502B has taken on increased importance in the Carter Administration.[50]

Having taken up military aid in 1974, Congress tackled economic aid the following year by enacting Section 310 of the International Development and Food Assistance Act of 1975.[51] Section 310 thereof requires the President to terminate such aid, under criteria similar to the ones found in Section 502B, "unless such assistance will directly benefit the needy people in such country." Again, this discretionary clause is subject to Congress' reserved power to overrule the President's determination by concurrent resolution.

The policy of intercession by threat of economic sanction gathered momentum in 1976 when Congress enacted legislation requiring the U.S. representatives on the Inter-American Development Bank and the African Development Fund to cast their votes against loans or assistance to any country engaging in gross violations of internationally recognized human rights.[52] Also in 1976 came two statutory provisions aimed at particular foreign states: Section 406 of the International Security Assistance and Arms Export Control Act of 1976[53] terminated military assistance and put a $27.5 million ceiling on economic assistance to Chile, while Section 505 of the Foreign Assistance and Related Programs Appropriation Act for 1977[54] cut off all military aid to Uruguay. Thus, by the end of 1976, a substantial amount of legislation, all initiated by Congress in spite of outright opposition or, at best, with tepid approval of the Executive, was in place and ready for the Carter Administration's use.

Barely a month passed before the new Administration took advantage of the legislation. In what the *New York Times* called "the first time in memory that any administration had publicly announced a reduction in foreign aid because of human rights considerations,"[55] Secretary of State Cyrus Vance in February 1977 announced reductions in assistance to Argentina, Uruguay, and Ethiopia.[56] Although the cuts were relatively small, their symbolic importance was enormous. Following the publication of Department of State human rights reports prepared for submission to the Senate Foreign Relations Committee, three more Latin American countries—Brazil, El Salvador, and Guatemala—saw the proverbial handwriting on the wall and, in a fine display of pique, announced that henceforth they would accept no further largesse from the United States.[57] Although the assistance boom apparently has not been lowered again, the message obviously has gotten through.[58]

Unilateral economic sanctions are a relatively new and admittedly tricky technique to use in the human rights area. They must be employed carefully if they are to achieve U.S. human rights goals without imperiling other foreign policy objectives. Especially in the area of economic assistance and loans, complicated issues are involved.[59] Not only will difficult decisions frequently be required, but innovative approaches also should be considered. For instance, the International League for Human Rights has suggested that "in some cases 'suspension' of aid by the Executive Branch may be more effective than bringing the matter to a point of Congressional reduction or termination of aid, thereby giving the offending country an incentive to improve conditions so as to end the suspension."[60]

Moreover, the carrot as well as the stick approach also should be kept in mind. The *New York Times* has observed that the behavior of governments toward their own peoples frequently can be improved "with promises of more aid, or credits for trading concessions (such as most-favored-nation tariffs to governments that relax emigration restrictions), or with favorable votes in multilateral institutions."[61] When such approaches are unsuccessful, however, the reduction or termination of assistance should be given serious consideration. Efforts should be taken, moreover, to prevent foreign countries from circumventing the effects of such reductions or cutoffs.[62] In short, while economic coercion is something to be avoided whenever possible, unilateral economic sanctions certainly are permissible when invoked to help promote internationally recognized human rights norms. They also represent the last stop on the intercessionary-intervention continuum short of humanitarian intervention itself.

II. Humanitarian Intervention

Humanitarian intervention, which generally involves the use or the threat of the use of force,[63] is much discussed by scholars[64] and rarely invoked by U.S. decision-makers.[65] Although, in Michael Reisman's words, "at least temporarily unthinkable,"[66] it is a doctrine that has been used in the past and is potentially useful for the future. Indeed, in view of the massive human rights deprivations that have taken place in recent years in such countries as Burundi, Uganda, and Uruguay—all small states where a well-executed intervention by a minimum number of troops might have saved a maximum number of lives—it is somewhat surprising that more consideration has not been given to its use by nation-states and international organizations, especially when intercessionary actions have been tried and found wanting.[67]

As far as humanitarian intervention's legality is concerned, the present writer concluded some years ago that "the doctrine appears to have been so clearly established under customary international law that only its limits and not its existence is subject to debate."[68] However, what has been the impact of the U.N. Charter upon this customary international law doctrine?[69] Here two problems arise. The first is whether such interventions still are lawful or whether they now are precluded by the U.N. Charter. The second, assuming that such interventions remain lawful, is what criteria should be used to judge a particular intervention's legality.

Although Article 1(7) of the U.N. Charter enjoins the United Nations itself not "to intervene in matters which are essentially within the domestic jurisdiction of any state,"[70] Article 2(4), which applies to member states, contains no mention of intervention. Rather, it requires states to refrain from "the threat or use of force against the territorial integrity or political independence of any state."[71] Although many commentators have concluded that this provision prohibits humanitarian intervention,[72] among those international lawyers who believe such intervention still is legal, at least four different legal theories have been advanced.

The first approach is that of the Australian jurist Julius Stone, who advocates a literal reading of the language of Article 2(4). It "does *not* forbid 'the threat or use of force' *simpliciter*," he contends; "it forbids it only when directed 'against the territorial integrity or political independence of any State, or in any other manner inconsistent with the Purposes of the United Nations.'"[73] In his opinion a humanitarian intervention would not be so directed and, hence, would not fall within the prohibition of Article 2(4).[74] Stone's view is consistent with Oppenheim's definition of intervention, which as mentioned above is limited to "dictatorial interference" in the affairs of other states.[75] Thus Stone finds little difficulty in justifying the use of armed force to further international human rights norms.[76]

The second approach employed to justify the claim that humanitarian intervention has survived the adoption of the U.N. Charter is that of Reisman. Adopting what some critics have labeled a "teleological"[77] interpretation, Reisman views Article 2(4) as an important part of the document, but still only a part. Looking at the Preamble, Article 1, and Articles 55 and 56, all of which evidence great concern for the advancement of human rights, he concludes that

> [T]he cumulative effect of the Charter in regard to the customary institution of humanitarian intervention is to create a coordinate responsibility for the active protection of human rights: members may act jointly with the organization in what might be termed a new organized, explicitly statutory humanitarian intervention or singly or collectively in the customary or international common law humanitarian intervention. In the contemporary world there is no other way the most fundamental purposes of the Charter in relation to human rights can be made effective.[78]

Reisman's approach is distinguished from Stone's in that humanitarian intervention is not unaffected by the charter as Stone thinks but, rather, is a logical extension of concern for norms that are rooted firmly in the charter. One must look to the dominant purposes of the charter as a whole and not blindly allow a single general principle like

Article 2(4)—admirable though that principle may be—to impede other major goals of the charter.

There is a third approach that stands apart from the first and perhaps from the second in that it does not necessarily accord a permanent status in international law to humanitarian intervention. Rather, this approach permits its substitution for the procedure contemplated by the charter, an emergency mechanism to be deactivated should the normal U.N. machinery in the Security Council ever begin to function smoothly. The problem with—and the virtue of—this approach is that it requires a rather sophisticated reinterpretation of the charter in light of events since 1945. Because the enforcement machinery of the Security Council has not worked out as planned or hoped, the argument goes, one is left with the undesirable choice of applying stopgap measures or doing nothing at all. Of these two choices, certainly the former requires adoption. As Richard Baxter, who has suggested this approach, puts it:

> Given the fact that we do live in an imperfect world, in which the United Nations is not operating as it should, it seems to me inevitable that there will be [humanitarian interventions]. It is almost as if we were thrown back on customary international law by a breakdown of the Charter system.[79]

The present writer, who has associated himself with this view in the past,[80] hereby reaffirms his support of it.[81]

A fourth approach by which humanitarian intervention might be condoned, if not actually justified, has been developed by Richard Falk[82] and, to a lesser extent, by Ian Brownlie.[83] Both scholars view the U.N. charter as prohibiting humanitarian intervention yet consider this broad prohibition potentially counterproductive. Thus, while not approving such interventions, Falk, by using a "second-order level of legal inquiry"[84] which involves criteria similar to ones suggested by advocates of humanitarian intervention,[85] nevertheless would not condemn them all. Brownlie, in a less sophisticated but nevertheless interesting analysis of the problem, compares humanitarian intervention to euthanasia. Both actions, he contends, are unlawful, but at the same time they are both moral actions which may find justification in higher considerations of public policy and moral choice.[86] Brownlie's variant of the fourth approach has been criticized by John Norton Moore and the present writer for its failure "to perform the ... intellectual task of trying to develop a set of criteria. You can't end it by saying it is illegal but also moral. We have to go beyond that and develop criteria for appraisal of the kinds of situations that we would recommend *ought to be* legal."[87]

The question of criteria raises the last issue to be considered in the essay, because no matter which of the above four approaches one adopts, one still is faced with setting legal standards for judging whether a particular humanitarian intervention really so qualifies. In 1966 Ved Nanda advanced five criteria for judging the legality of humanitarian interventions.[88] The following year the present writer recommended five of his own.[89] Subsequently, Moore synthesized the Nanda-Lillich criteria, with some additions and modifications.[90] Moore's synthesis in turn has been summarized most recently by Tom Farer:

That there be an immediate and extensive threat to fundamental human rights.
That all other remedies for the protection of those rights have been exhausted to the extent possible within the time constraints posed by the threat.
That an attempt has been made to secure the approval of appropriate authorities in the target state.
That there is a minimal effect on the extant structure of authority (e.g., that the intervention not be used to impose or preserve a preferred regime).
That the minimal requisite force by employed and/or that the intervention is not likely to cause greater injury to innocent persons and their property than would result if the threatened violation actually occurred.
That the intervention be of limited duration.
That a report of the intervention be filed immediately with the Security Council and, where relevant, regional organizations.

Space precludes elaborating on these criteria,[91] or even defending them against their critics.[92] Suffice it to say that the present writer rejects Farer's conclusion that "in the course of taming the doctrine, its partisans have managed to trivialise it as well."[93] The trivialization of the doctrine, as Farer's own text reveals, comes from the failure of states to resort to humanitarian intervention often enough, not from the efforts of commentators to limit the doctrine's potential for abuse.[94]

Another criticism of the doctrine, one more worthy of consideration, is that it never can be truly effective in protecting the human rights of individuals because it is an emergency measure, a "five minutes to midnight" sanction. One must admit that this argument is a telling one, yet if one looks at the problem of protecting human rights in a broader context than simply the single doctrine of humanitarian intervention, one sees that the argument, however large it may loom in isolation, is considerably reduced in size when regarded in proper perspective. It is true that humanitarian intervention is a last-ditch remedy; thus, there are serious situational constraints on how effective it can ever be in practice. One always must remember, however, that humanitarian intervention is not a doctrine unto itself: It is simply one part—not necessarily the most important or effective part—of a long continuum of possible strategies for influencing other states for human rights purposes. Certainly waiting until "five minutes to midnight" is an undesirable way to improve human rights situations throughout the world. This very fact, however, only adds strength to the arguments for developing and institutionalizing lesser but more effective means of interference by refining the techniques of humanitarian intercession. There is no requirement that the international community or concerned states wait until nearly the witching hour; lower level interference techniques can be mobilized much earlier in the evening. Rather than delaying until events reach crisis proportions, as is occurring in Rhodesia and may well happen in South Africa,[95] the international community, led by the United States, should apply all the intercessionary actions discussed in this essay in an attempt to achieve solutions before situations degenerate into ones where humanitarian intervention may be required.

III. Conclusion

In describing the international human rights policy of the Carter Administration, Secretary of State Vance has cautioned keeping in mind "the limits of our power and of our wisdom. A sure formula for defeat of our goals would be a rigid, hubristic attempt to impose our values on others. A doctrinaire plan of action would be as damaging as indifference."[96] He continued:

> If we are determined to act, the means available range from quiet diplomacy in its many forms through public pronouncements to withholding of assistance. Whenever possible, we will use positive steps of encouragement and inducement. Our strong support will go to countries that are working to improve the human condition. We will always try to act in concert with other countries through international bodies.
>
> In the end a decision whether and how to act in the cause of human rights is a matter for informed and careful judgment. No mechanistic formula produces an automatic answer.[97]

It is to be hoped that this essay, focusing as it does upon various action options available to the United States along the humanitarian intercession-intervention continuum, will help U.S. policy-makers in their search for informed, if not automatic, answers. From this and other efforts eventually will come the policy framework necessary to replace the vacuum left by the laissez-faire approach of prior administrations to the United States' role in promoting and protecting international human rights.

NOTES

1. See A. Hotchner, *Papa Hemingway* (New York: Bantam, 1967), p. 28.
2. T. J. Farer, "United States Foreign Policy and the Protection of Human Rights: Observations and Proposals," 14 *Virginia Journal of International Law* (Summer 1974): 623.
3. R. B. Bilder, "Human Rights and U.S. Foreign Policy: Short-Term Prospects," 14 *Virginia Journal of International Law* (Summer 1974): 597, 601; see also p. 604.
4. *New York Times*, May 23, 1977.
5. *Ibid.*, November 2, 1972 (emphasis added). For an incisive essay dismantling Nixon's (and, for that matter, Senator Fulbright's) jerry-built thesis that "[t]he 'national interest' is the only proper concern of this nation's foreign policy, and the 'national interest' should be narrowly construed to exclude moral commitments or 'causes' that do not promise a clear, direct, predictable payoff in increased security or prosperity for the nation," see "Is America's Business in Foreign Affairs Only Business?" *ibid.*, December 23, 1973; see Farer, *supra* note 2, pp. 625-628.
6. *Cf.* Bilder, *supra* note 3, p. 600.
7. Portions of the material in the balance of this essay are taken from a course of five unpublished lectures entitled "Humanitarian Intervention and Humanitarian Intercession," which the writer delivered at the International Institute of Human Rights, Strasbourg, July 18-22, 1977.
8. L. Oppenheim, *International Law*, Vol. 1 (New York: Longmans, Green, 1905), p. 181.
9. *Ibid*, p. 182.
10. *Cf. Banco Nacional de Cuba* v. *Sabbatino*, 376 U.S. 398, 410 (1964). Despite this traditional attitude, it should be noted, as a Department of State lawyer pointed out several years ago, that "most countries still regard statements directed to them about their activities involving the human rights of their own citizens as interfering in their own internal affairs and as politically unfriendly." International Protection of Human Rights, hearings before the Subcommittee on International Organizations and Movements of the House Committee on Foreign Affairs, 93rd Congress, 1st Session 95 (Washington, D.C., 1973) (statement of G. H. Aldrich). See text at notes 21-25 *infra*.
11. See R. Lillich, "Forcible Self-Help by States to Protect Human Rights," 53 *Iowa Law Review* (1967): 325. For a selected bibliography on the subject, see R. Lillich (ed.), *Humanitarian Intervention and the United Nations* (Charlottesville: University Press of Virginia, 1973), pp. 229-234. Compare I.

Brownlie, "Humanitarian Intervention," in J. N. Moore (ed.), *Law and Civil War in the Modern World* (Baltimore: Johns Hopkins Press, 1974), p. 217 with R. Lillich, "Humanitarian Intervention: A Reply to Dr. Brownlie and a Plea for Constructive Alternatives," in Moore (ed.), *Law and Civil War in the Modern World*, p. 229.

12. *Cf.* the 1975 *Digest of United States Practice in International Law* (Washington, D.C.: U.S. Government Printing Office, 1976), pp. 867-879.

13. On the need to place the "five minutes to midnight" situation in proper context, see *Humanitarian Intervention and the United Nations, supra* note 11, at 85-135 *passim.*

14. See *New York Times,* October 20, 1971.

15. See *ibid.,* February 20, 1976 and February 21, 1976.

16. *New York Times,* April 20, 1977.

17. See A. L. Lewis, "Law and the President," *New York Times,* April 19, 1973.

18. Ambassador's Sullivan's appointment was opposed by, among other persons, Richard Falk, during confirmation hearings before the Senate. Unfortunately, these hearings have not, and according to information given the present writer, will not be printed.

19. *New York Times,* February 18, 1977. It should be noted that the President did not answer a second letter from the leading Soviet dissident. *Ibid.,* May 11, 1977.

20. In a speech to the AFL-CIO, *ibid.,* October 4, 1975. Actually, Moynihan was quoting from a *New York Times* editorial of the previous day, *ibid.,* October 3, 1975.

21. See L. Oppenheim, *supra* note 9.

22. *New York Times,* March 22, 1977.

23. J. Carter, "Peace, Arms Control, World Economic Progress, Human Rights: Basic Priorities of U.S. Foreign Policy," 76 *Department of State Bulletin* (April 11, 1977): 329, 332.

24. International League for Human Rights, *Report of the Conference on Implementing a Human Rights Commitment in United States Foreign Policy* (March 4, 1977), p. 6 (hereinafter cited as *Conference Report*). See also *ibid.,* p. 55: "There is also much confusion on this issue in the United States press which often questions United States' 'interference' in the 'internal affairs' of another country. The point to be made is that 'interference' calling for observance of human rights is appropriate and justified because it seeks compliance with international standards on human dignity and freedom as called for by the Charter of the United Nations and other international agreements."

25. *New York Times,* February 1, 1977.

26. International League for Human Rights, *Conference Report, supra* note 24, p. 19. "This would be particularly true of career officers. Otherwise, the impression is created that the 'politicians' favor human rights but that the omnipotent 'career service,' does not," *ibid.,* pp. 19-20.

27. See, generally, C. Adler and A. Margalith, *With Firmness in the Right: American Diplomatic Action Affecting Jews, 1840-1945* (New York: American Jewish Committee, 1946).

28. See, e.g., Treaty of Peace with Bulgaria, February 10, 1947, Art. 31, 61 Stat. 1915, T.I.A.S. No. 1650, 4; C. Bevans, *Treaties and Other International Agreements of the United States of America 1776-1949* (Washington, D.C., 1970), p. 429.

29. Yuen-Li Liang, "Notes on Legal Questions Concerning the United Nations," 44 *American Journal of International Law* (January 1950): 100.

30. Interpretation of Peace Treaties with Bulgaria, Hungary, and Rumania (Second Phase), (1950) I.C.J. 221. See K. Carlston, "Interpretation of Peace Treaties with Bulgaria, Hungary, and Rumania, Advisory Opinions of the International Court of Justice," 44 *American Journal of International Law* (October 1950): 728.

31. Advisory Opinion on the Legal Consequences for States of the Continued Presence of South Africa in Namibia (South West Africa), (1971) I.C.J. 16.

32. *Ibid.*, p. 57. See E. Schwelb, "The International Court of Justice and the Human Rights Clauses of the Charter," 66 *American Journal of International Law* (April 1972): 337.

33. D. Fraser, "Freedom and Foreign Policy," 24 *Foreign Policy* (Spring 1977): 140, 152.

34. *Ibid.*

35. W. Korey, "The U.N.'s Double Standard on Human Rights," *Washington Post*, May 22, 1977.

36. E.S.C. Res. 1593, 58 U.N. ESCOR, Supp. (No. 1A) 8, *U.N. Doc.* E/4832/Add.1 (1970).

37. R. Goldman, *The Protection of Human Rights in the Americas: Past, Present, and Future*, Vol. 5 (New York: NYU Center for International Studies Policy Papers, 1972), pp. 36–41.

38. *Ibid.*, pp. 28–31.

39. S.C. Res. 232 (1965), November 12, 1965, 20 U.N. SCOR, Res. and Dec., at 8, *U.N. Doc.* S/INF/20/Rev. 1; S.C. Res. 232 (1966), December 16, 1966, 21 U.N. SCOR, Res. and Dec., at 7, *U.N. Doc.* S/INF/21/Rev. 1; S.C. Res. 253 (1968), May 29, 1968, 23 U.N. SCOR, Res. and Dec., at 5, *U.N. Doc.* S/INF/23/Rev. 1; S.C. Res. 333 (1973), May 22, 1973, 28 U.N. SCOR, Res. and Dec., at 14, *U.N. Doc.* S/INF/28/Rev. 1; and S.C. Res. 388 (1976), April 6, 1976, 31 U.N. SCOR, Res. and Dec., at 6, *U.N. Doc.* S/INF/32.

40. Res. I, *Ninth Meeting of Consultation of Ministers of Foreign Affairs, Washington, D.C., U.S.A., July 21–26, 1964, Final Act*, OAS Off. Rec. OEA/Ser. D/III 15 (English), p. 3 (1964).

41. Strictly speaking, the Byrd Amendment has not been repealed. In March 1977 the U.N. Participation Act was amended so that the amendment's strictures do not apply to any Executive order applying measures against Rhodesia pursuant to a U.N. Security Council resolution. Public Law 95–12, 95th Congress, 1st Session, 91 Stat. 22 (1977). Insofar as Rhodesian sanctions are concerned, then, the effect of the new legislation is to repeal the Byrd Amendment.

42. Res. I, *Sixteenth Meeting of Consultation of Ministers of Foreign Affairs*, San Jose, Costa Rica, July 29, 1975, Final Act, OAS Off. Rec. OEA/Ser. C/II. 16 [English], p. 4 (1975).

43. Foreign Assistance Act of 1973, Public Law 93–189, § 32, 87 Stat. 714 (1974) (found at 22 U.S.C. § 2151 note [Supp. V. 1975]). For discussion of this provision, see the 1974 *Digest of United States Practice in International Law* (Washington, D.C.: Government Printing Office, 1975), pp. 145–152.

44. Trade Reform Act of 1974, § 402, 19 U.S.C. § 2432 (Supp. V. 1975).

45. On the plight of Soviet citizens (primarily Jews) seeking to leave that country, see T. Taylor, *Courts of Terror: Soviet Criminal Justice and Jewish Emigration* (New York: Knopf, 1976).

46. See note, "An Interim Analysis of the Effects of the Jackson-Vanik Amendment on Trade and Human Rights: The Romanian Example," 8 *Journal of Law and Policy in International Business* (1976): 193.

47. Foreign Assistance Act of 1974, Public Law 93-559, § 46, 88 Stat. 1815 (1976), as amended, 22 U.S.C. § 2304 (Supp. V. 1975).

48. International Security Assistance and Arms Export Control Act of 1976, Public Law 94-329, § 301(a) 90 Stat. 729 (1976), 22 U.S.C.A. § 2304 (Supp. 1977).

49. *Human Rights and U.S. Policy: Argentina, Haiti, Indonesia, Iran, Peru, and the Philippines,* Reports on the House Committee on International Relations by the Department of State, 94th Congress, 2d Session (Comm. Print 1976).

50. See text at notes 56 and 57 *infra*.

51. International Development and Food Assistance Act of 1975, Public Law 94-161, § 310, 89 Stat. 860 (1975), 22 U.S.C. § 2151n (Supp. V, 1975).

52. Inter-American Development Bank Funds Act of 1976, Public Law 94-302 §§ 103, 211, 90 Stat. 592, 595 (1976), 22 U.S.C.A. §§ 283y, 290g-9 (Supp. 1977). The language employed was the same as that used in Section 602B of the Foreign Assistance Act of 1961 and Section 310 of the International Development and Food Assistance Act of 1975. See text following notes *supra* 47 and 51. Thus U.S. representatives, given the existence of gross violations of human rights, cannot cast affirmative votes "unless such assistance will directly benefit the needy people in such country." An attempt is pending to extend this approach to U.S. representatives on the World Bank.

53. International Security Assistance and Arms Export Control Act of 1976, Public Law 94-329, § 406, 90 Stat. 729 (1976), 22 U.S.C.A. § 2370 (Supp. 1977). Chile responded by formally notifying the United States that it did not want to receive any further economic assistance. *New York Times,* October 21, 1976.

54. Foreign Assistance and Related Programs Appropriation Act, Public Law 94-441, § 505, 94th Congress, 2d Session (1976). Uruguay reacted "with indignation" at this ban on military aid. *New York Times,* October 5, 1976. However, its indignation was not great enough to compel it to renounce anticipated economic assistance. That came later. See text at and accompanying note 56 *infra*.

55. *New York Times,* February 25, 1977.

56. *Ibid.* Argentina and Uruguay immediately announced that they wished to receive no further U.S. assistance. *Ibid.,* March 2, 1977. Ethiopia responded by ordering all U.S. military and diplomatic personnel out of the country, save for the staff at the Addis Ababa embassy, and by turning increasingly to the Soviet Union for assistance. *Ibid.,* May 1, 1977.

57. See *ibid.,* March 12, 1977 (Brazil) and March 18, 1977 (El Salvador and Guatemala).

58. Indeed, even before Secretary Vance's announcement, Paraguay and several other Latin American countries had released some political prisoners in the belief, which proved correct, that President Carter actually would prove to be "serious about human rights." *Ibid.,* February 24, 1977. See A. Lewis, "A Question of Humanity," *ibid.,* February 28, 1977.

59. Congressman Fraser has shown an appreciation of the difficulties of decision in this area. "Some aid is clearly humanitarian and reaches the people who need it. Other economic aid may be directly supportive of a repressive government and only indirectly benefit the people. There is a

difference, too, between finishing a partially completed project and starting a new one. With the limited amount of economic aid we have to dispense, governments with a poor track record on human rights should expect that record to weigh importantly in the allocation of new aid commitments," D. Fraser, *supra* note 33, p. 146.

60. International League for Human Rights, *Conference Report, supra* note 24, p. 28.

61. *New York Times,* January 27, 1977. See International League for Human Rights, *Conference Report, supra* note 24, pp. 28–29: "[P]ositive incentives and inducements may be more fruitful than negative sanctions. For example, inducements in the way of credits, commercial and technological aid, etc., could be offered to nations which make gains in human rights." In what may well be the most extreme instance of positive inducements, it has been reported that since 1961 West Germany literally has been buying (at prices ranging up to $15,000 a head) the freedom of "political prisoners" held in East Germany. *New York Times,* October 6, 1975.

62. "Conference members are of the view that countries which had military or economic aid cut off because of gross violations of human rights could circumvent the cut-off through purchases, private transactions and commercial traffic. It was recommended that with respect to such countries, other sources of military shipments, such as those purchased from DOD or elsewhere, should be reviewed. Some participants suggest that, in particularly egregious cases, private investments in and commerce to such country might be licensed and then scrutinized to see whether they were inconsistent with United States policy." International League for Human Rights, *Conference Report, supra* note 24, pp. 29–30.

63. See text at and following *supra* note 8.

64. See *supra* note 11.

65. The United States used the doctrine of humanitarian intervention and variations thereon to justify armed interventions in Lebanon in 1958, in the Congo in 1964, and in the Dominican Republic in 1965. See R. Lillich, *Forcible Self-Help to Protect Nationals Abroad,* chap. III (to be published by the Naval War College Press during 1979). See also text at *supra* note 12.

66. W. M. Reisman, "The Pragmatism of Human Rights," *The Nation,* May 1977, pp. 554, 555.

67. This essay focuses upon unilateral humanitarian intervention by states and purposely omits consideration of intervention for human rights purposes by the United Nations and regional international organizations. As B. H. Weston graphically states, "[I]f we are to limit humanitarian intervention to global organization intervention or its equivalent, then we are not talking about a real world. I don't think that we can expect the United Nations to intervene actively through the use of force except in the most limited circumstances. And if we shift to a regional organization type of intervention, such as might be undertaken by the OAS, then are we not risking a rubber-stamp operation such as prevailed in the Dominican Republic?" *Humanitarian Intervention and the United Nations, supra* note 11, pp. 85, 86. Of course U.S.-sponsored humanitarian intervention remains the ideal (see criteria 2 in the text at note 91 *infra*), but the likelihood of it happening is remote indeed, what with the Security Council "virtually paralyzed" and the General Assembly "incapable of action." R. R. Baxter, *ibid.,* p. 54.

68. R. Lillich, "Intervention to Protect Human Rights" 15 *McGill Law Journal* (June 1969): 205, 210.

69. For a comprehensive survey of the legal aspects of this question, see J. Fonteyne, "The Customary International Law Doctrine of Humanitarian Intervention: Its Current Validity under the U.N. Charter," 4 *California Western International Law Journal* (Spring 1974): 203.

70. U.N. Charter Art. 2, para. 7.

71. U.N. Charter Art. 2, para. 4.

72. See, e.g., I. Brownlie, *supra* note 11.

73. J. Stone, *Aggression and World Order* (Berkeley: University of California Press, 1958), p. 95.

74. See, W. Reisman, "Humanitarian Intervention to Protect the Ibos," in *Humanitarian Intervention and the United Natons, supra* note 11, pp. 177-178.

75. See text at *supra* note 8.

76. J. Stone, *supra* note 73, pp. 99-101.

77. T. Farer, "The Regulation of Foreign Intervention in Civil Armed Conflict," II *Recuell des Cours* (Hague Academy of International Law) (1974): 297, 389.

78. W. Reisman, *supra* note 74, p. 175.

79. R. R. Baxter, in *Humanitarian Intervention and the United Nations, supra* note 11, p. 54.

80. *Ibid.,* p. 61.

81. *Cf.* W. Reisman, *Nullity and Revision* (New Haven: Yale University Press, 1971), p. 850. "Only in the most exceptional cases will the United Nations be capable of functioning as an international enforcer; in the vast majority of cases, the conflicting interests of diverse public order systems will block any action. A rational and contemporary interpretation of the Charter must conclude that article 2(4) suppresses self-help insofar as the organization can assume the role of enforcer. When it cannot, self-help prerogatives revive."

82. R. Falk, "The Beirut Raid and the International Law of Retaliation," 63 *American Journal of International Law* (July 1969): 415. For a critical yet sympathetic evaluation of Falk's article, see D. Bowett, "Reprisals Involving Recourse to Armed Force," 66 *American Journal of International Law* (January 1972): 1.

83. I. Brownlie, *supra* note 11. See also I. Brownlie, "Thoughts on Kind-Hearted Gunmen," in *Humanitarian Intervention and the United Nations, supra* note 11, p. 139. Cf. T. Farer, "Humanitarian Intervention: The View from Charlottesville," *ibid.,* pp. 149, 163, 164.

84. Falk, *supra* note 82, p. 430, n. 39.

85. See text at note 91 *infra.*

86. I. Brownlie, "Thoughts on Kind-Hearted Gunmen," *supra* note 83, p. 146.

87. J. N. Moore, in *Humanitarian Intervention and the United Nations, supra* note 11, pp. 120-121. Accord, R. Lillich, *ibid., p. 118:* "[I]t does seem to me that we ought to clarify and establish criteria that will help decision-makers in the future, and we certainly are not helping them at all by saying 'Well, this was illegal but we morally approve of it.'"

88. V. Nanda, "The United States' Action in the 1965 Dominican Crisis: Impact on World Order, Part I," 43 *Denver Law Journal* (Fall 1966): 439, 474-479.

89. R. Lillich, "Forcible Self-Help," *supra* note 11, pp. 347-351.

90. J. Moore, "The Control of Foreign Intervention in Internal Conflict," 9 *Virginia Journal of International Law,* (May 1969): 205, 261-264. See

also J. Moore, *Law and the Indo-China War,* (Princeton, N.J.: Princeton University Press, 1972), pp. 182–186.

91. T. Farer, *supra* note 77, p. 394.
92. See, e.g., *ibid.,* pp. 394–402.
93. *Ibid.,* p. 395.
94. In fairness, Farer does admit that "[t]hese criteria do help to limit, although they by no means obviate, the danger of wide-ranging doctrinal abuse," *ibid.,* p. 394.
95. T. M. Franck, in Moore (ed.), *Humanitarian Intervention and the United Nations, supra* note 11, p. 90, "foresee[s] another massacre coming up, which would be a South African one, which could probably be stopped by some relatively low-level effective action on the economic plane. But the United States and most Western countries aren't prepared to do anything positive about that one."
96. C. Vance, "Human Rights Policy," 76 *Department of State Bulletin* (May 23, 1977): 505, 506.
97. See, e.g., J. Salzberg and D. Young, "The Parliamentary Role in Implementing International Human Rights: A U.S. Example," 12 *Texas International Law Journal* (Spring/Summer 1977): 251, 269–274.

Bibliography

"American Companies in South Africa and Human Rights," 15 *Howard Law Journal* (Summer 1969): 652.

BEITZ, C., *Human Rights and Foreign Policy: The Problem of Priorities* (College Park, Md., 1978).

BENNETT, W. T., JR., "United States Initiatives in the United Nations to Combat International Terrorism," 7 *International Lawyer* (October 1973): 752-760.

BILDER, RICHARD B., "Human Rights and U.S. Foreign Policy," 14 *Virginia Journal of International Law* (Summer 1974): 579-609.

BITKER, B., "Some Remarks on U.S. Policy of the Ratification of the International Human Rights Conventions," 2 *Human Rights, Journal of International and Comparative Law* (December 1969): 653.

BLOOMFIELD, L. P., *In Search of American Foreign Policy: The Humane Use of Power* (New York, 1974).

BUERGENTHAL, T., "International Human Rights: U.S. Policy and Priorities," 14 *Virginia Journal of International Law* (1974): 611-621.

FARER, T. J., "United States Foreign Policy and the Protection of Human Rights: Observations and Proposals," 14 *Virginia Journal of International Law* (1974): 623-651.

FISH, H., *Security Assistance in Perspective* (College Park, Md., 1978).

FREYMOND, J., "Confronting Total War: A 'Global' Humanitarian Policy," 67 *American Journal of International Law* (October 1973): 672-692.

HUMPHREY, J. (ed.), *Ratification of International Human Rights Treaties*, Committee on Human Rights, World Association of Lawyers (Washington, D.C., 1976).

LAKE, A., *Tar-Baby Option: American Policy Towards Southern Rhodesia* (New York, 1976).

LEFEVER, E., *Morality and Foreign Policy* (Washington, D.C., 1977).

———, "The Trivialization of Human Rights," 3 *Policy Review* (Winter 1978): 11-26.

LILLICH, R. B., "Human Rights, The National Interest, and U.S. Foreign Policy," 14 *Virginia Journal of International Law* (Summer 1974): 591-596.

MACLEAN, D., *Goals and Constraints: Moralism in U.S. Foreign Policy* (College Park, Md., 1978).

MISCHE, G., and Mische, P., *Toward a Human World Order: Beyond the National Security Straitjacket* (Ramsey, N.J., 1977).

SHUE, H., *Foundations for a Balanced U.S. Policy on Human Rights: The Significance of Subsistance Rights* (College Park, Md., 1977).

UTLEY, T. E., "A Reappraisal of the Human Rights Doctrine," 3 *Policy Review* (Winter 1978): 27-34.

Appendices

Commencement Address at the University of Notre Dame

MAY 22, 1977

PRESIDENT JIMMY CARTER

I WANT TO SPEAK TO YOU TODAY ABOUT THE STRANDS THAT CONNECT our actions overseas with our essential character as a nation. I believe we can have a foreign policy that is democratic, that is based on fundamental values, and that uses power and influence, which we have, for humane purposes. We can also have a foreign policy that the American people both support and, for a change, know about and understand.

I have a quiet confidence in our own political system. Because we know that democracy works, we can reject the arguments of those rulers who deny human rights to their people.

We are confident that democracy's example will be compelling, and so we seek to bring that example closer to those from whom in the past few years we have been separated and who are not yet convinced about the advantages of our kind of life.

We are confident that democratic methods are the most effective, and so we are not tempted to employ improper tactics here at home or abroad.

We are confident of our own strength, so we can seek substantial mutual reductions in the nuclear arms race.

And we are confident of the good sense of American people, and so we let them share in the process of making foreign policy decisions. We can thus speak with the voices of 215 million, and not just of an isolated handful.

Democracy's great recent success—in India, Portugal, Spain, Greece—show that our confidence in this system is not misplaced. Being confident of our own future, we are now free of that inordinate fear of communism which once led us to embrace any dictator who joined us in that fear. I'm glad that that's being changed.

For too many years, we've been willing to adopt the flawed and erroneous principles and tactics of our adversaries, sometimes abandoning our own values for theirs. We've fought fire with fire, never thinking that fire is better quenched with water. This approach failed, with Vietnam the best example of its intellectual and moral poverty. But through failure, we have now found our way back to our own principles and values, and we have regained our lost confidence.

By the measure of history, our Nation's 200 years are very brief, and our rise to world eminence is briefer still. It dates from 1945 when Europe and the old international order lay in ruins. Before then America was largely on the periphery of world affairs, but since then we have inescapably been at the center of world affairs.

Our policy during this period was guided by two principles: a belief that Soviet expansion was almost inevitable but that it must be contained, and the corresponding belief in the importance of an almost exclusive alliance among non-Communist nations on both sides of the Atlantic. That system could not last forever unchanged. Historical trends have weakened its foundation. The unifying threat of conflict with the Soviet Union has become less intensive even though the competition has become more extensive.

The Vietnamese war produced a profound moral crisis sapping worldwide faith in our own policy and our system of life, a crisis of confidence made even more grave by the covert pessimism of some of our leaders.

In less than a generation, we've seen the world change dramatically. The daily lives and aspirations of most human beings have been transformed. Colonialism is nearly gone. A new sense of national identity now exists in almost 100 new countries that have been formed in the last generation. Knowledge has become more widespread; aspirations are higher. As more people have been freed from traditional constraints, more have been determined to achieve for the first time in their lives social justice.

The world is still divided by ideological disputes, dominated by regional conflicts, and threatened by danger that we will not resolve the differences of race and wealth without violence or without drawing into combat the major military powers. We can no longer separate the traditional issues of war and peace from the new global questions of justice, equity, and human rights.

It is a new world—but America should not fear it. It is a new world—and we should help to shape it. It is a new world that calls for a new American foreign policy—a policy based on constant decency in its values and on optimism in our historical vision.

We can no longer have a policy solely for the industrial nations as the foundation of global stability, but we must respond to the new reality of a politically awakening world.

We can no longer expect that the other 150 nations will follow the dictates of the powerful, but we must continue—confidently—our efforts to inspire, to persuade, and to lead.

Our policy must reflect our belief that the world can hope for more than simple survival and our belief that dignity and freedom are fundamental spiritual requirements. Our policy must shape an international system that will last longer than secret deals.

We cannot make this kind of policy by manipulation. Our policy must be open; it must be candid; it must be one of constructive global involvement, resting on five cardinal principles.

I've tried to make these premises clear to the American people since last January. Let me review what we have been doing and discuss what we intend to do.

First, we have reaffirmed America's commitment to human rights as a fundamental tenet of our foreign policy. In ancestry, religion, color, place of origin, and cultural background, we Americans are as diverse a nation as the world has ever seen. No common mystique of blood or soil unites us. What draws us together, perhaps more than anything else, is a belief in human freedom.

We want the world to know that our Nation stands for more than financial prosperity. This does not mean that we can conduct our foreign policy by rigid moral maxims. We live in a world that is imperfect and which will always be imperfect—a world that is complex and confused and which will always be complex and confused.

I understand fully the limits of moral suasion. We have no illusion that changes will come easily or soon. But I also believe that it is a mistake to undervalue the power of words and of the ideas that words embody. In our own history, that power has ranged from Thomas Paine's "Common Sense" to Martin Luther King, Jr.'s "I Have a Dream."

In the life of the human spirit, words are action, much more so than many of us may realize who live in countries where freedom of expression is taken for granted. The leaders of totalitarian nations understand this very well. The proof is that words are precisely the action for which dissidents in those countries are being persecuted.

Nonetheless, we can already see dramatic, worldwide advances in the protection of the individual from the arbitrary power of the state. For us to ignore this trend would be to lose influence and moral authority in the world. To lead it will be to regain the moral stature that we once had.

The great democracies are not free because we are strong and prosperous. I believe we are strong and influential and prosperous because we are free.

Throughout the world today, in free nations and in totalitarian countries as well, there is a preoccupation with the subject of human freedom, human rights. And I believe it is incumbent on us in this country to keep that discussion, that debate, that contention alive. No other country is as well-qualified as we to set an example. We have our own shortcomings and faults, and we should strive constantly and with courage to make sure that we are legitimately proud of what we have.

Second, we've moved deliberately to reinforce the bonds among our democracies. In our recent meetings in London, we agreed to widen our economic cooperation, to promote free trade, to strengthen the world's monetary system, to seek ways of avoiding nuclear proliferation. We prepared constructive proposals for the forthcoming meetings on North-South problems of poverty, development, and global well-being, and we agreed on joint efforts to reinforce and to modernize our common defense.

You may be interested in knowing that at this NATO meeting, for the first time in more than 25 years, all members are democracies. Even more important, all of us reaffirmed our basic optimism in the future of the democratic system. Our spirit of confidence is spreading. Together, our democracies can help to shape the wider architecture of global cooperation.

Third, we've moved to engage the Soviet Union in a joint effort to halt the strategic arms race. This race is not only dangerous, it's morally deplorable. We must put an end to it.

I know it will not be easy to reach agreements. Our goal is to be fair to both sides, to produce reciprocal stability, parity, and security. We desire a freeze on further modernization and production of weapons and a continuing, substantial reduction of strategic nuclear weapons as well. We want a comprehensive ban on all nuclear testing, a prohibition against all chemical warfare, no attack capability against space satellites, and arms limitations in the Indian Ocean.

We hope that we can take joint steps with all nations toward a final agreement eliminating nuclear weapons completely from our arsenals of death. We will persist in this effort.

Now, I believe in détente with the Soviet Union. To me, it means progress toward peace. But the effects of détente should not be limited to our own two countries alone. We hope to persuade the Soviet

Union that one country cannot impose its system of society upon another, either through direct military intervention or through the use of a client state's military force, as was the case with Cuban intervention in Angola.

Cooperation also implies obligation. We hope that the Soviet Union will join with us and other nations in playing a larger role in aiding the developing world, for common aid efforts will help us build a bridge of mutual confidence in one another.

Fourth, we are taking deliberate steps to improve the chances of lasting peace in the Middle East. Through wide-ranging consultation with leaders of the countries involved—Israel, Syria, Jordan, and Egypt—we have found some areas of agreement and some movement toward consensus. The negotiations must continue.

Through my own public comments, I've also tried to suggest a more flexible framework for the discussion of the three key issues which have so far been so intractable: the nature of a comprehensive peace—What is peace? What does it mean to the Israelis? What does it mean to their Arab neighbors? Secondly, the relationship between security and borders—How can the dispute over border delineations be established and settled with a feeling of security on both sides? And the issue of the Palestinian homeland.

The historic friendship that the United States has with Israel is not dependent on domestic politics in either nation; it's derived from our common respect for human freedom and from a common search for permanent peace.

We will continue to promote a settlement which all of us need. Our own policy will not be affected by changes in leadership in any of the countries in the Middle East. Therefore, we expect Israel and her neighbors to continue to be bound by United Nations Resolutions 242 and 338, which they have previously accepted.

This may be the most propitious time for a genuine settlement since the beginning of the Arab-Israeli conflict almost 30 years ago. To let this opportunity pass could mean disaster not only for the Middle East but, perhaps, for the international political and economic order as well.

And fifth, we are attempting, even at the risk of some friction with our friends, to reduce the danger of nuclear proliferation and the worldwide spread of conventional weapons.

At the recent summit, we set in motion an international effort to determine the best ways of harnessing nuclear energy for peaceful use while reducing the risks that its products will be diverted to the making of explosives.

We've already completed a comprehensive review of our own

policy on arms transfers. Competition in arms sales is inimical to peace and destructive of the economic development of the poorer countries.

We will, as a matter of national policy now in our country, seek to reduce the annual dollar volume of arms sales, to restrict the transfer of advanced weapons, and to reduce the extent of our coproduction arrangements about weapons with foreign states. And, just as important, we are trying to get other nations, both free and otherwise, to join us in this effort.

But all of this that I've described is just the beginning. It's a beginning aimed towards a clear goal: to create a wider framework of international cooperation suited to the new and rapidly changing historical circumstances.

We will cooperate more closely with the newly influential countries in Latin America, Africa, and Asia. We need their friendship and cooperation in a common effort as the structure of world power changes.

More than 100 years ago, Abraham Lincoln said that our Nation could not exist half slave and half free. We know a peaceful world cannot long exist one-third rich and two-thirds hungry.

Most nations share our faith that in the long run, expanded and equitable trade will best help the developing countries to help themselves. But the immediate problems of hunger, disease, illiteracy, and repression are here now.

The Western democracies, the OPEC nations, and the developed Communist countries can cooperate through existing international institutions in providing more effective aid. This is an excellent alternative to war.

We have a special need for cooperation and consultation with other nations in this hemisphere—to the north and to the south. We do not need another slogan. Although these are our close friends and neighbors, our links with them are the same links of equality that we forge for the rest of the world. We will be dealing with them as part of a new, worldwide mosaic of global, regional, and bilateral relations.

It's important that we make progress toward normalizing relations with the People's Republic of China. We see the American and Chinese relationship as a central element of our global policy, and China as a key force for global peace. We wish to cooperate closely with the creative Chinese people on the problems that confront all mankind, and we hope to find a formula which can bridge some of the difficulties that still separate us.

Finally, let me say that we are committed to a peaceful resolution of the crisis in southern Africa. The time has come for the principle of majority rule to be the basis for political order, recognizing that in a democratic system the rights of the minority must also be protected.

To be peaceful, change must come promptly. The United States is determined to work together with our European allies and with the concerned African States to shape a congenial international framework for the rapid and progressive transformation of southern African society and to help protect it from unwarranted outside interference.

Let me conclude by summarizing: Our policy is based on an historical vision of America's role. Our policy is derived from a larger view of global change. Our policy is rooted in our moral values, which never change. Our policy is reinforced by our material wealth and by our military power. Our policy is designed to serve mankind. And it is a policy that I hope will make you proud to be Americans.

Law Day Address on Human Rights Policy

CYRUS R. VANCE
SECRETARY OF STATE

DEAN BEAIRD, STUDENTS, FACULTY AND ALUMNI OF THE UNIVERSITY of Georgia Law School, distinguished guests: I am delighted to be here with you on Law Day. And I am honored by the presence of my friend Dean Rusk, a distinguished member of your faculty.

I speak today about the resolve of this Administration to make the advancement of human rights a central part of our foreign policy.

Many here today have long been advocates of human rights within our own society. And throughout our Nation that struggle for civil rights continues.

In the early years of our civil rights movement, many Americans treated the issue as a "Southern" problem. They were wrong. It was and is a problem for all of us. Now, as a Nation, we must not make a comparable mistake. Protection of human rights is a challenge for all countries, not just for a few.

Our human rights policy must be understood in order to be effective. So today I want to set forth the substance of that policy and the results we hope to achieve.

Our concern for human rights is built upon ancient values. It looks with hope to a world in which liberty is not just a great cause but the common condition. In the past it may have seemed sufficient to put our name to international documents that spoke loftily of human rights. That is not enough. We will go to work, alongside other people and governments, to protect and enhance the dignity of the individual.

Let me define what we mean by "human rights."

Delivered at the University of Georgia's Law School, Athens, Georgia, April 30, 1977.

First, there is the right to be free from governmental violation of the integrity of the person. Such violations include torture; cruel, inhuman, or degrading treatment or punishment; and arbitrary arrest or imprisonment. And they include denial of fair public trial, and invasion of the home.

Second, there is the right to the fulfillment of such vital needs as food, shelter, health care, and education. We recognize that the fulfillment of this right will depend, in part, upon the stage of a nation's economic development. But we also know that this right can be violated by a Government's action or inaction—for example, through corrupt official processes which divert resources to an elite at the expense of the needy, or through indifference to the plight of the poor.

Third, there is the right to enjoy civil and political liberties—freedom of thought, of religion, of assembly; freedom of speech; freedom of the press; freedom of movement both within and outside one's own country; freedom to take part in government.

Our policy is to promote all these rights. They are all recognized in the Universal Declaration of Human Rights, a basic document which the United States helped fashion and which the United Nations approved in 1948. There may be disagreement on the priorities these rights deserve, but I believe that, with work, all of these rights can become complementary and mutually reinforcing.

The philosophy of our human rights policy is revolutionary in the intellectual sense, reflecting our Nation's origin and progressive values. As Archibald MacLeish wrote during our Bicentennial a year ago, "The cause of human liberty is now the one great revolutionary cause...."

President Carter put it this way in his speech before the United Nations:

> ... All the signatories of the United Nations Charter have pledged themselves to observe and to respect basic human rights. Thus, no member of the United Nations can claim that mistreatment of its citizens is solely its own business. Equally, no member can avoid its responsibilities to review and to speak when torture or unwarranted deprivation occurs in any part of the world....

Since 1945 international practice has confirmed that a nation's obligations to respect human rights is a matter of concern in international law.

Our obligation under the U.N. Charter is written into our own legislation. For example, our Foreign Assistance Act now reads: "A principal goal of the foreign policy of the United States is to promote the increased observance of internationally recognized human rights by all countries." In these ways our policy is in keeping with our tradition, our international obligations, and our laws.

In pursuing a human rights policy, we must always keep in mind the limits of our power and of our wisdom. A sure formula for defeat of our goals would be a rigid, hubristic attempt to impose our values on others. A doctrinaire plan of action would be as damaging as indifference.

We must be realistic. Our country can only achieve our objectives if we shape what we do to the case at hand. In each instance we will consider these questions as we determine whether and how to act:

First, we will ask ourselves, what is the nature of the case that confronts us? For example, what kind of violations or deprivations are there? What is their extent? Is there a pattern to the violations? If so, is the trend toward concern for human rights or away from it? What is the degree of control and responsibility of the Government involved? And, finally, is the Government willing to permit independent, outside investigation?

A second set of questions concerns the prospects for effective action. Will our action be useful in promoting the overall cause of human rights? Will it actually improve the specific conditions at hand? Or will it be likely to make things worse instead? Is the country involved receptive to our interest and efforts? Will others work with us, including official and private international organizations dedicated to furthering human rights? Fnally does our sense of values and decency demand that we speak out or take action anyway, even though there is only a remote chance of making our influence felt?

We will ask a third set of questions in order to maintain a sense of perspective. Have we steered away from the self-righteous and strident, remembering that our own record is not unblemished? Have we been sensitive to genuine security interests, realizing that outbreak of armed conflict or terrorism could in itself pose a serious threat to human rights? Have we considered all the rights at stake? If, for instance, we reduce aid to a Government which violates the political rights of its citizens, do we not risk penalizing the hungry and poor who bear no responsibility for the abuses of their Government?

If we are determined to act, the means available range from quiet diplomacy in its many forms through public pronouncements to withholding of assistance. Whenever possible, we will use positive steps of encouragement and inducement. Our strong support will go to countries that are working to improve the human condition. We will always try to act in concert with other countries through international bodies.

In the end a decision whether and how to act in the cause of human rights is a matter for informed and careful judgment. No mechanistic formula produces an automatic answer.

It is not our purpose to intervene in the internal affairs of other countries, but as the President has emphasized, no member of the United Nations can claim that violation of internationally protected human rights is solely its own affair. It is our purpose to shape our policies in accord with our beliefs and to state them without stridency or apology when we think it is desirable to do so.

Our policy is to be applied within our own society as well as abroad. We welcome constructive criticism at the same time as we offer it.

No one should suppose that we are working in a vacuum. We place great weight on joining with others in the cause of human rights. The U.N. system is central to this cooperative endeavor. That is why the President stressed the pursuit of human rights in his speech before the General Assembly last month. That is why he is calling for U.S. ratification of four important human rights covenants and conventions, and why we are trying to strengthen the human rights machinery within the United Nations.

And that is an important reason why we have moved to comply with U.N. sanctions against Rhodesia. In one of our first acts, this Administration sought and achieved repeal of the Byrd amendment, which had placed us in violation of these sanctions and thus in violation of international law. We are supporting other diplomatic efforts within the United Nations to promote basic civil and political rights in Namibia and throughout southern Africa.

Regional organizations also play a central role in promoting human rights. The President has announced that the United States will sign and seek Senate approval of the American Convention on Human Rights. We will continue to work to strengthen the machinery of the Inter-American Commission on Human Rights. This will include efforts to schedule regular visits to all members of the Organization of American States, annual debates on human rights conditions, and the expansion of the inter-American educational program on human rights.

The United States is seeking increased consultation with other nations for joint programs on economic assistance and more general efforts to promote human rights. We are working to assure that our efforts reach out to all, with particular sensitivity to the problems of women.

We will meet in Belgrade later this year to review implementation of the Final Act of the Conference on Security and Cooperation in

Europe—the so-called Helsinki conference. We will take this occasion to work for progress there on important human issues: family reunification, bi-national marriages, travel for personal and professional reasons, and freer access to information.

The United States looks to use of economic assistance—whether bilateral or through international financial institutions—as a means to foster basic human rights.

• We have proposed a 20 percent increase in U.S. foreign economic assistance for Fiscal Year 1978.

• We are expanding the program of the Agency for International Development for "new initiatives in human rights" as a complement to present efforts to get the benefits of our aid to those most in need abroad.

• The programs of the U.S. Information Agency and the State Department's Bureau of Educational and Cultural Affairs stress support for law in society, a free press, freedom of communication, an open educational system, and respect for ethnic diversity.

This Administration's human rights policy has been framed in collaboration and consultation with Congress and private organizations. We have taken steps to assure firsthand contact, consultation, and observation when members of Congress travel abroad to review human rights conditions.

We are implementing current laws that bring human rights considerations directly into our decisions in several international financial institutions. At the same time, we are working with the Congress to find the most effective way to fulfill our parallel commitment to international cooperation in economic development.

In accordance with human rights provisions of legislation governing our security assistance programs, we recently announced cuts in military aid to several countries.

Outside the Government, there is much that can be done. We welcome the efforts of individual American citizens and private organizations—such as religious, humanitarian, and professional groups—to work for human rights with commitments of time, money, and compassion.

All these initiatives to further human rights abroad would have a hollow ring if we were not prepared to improve our own performance at home. So we have removed all restrictions on our citizens' travel abroad and are proceeding with plans to liberalize our visa policies.

We support legislation and administrative action to expand our refugee and asylum policies and to permit more victims of repressive regimes to enter the United States. During this last year, the United States spent some $475 million on assistance to refugees around the world, and we accepted 31,000 refugees for permanent resettlement in this country.

What results can we expect from all these efforts?

We may justifiably seek a rapid end to such gross violations as those cited in our law: "... torture, or cruel, inhuman or degrading treatment or punishment, or prolonged detention without charges...." Just last week our Ambassador at the United Nations, Andrew Young, suggested a series of new ways to confront the practice of torture around the world.

The promotion of other human rights is a broader challenge. The results may be slower in coming but are no less worth pursuing, and we intend to let other countries know where we stand.

We recognize that many nations of the world are organized on authoritarian rather than democratic principles—some large and powerful, others struggling to raise the lives of their people above bare subsistence levels. We can nourish no illusions that a call to the banner of human rights will bring sudden transformations in authoritarian societies.

We are embarked on a long journey. But our faith in the dignity of the individual encourages us to believe that people in every society, according to their own traditions, will in time give their own expression to this fundamental aspiration.

Our belief is strengthened by the way the Helsinki principles and the U.N. Declaration of Human Rights have found resonance in the hearts of people of many countries. Our task is to sustain this faith by our example and our encouragement.

In his inaugural address, three months ago, President Carter said: "Because we are free, we can never be indifferent to the fate of freedom elsewhere." Again, at a meeting of the Organization of American States two weeks ago, he said: "You will find this country ... eager to stand beside those nations which respect human rights and which promote democratic ideals."

We seek these goals because they are right, and because we too will benefit. Our own well-being, and even our security, are enhanced in a world that shares common freedoms and in which prosperity and economic justice create the conditions for peace. And let us remember that we always risk paying a serious price when we become identified with repression.

Nations, like individuals, limit their potential when they limit their goals. The American people understand this. I am confident they will support foreign policies that reflect our traditional values. To offer less is to define America in ways we should not accept.

America fought for freedom in 1776 and in two World Wars. We have offered haven to the oppressed. Millions have come to our shores in times of trouble. In time of devastation abroad, we have shared our resources.

Our encouragement and inspiration to other nations and other peoples have never been limited to the power of our military or the bounty of our economy. They have been lifted up by the message of our Revolution, the message of individual human freedom. That message has been our great national asset in times past. So it should be again.

Universal Declaration of Human Rights

U.N. GENERAL ASSEMBLY

Now therefore The General Assembly proclaims

This Universal Declaration of Human Rights as a common standard of achievement for all peoples and all nations, to the end that every individual and every organ of society, keeping this Declaration constantly in mind, shall strive by teaching and education to promote respect for these rights and freedoms and by progressive measures, national and international, to secure their universal and effective recognition and observance, both among the peoples of Member States themselves and among the peoples of territories under their jurisdiction.

Article 1. All human beings are born free and equal in dignity and rights. They are endowed with reason and conscience and should act towards one another in a spirit of brotherhood.

Article 2. Everyone is entitled to all the rights and freedoms set forth in this Declaration, without distinction of any kind, such as race, colour, sex, language, religion, political or other opinion, national or social origin, property, birth or other status. Furthermore, no distinction shall be made on the basis of the political, jurisdictional or international status of the country or territory to which a person belongs, whether it be independent, trust, non-self-governing or under any other limitation of sovereignty.

Article 3. Everyone has the right to life, liberty and security of person.

Article 4. No one shall be held in slavery or servitude; slavery and the slave trade shall be prohibited in all their forms.

Article 5. No one shall be subjected to torture or to cruel, inhuman or degrading treatment or punishment.

Article 6. Everyone has the right to recognition everywhere as a person before the law.

Article 7. All are equal before the law and are entitled without any discrimination to equal protection of the law. All are entitled to equal protection against any discrimination in violation of this Declaration and against any incitement to such discrimination.

ARTICLE 8. Everyone has the right to an effective remedy by the competent national tribunals for acts violating the fundamental rights granted him by the constitution or by law.

ARTICLE 9. No one shall be subjected to arbitrary arrest, detention or exile.

ARTICLE 10. Everyone is entitled in full equality to a fair and public hearing by an independent and impartial tribunal, in the determination of his rights and obligations and of any criminal charge against him.

ARTICLE 11. (1) Everyone charged with a penal offence has the right to be presumed innocent until proved guilty according to law in a public trial at which he has had all the guarantees necessary for his defence. (2) No one shall be held guilty of any penal offence on account of any act or omission which did not constitute a penal offence, under national or international law, at the time when it was committed. Nor shall a heavier penalty be imposed than the one that was applicable at the time the penal offence was committed.

ARTICLE 12. No one shall be subjected to arbitrary interference with his privacy, family, home or correspondence, nor to attacks upon his honour and reputation. Everyone has the right to the protection of the law against such interference or attacks.

ARTICLE 13. (1) Everyone has the right to freedom of movement and residence within the borders of each state. (2) Everyone has the right to leave any country, including his own, and to return to his country.

ARTICLE 14. (1) Everyone has the right to seek and to enjoy in other countries asylum from persecution. (2) This right may not be invoked in the case of prosecutions genuinely arising from non-political crimes or from acts contrary to the purposes and principles of the United Nations.

ARTICLE 15. (1) Everyone has the right to a nationality. (2) No one shall be arbitrarily deprived of his nationality nor denied the right to change his nationality.

ARTICLE 16. (1) Men and women of full age, without any limitation due to race, nationality or religion, have the right to marry and to found a family. They are entitled to equal rights as to marriage, during marriage and at its dissolution. (2) Marriage shall be entered into only with the free and full consent of the intending spouses. (3) The family is the natural and fundamental group unit of society and is entitled to protection by society and the State.

ARTICLE 17. (1) Everyone has the right to own property alone as well as in association with others. (2) No one shall be arbitrarily deprived of his property.

ARTICLE 18. Everyone has the right to freedom of thought, conscience and religion; this right includes freedom to change his religion or belief, and freedom, either alone or in community with others and in public or private, to manifest his religion or belief in teaching, practice, worship and observance.

ARTICLE 19. Everyone has the right to freedom of opinion and expression; this right includes freedom to hold opinions without interference and to seek, receive and impart information and ideas through any media and regardless of frontiers.

ARTICLE 20. (1) Everyone has the right to freedom of peaceful assembly and association. (2) No one may be compelled to belong to an association.

ARTICLE 21. (1) Everyone has the right to take part in the government of his country, directly or through freely chosen representatives. (2) Everyone has the right of equal access to public service in his country. (3) The will of the people shall be the basis of the authority of government; this will shall be expressed in periodic and genuine elections which shall be by universal and equal suffrage and shall be held by secret vote or by equivalent free voting procedures.

ARTICLE 22. Everyone, as a member of society, has the right to social security and is entitled to realisation, through national effort and international co-operation and in accordance with the organisation and resources of each State, of the economic, social and cultural rights indispensable for his dignity and the free development of his personality.

ARTICLE 23. (1) Everyone has the right to work, to free choice of employment, to just and favourable conditions of work and to protection against unemployment. (2) Everyone, without any discrimination, has the right to equal pay for equal work. (3) Everyone who works has the right to just and favourable remuneration insuring for himself and his family an existence worthy of human dignity, and supplemented, if necessary, by other means of social protection. (4) Everyone has the right to form and to join trade unions for the protection of his interests.

ARTICLE 24. Everyone has the right to rest and leisure, including reasonable limitation of working hours and periodic holidays with pay.

ARTICLE 25. (1) Everyone has the right to a standard of living adequate for the health and well-being of himself and of his family, including food, clothing, housing and medical care and necessary social services, and the right to security in the event of unemployment, sickness, disability, widowhood, old age or other lack of livelihood in circumstances beyond his control. (2) Motherhood and childhood are entitled to special care and assistance. All children, whether born in or out of wedlock, shall enjoy the same social protection.

ARTICLE 26. (1) Everyone has the right to education. Education shall be free, at least in the elementary and fundamental stages. Elementary education shall be compulsory. Technical and professional education shall be made generally available and higher education shall be equally accessible to all on the basis of merit. (2) Education shall be directed to the full development of the human personality and to the strengthening of respect for human rights and fundamental freedoms. It shall promote understanding, tolerance and friendship among all nations, racial or religious groups, and shall further the activities of the United Nations for the maintenance of peace. (3) Parents have a prior right to choose the kind of education that shall be given to their children.

ARTICLE 27. (1) Everyone has the right freely to participate in the cultural life of the community, to enjoy the arts and to share in scientific advancement and its benefits. (2) Everyone has the right to the protection of the moral and material interests resulting from any scientific, literary or artistic production of which he is the author.

ARTICLE 28. Everyone is entitled to a social and international order in which the rights and freedoms set forth in this Declaration can be fully realised.

ARTICLE 29. (1) Everyone has duties to the community in which alone the free and full development of his personality is possible. (2) In the exercise of his rights and freedoms, everyone shall be subject only to such limitations as are determined by law solely for the purpose of securing due recognition and respect for the rights and freedoms of others and of meeting the just requirements of morality, public order and the general welfare in a democratic society. (3) These rights and freedoms may in no case be exercised contrary to the purposes and principles of the United Nations.

ARTICLE 30. Nothing in this Declaration may be interpreted as implying for any State, group or person any right to engage in any activity or to perform any act aimed at the destruction of any of the rights and freedoms set forth herein.

Biographical Sketches

ROBERTA COHEN is currently a human rights officer in the Department of State. She was Executive Director of the International League for Human Rights for seven years and has been active in the field of international human rights for many years. She holds degrees from Barnard College and Johns Hopkins School of Advanced International Studies. She has written several articles and documents in the field of international politics and human rights, including "International Human Rights: A Role for the United States," which she co-authored for the *Virginia Journal of International Law* (1974).

TOM J. FARER is Professor of Law at Rutgers (Camden) School of Law. He is a graduate of Princeton University and the Harvard Law School. In addition to practicing law he has held several positions in the federal government, most recently as Special Assistant to the Assistant Secretary of State for Inter-American Affairs. He is currently a member of the Inter-American Commission on Human Rights and a member of the Council on Foreign Relations. He is the author of several books and articles dealing with human rights, economic development, and U.S. foreign policy.

DONALD M. FRASER has been a member of the U.S. House representing the Fifth District of Minnesota since 1962. He received his undergraduate and law degrees from the University of Minnesota. He was a U.S. delegate to the 30th Session of the United Nations General Assembly, 1975, and acted as Congressional Advisor to the U.S. Delegation to the United Nations Conference on Disarmament, 1968–1973, to the U.S. Delegation to the Law of the Seas Conference, 1972–1975, and to the U.N. Commission on Human Rights, 1974. He is chairman of the International Organizations Subcommittee, which has held over

100 human rights hearings during the past several years, and is the leading spokesperson in the U.S. Congress on human rights issues.

RITA E. HAUSER is a partner in the law firm of Stroock, Stroock and Lavan, New York City. She holds degrees from Hunter College, the University of Strasbourg, and Harvard and New York University Law Schools. From 1969 to 1972 she served as United States Representative to the United Nations Commission on Human Rights. She has held numerous other public positions and is extremely active in legal and human rights professional organizations.

DONALD P. KOMMERS, Director of the Center for Civil Rights at the University of Notre Dame, is also Professor of Law and Professor of Government and International Studies at Notre Dame. He received his Ph.D. from the University of Wisconsin, where he also studied law. More recently, he has been a scholar in residence at the West German Federal Constitutional Court and an Alexander von Humboldt Fellow in the law school of the University of Cologne. His published works include several books and articles on American civil rights, comparative constitutional law, and German law and politics.

RICHARD B. LILLICH is Professor of Law, University of Virginia Law School. He is a graduate of Oberlin College and received law degrees from Cornell, and New York University School of Law. He is President of the Procedural Aspects of International Law Institute and chairman of the Committee on Human Rights, American Branch, International Law Association. Editor of the Procedural Aspects of International Law Series from 1962 to 1977, he is the author of five of its titles and of numerous articles and legal studies.

G. D. LOESCHER is Assistant Professor in the Department of Government and International Studies and Assistant Academic Dean of the College of Arts and Letters at the University of Notre Dame. He holds a Ph.D. in International Relations from the London School of Economics and Political Science and is the author of articles on human rights and Asian affairs. Currently a Dorothy Danforth Compton Fellow (Institute for the Study of World Politics), he is spending 1978-1979 as a Research Associate of the Centre for International Studies at the LSE writing a book on U.S. human rights policy.

PETER REDDAWAY is Senior Lecturer in Political Science at the London School of Economics and Political Science. He graduated from

Cambridge University and has done graduate work at Harvard University, Moscow University, and LSE. He is active in international human rights organizations. A noted authority on the Soviet human rights movement, he is the author of *Uncensored Russia: The Human Rights Movement in the Soviet Union* (1972) and *Psychiatric Terror: How Soviet Psychiatry is Used to Suppress Dissent* (1977) as well as numerous articles.

ARTHUR H. ROBERTSON is Professor of Law at the University of Paris. After receiving his B.A. at Magdalen College, Oxford, he earned advanced law degrees at Oxford and Harvard Universities. An international lawyer and diplomat, he has held several positions in the United Nations and the Council of Europe. From 1962 to 1973 he was Head of the Council's Directorate of Human Rights. He is currently chairman of the Editorial Committee of the European Yearbook and a member of the Council of the International Institute of Human Rights. Among his several books are *Human Rights in the World* (1963) and *Human Rights in Europe,* 2d edition (1977).

NIGEL S. RODLEY is the Legal Adviser of Amnesty International and a part-time lecturer in law at the London School of Economics and Political Science. He holds law degrees from Leeds University and Columbia University. He has taught at Dalhousie University Law School, the New School for Social Research, and the University of Notre Dame London Center for Legal Studies. His published work has covered various aspects of international law, international organization and international economic law as well as the international protection of human rights.

HARRY M. SCOBLE is Professor of Political Science at the University of Illinois at Chicago Circle. He holds degrees from Williams College and Yale University Graduate School. He has taught at the University of North Carolina, Boston University, the University of Wisconsin at Madison and UCLA. He co-founded, with Laurie Wiseberg, the Human Rights Internet within the International Studies Association, and they are currently the co-editors of *The Human Rights Internet Newsletter.* He is the author of numerous articles and monographs and has particular interest in human rights NGO's, policy-evaluation and impact-analysis and the interactions of social scientists and political elites.

VERNON VAN DYKE is Professor of Political Science at the University of Iowa. He received his Ph.D. from the University of Chicago. He has been President of the International Studies Association and the Midwest Political Science Association. He is the author of several books, including *Human Rights, the United States, and the World Community* (1970), and several recent articles on the requirement of the U.N. Charter that members shall promote human rights without distinction as to race, sex, language, or religion.

BEN WHITAKER is Director of the Minority Rights Group in London and a member of the U.N. Human Rights Subcommission. He was formerly a Barrister, an Extramural Lecturer in Law for London University, and a Member of Parliament for Hampstead (Labor) from 1966 to 1970. He is the author of several books on contemporary social problems and currently specializes in the problems of minorities around the world.

LAURIE S. WISEBERG is Assistant Professor of Political Science at the University of Illinois at Chicago Circle. She received her Ph.D. in Political Science from the University of California, Los Angeles, and has taught in Wales, Nigeria and the United States. She co-founded, with Harry Scoble, the Human Rights Internet within the International Studies Association, and they are currently the co-editors of *The Human Rights Internet Newsletter*. She is the author of numerous articles on international human rights nongovernmental organizations, international relations, and African affairs.

EDDISON J. M. ZVOBGO is a leading member of the Zimbabwe African National Union (ZANU) in Mozambique. He holds degrees from London University, Harvard Law School, and the Fletcher School of Law and Diplomacy. For seven years he was a political detainee of the Rhodesian Authorities and in 1970 was named Prisoner of Conscience of the Year by Amnesty International. He was recently an Associate Professor of Law at Lewis University. He has written a number of articles on African affairs and human rights.

Index

Abourezk, James, 236
Affirmative action, 11, 33, 43, 47, 56–57, 66
Africa, 3, 81–82, 94–104
African Development Fund, 286
African liberation movements, 99
Agency for International Development (AID), 181, 219, 233, 252
Agnew, Spiro, 280
Albania, 115, 130
Aliens, 88
Allende, Salvadore, 162
American Association for Advancement of Science, 185
American Civil Liberties Union, 72, 186
American Convention on Human Rights of 1969, 18–19, 176, 284
American Declaration of Independence, 85
American Declaration on the Rights and Duties of Man, 18
American Indians, 46
American National Council of Churches of Christ, 185
Amin, Idi, 93, 100, 101, 104, 281
Amnesty International, 6, 7, 24, 102, 175–77, 182, 192, 193, 194, 195, 198, 249
Anglo-Iranian Oil Company, 265
Angola, 96, 115, 167, 201, 259, 265, 267, 268
Anti-Semitism, 63
Anti-Slavery Society, 187, 192

Apartheid, 6, 63, 96, 139, 186
Arab republics, 94
Argentina, 7, 165, 185, 192, 198, 224, 232, 237, 250, 285, 286
Argus, The, 169
Arms embargo, 139
Arms Export Control Board, 233
Asia, 94
Assimilation, 34, 67
Assistance programs, 182, 191, 201, 214, 219, 220, 221, 222, 228–29, 231, 232, 237, 248, 285, 286
Australia, 94
Austria, 15, 16, 144

Badillo Amendment, 201
Baldwin, Roger Nash, 186
Banda, Kamuzu, 99, 102
Bangladesh, 69, 279
Barker, Ernest, 40, 41, 42, 48, 49, 50
Basques, 65
Baxter, Richard, 289
Belgium, 15, 16, 45–46, 48, 53, 55
Biafra, 69
Bilder, Richard, 278
Black Panther Party, 181
Bolsheviks, 116, 117
Bozovic, Aleksander, 168
Brazil, 7, 225, 250, 271, 280, 286
Bretons, 65
Brezhnev, Leonid, 130, 132, 281
Brownlie, Ian, 289
Brzezinski, Zbigniew, 226

325

Bukovsky-Corvalan prisoner exchange, 136, 137, 138, 221, 223
Bulgaria, 115, 137, 283
Bureau of Near Eastern Affairs, 231
Burundi, 98, 100, 287
Byrd Amendment, 278

Cambodia, 7, 115, 201, 259, 279, 280
Cameroun, 98, 102
Canada, 22, 130, 132, 170
Capitalism, 273
Capotori, Francesco, 64
Carter, President Jimmy
  administration, 133, 144, 156, 179, 194–95, 199–202, 212–17, 222–26, 233–35, 239–40, 249, 261–62, 278, 282, 285, 286, 291–92
  American Convention on Human Rights, 19
  foreign aid, 7
  Helsinki, 136, 138
  speeches, 10, 74, 140, 141–42, 223, 258, 281–82, 302–308
Cassin, René, 6, 139–40
Castro, Fidel, 266
Chad, 98
"Charter 77," 135–36
Chile, 6, 19, 138, 153, 162, 169, 179, 181, 182, 191, 192, 198, 220, 222, 230, 231, 234, 248, 249, 265, 269, 274, 284
Chinese-Americans, 68
Christian Democratic World Union, 144
Christopher, Warren, 231
Churchill, Winston, 13
CIA, 89, 200, 235
Clark, Mark, 180
Cohen, Roberta, 212, 214, 215, 216–40
Cold War, 94, 131, 201, 263
Colombia, 19, 271
Colonialism, British, 44–45
Committee on the Present Danger, 201

Communist parties
  Soviet Union, 116–20
  Western Europe, 112, 126, 136
Communist Party Programme, 118–19
Communalism, 55–59
Cook Islands, 52
Costa Rica, 19, 142
Council of Europe
  Convention on Human Rights, 14–15, 253
  creation of, 13
  Cyprus, 48
  monitoring human rights, 159, 253
Counterinsurgency, 259, 265–66
Crimean Tartars, 121
Cuba, 7, 115, 201, 223, 259, 266, 269, 284
Cyprus, 48, 153, 163–64
Czechoslovakia, 50, 115, 126, 135, 136, 223, 275

Daalder, Hans, 54
Dahomey, 98
Declaration on the Establishment of a New International Economic Order, 83
Decolonization, 65, 94, 96–97, 185
DeFunis case, 57
De Gaulle, Charles, 87
Denmark, 15, 16, 22, 144
Derian, Patricia, 233, 234
Détente, 131, 220, 223
Detention centers, 7
Dominican Republic, 19, 265
"Double minority," 63, 69
Dubcek, Alexander, 136
Dunant, Henry, 24

East Germany, 115, 136
Eastern Europe, 113, 114, 136, 181
Economic aid, 182, 191, 201, 221, 224, 237, 248
Economist, The, 274

Ecuador, 19
Eisenhower, Dwight, 269
El Salvador, 19, 250, 286
Embargo, 271
English Bill of Rights, 80
English Petition of Rights, 80
Ennals, Martin, 188
Eritreans (secessionists), 35
Ermacora, Felix, 157
Ethiopia, 35, 94, 98, 101, 224, 232, 237, 286
Ethnic community
 consent, 51-52
 definition, 37-38
 group rights, 54-59
 liberal theory, 39-42
 practices, 42-48
Ethnic separatism, 35
Euro-communism, 112, 126, 136
Europe
 Convention on Human Rights, 13-17
 EEC treaty, 17-18
 Helsinki, 18
 history of human rights, 85-89, 90-92
 protection of human rights, 5
European Charter on Human Rights, 13
European Commission on Human Rights, 13, 14, 15, 176
European Committee of Foreign Ministers, 14, 15, 17
European Communities, law of, 17, 18
European Convention for the Protection of Human Rights and Fundamental Freedoms
 application, 73
 guarantees, 13-14, 94
 monitoring, 159, 176
 origin of, 13
 procedure, 14-16
 relationship to EEC law, 17-18
 signature of, 14-15
European Court of Human Rights, 13, 15

European Organization for Nuclear Research, 137
European Social Charter of 1961, 16
Export-Import Bank, 182

Farer, Tom J., 259, 263-77, 290
Fascell Commission, 247
FBI, 89, 181
Fiji, 45, 48, 55
Finland, 22, 50
First World
 history, 85-88, 90-92
 personal liberty, 85
 traditional liberties, 85-89
Fiss, Owen M., 47
Flemish, 53
Ford, Gerald, 130, 179, 199, 216-22, 225, 248, 249, 285
Foreign Assistance Act, 180, 219, 221, 222, 227, 234, 248, 250, 260, 285, 286
"Four Freedoms," 91
"Fourteen Points," 91
France, 22, 52, 87
Franco, Francisco, 275
Fraser, Donald, 179, 196, 212-13, 214-15, 218, 247-54, 284
"Free World Coalition," 263
Freedom of Information Act, 181
Freedom of Thought Foundation, 72
French and Dutch Cultural Councils, 46
French Declaration of the Rights of Man, 80
French Revolution, 43, 85

Gandhi, Indira, 195
Gandhi, Mohandas K., 63
Geisel, General Ernesto, 193
Ghana, 100-102
Ginzberg, Alexander, 136
Giscard d'Estaing, Valéry, 130, 137
Goma, Paul, 136
Granada, 19

Greece, 14, 48, 87, 167, 265, 280
Guatemala, 7, 19, 250, 265, 266, 286
Guinea-Bissau, 96, 167
Gulf Oil Company, 268
Guyana, 265

Haiti, 19, 167, 285
Hague Congress, 13
Hampton, Fred, 180
Harkin Amendment to International Development and Food Assistance Act, 180, 201
Hasidic Jews, 57
Hauser, Rita, 80, 85–89
Helsinki Conference
  Final Act, 18, 111, 130–34, 144–46, 202, 236, 247, 253, 282
  future developments, 141–44
  participants, 130–31
  repercussions, 112–14, 134–40
Hesburgh, Theodore M., 239, 252
Ho Chi Minh, 266
Hobbes, Thomas, 36, 39, 40
Honduras, 19
Human Rights Internet, 184
Human rights lobbies, 156, 187–89
Human Rights Working Group of Coalition for a New Foreign and Military Policy, 184, 188, 191
Humphrey, Hubert, 237
Hungary, 115, 283
Hutu, massacre of, 100

Iceland, 15
Indemnity Acts in Southern Africa, 103
India, 94, 195
Individualism, 54–59
Indonesia, 7, 94, 181, 182, 285
Ingersoll, Robert, 219
Integration, 67
Interagency Committee on Human Rights and Foreign Assistance (State Department), 233

Inter-American Affairs Bureau, 234
Inter-American Commission on Human Rights, 18, 190, 284
Inter-American Council of Jurists, 18, 19
Inter-American Court of Human Rights, 284
Inter-American Development Bank, 182, 286
Intercession
  definition, 279
  humanitarian, 280–87
International Commission of Jurists, 24, 70–71, 144, 154, 175–77, 182, 192, 195, 197, 198
International Court of Justice, 131, 154, 283
International Development and Food Assistance Act, 252, 260, 285
International Development Association, 182
International Federation for Human Rights, 186, 189
International Finance Corporation, 182
International Institute of Human Rights, 6, 24
International Labor Organization (ILO), 17, 123, 173, 175, 176–77
International League for Human Rights (ILHR), 183, 185–86, 189, 192, 193, 195, 231, 282, 286
International political movements, 253
International Red Cross, 24, 184, 196–97
International Security Assistance and Arms Export Control Act of 1976, 180, 260, 286
Internationale Handels-gesellschaft Case of 1970, 17
Internment, 14
Internship programs, 193–94
Interrogation of prisoners, 15
Intervention, 54, 260, 279, 287–91
Investment, foreign, 268–73

Iran, 7, 181, 192, 197, 224, 229, 271, 281, 285
Iraq, 7, 231
Ireland, Republic of, 14, 15
Israel, 22
Italy, 15, 143
Ivory Coast, 98, 102

Jackson, Henry, 181
Jackson-Vanik Amendment, 114, 260, 285
Jefferson, Thomas, 36, 43, 51
Jenks, Wilfred, 144
Judeo-Christian environment, 90

Kenya, 69, 98, 101, 102, 104
KGB, 120, 125
Kapwepwe, Simon, 102, 104
Kaunda, Kenneth, 99
Kenyatta, Jomo, 99
Khrushchev, Nikita, 119-21, 126
Kievan Russia, 115-16
Kikuyu, 69
Kissinger, Henry, 212, 217, 219, 221, 222, 226, 231, 239, 252, 263, 280
Kurdish refugees, 231
Kuwait, 268

Laissez-faire economy, 87
Laos, 115, 201, 259
Latin America, 94, 182, 225, 266, 270, 278
Lawyers' Committee on International Human Rights, 194
Lebanon, 55
Lelio Basso International Foundation for the Rights and Liberation of the Peoples, 186
Lenin, 117
Lenschina, Alice, 100, 102
Liberal International, 253
Liberalism, 33, 36, 37, 38-42
Liberia, 94
Libya, 268
Liechtenstein, 130

Lijphart, Arend, 53
Lillich, Richard, 212, 260-61, 278-98
"Linkage" argument, 222
Lobbies, 156, 187-89
Locke, John, 36, 39, 40, 41
Lodge, Henry Cabot, 139
London *Daily Telegraph*, 170
London *Guardian*, 170
London *Sunday Times*, 169
London *Times*, 73, 169
Lorwin, Val R., 53
Lumpa Church, 100
Luo, 69
Luwum, Archbishop, 170
Luxemburg, 15
Luxemburg Court, 17-18

MacDermot, Naill, 188
McRae, Kenneth C., 54
Magna Carta, 80, 85, 90
Malawi, 98, 102, 104
Mali, 98
Marxism, 270, 276
Marxist-Leninist states, 115
Mashawira, Alexander, 104
Mauritania, 98
Mayotte, 52
M'Baye, Keba, 170
Melting pot, 58
Meskhetians, 121
Mexico, 271
Middle East, 94, 153, 162, 164, 169
Military aid, 219, 221, 222, 224, 229, 232, 237, 249, 250, 286
Mill, John Stuart, 40, 41, 49
Minorities, 33, 34, 41
  assimilation, 67-69
  case studies, 71-73
  "cognizable group," 34, 47, 57
  consent of governed, 51
  definition, 63-66
  demands, 69-71
  discrimination, 66-67
  groups as right-and-duty-bearing units, 33, 36, 37, 54-59
  self-preservation, 65-66

Mobutu, 99
Monaco, 130
Moon, Rev. Sun Myung, 72
Moore, John Norton, 289, 290
Moros, 69
Mossadegh, Mohammed, 265
Movement for European Unity, 13
Movement of Catholic Lawyers, 186
Moynihan, Daniel Patrick, 201, 239, 281
Mozambique, 96, 115, 167, 201, 267
Multi-national corporations, 75, 182, 191, 269
Muslims, London, 72

Namibia, 6. 96, 161, 192, 283
Nanda, Ved, 290
National Academy of Science, 185
National security, 229, 237, 266, 267–73
National Security Council, 226, 236
Nationalization, 268–73
Netherlands, 14, 15, 16, 143
Newman, Frank C., 169, 194
New York Times, 181, 196, 229, 282, 286, 287
New Zealand, 22, 52, 53, 94
Nicaragua, 237, 250
Niger, 98
Nigeria, 98
Nixon, Richard, 179, 199, 216–22, 225, 248, 279, 280
Nkrumah, Kwame, 99, 102, 264
Nold Case in 1974, 18
North Korea, 115
North Marianas Islands, 52
Northern Ireland, 14, 15, 22, 68, 69, 113
Norway, 14, 15, 22
Nyerere, Julius, 99, 100

O'Brien, Conor Cruise, 66, 68–69
Old Order Amish, 57, 59
Ombudsman, 19–23
OPEC, 271
Oppenheim, Lassa, 279, 288

Organization for African Unity, 96
Organization of American States (OAS), 19, 155, 190, 191, 218, 283, 284
Orlov, Youri, 136, 137
"Ostpolitik," 131
Overseas Private Investment Corporation, 182

Pacem in Terris, 23
Pakistanis, 68, 279
Palestinians, 49, 51
Panama, 19, 181
Papua New Guinea, 94
Paris treaty of 1951, 17
Park, Chung Hee, 196, 280
Pateman, Carole, 55
Patocka, Jan, 136
Paul VI, Pope, 16, 130
P.E.N. International, 186, 193, 197
Pentagon, the, 229
People's Republic of China, 89, 94, 115, 266
People's Republic of the Congo, 98, 265
Peru, 285
Peter the Great, 115
Philippines, 69, 143, 181, 182, 198, 224, 250, 285
Pinochet, General Augusto, 191, 193, 274
Pitkin, Hanna, 54
Plamenatz, J. P., 55
Plebiscites, 50
"Pluralism," 53, 275
Poland, 50, 115, 136, 265
Political prisoners, 7, 136, 195
Portugal, 14, 87
"Prague spring," 136

"Quiet diplomacy," 156, 193, 196, 261, 262

Racial discrimination, 6, 11, 33, 97
Rawls, John, 39, 54
Reddaway, Peter, 110, 115–29

Regional devolution, 65
Reisman, Michael, 287, 288
Rhodesia, 96, 101–104, 167, 284
Rights,
  to counsel, 16
  of due process, 86
  to equal opportunity, 67
  to fair trial, 6, 15, 101, 103–104
  of individual petition, 14–15
Robertson, Arthur H., 3–4, 5–28, 80, 112, 113, 130–48, 152
Rodley, Nigel, 152, 153, 157–78
Roman Catholic church, 184
Romania, 115, 136, 283, 285
Roosevelt, Franklin Delano, 91
Rostow, Walter, 266
Rousseau, Jean-Jacques, 39, 40
Ruttili Case in 1975, 18
Rwanda, 98, 100

Sabine, G. H., 39
Sakharov, Andrei, 126–27, 136, 137, 138, 223, 281
SALT, 112, 114, 222, 225
San Marino, 130
Sartre, Jean-Paul, 65
Saudi Arabia, 271
Scandinavia, 14
Scarman, Lord Justice Leslie George, 73
Schmidt, Helmut, 130
Schoultz, Lars, 182
Scoble, Harry, 152, 155, 156, 179–208, 212, 214
Scots, 65
Secession, 68–69
Self-determination, 33, 34, 49–52, 68, 73, 81
Senegal, 98, 102
Shah of Iran, 197
"Sharpeville massacre," 139, 198
Shestack, Jerome, 188
Sierra-Leone, 98
Six-Day War, 162
Smith, Ian, 101
Sneider, Richard L., 196
Social contract, 39

Socialist International, 253
Sohn, Louis, 142
Solzhenitsyn, Alexander, 7, 220, 223
Somalia, 35, 98
Soul City, 57
South Africa, 59, 96, 101–104, 138–39, 167, 181, 182, 192, 228, 283
South America, 186
South Korea, 181, 182, 196, 221, 222, 223, 224, 229, 248, 249, 280
Southern Africa, 6, 153, 162, 169, 181, 186, 191, 198, 229
Soviet Baptists, 121
Soviet Germans, 121
Soviet Jewry, 122, 186, 282
Soviet nationalist movements, 121, 122
Soviet religious movements, 121, 122
Soviet Union
  criminal code, 111, 123–24
  detention centers, 7
  dissidents, 112, 120–22, 186, 223
  Helsinki, 137
  history, 115–16, 265
  human rights, 110–14, 123, 223, 225
  monitoring human rights, 154, 181, 185, 192
  socialist ideology, 116–20
  Third World, 263, 265, 266, 270
Spain, 14, 87, 275
Stalin, 117, 120, 121
Stettinius, Edward R., 91
Stevenson Amendment, 114
Stone, Julius, 288
Sudan, 98
Sullivan, William, 280–81
Swaziland, 102
Sweden, 15, 16, 19–22, 87
Switzerland, 15, 22

Tanzania, 44, 48, 82, 102, 104
Third World
  decolonization, 96–100, 185
  economic assistance to, 182
  human right violations, 100–103

Third World, *continued*
  monitoring human rights, 181, 187, 189
  security interests in, 258–59, 263–76
  Southern Africa, 101, 103–104
  U.N. Charter, view of, 66, 74, 84, 92–96
Tito, Marshal, 264
Togo, 98
"Tokenism," 200
Torture, 75, 88, 181, 240
Trade union rights, 16, 86, 162, 173
Turkey, 48, 164
Tutsi people, massacre of, 100
Two treaties of Rome of 1957, 17

Uganda, 6, 98, 100, 101, 104, 153, 165, 170, 223, 230, 287
Ukraine, 121, 192
Unification Church, 72
United Kingdom, 14, 15, 16, 22, 41, 53, 87, 170, 188
United Kingdom's Education Act, 73
United Nations, 8–12, 91, 152–56, 157–72, 284
  Charter, 11, 23, 33, 49, 91, 94–96, 138, 161, 222, 258, 260–61, 282, 287, 288
  Commission on Human Rights, 7, 9, 11, 12, 74, 142–44, 153, 162, 163, 165, 166, 167, 168, 169, 172, 173, 190, 281
  Committee on Human Rights, 9, 10, 159
  Committee on the Elimination of Racial Discrimination (CERD), 10, 11, 159, 160–61, 177
  Decade of Development, 191
  Economic and Social Council (ECOSOC), 9, 10, 11, 12, 142–43, 152–53, 160, 162–68, 171–72, 190, 192, 284
  General Assembly, 2, 8, 11, 49, 51, 283
  General Assembly's Special Committee of Twenty-Four, 161
  High Commissioner for Namibia, 6, 161
  High Commissioner for Refugees, 165
  International Covenant on Civil and Political Rights, 8, 9, 23, 64, 71, 140, 158, 159, 160, 284
  International Covenant on Social, Economic, and Cultural Rights, 8, 9, 23, 140, 158, 160, 284
  International Convention on the Elimination of All Forms of Racial Discrimination, 10, 11, 48, 158, 159, 176, 284
  Minority Rights Group, 64, 192
  Secretary General, 12
  Security Council, 289
  Special Committee on Discrimination in Education, 173–74
  Sub-Commission on Prevention of Discrimination and Protection of Minorities, 12, 48, 123, 153, 158, 164, 167, 190
  Trusteeship Council, 143, 144, 161
  Universal Declaration of Human Rights, 2, 13, 22, 38, 66, 71, 74, 86, 87, 92, 94–95, 158, 186, 261, 282
UNESCO, 173–75
United States, 4, 6, 22, 48, 130, 132, 291–92
  Army School of the Americas, 181
  Bill of Rights, 80, 91, 94
  Commission on Civil Rights, 239
  Congress, 179–82, 201, 212, 214–15, 219–22, 236–38, 247–54, 260, 271, 285
  State Department, 155–56, 200, 213, 214, 218–22, 224–26, 227–35, 261, 286
  Supreme Court, 34, 46–47, 57
University of Georgia, 258, 261, 309
University of Notre Dame, 258, 278, 302

Uruguay, 7, 19, 185, 222, 224, 232, 237, 249, 286, 287

Van der Stoel, Max, 136
Van Dyke, Vernon, 33, 36–62
Vance, Cyrus, 212, 216, 223, 225, 227, 230, 231–32, 286, 291, 309–15
Vatican, 7, 184
Vatican Commission on Justice and Peace, 23, 185
Venezuela, 19, 271
Vicariate of Solidarity, 191
Videla, General Jorge, 193
Vietnam, 115, 179, 199, 201, 266, 269, 279
Vorster, John, 101
Vyshinsky, Andre, 138

Walloons, 53
West Germany, 15, 16, 22
Western Sahara, 164

Whitaker, Ben, 33, 63–76, 188
Wilson, Harold, 130
Wilson, Woodrow, 49, 68, 91
Wiseberg, Laurie, 152, 155, 156, 179–208, 212, 214
World Bank, 182, 191, 237, 269
World Council of Churches, 185, 195
World Union of Christian Democrats, 253
World War I, 50, 68, 91
World War II, 13, 24, 50, 69, 87, 131, 135, 194, 197, 231, 263, 266, 279

Young, Andrew, 200, 279
Young Communist League, 125
Yugoslavia, 115

Zaire, 98
Zambia, 98, 100–101, 102, 103
Zimbabwe, 96
Zvobgo, Eddison, 81, 90–106